Phantom Spies,
Phantom Justice

Phantom Spies, Phantom Justice:
Revived McCarthyism And My Prosecution That Was The Rehearsal
For the Rosenberg Trial –
Updated edition

Published by:
The Justice Institute; PO Box 68911; Seattle, WA 98168
www.justicedenied.org
info@justicedenied.org

First updated edition, June 2012
(Text corrections only May 2014)

Trade Paperback ISBN: 0-9855033-0-0
Trade Paperback ISBN-13: 978-0-9855033-0-7
LCCN: 2012939448

Backcover photograph by Steve Burns
Cover photo courtesy of Getty Images

Printed in the U.S.A.
This book is printed on acid free paper
.

Phantom Spies, Phantc

How I Survived McCarthyism And My F
Was The Rehearsal For The Rose

Updated with new chapter

By Miriam Moskowitz

For my beloved parents, the late Sigmund J. and Rose H. Moskowitz, who gave me unconditional love and support even though they had always believed that the United States government could do no wrong.

Table of Contents

Preface 1

Foreword 2

Introduction 6

Part I – A World Gone Awry 7

    Chapter 1 – July 1950 – A Midsummer Madness 9

    Chapter 2 – A Blanket of Fear 22

    Chapter 3 – In The Beginning 32

    Chapter 4 – Jailhouse Blues 38

    Chapter 5 – With Justice for All 42

Part II – Kaufman's Court 45

    Chapter 6 – Setting the Stage 47

    Chapter 7 – Elizabeth, the Queen 49

    Chapter 8 – Harry Gold, "I Lied Desperately" 58

    Chapter 9 – The Majesty of the Law 104

Part III – Women In Detention 108

    Chapter 10 – Jail – New York City, 1950 109

    Chapter 11 – Bernice 116

    Chapter 12 – Sabine 118

    Chapter 13 – Ethel Rosenberg 120

    Chapter 14 – And in the End, the Sisterhood 125

Part IV – Serving Serious Time 127

    Chapter 15 – Shirley 128

    Chapter 16 – Christmas with Iva 131

    Chapter 17 – Lady Lily and the End of the Line 135

    Chapter 18 – Reconnections 141

    Chapter 19 – Hope Is For Fools 143

    Chapter 20 – Surrogate Living 145

Part V – Life Resumes Among The Lawful 156

    Chapter 21 – Working 157

    Chapter 22 – Broken Shadows 166

    Chapter 23 – Abraham Brothman 170

    Chapter 24 – Enter Venona 182

Part VI – A Confluence Of Toads 188

    Who Benefited? 189

    Chapter 25 – Elizabeth Bentley 190

Chapter 26 – Harry Gold.. 204
Chapter 27 –… And The Real Harry Gold 210
Chapter 28 – Roy M. Cohn, Assistant Prosecutor 234
Chapter 29 – Irving H. Saypol, Prosecutor............................ 242
Chapter 30 – Irving R. Kaufman, the Judge 244

Epilogue 248

Afterword.. 250

Appendix A.. 253

Appendix B 254

Appendix C 256

Appendix D 258

Acknowledgments.. 263

About the Author 264

Photos and Images 265

Endnotes.. 266

Index 285

Preface

"... The Brothman-Moscowitz (sic) case was a dry run of the upcoming Rosenberg trial. We were able to see how Gold and Bentley fared on the stand, and we were able to see how we fared, Saypol and I."[1]
Roy M. Cohn

The wind was a month ahead of schedule gusting in a frenzy and seeming to question why she had chosen to stand on this east side upper Manhattan corner and why on this particular morning. No spot of sun lingered in front of the funerary where she kept vigil and the wind blew shafts of cold at her like trumpets bellowing a finale before the cymbals crash to signal the end of the opus. Ignoring the inconvenience of her seventy-five years she flitted wraithlike from spot to spot, losing her balance in the unforgiving wind, regaining it and edging towards another, perhaps more benevolent space where the fury of the weather might not find her. And inside, the funeral service for the man who was being mourned but not by her proceeded with ritualized pomp and extravagant eulogies.

February 3, 1992 at the funeral service for Judge Irving R. Kaufman (See Chapter 30)

Foreword

The remaining survivors of the United States' mid-20th century political crusade against "subversion" and "communism" are few in number but great in age. The ages range from the very young to the very old, and include the "Occupier" partisans who have made the clearest and most accurate description of the current division of humanity: The amoral jungle wars of the 1% determine the lives and deaths of the 99%.

These thoughts crowd the mind in reading *Phantom Spies, Phantom Justice*, by Miriam Moskowitz.

In perilous and unquiet mid-20th century America, when she was a young woman, she chose a path she knew might make her a public pariah and a federal prison inmate. The details abound in her fascinating book and, read together with other histories and memoirs of women and men taken prisoner by the 1%, the reader is struck by two related phenomena: first, the portfolio of illegalities, cruel deceptions and gall which nervous 1% governments use to punish unrest and resistance to dangerous agendas, and second, the honorable conduct displayed by most Americans who faced arbitrary and wrongful arrest and punishment.

The crusade against falsely labeled "disloyalty" in mid-20th century United States began within weeks of the American-British-Soviet victory over the Germans and Japanese in 1945. Almost overnight, our media was ablaze with tales of "Soviet hostility" and "communist treason" against the United States. There was, simultaneously, a spate of loyalty oaths, arrests, finger-pointing accusations, firings of hundreds of "suspect" teachers and other professionals, removal of "suspect" books from classrooms and libraries, the parading on television of persons who were not charged with treason but who "might" commit treason in the future, and requests by President Truman for citizens to be alert to the possibility that their neighbors were traitors. The media began estimating the number of casualties we might expect from atomic bomb attacks against New York, Washington, and other cities, and the estimates never fell less than in the millions.

In the midst of the fear of war and the passions generated against suspect relatives, neighbors and colleagues, the Department of Justice staged a number of treason-oriented trials in which jurors were compelled to choose between determining the facts, as the Constitution required them to do, or acting on the principle of "better safe than sorry" by siding with the prosecutors in the belief that they were protecting the lives of their children, their spouses and their own.

In the fifth year of the dragnet search for "disloyals", Ms. Moskowitz was abruptly taken from the rounds of her daily life to spend two years in federal prisons, was heavily fined, and suffered years of harassment by the FBI after her release. Her account is both singular and universal among the many American women and men who, confronted with politically motivated arrests and indictments, took the honorable road of refusing to obtain their freedom by becoming prosecution witnesses—"informing" against innocent persons.

As the reader will discover in *Phantom Spies, Phantom Justice*, a deliberately created vagueness marked the government's accusations in its "disloyalty" cases. Typically, the indictments avoided charging the defendants with any specific acts of disloyalty. Instead, they were charged with "conspiring" to commit acts of the mind, such as being "motivated" to be disloyal or of harboring "allegiance" to Russia. In the Brothman-Moskowitz case, the indictment read "conspiracy to obstruct justice"; in the Rosenberg-Sobell case which followed four months later, it was "conspiracy to commit espionage."

Ms. Moskowitz' trial did not stem from anything she was charged with doing. She had been a secretary and friend to Abraham Brothman Three years earlier, in 1947 Brothman, a chemical engineer, and Harry Gold, a chemist employed in Brothman's firm, were called to testify before a grand jury that was investigating Soviet espionage. Gold had been a Soviet spy in the years before he met Brothman. The grand jury declined to indict them. Three years later, in 1950, an indictment was drawn charging that the two men had conspired to lie to the 1947 grand jury, and charging that Ms. Moskowitz had known about the conspiracy.[1] The sole proof brought by the prosecution against Ms. Moskowitz was unsupported testimony by Harry Gold that she had been present at a conversation between him and Brothman when they agreed to lie.

Gold had earlier confessed to having been a Soviet spy, a crime for which he might be sentenced to death. At the time he testified against Ms. Moskowitz, however, he had not yet been sentenced. Understandably, his desire to cooperate with the government was guaranteed. Gold's court-appointed attorney, John D.M. Hamilton, former chairman of the National Committee of the Republican Party, told the judge at Gold's trial that his client was:

> *perfectly willing to accept any statement of the crime that he [the prosecutor] might make, without supporting evidence.*[1]

A prosecutor lacking evidence of a crime could not ask for a greater gift. After his testimony against Ms. Moskowitz, Harry Gold was sentenced to

---

[1] The indictment identified Gold as an unindicted co-conspirator.

30 years imprisonment. Having escaped a death sentence, Gold now prepared himself to merit a reduction in his sentence. The Rosenberg/Sobell trial, held four months after the Brothman/Moskowitz trial, gave him that opportunity, although, by his own account, he had never met or even heard of the Rosenbergs or Sobell. At their trial, he testified he had met with David Greenglass (another witness facing a death sentence) and his wife, Ruth Greenglass, to obtain classified data on the atom bomb. He introduced himself to Greenglass and his wife, neither of whom he had met before, with the words, "I come from Julius."[2] That testimony had taken shape only after hours Gold had spent with the prosecution to prepare for his court appearance.

Just as Gold had falsely "placed" Ms. Moskowitz at a conversation between Brothman and himself, he now injected Julius Rosenberg, by way of a false greeting, into a meeting between Gold and David Greenglass. This was the prosecution's deceptive way of conveying to the jurors that Julius Rosenberg was involved in atomic espionage without having to offer proofs of any kind. Greenglass, who was also desperate to dodge a death sentence, had named Julius Rosenberg and his sister, Ethel Rosenberg, as his co-conspirators. He was rewarded with a fifteen-year sentence in place of the death sentences given to the Rosenbergs.

As Ms. Moskowitz demonstrates in her book, time was not as forgiving as the prosecutors, the judge, and the pliant witnesses expected. For one thing, in the 1970s the Freedom of Information Act disgorged many hundreds of government documents that revealed prosecutorial and judicial deceptions, perjuries and other misconduct in the "loyalty" trials. Miss Moskowitz used those files to form the background to her book. Also, public knowledge revealed that the chief prosecutor, Irving Saypol, who was rewarded with a New York State judgeship after the trials, was subsequently indicted in 1972 for bribery and perjury. The assistant prosecutor, Roy Cohn, was disbarred for theft of client funds and other ethical misconduct. In 2001 David Greenglass confessed in a book by a *New York Times* reporter, and on CBS' *60 Minutes* television show that he had perjured himself in his 1951 testimony against his sister and her husband, Ethel and Julius Rosenberg.

A few simple questions may occur to readers after they turn the last page of *Phantom Spies, Phantom Justice*: How did all this happen? What happened to the Constitution? What happened to the conventional concept of Americanism? Where was our vaunted media? Where were the whistleblowers?

President Eisenhower pointed to a clue to the answers. When he left office he cautioned the nation against what he called the "military-industrial complex", and warned that "We must never let the weight of this combination endanger our liberties or democratic processes."[3] Sadly, from the day we and Great Britain and the Soviet Union declared victory over

Nazism and fascism, the "combination" undertook a massive ousting from public life of any and all critics who opposed the belligerent "military-industrial complex" agenda for creating a worldwide American empire. Loyalty was equated with support for the empire-building complex, which the current generation has rightly labeled the "1%".

Among the changes the belligerent 1% imposed on the nation was the denigration of the right of Americans to fair and transparent trials by arguing that the Constitution was not a suicide pact, that free speech and honest trials were a menace to our security, that the Bill of Rights is dangerous to our survival, that democracy is a slippery slope at the bottom of which the nation will find itself in servitude (in the second half of the 20th century) to Russia and (in the 21st century) to Islam. The 1% has told two generations of Americans that "It's better to be safe than sorry", by which the 1% means that it's dangerous to ask questions, even more dangerous to express doubts and, most dangerous of all, to regard family life, educating the young, healing the sick and keeping the peace a better agenda than one that keeps the 1% cash rich, armed and unregulated.

We have an example before us of the truth that acting on one's beliefs is better than being silently "safe" and sorry. Miriam Moskowitz' beliefs, an amalgam of civics class lessons in Americanism, Old and New Testament teachings and socialist economics, are clear: respect free speech, be a good neighbor, you are your brother's keeper, do not bear false witness, do unto others as you wish them to do unto you, the laborer is worthy of his wages, respect the equality of all human beings.

Miriam Moskowitz' book lights the way.

David Alman[2]
February 2012

---

[2] In 1951 David Alman and his wife, the late Emily Arnow Alman, co-founded the National Committee to Secure Justice in the Rosenberg Case. They also co-authored, *Exoneration: The Trial of Julius & Ethel Rosenberg and Morton Sobell*, published in 2010 by Green Elms Press (Seattle).

Introduction

To us who were involved and to many political watchers on the sidelines it seemed inescapable that the Abraham Brothman and Miriam Moskowitz prosecution was, in reality, an excuse for an attack of McCarthyite political intimidation and repression in the guise of a hunt for spies and traitors.

My book was first proposed by a loyal friend and dear departed old union buddy, Milt Ost, shortly after I was released from prison. He regularly reminded me I had a story to tell. Because I needed time to reorganize my life and also because I was reluctant to dredge up the events which had caused so much pain, it took a large chunk of time for me to come to terms with the task.

The appearance of a number of historically revisionist references to the Brothman/Moskowitz case finally convinced me it needed to be done. It was not only the factual distortions those books presented, it was also that some of them credited me with opinions I never expressed and interviews I never gave. In one instance I protested to the author and his publisher and asked for a correction, but those protests went unanswered. Clearly, it was time for me to set straight a small but significant bit of American history.

For the record, it must be said that I found the services of the Federal Bureau of Investigation sorely wanting in filling my requests for copies of files. Under the Freedom of Information Act I was entitled to copies of the material they had generated about me. It took almost three years and repeated telephone calls before I received the first batch of files; others came even later and some not at all. Those, the FBI said, were no longer available but gave no sensible explanation of why. Much of what did reach me was heavily redacted with critical information blacked out, thus rendering the material useless. It must also be acknowledged, given the culture of the FBI, that no one will really ever know if, in fact, they provided me with all the material I was entitled to or whether they withheld some in contravention of the law.

Miriam Moskowitz
January 2012

PART I

A WORLD GONE AWRY

REDS SMASH ON IN FLANK ATTACK

Story on page 3

Nab Man, Woman in Spy Plot

Story on page 2

'Shades' on Spy Case Lifted

Miriam Moskowitz, 34-year-old stockholder in a chemical firm, is taken to Federal Courthouse here by FBI agent [▲]. Also showing up at the courthouse was Abraham Brothman, 36 [◄—] of Sunnyside, Queens. Both were indicted on charges of obstructing justice by helping to conceal the spying activities of Harry Gold, 39-year-old chemist who is awaiting sentence for giving atomic secrets to the Russians. —*Story on page 3*

Abraham Brothman is in lefthand photo, and Miriam Moskowitz is being escorted by an FBI agent. (*New York Daily News*, July 30, 1950)

Chapter 1

July 1950 – A Midsummer Madness

From nowhere they came, like a biblical plague of locusts and they seemed to be all over my landscape. They had followed me for days wherever I went—by car, by subway, on foot—and they made no effort to be invisible, as though they were deliberately trying to unhinge me. They were neatly dressed in subdued ties and dark, funereal suits and they wore hats, felt hats with wide brims. They were FBI agents and I knew who they were because I had met their counterparts when they interrogated me weeks earlier; their presence now was ominous but I did not know why they were stalking me. I had a numbing fear that they were on a mission of ambush and I was their quarry.

On Friday afternoon, July 28, they telephoned me at the office to ask if Abraham Brothman would be available for another round of questioning the following week. I was Abe's secretary; we were close friends and because of that I was alarmed. They were taking too much time from him and seriously disrupting his work schedule. Nevertheless, I said I thought he would be available and then telephoned Abe. He was on site in New Jersey supervising the installation of a chemical plant he had designed to manufacture thioglycolic acid, a hair preparation. I gave him my news but he was noncommittal. I guessed he did not welcome it.

Abe was to return to Manhattan that evening and pick me up for dinner. He was late and as I waited in front of the building where I lived on Eighth Avenue in Chelsea I saw the hats and suits in a car across the avenue. Abe finally arrived and we drove off. He noticed our escorts immediately and we did not speak. Dinner now out of the question, we were no longer hungry. We zigzagged in and out of streets aimlessly and they followed close behind. We drove uptown to see if friends were home. I parked the car and remained while Abe went into the building. He returned immediately; they were not home. In the meantime the hats and suits had drawn up in front of us. When I started the car it lurched forward and rammed them. They never got out to complain.

Abe took the wheel and drove downtown to a restaurant; we couldn't think of what else to do. It was now about nine in the evening. On Second Avenue on the lower East Side, Abe stopped to telephone our lawyer. He told Abe to get out of town, to go anywhere, perhaps to his summer place in the country, or to a movie. The lawyer said to behave as if nothing were happening. His advice was useless and I thought he was panicking worse than we were.

We parked the car and headed for a corner restaurant on foot. We went in through the front door and out the side door. Then we walked around the block, talking, trying to bolster each other's courage and desperately reaching for some kind of emotional equilibrium. We had lost the stalkers but we knew that would be only temporary. We did not know what to do and while I could not understand why they were pursuing us, I think Abe realized what awaited us. We walked for hours, loathe to return to the car. When we did, they were still there. Abe drove me home and when he got to his place he telephoned to say he was all right. It was now well past midnight. Perhaps they would disappear by morning, I hoped.

Abe was to pick me up the next morning to accompany him to the plant. Before he arrived, I trotted some wash down the block to the laundromat. A different car, parked outside my building, rolled with me as I made my way along the busy avenue and as I returned with my clean wash it accompanied me. Abe arrived and we headed for the Holland Tunnel. The stalkers drove behind us all the way to the plant.

It was a bit before noon when we arrived and Abe went about the task of inspecting and steadying the equipment and conferring with the workmen. We were nervous and exhausted and bewildered. It was a hot day and I had changed from street clothes to shorts and a shirt. When I drove off to get sandwiches and coffee for all of us, the stalkers followed. When I returned they parked about five hundred feet away under the trees, hats and jackets off, ties loosened. The plant was in the middle of a vacant, sandy field with no other buildings nearby so their view of us was clear and unobstructed. From time to time they would start up the car and circle around the plant.

We had a folding cot in the plant and at about three in the afternoon Abe used it to rest. He had one of his blinding headaches. I sat on the sand in front of the building watching the watchers, wondering, always wondering what they would do next. Suddenly they were joined by two other cars and then the three gunned their motors and roared across the field toward the plant. They jolted to a stop in front of me. I ran inside and called Abe.

"They're here," I said. He rose quickly.

There were nine of them and they seemed to swarm all over the place. Four of them took Abe to one side and searched him; another two lined up the four plant workers and another three separated me from the others. The telephone rang, but they would not let me answer it. The plant manager urged them quietly to let him answer it and after several rings they agreed. It was my father; he was an investor in the plant. He wanted to know if everything was going well and did it look like startup would go as scheduled next week? The plant manager assured him all was well.

I asked the agents what they wanted of me and they said, "Miss, don't you understand? You're under arrest!"

I was dumbfounded. "Why?" I asked.

"Conspiracy to Obstruct Justice," they replied. I asked about Abe and they said, he too, was under arrest for the same charge. I shouted that over to Abe in case he hadn't yet been told. Knowing the charge was reassuring; how bad could such a charge be? I hallucinated that it sounded like a traffic violation.

I thought to ask them for warrants but they had none; the warrants were back in New York City, they said. I shouted that over to Abe but I wasn't sure he was hearing me. He seemed dazed and barely functioning. I argued with my guards that they could not arrest me without a warrant but they ignored me. I gave up because they were nine and we were two.

In an other-world sound chamber it seemed to me I heard them say that I had to get into the car with them but I needed to change back into street clothes. They took me to the bathroom and remained while I dressed, discreetly averting their eyes. Then they took Abe in one car, me in another; three of them accompanied each of us. The third group shook hands with the men who now took charge of us and there were congratulations back and forth as though they had just accomplished a dangerous mission. Then the third group left.

The two cars traveled close to each other and the drive seemed to me to be unduly leisurely, I gestured to Abe through the car window from time to time but he was unresponsive. If I appeared self-possessed, I was in fact numb with shock and holding on to my composure with effort. My escorts, the FBI agents, offered mints and cigarettes; I did not want any. As we cleared the Holland Tunnel into Manhattan, I began to repair my make-up and comb my hair—random acts meant to stave off the fear that was beginning to paralyze me. They thought the primping was funny. As we headed across town the car's two-way radio began to crackle and they talked with their headquarters in police jargon. When we approached our destination, the Foley Square Courthouse and FBI headquarters, I saw the waiting reporters and cameramen. It was not quite six p.m.—just in time to make the evening news and tomorrow's morning papers.

With the reporters in pursuit we climbed the long, imposing stone staircase, past the massive columns of this simulated Greek temple, and into a cavernous hall. The elevator that carried us upstairs was like an urn carrying me to my entombment. The somber personnel accompanying me were my charnel house ushers.

The agents took me to the fingerprinting room and the process of destroying my persona began. They took my prints but I would not sign the fingerprint card. They took my purse, but I would not sign a receipt for it. They were visibly annoyed; I was upsetting their routine but I would not yield. I was frightened but I was also angry and I rejected the presumed legitimacy of what they were doing to me.

Their arrest log says, "…she was advised of her rights…" No such advice was given to me.[1]

They took me for mug shots and then into their office where they asked if I wanted to make a statement. I declined.

They gave me permission to call our attorney but, would not let me call my parents. The arrest log says: "7:25 p.m.: Subject put through a call to family…but could not reach them."[2] That was not true. They told me I could call my family from the jail which was also not true but I did not know it then. No personal calls were permitted out of the jail, ever.

It was about eight o'clock in the evening when they delivered me to the Women's House of Detention near Christopher Street and Sixth Avenue in Manhattan. The agents turned me over to the matron in charge and left. As I watched them go I momentarily wanted to cry out, "Don't leave me!" Whatever I had to face now I'd be alone and in a new kind of hostile territory.

The matron took me into an examining room where I had to strip and shower while she examined my clothes minutely, even the seams, presumably for drugs. Then she ushered me into a small room, put me up on an examining table and gave me an enema. After that she led me into a holding room where other prisoners were awaiting processing. Some of them looked incredibly young, still in their teens, with beautiful smooth skin, bright eyes, full of muscle and strength and the glow of youth – and with needle-pricked arms. Most were African-Americans. They all looked as forlorn as I felt.

In my turn, the nurse weighed me but recorded my weight at about ten pounds less than the scale showed. A doctor then examined me. She checked my teeth. "Teeth well cared for!" she called in a thick German accent to the recording nurse. One of Hitler's refugees, I surmised. She also checked my ears and hair and gave me a pelvic examination. During that procedure she asked what my name was and when I told her she spat out, "SPY!" and jabbed me with the speculum. I throttled a cry but my body gave and I jumped reflexively on the table.

During this dehumanizing business I was seized with the notion that I was observing these curious events from outside my own self; I was not me and all this was happening to someone for whom I felt very sorry. As I dressed I fought against the feeling of humiliation but it was indisputable that I was now totally in control of others. It was indeed a midsummer madness.

A guard made out an identity card for me while I answered her routine questions. She gave me a pair of sheets, a pillow slip and two thin blankets; but took my cigarettes and cosmetics. Since the FBI agents had already relieved me of my purse with all its other contents, I was now shorn of all personal belongings except the clothes I was wearing.

The guard took me up to the fifth floor and delivered me to another guard, who took me to a cell, Number 53. It was now almost nine o'clock and the inmates were already locked in their cells for the night. The guard told me to hurry to make up the cot because the lights would go off soon and it would be too dark to see. Hypnotized, I watched her pull the heavy metal gate of my cell to a percussive close and lock it with huge keys. Other inmates, standing at the bars of their cells eyeing me, began to hoot:

"New meat! New meat!"

It was Saturday night. One wag called to me that next Saturday we'd be let out in the evening to go to a restaurant and then to a show. I sensed she was performing some rite of initiation; the other women howled with laughter as they watched my expression. The young woman in the cell next to me, who I could not see, asked me quietly what I had done to be arrested.

"Nothing!" I replied.

There was more hooting. She asked what I had been picked up for and I answered, "Conspiracy to Obstruct Justice."

No one understood that and I said I did not understand it either. They asked how much time I was facing and I told them I had no idea. Someone at the far end of the cell block snorted with disgust:

"New meat! This fancy white chick she ain't done nothin', she don't know nothin', she sure ain't got nothin' but here she be in this rat hole just like the rest of us."

And that was true.

I asked if anyone had a cigarette and my next door neighbor squeezed one over to me though the front bars of our adjoining cells. Then she sent me two or three loose matches and an empty match folder. She apologized; matches were scarce and a book of them cost extra at Commissary here. She asked if I had any money with me and I told her the FBI agents had taken it. The others promptly had advice: I'd better send for some because I'd need it here. They explained how Commissary worked. One could buy cigarettes, matches, cosmetics, sandwiches, cake and coffee but not until Monday. Since this was only Saturday I did not know how I'd do without cigarettes until then. My panic button wailed.

The cot was about two feet wide; its thin mattress enclosed in plastic. It felt cold and clammy despite the July heat. I made up the cot before the lights went out and I lay down.

"This is silly," I thought. "I'm never going to be able to sleep."

I got up and sat on the table which pulled down from the window. The window looked down on Christopher Street near the corner of Greenwich Avenue. I watched the Bun'n' Burger coffee shop across the street; I had been there only a few evenings earlier. How normal the flow of life seemed down there! I sat up all night watching the people and the traffic, desperately wanting to share in the banality of that street life. I thought about all the people I knew and wondered if any of them would come forward now to try to help. Surely they would know that none of the accusations against me were true. I thought of my parents and the pain I was causing them now, and I writhed with anguish. I had propelled them from middle class suburban Jewish respectability, a condition they set great store by, to disgrace and as it would turn out, financial ruin. It was devastating.

I was sure that people would rally the next morning in front of the jail to denounce the fake accusations and demand my release, and I sat on that table impatiently waiting for the sunrise. And as I fantasized, I reviewed everything I might have done to cause this calamity.

First, what did the charge, "Conspiracy to Obstruct Justice," mean? Was it because I had tried to deflect the FBI agents from continuing to harass Abe so that he could uninterruptedly complete the design work on the plastics plant for the new Swiss account? We had a lot riding on that business. It would pay off a mountain of debt and give long-term stability to the firm.

Should I not have forced a showdown with the agents to get them out of the office and should I not have been so defiant in refusing to continue to let them harass him? I made no sense out of this situation. Abe had accommodated their requests for interviews and he had patiently answered all their questions. But the FBI never seemed satisfied; the agents would return for yet another interview and it was disrupting Abe's work schedule and a deadline he was facing. I finally told them he was too busy to continue and I ushered them out of the office. I wondered: was this what constituted "Conspiracy to Obstruct Justice?"

Abe Brothman was a chemical engineer who had worked for a design and equipment manufacturer in New York City in the late 1930s and early 40s. Part of his income accrued through sales commissions. The firm advertised in trade and professional journals and it was through such means, Abe had told the FBI, that a man called on him in early 1940 who said he had business connections with the Russian Trade Commission (Amtorg) in New York. The man's name was John Golos; in return for his obtaining business from Amtorg he and Abe agreed that he would be paid the usual finder's fee of ten percent. Abe welcomed his offer; he had previously tried to interest the Russians in doing business with him but could never get past their reception desk.

Subsequently Golos' secretary, Helen, called on Abe when Golos himself was not available. From time to time Abe provided her with technical proposals and blueprints of flow sheets. It was his own work, it was not connected with any government project and it was neither secret nor classified information. There was no reason to believe then, and especially after Pearl Harbor when the Soviet Union was a wartime ally, that his efforts would be regarded with disfavor by the United States government.

Abe would dictate explanatory notes on his material to Helen because he was unwilling to devote excessive time to speculative sales efforts by preparing these notes himself. He quickly found this arrangement unsatisfactory so he asked Golos to send him someone with a technical background who would understand his verbal descriptions of the material he was submitting. In the fall of 1941 a chemist by the name of Frank Kessler took Helen's place and the two men met sporadically thereafter.

No business resulted from this and the Golos/Helen contact seemed to lapse. However, Abe found it useful to employ Kessler from time to time as a freelancer when his engineering work required chemical analyses. He had no chemical laboratory and Frank had the use of the one which employed him in Philadelphia. It was a mutually beneficial business arrangement; Abe gained the professional services of a chemist when he needed it, and the chemist gained extra income. Whenever Abe needed to contact Kessler he used a mail drop Kessler had given him in care of one, Harry Gold. Eager to keep the Amtorg possibility alive and needing the chemist's services Abe did not question this.

In August 1944 Abe set up his own consulting engineering business in midtown Manhattan with several other engineers as nominal partners. In October I came to work for him. A year and a half later Abe opened a chemical laboratory in Elmhurst, Queens. He needed a chief chemist and offered the job to Kessler. The wartime shortage of civilian labor particularly technically trained people, had lingered into the postwar era and qualified technical personnel were not easily obtainable.

Kessler came to work for Abe in May 1946. It was then he revealed his true name. He had been unwilling to do so earlier, he said, because he did not want his employer to learn of his moonlighting. His real name was Harry Gold.

In November 1945 Helen, under her true name of Elizabeth Bentley, called on the FBI to confess that she had been a Soviet spy courier in the late 1930s and early 40s. She implicated a number of government employees who, she said, had given her classified information for her boss, Jacob (John) Golos, to transmit to the Soviet Union. She said that Golos, now dead, had been an important member of the American Communist Party.

She also implicated Abraham Brothman, although he was not a government employee. She said she had collected technical material and drawings for industrial designs from him. But it was not until two years later that Abe and then Harry Gold were questioned by the FBI.

On July 22, 1947 Abe was called before a grand jury which had been convened to investigate espionage, based on Elizabeth Bentley's testimony. Abe told the grand jury the facts as he had given them to the FBI. He denied he was a member of the Communist Party although he admitted having belonged to the Young Communist League while a teenage student.

Some nine days later Gold was also summoned to appear before the same grand jury.

I was not called before the grand jury until three years later; but I judged it to be a fishing expedition and not truly a pertinent investigative event. The jury asked me questions concerning my personal beliefs and political activities then deemed heretical and un-American so I took refuge in the Fifth Amendment and refused to answer. One juror was incredulous; why, she asked, would I not answer if I had nothing to hide? Another asked if it would "degrade" me to admit that I had worked for the government. These jurors clearly did not understand that the Fifth Amendment guarantees the right not to have to testify against oneself as a protection against arbitrary government abuse or capricious investigation. My lawyer had not been permitted to be present (grand jury hearings do not allow attorneys to be present) — and the prosecutor who presented the case did not instruct the jury on the legitimate use of the Fifth Amendment. He allowed the panel to believe that one who takes the Fifth must have something to hide and therefore must be guilty. In the meantime, I was not permitted to know what testimony had been offered against me nor by whom, nor was I entitled to a transcript of such testimony. The grand jury was the tool of the prosecutor.[3] Abe called the grand jury hearings, "Star Chamber proceedings."[4]

In 1947, however, the government did not seem to be interested in following up on Harry and Abe's grand jury appearances. No indictments were issued. (Later, in 1948, Elizabeth Bentley would publicly surface as a witness before Senate and House investigative committees. The Republican-led committees sought to exploit her testimony to support their accusations that the Truman administration was lax in its internal security procedures.[5])

Abe was nevertheless uneasy about where the investigations into his business affairs would lead. Early in 1946 he had been solicited by two men who, the Brothman staff was told, were from the Jewish Agency for Palestine. They asked Abe for the design of a plant to manufacture fertilizer from potash of which there were abundant deposits in that land. The Jewish government was two years away from becoming the State of Israel, *de jure*, but it was functioning *de facto* and was building a basic industry. The work Abe was asked for had to be done quickly, and except for the salaries of the staff who worked on the project, it had to be pro bono as well as spare and unadorned. The materials to build it had to be mostly what was readily available since the British had the area under blockade and importation of equipment would be impossible. The work involved uncomplicated textbook chemistry.

Abe labored intensively on the plant designs, the equipment specifications and the operating manuals, putting aside bread-and-butter work. When the project was completed one of the men picked up the material. He and Abe shook hands and drank a toast; he left and we never saw him again.

It concerned Abe that the FBI not learn of this work because the men who had called on him were, he knew, not from the Jewish Agency but rather from the Haganah, the Jewish defense force in Palestine which the British had outlawed. The plants were designed to produce not fertilizer, but explosives. While Abe had broken no laws in providing these designs, the juxtaposition of this event with the FBI implication that he had engaged in espionage might have lent credence to Bentley's accusations. Moreover, such publicity would not have been helpful to the fledgling Jewish state.

The grand jury inquiry interfered with Abe's ability to resume the rhythm of disciplined work. Although he seemed to be summoning hidden reserves of self-confidence he was frequently uneasy and distracted. Income began to dry up and one by one the staff left. Worse yet, by 1948 the trusting relationship Abe had had with Harry Gold had significantly soured because of the firm's straitened finances. Gold accused Abe of management irregularities and Abe, in turn, locked Gold out of the laboratory. Gold thereupon left amid threats to sue. Abe assumed the research tasks as well as the equipment design work and hopped from laboratory to office desperately trying to keep his business on track.

In September 1949 the United States was shaken by the news that the Soviet Union had exploded an atom bomb. A few months later, in February 1950, amid intensifying hostility towards the Soviet Union, the world learned that an English nuclear physicist, Klaus Fuchs, was arrested in England. It was reported he confessed to having given information on the American-led A-bomb project to a courier for transmittal to the Soviet Union.[6] Abe had had no involvement in any aspect of the work relating to the bomb, but because the news each day was dominated by the intensifying anti-Soviet hysteria he thought he had much to be concerned about.

It was as he expected.

Elizabeth Bentley came forward again, in 1950, as the media darling. She claimed to have new revelations and fresh expertise on American "subversives" and their involvement in Soviet espionage. FBI chief, J. Edgar Hoover fed those stories to his favorite newspaper columnists. They, in turn, predicted ominously that new disclosures and arrests were imminent. The increasingly overwrought accusations of Senator Joseph McCarthy, who headed a Senate subcommittee investigating communists in government, helped keep the pot boiling. President Truman announced that the United States would build a hydrogen bomb many times more powerful than those that had destroyed Hiroshima and Nagasaki. The Korean War, blamed on Red China, had begun and was threatening to escalate into World War III.[7]

Earlier, in March 1947, President Truman had instituted Executive Order #9835 which established the Federal Employees Loyalty Program.[8] It barred communists or those aiding or sympathetic to communists from employment in federal, state or local governments as well as in the military and in industries which had defense contracts with the government. The proscription was not confined merely to card-carrying communists. Anyone could be accused of being subversive, sometimes by faceless informers. The irony appeared to escape most Americans that a loyalty oath was deemed necessary in 1947 *after* the war but had not been thought vital to the nation's security *during* the war from 1941 to 1945.

The bandwagon was rapidly filling up. In 1947 the darling of the liberal establishment, Senator Hubert H. Humphrey of Minnesota, proposed making Communist Party membership a crime.[9] Americans did not question this proposed infringement on the Bill of Rights, and Americans for Democratic Action (ADA) and the American Civil Liberties Union not only failed to raise their voices in protest, they ratcheted up the witch-hunt with their own denunciations. Some members of the ACLU leadership, like Morris L. Ernst, even cultivated cordial and confidential relationships with the FBI.[10]

In October 1949 eleven top Communist Party leaders were convicted under the Smith Act of conspiring to teach and advocate the overthrow of the United States government by force and violence.[11] In 1950 the McCarran Internal Security Act required that all communist and communist-dominated organizations register the names of members and contributors with the federal government.[12] Later the Communist Control Act of 1954 would further strengthen the provisions of the McCarran legislation by providing severe penalties for failure to register; it also denied collective bargaining power to communist-dominated unions, however loosely any communists were identified.[13]

It was never foreseen that one of the byproducts of this obsessive frenzy would be the requirement that teachers instruct their pupils how to hide under their desks in the event of a nuclear war, the absurdity of that and the impossibility of survival notwithstanding. The potential need to build private bomb shelters would also become an item in the lives of some frightened Americans which would, in turn, give rise to some knotty moral questions: What if one's shelter were large enough to hold only one's own family and what if stampeding, shelter-less friends or neighbors would try to gain access during a bomb attack? Along with food and water, one would clearly have to stock the shelter with arms and ammunition and be prepared to use them to keep out persons for whom there would be no room in the event of a nuclear war.

The corrosive, morally crippling effect of the witch hunt did not appear to be a concern to most Americans and there were few voices of sanity. But the fear in the land was palpable and most of it was generated out of the nation's capital. Some members of Congress, not to be outdone by J. Edgar Hoover or Joseph McCarthy, urged passage of legislation to round up communists and others suspected of treason, to corral them into detention camps.[14] They were inventing a danger and then rising to vanquish it.

The onset of the Korean War on June 25, 1950 resulted in increased hostility towards communists and anyone who questioned the justification for American intervention in what was, basically, a quarrel between North Korea and South Korea. Americans rallied to support President Truman as American servicemen left for Korea. After the North Koreans overran most of South Korea, and American forces pushed them back almost to the Yalu River border with China, the lines froze along the 38th parallel. In 1951 negotiations were begun for a cease-fire and after much difficulty it was accomplished on July 27, 1953, almost two years later. The terms were basically what had been originally proposed.[15] Nevertheless, anyone who had questioned American involvement was regarded as a communist and a potential traitor to American values.

In this fateful period, the late spring of 1950, the FBI returned to Abe and to me for questioning. We were unaware that they were also questioning Harry Gold in Philadelphia. About a week later, on May 22, 1950, Gold confessed that he had been the Soviet contact with Klaus Fuchs, the British atomic scientist and confessed spy. Gold said he had also collected information from David Greenglass, the brother and brother-in-law of Ethel and Julius Rosenberg. Included in his confession was a statement that he had purchased industrial manufacturing information from Alfred Dean Slack, a chemist, about the commercial production of RDX, an explosive more powerful than TNT. Glossed over in the news reports was that Slack had no involvement in the A-Bomb project.[16]

(The chemistry of RDX was available in any public library and had been known since before the first World War. Its mass production problems had not been solved commercially in the United States until World War II but that appeared to be merely a question of time. Nevertheless, the press created the impression that vital security secrets had been lost to the Russians in the matter of RDX.)

In quick succession a number of arrests occurred all accompanied by sensational headlines about the theft of American atomic secrets and the culprits who had made that possible. Slack was arrested on June 15 in Syracuse, New York where he lived. Greenglass was arrested the next day in New York City and he implicated Julius Rosenberg. David's wife, Ruth Greenglass, was not arrested but she implicated Ethel Rosenberg (her husband's sister and wife of Julius). Julius was arrested on July 17, 1950 and Ethel on August 11, 1950. All of them were charged with conspiring to commit espionage. On August 18 Morton Sobell, a college classmate and friend of Julius was arrested. News reports identified him as another member of the "spy ring."[17]

Gold also confided to the FBI that he would have confessed three years earlier when the 1947 grand jury first questioned him, but Abraham Brothman had induced him to concoct a false story and that he had agreed with Abe that they would both lie to the grand jury. Furthermore, Gold said I had known that the two of them would lie and, by implication, I supported their efforts.

Abe and I were arrested on July 29, 1950. (For Abe, this was the last possible day before a three-year statute of limitations dating from his and Gold's 1947 grand jury testimony would have tolled and made prosecution impossible. The Statute of Limitations did not apply to me since I had not testified in 1947.) J. Edgar Hoover announced with great triumph that we were two more links in the Soviet atomic spy chain. The following are typical headlines announcing our arrests:

"NEW SPY ROUND UP BRINGS 2 ARRESTS; OTHERS DUE SOON: Engineer and Woman once in US employ seized after hurried indictments. Link with Gold charged," (photographs with story) *The New York Times*, July 30, 1950.

"NEW YORKERS SEIZED IN SPY ROUNDUP EN ROUTE TO DETENTION PEN (headline under photograph) FBI Agents Close in on Abraham Brothman and Miriam Moskowitz Adding Two More Names to Growing Spy Ring," *The New York Daily Mirror*, July 30, 1950.

"SPY DATA COMING IN BY THE HOUR, SAYS SAYPOL," *The New York Daily Mirror*, August 1, 1950.

The headlines and news reports were similar across the country. Despite the headlines, however, neither Abe nor I were charged with espionage but, rather, with having conspired to obstruct justice. Even then, on the very day of the indictment, the government attorneys were still not sure what statute they would use for the indictment. In the peculiarities of the law, obstruction of justice under Section 1503 of the 1947 edition of the U.S. Code was merely a misdemeanor while conspiracy to obstruct under Section 88 of Title 18 of the 1946 edition was a felony, according to the U.S. Attorney in the Southern District of New York. [18] It is also legal lore that a prosecutor prefers a conspiracy charge when evidence is inconclusive because the rules of evidence in conspiracy cases are less demanding. And no ambitious prosecutor would pursue a misdemeanor, given a choice, when a felony would net him more attention and, if he won his case, far more prosecutorial prestige. So, with some painstaking research and zealous creativity, the United States Attorney's Office was able to fit the crime to the punishment and we were indicted under the conspiracy charge—a felony.

The heart of the accusation was that Abe and I had conspired to impede a grand jury investigation into espionage in 1947: Abe and Harry Gold had agreed to lie to the grand jury and I had known about it. A second count against Abe said that he had influenced Harry to lie, in effect, a subornation of perjury. Bail was set at $25,000 each, a staggering sum in 1950, especially for such a charge. It gave credence to the government's claim, which FBI Chief J. Edgar Hoover and the prosecution hammered to the press, that we were dangerous criminals.

And so we were now behind bars.

Chapter 2

A Blanket of Fear

My arrest and criminal notoriety, with all its punitive aftershocks, resulted from my relationship with my co-defendant, Abraham Brothman.

Abe was married and the father of two young children He was devoted to his family but always seemed more preoccupied with his work, spending his days and most evenings at the office, or in the company of professional colleagues. Even on weekends or holidays one could invariably find him bent over his drawing board. I was hired in October 1944 to handle his office work, and was immediately aware that his professional absorption to the exclusion of a normal family life was a defining mode for him.

Abe was usually out of the office during the day calling on accounts or at client meetings and he would return just as I would be packing up for the day. I began to adjust my hours to accommodate his routine. We often worked late, went to dinner together, and I found charming his endless stories of his childhood in an extended family. I was dazzled also by his erudition in science and mathematics, by the reach of his mind in history, and his canny perceptions of the events of the day. He was the liveliest conversationalist and the most indefatigable I had ever known. When he also turned out to be musically gifted—he had studied voice and could impressively render Schubert or Puccini or Cole Porter—it seemed a superabundance of gifts had been lodged in this person and I was awed. He was amusing, too; his irreverent quick humor skewered the shams of modern life, and I learned to laugh with him at the contradictions we had to cope with.

Before Abe, I had worked for the government as a clerk, first for the Immigration and Naturalization Service, then for the Social Security Board, and finally for the War Manpower Commission. My life centered around my job and the union I belonged to, a CIO affiliate, the United Federal Workers of America. On Wednesday evenings at the union hall we had folk or square dancing; on Saturday evenings we ran social events, even a theater party now and then; summer Sundays were for beach parties; and in between we worked on grievance strategies, held business meetings, or ground out leaflets on the mimeograph machine in support of a union action. The young men in my life, most of whom I had met either at City College of New York where I was an Evening Session student or through union activities, were now in uniform preparing to fight World War II. When they came home on leave I dragged them to the union hall for whatever was going on there, or we went to the movies and later, over coffee, I listened to their accounts of army life. They were unenthusiastic soldiers, perhaps, but always brave and I ached for them, so innocent and unknowing about what awaited them overseas.

And while I was veering leftward in my political perceptions I was also dipping into interests that were not remotely concerned with causes or social problems. One of the young men would take me to Nick's Bar in the Village on Tenth Street and Seventh Avenue on Saturday evenings or to Jimmy Ryan's on West 52 Street on Sunday afternoons where for the price of a beer at Nick's, or a fifty-cent admission at Ryan's, we would listen with total rapture to Eddie Condon and Pee Wee Russell and Sidney Bechet and Max Kaminsky and other giants of jazz whose names I no longer remember. They gave us haunting, heart-stopping, bluesy improvisations; their interactive exchanges finding harmonies that could have been Debussy's or Ravel's while a clarinet quivered and a velvety trumpet reached achingly for a resolution. All the while the percussive tempos, now driving, now mellow, combined to offer mood and music that was the new aesthetic joy of the forties' jazz, totally unlike anything we had ever heard and we were captivated and shaken to such emotional depths as we had never known before.

In 1944 I became restless in my government job, left it, and found one

Miriam Moskowitz and Abraham Brothman at The Palmer House in Chicago, June 1946, unaware that seven months earlier, Elizabeth Bentley had put Brothman in the cross-hairs of the FBI. (Miriam Moskowitz)

with Abe Brothman. Suddenly my good old friends all seemed like sandbox playmates; Abe and his universe were closing them out. Over several months our relationship took a more personal turn. I was twenty-eight, he was thirty-one; it was an unchartered course and neither of us recognized the dangers.

I was also not paying attention to the clouds mottling my horizon: the growing intensity of an anti-communist fever claiming national front and center stage attention. I read disbelievingly the escalating accusations of communists corrupting the corridors of government. It could not possibly last, I thought, no one would believe such nonsense. Growing up in the 1930s, I had observed the Communist Party, a legal entity, to have been consistently in the forefront of social and economic struggles affecting the vulnerable and the voiceless. I had read in the left press of communists who had joined picket lines in solidarity with strikers in front of steel mills or coal mines, who risked their lives to help distribute leaflets, and who collected food for hungry families. I remembered the stories of valiant volunteers, communists, who helped desperate farmers in the Midwest during the Depression to shoulder rifles against the sheriffs at the mortgage foreclosures ordered by banks.[1] The Communist Party had organized the campaign to free the Scottsboro Boys, the nine black teenagers who faced a legal lynching in Alabama on false rape charges. It was among the first to sound the alarm against the professional anti-Semites, Father Charles Coughlin and Gerald L. K. Smith, who were spewing their poison on radio or in print. American communists had fought as volunteers in the Spanish Civil War against the first fascist attack before World War II. The Communist Party had guarded the interests of labor – some of the most militant and dedicated union members were Party people. It had organized unemployed councils which developed campaigns for government relief for the unemployed, and it had led rent strikes and eviction resistance against gouging landlords. Pete Cacchione, a labor leader from Brooklyn, and Benjamin Davis, Jr., a lawyer and an African American from Harlem, were elected on the Communist Party ticket to the New York City Council in the nineteen-forties; there they led a successful struggle to establish rent control. It still protects tenants to this day.

Nevertheless, the fever was gaining virulence; anti-communism dominated the news each day. Harry Bridges, the west cost longshoremen's union leader, was being investigated for communist ties with a view to deporting him back to his native Australia. Other unions were being "cleansed" of militant leaders, teachers were being fired for leftist leanings, and Paul Robeson, the noted African-American actor and singer who had supported left causes and had expressed admiration for the Soviet Union because, he said, it did not discriminate against black people—he and an audience had been threatened by a vigilante mob when he was to sing at an outdoor concert in Peekskill, New York, in September 1949.

The antipathy had started right after the victory of the Russian revolution of 1917-1918. Anti-communist, xenophobic fervor had simmered throughout the 1920s and 30s during the Depression, and it was made more acute with the election of Franklin Delano Roosevelt as President in 1932. One of the first acts of his administration was to recognize the USSR in 1933, an event which angered the right even though it was good for American business. Sharpening the hostility was the formation of the Congress of Industrial Organizations (CIO) in the mid-30s. It had broken away from the old-line American Federation of Labor and was more militant. Conservatives saw the passage of the Wagner Labor Relations Act in 1935 giving workers the right to organize and to bargain collectively as robbing business of its accustomed hegemony over the workplace.[2-5, 7]

Succeeding New Deal legislation exacerbated the right wing hostility to the Roosevelt administration even more. The establishment in 1935, by Executive Order, of the Works Project Administration (WPA), putting millions of the unemployed on the federal payroll, the social gains provided by the New Deal programs threatened hitherto unrestricted corporate power. Roosevelt termed the capitalist overlords malefactors of great wealth and they called Roosevelt a communist, coddling labor, extravagant with public funds and wooing minorities. They complained also that there were too many Jews in Washington, that his administration was under the thumb of Catholics and that Mrs. Roosevelt ought to stay at home instead of gadding about with her do-good activities.[6]

The New Deal programs were designed to be economic investments to relieve the suffering and to put people back to work, to calm the mounting fear and to rout the sense of hopelessness, unrest and hardship caused by the Depression. They were unprecedented and they permanently altered the economic, social and governmental landscapes. They included Social Security, Unemployment Insurance, farm price supports, and rural electrification through the Tennessee Valley Authority. The programs also instituted government regulation of banking and the stock market to protect bank depositors against bank failures (which occurred frequently after the stock market crash of 1929) and investors from stock market failures, then a common Wall Street nightmare. In addition, the New Deal created the National Housing Act under which the Federal Housing Administration offered home loans and mortgage insurance to benefit mostly low- and middle-income home buyers.

The massive spending stimulated recovery by funneling money into the economy as payments for material, equipment and labor. It thus increased the national purchasing power until the economy could expand and private industry could recover enough to begin hiring again. At the same time the WPA programs took care of the needs of some of the country's infrastructure including the construction of public buildings, bridges, roadways and airports as well as conservation work in the national parks and forests. It also conducted an education program through the National Youth Administration, training young men and helping them find work. More critically, the New Deal Farm Security Administration provided emergency loans to farmers to rescue them from impending bankruptcy.

Not least among the programs was the Federal Arts Project; it gave dignified and creative work to scores of unemployed theater people, artists, writers, teachers and musicians and it brought the arts to millions of Americans.[7, 8] For example: The Music Project's many symphony orchestras gave about four thousand performances a month before hundreds of thousands of people, more than half of whom had never heard a live orchestra before. Thousands more learned to play or sing at its many teaching centers.

The Theater Project's companies played to over 25 million people, most of whom had never seen a stage play before. Some of their productions were highly innovative. Among those who got their start here were Orson Welles, John Houseman, John Huston and Norman Lloyd.

The Art Project's artists produced nearly a million works of visual art which were exhibited and used by schools, courthouses, hospitals, libraries, post offices and other public buildings. And each month 60,000 people came to the free art classes offered by the Art Project. Some of the artists and photographers who emerged from this program included Franz Kline, Willem de Kooning, Ben Shahn, Hugo Gellert, Miguel Coverrubias, Al Hirschfield, Gordon Parks, Dorothea Lange and Arthur Rothstein. Much of the art produced under the aegis of the Art Project provided a vivid record, otherwise unobtainable, of life during the Depression.

The Writers' Project employed workers of literary competence and included many teachers who could not find teaching jobs. Some of these writers trekked the countryside, discovering untapped fountains of folklore and history, wrote about them and provided invaluable data for later researchers of Americana. Writers who came out of this program included Conrad Aiken, Saul Bellow, Studs Terkel, Richard Wright, Nelson Algren, Ralph Ellison, John Cheever and Malcolm Cowley.

The Federal Arts Projects collectively became one of the mot culturally productive and creative periods in American history. Nevertheless, it faced considerable opposition in Congress almost from the first days of its creation. The opposition had two roots: the idea that work relief was not something the government should be involved in and the accusation that the WPA projects constituted a network for militant trade unionists and communists. In 1939 the House Investigative Committee began a campaign of intimidation by questioning Federal Arts Project employees regarding their union and political activities, hoping to rouse support for eliminating the programs. The Senate joined in the harassment. As a result, in 1939 the WPA appropriations were cut and the Federal Arts Project died. The WPA itself went out of business officially in 1943.[8]

The New Deal was, in almost every aspect, revolutionary in scope and it was fought bitterly by America's right wing politicians. (What remains of it today is still under attack: witness the drive to scuttle Social Security, as well as Medicare passed in the Johnson era.)

In the meantime, World War II had taken center stage.

While the economies of Europe became devastated, American industry by the war's end had prospered as the government built up its armed forces and produced war materiel. American farms and factories began to hum as they had not before. Unemployment fell to statistical negligibility and personal income rose to unprecedented highs.[9]

On April 25, 1945 the armies of the Soviet Union in the eastern sector of the European theater of war, and those of Great Britain, France and the United States in the west met in jubilant, fraternal victory on the banks of the Elbe in eastern Germany. The event, while generating euphoric joy throughout the world, portended trouble. At stake now was the political form of the postwar world and how it would be affected by where the different armies had planted their feet at war's end. With the Soviet armies having fought their way so far west of its borders, Washington and London could see eastern European markets in danger of being lost to the Russians once peace was formalized.

A concomitant fear in Washington was that with the advent of peace the country would not be able to absorb returning servicemen into the labor market; or be able to find markets for its war-expanded production capabilities. Domestic markets alone would not be able to absorb all that America could now produce. The prospect existed that the economy would sink back into a depression, factories would become idle, mass unemployment would return, and an unstable economy once again would tear at the social fabric of the nation. American capitalism had been near collapse in 1932 when Roosevelt rescued it with the extraordinary measures of the New Deal. The situation was now ominous, and always hovering over it was the inchoate fear of American business that American workers might look to their Soviet counterparts for political lessons. It became strategically imperative for American corporate, military and political leaders to maintain American economic hegemony, not only in Europe but globally, through acquisition of foreign markets.[10]

The Marshall Plan resulted. It was an immense program of foreign aid in the form of American goods and services, ostensibly idealistic and designed to rebuild Europe, but it was hardly without self-interest. Since the Marshall Plan demanded the opening up of European markets to American penetration, the Soviet Union saw it as a hostile, predatory maneuver and declined to participate. It also loudly denounced it. On the other hand, the

Plan's anti-Soviet nature was barely concealed with thinly veiled warnings about countries seeking to gain political ends through human misery. By clever maneuvering America's political leaders also kept the Marshall Plan out of the United Nations where it would have logically belonged, but where the Soviet Union with its powerful voice and decisive vote could have kept it stillborn.[11]

Thus began the superpower rivalry, pitting the two principle victors against each other. One, the United States, at the end of the war was preeminently powerful (despite its significant war casualties: 400,000 killed and 700,000 wounded).[12] It was blessed with a thriving agriculture, an efficient, modern industrial complex, an effective transportation network, access to raw materials, a trained and healthy workforce, intact national boundaries and, not least, a nuclear monopoly. The other, the Union of Soviet Socialist Republics, had defeated the Wehrmacht on its western front at staggering cost. Russian army casualties, conservatively estimated at 29 million, represented more than three-quarters of all Allied casualties in the war – without counting civilians, said to have been over 17 million.[13] Moreover, its people were ill and exhausted, its land scorched, and those of its industries that had not been moved to its eastern interior in shambles.

World War II also represented the second time in some twenty years that the USSR had endured a foreign invasion. Soon after the Communists took power in 1917, British, American and French Allies occupied Murmansk and Archangel in the north, while additional British and French forces occupied Odessa and the Crimea in the south and part of the Caucasus. In Siberia, the Czech Army controlled the railroad, while Japanese and American troops spread from the Pacific westward. It was not until 1920 that the last of the invaders was driven out.[14]

The Russians never forgot this attempt to reverse their revolution. Now, in their 1945 victory, they were suspicious and determined to protect their borders by occupying neighboring states until those states developed benign and cooperative governments. They were particularly concerned about Poland with which there was a long history of thorny relations.[15] For the Russians they would thus seek a new *cordon sanitaire,* a buffer against possible new aggressors. To the U.S. and Western Europe, this westward sweep of the Soviet military and its subsequent occupation of neighboring states was perceived as a threat. For its part, the United States built a franchise of geopolitical influence through alliances, from North America through Greenland and Iceland, to Europe from Norway south to Portugal, eastward across Europe to the Middle East and thence to Pakistan and India. On Asia's Pacific coast it enfolded South Korea and Japan in its embrace.[16] Thus it surrounded the USSR with military bases legitimized as a way of protecting the world from the spread of communism.

And so, with the juxtaposition of the USSR's cordon sanitaire, and the

U.S. policy of containment, the Cold War was launched.

Matters were shaping up domestically, as well. Enemies of New Deal programs found they could delegitimize those programs by associating them with communism. A new and dangerous precedent now gained traction in the Cold War atmosphere: accusation without proof, labeling without reason, and demonizing of non-conformist political beliefs. These tactics, abetted by a pervasively intensifying anti-Soviet animus, became a vital part of the anti-Communist crusade. The mid-1930s had seen the creation of congressional committees that investigated subversive activities, initially those of fascist sympathizers like the German-American Bund. The House Committee on UnAmerican Activities (HUAC) was soon beating an unremitting drum roll denouncing the Red Menace.[17] J. Edgar Hoover, Director of the FBI, not to permit anyone to steal his spotlight, worked closely with HUAC and monitored the personal and political activities of prominent citizens including Eleanor Roosevelt, Democratic presidential candidate Adlai Stevenson II, Thomas Mann (a celebrated writer who had fled Germany to come to the United States in 1938), and Albert Einstein (and later the Reverend Dr. Martin Luther King, Jr.) among others. Mann, who had won the Nobel Prize for literature in 1929, moved to Switzerland in 1953 because of America's political climate. Einstein considered looking for a country with greater intellectual freedom but decided to stay.[18]

The problem was there was never a clear understanding of what constituted a communist, or even a justification for branding people as subversive or un-American because of their non-conformist views. Card carrying CPUSA (Communist Party of the USA) members were not the only ones denounced. Informers labeled people as subversives or as communists whimsically, their uncorroborated accusations uncritically accepted. Prominent among the informers were Louis Budenz, John Lautner, Elizabeth Bentley, Whittaker Chambers, Herbert Philbrick, Harvey Matusow, J. B. Matthews, Matt Cvetic and Paul Crouch. Many of them made a career out of denouncing and the Red Scare became good business.[19]

Playing on the fears of a trusting American electorate also proved to be a useful route for ambitious politicians. As an opportunity for self-promotion it was a political gold mine. For example: A successful practitioner of hunting communists and a rabid foe of Roosevelt was Republican Congressman J. Parnell Thomas from New Jersey. Thomas gained national approval and an ever-increasing budget and staff as head of HUAC from 1937 to 1949. This protector of the American way was later sentenced to six to eighteen months in prison for padding his payroll and pocketing salary kickbacks.[20]

Senator Lyndon Johnson from Texas, gained the support of the Texas oil crowd by calling Leland Olds, head of the Federal Power Commission, a communist. Olds had stood fast against the drive of the monopolies to increase consumer prices for oil and gas. Johnson knew Olds was not a subversive, but when he finished red-baiting him Olds was not reappointed. Olds was 58 when his career ended. He died in 1960, a poor man, snubbed by old friends and neighbors because of the communist taint. The policies and regulations he had instituted to break the grip of the private utility monopolies were reversed by his successor.[21] Johnson, however, secured his senate seat, and then his step up to the vice-presidency with the help of his friends in the energy business. He succeeded to the presidency when John F. Kennedy was assassinated.[22]

An even greater threat to American political stability came from a senator from Wisconsin. Senator Joseph McCarthy found a secure niche in the Senate in 1950, an ever-increasing share of the Senate budget for his permanent investigation subcommittee—and growing prominence for himself—as he intoned his sensational revelations of spies in the government. He wielded great power and the term, "McCarthyism," became a pejorative for the use of personal attacks through widely publicized, indiscriminate allegations which were never based on substantiated charges. It was not until he took on the United States Army with allegations of being sympathetic to and employing a communist that his power waned. McCarthy unraveled and lost support, but not before he had ruined the reputations and lives of many innocent people and spread a blanket of fear across the land.

Richard M. Nixon began his leap to national attention by red-baiting competitors for office, first Jerry Voorhees and then Helen Gahagan Douglas. In both cases he won election by inflicting lasting political damage. His technique of slander and demagogy, earned him the sobriquet, "Tricky Dick," and it tagged him for the rest of his political career.[23] Nixon came to national prominence for his work on the House UnAmerican Activities Committee where he was credited with forcing a confrontation between Alger Hiss and Whittaker Chambers, who had accused Hiss of having given him State Department secrets for transmittal to the Russians during the Roosevelt administration. Hiss was charged with perjury in denying association with Chambers in the 1930s. In the first of two trials the jury disagreed and the case was discharged. In January 1950, in a second trial, Hiss was found guilty and went to prison.

Nixon was elected President in 1968 and in the spring of 1970 expanded the Vietnam War by invading Cambodia. Students all over the United States, already worried about their vulnerability as fodder for a war that increasingly made little sense, demonstrated against the decision. Nixon called the protesting students, "bums." His inflammatory rhetoric helped create intolerable national stress which could have no benevolent result. On May 4, 1970, the Ohio National Guard fired tear gas grenades into a rally of about 300 unarmed students at Kent State University and then without warning they fired their M-1 rifles. Sixty-seven shots were fired in 12 seconds. When they finished, four "bums" lay dead and nine were wounded.[24]

The Watergate debacle in 1973 ended Nixon's presidency. Because of his complicity in criminal activities, Nixon became the first and only president to resign office in disgrace, which he did in August 1974, just ahead of an impeachment vote by the U.S. Senate.[25]

The parade continued.

A photogenic actor known mostly for his roles in Grade B movies, Ronald Reagan, as president of the Screen Actors Guild, gained national prominence when he testified before HUAC in 1947. The Guild had a tradition of supporting actors who had been targets of the vigilante blacklists resulting from the HUAC investigations. Reagan accommodated the studios that blacklisted actors, producers and writers who did not cooperate with HUAC.[26] Ten actors, writers and directors were jailed for contempt of congress when they refused to testify, and the studios fired them, with Reagan's support. Thereafter they were blacklisted, some never to work at their craft again.

On June 10, 1950, the first two of the Hollywood Ten, John Howard Lawson and Dalton Trumbo, began serving their prison terms. Two months later President Truman dispatched the first troops to Korea. Within a matter of a few weeks, nine Americans were arrested for allegedly stealing atom bomb secrets. The author William A. Reuben commented, "It is a safe bet that historians will agree that the summer of 1950 was the most hysterical period in the history of the United States. And the most shameful."[27]

In his appearance before the House UnAmerican Activities Committee, Reagan had not publicly named names, but he had done so secretly to the FBI.[28] Thus, he went from New Deal enthusiasm and union militancy to political informer and eventually, as president of the United States, to strikebreaker, firing PATCO union air traffic controllers in August 1981 when they struck for better pay and working conditions.[29]

At the end of 1991, what had been apparent for some time to Soviet watchers came to a head: the USSR dissolved and became a commonwealth of independent states. The Cold War was now over but left in its wake a legacy of fear, ruined lives, lost careers, trust and hope maimed beyond repair.

I was among those wounded.

Chapter 3

In The Beginning

When the FBI agents first called on me in May 1950 I talked to them. I had not understood that I had the constitutional right not to talk to them and that it was my equally important right to be left in peace and not to be harassed. I had been apprehensive that if I had refused to talk it would surely have convinced them that I was hiding important information. The badges they flashed and their authoritative manner were intimidating. I also did not realize that their motivation was not to establish a true picture of events but, rather, to justify their preconceived bias. Later I refused to continue the interviews; but talking to them at all was a major tactical mistake.

During their interviews the agents generated an aura of undefined danger; conveying an ominous sense of knowing something damning about me. They repeated their questions in different ways as though trying to trick me. They showed me pictures of people I did not know and had never met; but I was never sure they believed me when I said so. And they seemed to put a threatening spin on my most innocent doings.

They took a detailed accounting from me of my education, my work history, my family, what the source of Abe's income was, a list of employees and business associates, and asked me how Abe came to know Harry Gold. I could not tell them that for I did not know. I had never asked Abe and it was never a topic of conversation between us. They asked me about a discussion between Abe and Harry on a particular evening—did we not all go to dinner that night? We could have, but I did not remember specifically. And then:

"Did Mr. Brothman discuss the details of his grand jury appearance with you?" I could not remember.

"But would it not have been unusual for him not to discuss this with you?" No, he did not discuss a lot of things with me.

"Did he tell you what it was about?" He dismissed it as spy-scare stuff—silly and not pertinent to anything in his life.

"Are any of the Brothman employees members of the Communist Party?" No, they were not, so far as I knew.

"And you, Miss Moskowitz, are you a member of the Communist Party?" I answered no quickly, almost too quickly. I tried to remind myself that I had done nothing wrong and had nothing to fear. They had not named a crime and they had not accused me of anything.

"Did Mr. Brothman ever discuss communist ideas with you?"

"No."

I wondered. What were the FBI's notions of communist ideas? If I had spoken of how troubled Abe had been over the use of atom bombs on Hiroshima and Nagasaki in August 1945, and his fear that in the wrong hands the bomb could be used someday against civilian targets again, would they have branded that as a communist idea? Or that he fumed over Winston Churchill's Iron Curtain speech in 1946 in Fulton, Missouri because he believed it would destabilize world peace, would that have made him unpatriotic? Or that he regarded the Truman Doctrine of 1947 as unnecessarily provocative, would that, too, have stamped him as disloyal? If Abe Brothman had not held with the orthodoxies of the moment would that have made him an ideological outlaw?

"One night in May 1947 you and Gold and Brothman worked late in the laboratory. Brothman drove the two of you to Manhattan to drop Gold off at Penn Station and then to take you home. Do you recall that in the car Brothman and Gold had a violent argument and almost came to blows?"

"No, such an event never took place. They never argued."

"And you did not try to calm them down?"

"No. I never took part in their conversations because they were usually about technical matters. Also, that evening I would not have heard them. I was curled up on the back seat fast asleep. They were in the front, murmuring. It was four in the morning."

It had begun as a mildly disconcerting event, intrusive and annoying but one I regarded as a temporary inconvenience. The United States government in all its majesty could not seriously be poking through my insignificant

The subpoena demanding Miriam Moskowitz' appearance before the Grand Jury on July 17, 1950.

world expecting to uncover grand scale perfidy. But the questions were repetitive; as they gained intensity I felt threatened and uneasy.

Having talked to them, nevertheless, I had told one lie. I denied that I was a communist when in fact I was. I did not like disowning my ideological convictions. I thought they merited respect and would have preferred to deal with the question openly. I sensed, however, that it would distort the inquiry. It would immediately becloud the question of my innocence in what seemed to be a festering political toxemia and it would have subjected me to demands to name others, which I would not do. I thought that in turn might have escalated into contempt-of-court citations, if a judge had ordered me to give information and I refused. The only course I had to prevent this situation from spiraling out of control was to refuse to speak further and to say nothing about my politics – or anyone else's.

It was the Depression and then World War II which had shaped my turning to the political left.

I had never forgotten the bread lines of the Depression and the men in threadbare suits and ties—the trappings of their dwindling claim to middle class respectability—who were selling apples on the street, or the families who were lining up at soup kitchens in the dead of winter. I remembered the newspaper pictures of furniture and household belongings piled on the sidewalk, and frightened children clustered around them in evictions of families who could not pay their rent.

I had an indelible memory of having taken the elevator to the top of an office skyscraper in downtown Manhattan. It was soon after I had graduated from high school. I had been making the rounds of the employment agencies but was infrequently being sent out for job interviews because there were so few jobs and so many applicants. I had descended the stairway on foot and visited each office, floor by floor, asking if there was a job I could fill. And I had never forgotten having sought shelter in Trinity Church nearby on that cold and rainy November day and having wept despairingly as I sat in the dark and contemplated my bleak future. I was all of eighteen.

My father was a salesman for wholesale meat packers. He would come home late in the day with fearful stories of butcher shops closing because the owners were not doing enough business to pay their bills. Because Dad made the rounds of the trade he knew where there was a chance job opening; as a result, every night before he sat down to supper he would field telephone calls from men desperate for a job or even a day's work, who hoped he might be able to put them on to one. There was no effective social safety net and unemployment insurance was regarded as a presumptuous idea promoted by a bunch of wild-eyed radicals looking to freeload on those who had been more provident.

I listened to those calls and saw my father's face grow longer as he worried about whether his own job would last out the crisis, and I watched my mother share his concern and maneuver with his shrinking income to produce a meal that would feed six of us. I was growing up in a wretched time.

I remembered that dear young man who worked in the same government office as I did a few years later—the Immigration and Naturalization Service—and who rode the subway with me after work. We were both attending classes at the City College of New York, pursuing degrees at night. He was ever so circumspect in his overtures of friendship as I was in receiving them. It was a reminder of how the social sickness of race prejudice could undo a potential friendship—for he was black and I was white. Because we were young, we were brave and dated cautiously. Subsequently his parents invited me to dinner at their home and I went, but I could not return the invitation to him. We went to our graduation gala, not together but with other companions, and we eyed each other from opposite sides of the dance floor and opposite ends of the bar. When we did go out together we remained within the ring of safety the Harlem ghetto provided; we dared not go downtown to a movie or the theater and risk stares and provocations. When he took me back to my apartment – I was now sharing a place in Manhattan – in his rinky-dink old heap of a car after class or at the end of an evening out, he would park half a block away and murmur an endearing, quick goodnight. We could never linger over farewells for we might be observed by a passerby and there was danger in that. In the car he would watch me protectively as I walked down the block to my door alone in the dark.

The head of our office took to calling arbitrary and unpaid overtime, and without advance notice. My young friend and I had evening classes to get to and some of the women in the office had children in day care, institutions with inflexible closing hours. It became an intolerable situation. I chose to join the union, a local affiliate of the CIO, and to solicit membership among my coworkers so that the union would handle our complaint. To negotiate our complaint we needed a grievance committee and I became a member of it. I also ground out the publicity for our action.

But my young man wanted no part of the union or of anything that grazed near a field of political controversy. I caught a faint whiff of disdain for it from him and thought I understood. His personal anemometer for judging political winds was actuated by how they affected him as a black American for he judged all of them, the union and anything else, to be potential trouble.

My liberal leanings amused him and he twitted my efforts to blend my middle class background with a left perspective. He teased me, calling me, "Mrs. Babbitt," a reference to Sinclair Lewis' satirical novel, *Babbitt*, which derided middle class, liberal pretensions. And as we contemplated our career moves after graduation my options as a woman were limited, but his were even more so.

When he was drafted he became an officer in the United States Army— in a black unit because the Army was still segregated. And because he was black and I was white our relationship was approaching a dead end. The frustrations of trying to be like any other young couple with foreseeable goals were becoming insurmountable. When he left for the Army our goodbyes were wistful and hopeful yet we knew, I think, that we would never see each other again.

While I was active in the union I marched with my local in a May Day parade behind banners of peace and equality. May Day had its origins in medieval England where it was celebrated on May First as a festive holiday. The Socialist International in 1889 adopted May Day as a workingman's holiday.[1] It was also celebrated in most of Europe, especially in the former USSR, and before the Cold War it was celebrated in working class communities in the United States. My colleagues and I chanted:

"OPEN UP THAT SECOND FRONT!"
or "JIM CROW MUST GO!"

We sang the songs of our time: *"JOE HILL," "SOLIDARITY FOREVER," "WHICH SIDE ARE YOU ON." "IF I HAD A HAMMER,"* and those of international peace and freedom—*"PEAT BOG SOLDIERS,"* or *"DIE GEDANKEN SIND FREI"* and out of the Spanish Civil War, *"VIVA LA QUINTE BRIGADA,"* stirring songs full of hope and humanity. Harry Bridges was our worker hero and Paul Robeson our cultural icon.

I also admired the bravery of the Russian people during the war; the siege of Leningrad, in particular, roused my sympathy. In August 1941 the Germans cut off the city from the rest of Russia and for almost two years the citizens withstood daily shelling and air raids, while no food or supplies could get through. General Eisenhower cited casualty figures of 350,000 who had died of starvation alone, with many more killed and wounded. He wrote: "The extraordinary suffering of the population and the length of time that the city endured the rigors and privations of the battle combined to make the operation one of the memorable sieges of history; … it is without parallel in modern times."[2]

One had to salute such grit. In solidarity I wrote letters to my legislators urging the opening of the Second Front to take some of the pressure off the Russians, and I gave scarves and gloves for Russian War Relief.

In this period I also signed numerous social action petitions. It was a turbulent time forged in Depression, insecurity and war, and my union comrades and I had become social idealists.

One summer day in 1946 I walked into a neighborhood office of the Communist Party and asked to join. Somewhat startled, a man handed me a membership application which I filled out and signed. When I left I felt the day had been well spent.

My active contributions were thin and when I went to meetings I found the rhetoric obscure, stylized and usually bombastic, although centered on real problems. Mostly it concerned Washington's support of the growing assault on the gains of unions, as well as the threat to subvert the peace in this post-Roosevelt era. We were also concerned with local issues; the need for jobs and inexpensive housing for returning veterans, the increased cost of a subway ride, and always the stubborn issues of racial and religious discrimination. On several Sunday mornings I solicited subscriptions to the *Daily Worker* and peddled Marxist literature. They were not tasks I particularly relished but I had a strong personal ethic and I recognized that my life was now richer for a responsible commitment I had not had before.

I also joined the short-lived Progressive Party (in New York State it merged with the American Labor Party) in 1948, and I courted signatures on election petitions for it. As a third party opposition to President Harry Truman and his new Cold War agenda, the Progressive Party recognized by 1946 – soon after he took office on the death of Roosevelt – that his postwar presidency was undoing the enlightened New Deal policies. It was also accompanied by an increase in violence towards African-Americans. The Progressive Party's platform endorsed peace, the right of workers to organize and strike against oppressive working conditions, and it opposed racial discrimination.

My colleagues and I saw our convictions giving new meaning to our lives. We had no way of knowing, and would never have believed that revolution and reform could ever be twisted to become the savage despotism it became under Stalin. Soon after I joined the Communist Party, however, it seemed to undergo serious ideological ferment. Earlier, criticisms had been leveled against it by some of the fraternal European organizations and that criticism was still ricocheting among the rank and file in the local clubs. At meetings I asked questions, but the answers were obscure and not forthcoming. My repeated questions were regarded with suspicion, which escalated; almost immediately I was accused of acting in concert with enemy agents and I was expelled.

But this was a dispute over ideas and it is not the business of government to censor ideas or to monitor thought. When the FBI questioned me, therefore, I refused to discuss my political beliefs or activities or those of others. I wondered simplistically when I was arrested, would this have been the basis for charging me with having conspired to obstruct justice?

Sitting in jail that long sleepless night of my arrest I found it impossible to unravel this bizarre turn of events. And as I greeted the dawn, perched impatiently on the table watching the street below, it blew over me with the force of a hurricane that I would have to fend for myself; blind-sided and politically powerless, alone and without resources, I would be unable to overcome the distorted view the world would be fed of who I was.

Chapter 4

Jailhouse Blues

Even before the morning wake-up call a storm of obscenities erupted in the cellblock and crowded out all purposeful reflection. As the women stirred, one cursed and yelled to the guard to open the gates: "Hey, lady! Let me out! I be gittin' sick in heah!"

Her cell neighbor groaned in protest: "It's Sunday, girl. Breakfast ain't for 'nother hour. Be quiet and let me sleep!"

But the savage brutishness intensified and someone farther down the cellblock shouted a reprimand: "Shut yer mouth, girl! Hush up! You be makin' too much damn noise and it's only six in the mohnin'!"

Now a threatening interchange layered over the universal noise and the cellblock roared to life. A young woman, seemingly not out of her teens whom I had heard weeping during the night, moaned: "I wanna go home! Dear God. Please. I wanna go home!"

At the other end there was commiseration: "Ain't that chile never gonna stop cryin'? Don' cry, honey. It don' do no good. You'll get used to it heah."

A perceptive soul summed it all up: "Shee-it! This ain't no place to be on a Sunday."

So began my first day in jail.

"Hey, miss, you white chick with them fancy ways. What they really grab you fer?"

I was tired and frightened and the wretchedness of my surroundings and the agitated women added to my unease. I did not answer. But they were not letting me hide.

"Hey, lady..." someone else called to me. "It's only a half-hour to breakfast. Better git yo' order in to the guard. Tell her whether you wants bacon and eggs or sausages and pancakes. Do it now, quick! I be tellin' ya fer y'own good, honey. Otherwise ya gits only leftovers!"

Screeching laughter told me I was being led into a booby trap. I forced myself to be flippant but I was angry: "Thanks, but I'm not hungry. Had too much steak and chocolate cream pie last night and I'm still full. You can have my share."

Again they screamed with laughter. Some of the women repeated what I had said, imitated my speech and mocked me with a hip flounce. Their fun at my expense was another probe pecking at my wounds.

"Why are you doing this to me?" I thought. "You're just a bunch of miserable lowlifes, a pack of losers and I hate you all!"

I waited my turn and then showered and dressed. Just when I was ready our cellblock was called to breakfast. I wanted only coffee. As we filed past the guard monitoring the chow line I glanced at the front page of a tabloid on her desk. My picture on one side and Abe's on the other filled the whole page. It had been taken as we hurried up that long, stone stairway into the Foley Square Courthouse the evening before. The headlines said two more A-bomb spies had been caught.

I thought the guard looked at me with loathing but it was the front page and its headlines that made me ill. I got off the chow line and hurried back to my cell where I retched. No longer did I want any coffee. I wondered how the plant in New Jersey would continue to function. My father's savings were invested in it; he had recently been excessed out of his job, and without a pension. I wondered about the Swiss clients and how soon and how successfully Abe would be able to reassure them that this scandal wasn't real; that it had been fabricated. I had not yet begun to realize that everything I had worked for so long, every sacrifice I had made was hopelessly, irretrievably gone now.

I returned to the officer's desk. She was supervising breakfast, so did not notice my standing over her newspaper. I read quickly and the paragraph that told how much time might be meted out to us it was another blow. Two years for me on a single count and two plus five for Abe on two counts. There could also be a fine of $10,000 for each of us plus an extra $5,000 for Abe on the second count. I had no idea how I'd ever pay that sum of money; the insanity of it suggested I could be incarcerated forever.

When the women returned to the cellblock after breakfast I questioned them and they proved to be wise and knowledgeable; knowledge was survival and they were clearly survivors. Some of them knew that if I did not have the money to pay the fine I would have to sign a Pauper's Oath, do thirty days extra and the government would have to release me. (What they did not know was that the extra thirty days would not be forgiveness time; the government would want that money out of any future income I might acquire once I was free.)

Someone handed me a cigarette. I did not ask for it but I was grateful. Before I lighted up, I drank a quantity of water to fool my stomach into thinking it was full so that the cigarette would not make me nauseous. I collected a supply of about six cigarettes and some matches but I never knew who my benefactors were. I began to realize there was a well of sisterly kindness here—seared, flinty, jeering, suspicious and unsentimental—and I had somehow tapped into it.

I determined that my meager supply of smokes would have to last until the afternoon of the next day when Commissary would appear. I was sure my parents would come to see me as soon as possible, and they did. But with only six cigarettes until then I could not smoke more than once an hour, and then only a few puffs at a time. I would take a hungry drag or two and then carefully pinch the burning end of the cigarette to put it out.

In the afternoon newspapers arrived for those inmates who had ordered them the day before and I borrowed one to read the details of my arrest. It was more of the same. I was an atom-bomb spy. I was a communist. I was an enemy of my country. This went beyond the mere marketing of news; the press had gone berserk. It had jettisoned established journalistic standards and was behaving like the prosecution's pet poodle. It uncritically accepted the self-congratulatory press agentry from J. Edgar Hoover and his cohorts and it seemed to me it was without honor or conscience.

Some of my sister jail mates were unimpressed by what they read. They had their own experiences and knew almost instinctively that not everything the press printed was believable. They knew also that truth and justice and the law were frequently unrelated concepts. However, a few muttered ugly threats calling me, "SPY!" or "TRAITOR!" They were big and burly and mean-looking, and I was fearful. My cell neighbor warned me to keep my wits about me and not answer or provoke them for they would welcome an excuse to corner me and beat me up – or worse. I made sure never to get caught in the communal shower room when one of them was there, and I was wary of their presence on the chow line even though it was supervised by the guards. In the afternoon when we were allowed to go up to the roof for recreation hour, I never got on the same elevator with them. In the day room after supper, I sat far away from them or stayed in my cell. Ultimately they were sentenced and transferred to other institutions and I was free of their menace. With vigilance and help from sister inmates I had managed to navigate clear of jailhouse problems.

In the meantime my parents, my sister and my brothers took turns visiting me, which made life bearable. My attorney also appeared to tell me what he was doing, so I knew I was not alone and that a defense was being planned. No other visitors were allowed.

Eighteen days after my arrest a guard came for me during afternoon lockup. "Get your things together, Moskowitz, and strip your cot. You're going out on bail."

In an instant I gathered up the change of clothes my sister had brought and rolled it into a tight wad. I couldn't find the letters and notes I had kept on an open shelf—the only storage space in the cell. I needed that material to discuss with my attorney and for the future, and I realized with dismay that I would have to re-create it. (I found that material years later, in the FBI file, some of which became available to me in May 2001.[1] The jail had turned it over to the U. S. Marshal; his cover note implied that I had forgotten it. But I did not forget it; it had been stolen from me.)

I stripped the cot, folded the sheets and laid them on top of the pillow, yanked out the newspaper padding I had used under the mattress to even out the well of the sagging spring and fled down the corridor. The cellblock was uncharacteristically quiet as the women watched, and I was sad for them. Few others would be able to make bail.

My cell neighbor called softly after me, "Good luck, girl!

I spun around, ran back to her, held her arms through the bars and tried to embrace her as our cheeks brushed and our tears mingled. I gave her my cigarettes—and the matches—then resumed flight. Down the elevator, through the office and out into the waiting marshal's car which would whisk me to court where I would be released. My parents and my attorney were waiting for me and together we walked into the free world and fresh air, benevolent sunshine and the bliss of freedom.

It had been a long and unforgettable eighteen days.

Chapter 5

With Justice for All

A few weeks after my arrest, in September 1950, Alfred Dean Slack pleaded guilty to having conspired to commit espionage. He then tried to retract his plea on a claim that he had had inadequate legal representation. He had been coerced into pleading guilty, he told the court, but in fact he was not guilty. He maintained and the prosecution knew that he had never been associated with the atom bomb project; his activities had been unrelated to Klaus Fuchs or spy rings or any government secrets. He had known Gold only as a purchaser of commercial manufacturing data. The judge refused to allow him to change his plea. At sentencing the prosecutor recommended a ten-year jail term; the judge imposed fifteen.[1]

On September 28, 1950, a week after Slack's sentencing, the ninth victim was arrested. He was Oscar J. Vago, a former partner of Abe's with whom Gold had been friendly while he worked for Abe. Vago had been interrogated by the grand jury and was now charged with having lied to it. He was a naturalized citizen, having been born in Hungary, and he had come to the United States on a student visa in the mid-1920's. He dropped his college courses when he found them too elementary, but this had the effect of canceling the validity of his student visa.

Nevertheless, Vago remained in the United States and worked as an engineer under an assumed name. He also paid taxes under that name. In 1928 he married, but used his correct name. His bride was also a Hungarian immigrant, but she became a citizen in 1931. In 1933 the couple went to Hungary for a visit. When they returned to the United States Vago was now a legal immigrant, the husband of a citizen. But with this trip he had one too many entry dates. In his application for citizenship he used the second date.[2]

At a grand jury hearing in September 1950 Vago, an extremely nervous man with a nervous tic, gave the earlier entry date without explaining the ambiguous events. Voluntarily, a few days later he requested an appearance before the grand jury to correct the record. He was never given a chance. He was seized, instead, as another suspect in the spy ring, and held in $50,000 bail on a charge of perjury.

Unsuccessful in getting bail reduced and unable to raise the $50,000, Vago was held for twenty-one months until after the Brothman/Moskowitz and the Rosenberg/Sobell trials had been disposed of. In June 1952 Judge Sylvester J. Ryan heard the perjury case against Vago in lieu of a jury. He chastised the prosecution for its delay in bringing the case to court and imposed a suspended sentence. Judge Ryan also noted that Vago's indictment had had nothing to do with espionage.[3]

Nevertheless, within a time frame of four months in 1950 there were nine arrests of Americans, the arrests made to appear connected with Soviet atomic espionage and the Fuchs event. The newspaper headlines were consistently lurid. Each arrest appeared to have been staged to follow on the heels of the one before it and the public accepted the barrage of fearful news without question or analytic wonder. Hard facts were never offered, only sensationalized, ominous hints and innuendoes. (In the meantime, the lawyer we had used for business dealings obtained a trial lawyer for us and we began meeting with him. My parents took a mortgage on their house to pay my share of the costs. Abe raised money by borrowing, but I never knew from whom.)

In October 1950, in preparation for trial, our attorneys petitioned for a Bill of Particulars, the granting of which we expected to be routine. Judge Edward Weinfeld denied the petition.[4]

Our trial began on November 8, 1950. Judge Irving R. Kaufman presided and his first act was to remand Abe and me to jail even before jury selection. We had been free less than three months. Sending us back to jail buttressed the prosecution's claim that we were dangerous criminals. In his argument opposing commitment our attorney complained to the court that a prospective defense witness had refused to talk to our investigator. Our attorney said the FBI was intimidating our witnesses. Judge Kaufman rejected the accusation; he said the FBI did not intimidate witnesses.[5]

The backdrop to our trial was the vivid culmination of all the arrests. The newspaper headlines, like incendiary blowtorches, propelled this case to the outer limits of absurdity and the prospective jurors would have been unable to avoid seeing them:

"3 ATOMIC SPY SUSPECTS DUE IN COURT TODAY'
– *New York Daily News*, November 8, 1950

"GOLD PREPARES TO TESTIFY AGAINST 2 IN ATOM SPY RING'
– *New York Daily News*, November 8, 1950

"BAIL CANCELLED FOR 2 ON TRIAL IN ATOM PLOT"
– *New York Daily News*, November 9, 1950

"2 GO ON TRIAL IN ATOMIC SPY CASE, LOSE BAIL— SAYPOL LINKS BROTHMAN AND MISS MOSKOWITZ TO 'WORLD COMMUNIST CONSPIRACY'"
– *New York Herald Tribune*, November 9, 1950

The prosecution team was headed by Irving H. Saypol and included Roy

M. Cohn, John M. Foley, Myles K. Lane and Thomas Donegan. Our attorneys were William W. Kleinman, (a former Brooklyn District Attorney), his assistant, Mortimer Sattler, and William L. Messing. There were two and only two prosecution witnesses: Elizabeth Bentley and Harry Gold. It would be the same core cast that four months later would try, prosecute, or testify against Julius and Ethel Rosenberg. The conclusions were inescapable: our trial was a necessary dress rehearsal for that later event and our conviction was critical to the prosecution's success in those proceedings.

Even before our trial opened and unremittingly as it progressed, the FBI and Saypol's office leaked misinformation to the press. Walter Winchell, the gossip columnist and radio personality (and nightclub companion of J. Edgar Hoover and Roy Cohn) mirrored the prevailing hysteria, daily predicting revelations of heinous crimes the government would prove we had committed. The rest of the media, ever eager for Hoover and Company's handouts, tumbled over each other to acquire more of the offal. None of the promised revelations ever materialized, but the relentlessly poisonous pre-trial notoriety guaranteed that we would find it difficult, if not impossible, to acquire a panel of unprejudiced jurors. It also made a sham of the uniquely American doctrine of presumption of innocence; that is, a defendant is innocent until proved otherwise.

```
UNITED STATES DISTRICT COURT

SOUTHERN DISTRICT OF NEW YORK.

------------------------------x
                              :
UNITED STATES OF AMERICA      :
                              :
          vs.                 :    C. 133-106
                              :
ABRAHAM BROTHMAN and MIRIAM   :
MOSKOWITZ.                    :
                              :
------------------------------x

Before:

        HON. IRVING R. KAUFMAN
                District Judge.


                    New York, November 8, 1950, 11:00 a.m.


                    APPEARANCES:

IRVING F. SAYPOL, ESQ., United States Attorney,
                    for the Government:
By Irving H. Saypol, Esq.; U. S. Attorney,
    Roy M. Cohn, Esq., and
    John M. Foley, Esq., Assistant U. S. Attorneys.

WILLIAM MESSING, ESQ.,
WILLIAM W. KLEINMAN, ESQ., and
MORTIMER SATTLER, ESQ.,
                    Attorneys for the Defendants.
```

PART II

KAUFMAN'S COURT

Chemical engineer Abraham Brothman and his former business partner, Miriam Moskowitz, arriving in Federal Court.
(Mirror Photo)

2 in Spy Case Sent To Jail as Trial Begins

Chemical engineer Abraham Brothman and his former business partner, Miriam Moskowitz, went on trial in Federal Court yesterday on charges of conspiring to obstruct justice during an investigation of Soviet espionage. Judge Kaufman promptly cancelled their $25,000 bail and directed they be jailed during the trial.

The remanding of the 36-year-old Brothman, of 41-08 42d St., Sunnyside, Queens, and Miriam, 34, of 151 Eighth Ave., was requested by U. S. Attorney Saypol, who said the case is tied up with the world Communist movement. He charged the defendants' Red leanings prompted them to "obstruct justice by misleading a Federal grand jury."

Judge Kaufman directed that selection of a jury begin tomorrow. His action in revoking bail was protested by the defense counsel, William Kleinman. Kleinman contended that the bail of the 11 Communist leaders convicted last year was not revoked until they became obstreperous in court and that Alger Hiss remained at liberty during trial.

Further protest was cut off by Judge aKufman, who told both sides to submit questions to be put to prospective jurors. He directed that Brothman and Miss Moskowitz be permitted to consult with their attorney.

Named as a co-conspirator, but not a co-defendant, is Harry Gold, the Philadelphia biochemist who has pleaded guilty to passing atomic secrets to Dr. Klaus Fuchs, the British scientist now serving a prison term

in England for espionage.

The indictment charges that Brothman, Miss Moskowitz and Gold conspired to "defraud the U. S. of the government function of enforcing the Federal criminal law," and that Brothman persuaded Gold to give false testimony before a grand jury.

Target in Crime Probe Defeated

GARY, Ind., Nov. 8. (AP).—The Democratic prosecutor of Lake County, who has been the target of the Gary Crime Commission, lost his bid for reelection yesterday.

Prosecutor Ben Schwart lost to David P. Stanton, a Republican, by more than 6,000 votes despite the fact that the Democrats swept most other offices in this county adjacent to Chicago.

The Crime Commission had charged that there was a connection between the prosecutor's office and organized crime.

An amateur can buck a professional in the spot news field. The MIRROR pays both well. Phone MU. 2-1000, Ext. 14.

(New York Daily Mirror, November 9, 1950)

Chapter 6

Setting the Stage

U nited States Attorney Irving H. Saypol opened the trial with a statement which dealt with "the world-wide quest for communist totalitarian domination..." putting the case against us in the context of the rabid anti-communism enflamed by McCarthy and the press. The background to our indictment, he said, concerned a grand jury investigation into espionage conducted for the Soviet Union by American communists. He spoke of "... a world communist movement whose purpose it is by treachery, deceit, infiltration by other groups, espionage, sabotage, terrorism, and other means... to establish a communist totalitarian dictatorship..." He said that by inducing a witness to lie about espionage matters we had accomplished a diversion of the jury's attention to a false track, delaying justice for more than three years. He did not accuse us directly of being communists but delivered a clear implication that we were, and that that was our motivation for the crime.

The lead-up to the trial included the reading of the testimonies of the FBI agents who had originally questioned Abe and Harry and then, of Abe and Harry's grand jury testimony in July 1947. There was nothing different or new about those testimonies. Abe had told them that Golos offered sales services which he accepted. Golos introduced his secretary, Helen, who would pick up any of Brothman's offerings when he, Golos, was not available. Ultimately Harry Gold took Helen's place because Abe needed to discuss his material with a technical person. In his grand jury testimony Abe had also said that whatever material he gave Golos or Helen he had also published in established, professional engineering journals; a matter of some twenty-four technical articles.

After a flurry of interest Golos seemed to have lost any desire to mine this source of business, and he (and Helen) faded out of the picture. However, Abe and Harry had professional interests in common and over the next year or two Abe had used Harry on a freelance basis from time to time. At the end of 1945 Abe set up his own laboratory and invited Harry Gold to head it. In May 1946 Harry Gold came to work for Abe.

In that testimony Abe denied that he was a member of the Communist Party but admitted that he had belonged, briefly, to the Young Communist League when he was a student, that he had probably signed petitions of various organizations, and that this was the sum total of his political affiliations.

Harry Gold's testimony before the 1947 grand jury included a resume of his education. He attended a year and a half at the University of Pennsylvania; then from 1933 to 1936, earned a diploma in chemistry at Drexel Institute in Philadelphia. From 1939 to 1940 he attended Xavier University in Cincinnati, where he obtained a bachelor of -science degree in chemistry. Between Drexel and Xavier he also took a course in psychology, an organic chemistry course at Columbia, and at St. Joseph's School in Philadelphia he took courses in engineering management, science, a war training program, fermentation chemistry, distillery operation and laboratory glass-blowing.

Gold had testified that he met Golos in the fall of 1940 at a meeting of the American Chemical Society in Philadelphia, having been introduced to him by a colleague, Carter Hoodless. Gold went to dinner with Golos, during which the latter proposed a business arrangement. He needed someone to check on the technical validity of some proposals and related drawings of chemical processes which an engineer by the name of Abraham Brothman was submitting to him, and he was willing to pay for those evaluations. Golos gave him Brothman's telephone number and asked him to call. Gold said he thought some of the evaluations might involve "paper chemistry" but some would have to be checked in a laboratory.

Gold further testified that Golos never told him what his own connections were and that he never mentioned any Russian affiliation.

Gold testified that he met with Brothman some six months later, about the late spring of 1941. He never saw Golos again, however. Golos did telephone Gold at his home several times but never renewed their arrangement so Gold concluded that Golos "was a phony, (sic) just another one," in an apparently long string of fly-by-nighters whom he had met over the years. In the meantime his friendship with Brothman and their professional relationship had borne fruit. He was now Brothman's chief chemist.

Gold also testified that he had never been a member of the Communist Party nor ever belonged to a communist front organization.

That ended the reading of the 1947 grand jury testimony of Abraham Brothman and Harry Gold. I had not been summoned to appear before this grand jury, but I was summoned three years later, in 1950. During this trial, however, no one, least of all the judge, asked whether I had appeared in 1947 (or at any other time), and what had been my testimony. I sensed that I was becoming a non-person in this court even though I was seated at the defendants' table. For the moment that seemed to be an advantage.

Now we moved to a juicier phase of the trial. The courtroom audience and the media people were eagerly awaiting this.

Chapter 7

Elizabeth, the Queen

The prosecution then brought Elizabeth Bentley to the stand.[1] Bentley had voluntarily confessed to the FBI in November 1945 that she had received secret government information from Americans for transmittal to the Soviet Union. She had been testifying about her activities before various congressional committees since 1947. When she appeared at our trial she was already well known as a self-confessed ex-Communist spy courier. The tabloids referred to her as the "Red Spy Queen." Among those she had testified against were United States government employees Alger Hiss, William Remington, Nathan G. Silvermaster, Victor Perlo and Harry Dexter White. She had also testified against Earl Browder, former head of the American Communist Party.

During her many congressional appearances, no one had ever challenged her veracity and she was protected, by immunity, from prosecution for perjury. As a witness in our trial, however, she was not so protected. Thus, her appearance against us had an unquestioned aura of legitimacy; she was heralded in the media as the definitive, unimpeachable witness. And as an expert on communist espionage her opinions at our trial, in the form of testimony were given the weight of hard evidence.

On direct examination Bentley gave her background. She had graduated from Vassar College in 1930, taught at a private school for girls for two years and then took a master's degree at Columbia University. She spent the following academic year, 1933-34, in Italy at the University of Florence.

Prosecutor Saypol drew from her that she had joined the American Communist Party in March 1935 when she returned to the United States. He then led her to testify about some of her activities in the Party. Kleinman, our attorney, who had begun to object earlier when the prosecutor introduced this line of testimony, became more insistent. He said Bentley's information was irrelevant, immaterial and had nothing to do with us. Also, he pointed out, the date of her joining the Communist Party, March 1935, much predated the time frame specified in the indictment. Kaufman overruled him. However, it was clear that Bentley's testimony served the purpose of putting the issue of communism squarely before the jury. Without Bentley's remarks the prosecution could not have introduced it.

While a member of the Communist Party she obtained a job in July 1938 as a secretary and researcher in the Italian Library of Information in New

York City. The Library, she explained, was a fascist propaganda outlet for the Italian government in the United States. Thereupon she sought out someone at Communist Party headquarters in New York and connected with a Mr. F. Brown who told her to collect whatever literature and propaganda she thought would be interesting. As Mr. Brown seemed to have no time for her subsequently, she was referred to Jacob Golos, to whom she thereafter delivered her material. (Under cross examination she said that soon after meeting Golos they became lovers, although they did not live together.)

She met Abraham Brothman through Jacob Golos, who introduced her as "Helen." The meeting occurred about the spring of 1940. Her description of the meeting was specific:

Q. (by Mr. Saypol): "Will you tell us what circumstances under which you met Mr. Brothman first, and when?"

A. "Yes, in the spring of 1940 after a conversation with Mr. Golos, I met Mr. Brothman at a Chinese restaurant which is on 33rd Street between Sixth and Seventh Avenues on the second floor. We had a meal there and after that we had a long discussion."

Q. "Before you had the meal, was there an introduction all around?"

A. "Yes, Mr. Golos introduced Mr. Brothman as Abe Brothman, and he introduced me as 'Helen.'"

Q. "Did he mention your second name?"

A. "No, he did not."

Q. "How did Brothman refer to Mr. Golos?"

A. "He referred to him as John."

Q. "Now go on and tell us, the introductions having been effected, the dinner having been had, what was the conversation amongst the three of you?"

A. "Mr. Golos explained to Mr. Brothman that it would be rather difficult for him in the future to see him each week or each two weeks, and that therefore I would take his place in order to bring him directives from the Communist Party, to collect his Communist Party dues and to collect any material that he had to be relayed to Mr. Golos."

Q. "How long did these meetings continue from the time of the first meeting in the spring of 1940?"

A. "Until the early fall of 1941."

Bentley went on to state that she continued to meet with Brothman almost weekly after that, usually around 8 o'clock in the evening. They would have dinner during which she would explain the latest Communist Party policy and theories to Brothman. He would then hand her some blueprints and would dictate technical explanations of them to her.

Brothman asked her once or twice, said Bentley, whether the engineers at

Amtorg were satisfied with his work. (Her remarks substantiated his statements that he hoped to please Amtorg because he was seeking business from them.)

He soon became dissatisfied in dealing with her, Bentley said, because she did not understand his technical explanations. He asked Golos to put him in touch with an engineer, instead.

(Brothman was obviously asking for a direct sales contact with the prospective client but he may have also had a more personal reason. During this period, he once told Gold, Bentley had tried to seduce him, thus presenting him with an awkward situation.[2] It was then that Brothman asked for a replacement. Now, as she testified against him, he felt that his lack of personal interest in Bentley accounted for the hostility manifest in her trial testimony.)

Subsequently, Bentley arranged for a replacement but when Brothman demurred, inexplicably, despite his request for a change, Bentley chastised him. Unless he followed orders, she testified, "we would be forced to the unpleasant conclusion that he was not a good communist." Brothman finally yielded.

As described by Bentley, the method of connecting with the new contact had strange, clandestine overtones. Brothman was to park his car on a particular street in Manhattan on a particular night and at a particular hour. At the appointed time the new contact would slide into the front seat alongside him and say, "I bring greetings from Helen."

Bentley asked Brothman for his car's license number so that it could be passed to the new contact. Brothman again objected, she said; he did not understand why he had to meet people in such an odd way and why couldn't she or Golos do the introducing. They, in turn, argued with him and said that as a good communist he should follow orders. Eventually, and again reluctantly, he gave her his license number.

Bentley denied knowing Harry Gold or ever having met him even though he was her successor. The last time she saw Brothman was about the early fall of 1941.

On cross-examination Bentley became confrontational, seeming to relish the courtroom combat. Our attorney, Kleinman, elicited from her that she was forty-two years old, that she had been living intermittently in an apartment for the past twelve or more years which belonged to a relative and for which she paid no rent. She appeared to have other addresses as well and she had had a succession of temporary jobs. She admitted again that she had worked for the Italian Library of Information for some nine or ten months and stole literature and copies of correspondence from them.

About the last day of July or the first of August, 1949, she said, she began testifying before several congressional committees in Washington, including the House UnAmerican Activities Committee, the Senate

Investigations Committee and Senator McCarran's Committee on Immigration and Naturalization. She had also testified before several grand juries beginning in June 1947.

Kleinman asked Bentley if she had testified in 1947 about Harry Gold; the information would enable him to then match that testimony with what she was now offering to determine if she was consistent. Bentley ducked answering; she said she could not remember. Kleinman continued:

Q. "But sometime in 1950 did you testify…. Were you asked any questions concerning Harry Gold?"

A. "I think I was; I can't recall."

Q. "Well, at that time the name Harry Gold did have some significance to you, did it not?"

A. "Well, very vaguely, Mr. Kleinman."

Q. "Well, you read the newspapers don't you?"

A. "I was in Connecticut and not reading anything but the Norwalk News which didn't go into things like that."

Q. "You mean it was not reported in that newspaper that a man had been arrested for spy activities in May of (that) year?"

A. "Very vaguely; I paid little attention to it."

Q. "Miss Bentley, you have been interested in these activities for a good many years, haven't you?"

A. "I was on vacation from it."

Q. "But you have been interested in spies and espionage?"

A. "I was interested, Mr. Kleinman."

Q. "In foreign agents?"

A. "I was."

Q. "Weren't you interested in finding out if any of your friends were involved with Harry Gold or any of your former friends?"

A. "No, I wasn't."

That was false testimony.

Starting in November 1945 the FBI was in almost daily contact with Bentley, and from 1948 and for the next several years she testified frequently before various government committees. In 1950, at the time of Gold's arrest, she was testifying before the grand jury that would indict us as well as William Remington. In the spring of 1950 she also contracted with a publisher to write the story of her communist activities. She was on no vacation from any interest in these events; she was vitally involved.

The FBI's own files corroborate this. In March 1950 an FBI memorandum states: "Gold, according to Confidential Informant Gregory, (the FBI's code name for Bentley) acted on behalf of Jacob Golos, known Soviet Agent now deceased in 1940 and 1941, in picking up blue prints from Abraham Brothman."[3]

She had indeed been paying attention to the subject of Harry Gold and the prosecution and the FBI knew that her testimony on this was false.

Under cross-examination Bentley was Saypol's most skillful, well-rehearsed witness. She was by turns waspish with Kleinman, scornful, condescending and supremely artful at parrying his questions and handing him non-committal answers. When Kleinman asked her a repetitive question she snapped, dismissively, "I just mentioned, some nine or ten months."

When he asked about her ethics in stealing papers from the Italian Library she replied: "I was a communist in those days and those were and still are communist ethics."

Q. (by Kleinman) "I take it that communism was a religion with you..."

A. "Communism was a religion with me as it was with most communists."

Q. "I am speaking now of you, Miss Bentley. Was it true of you that it was a religion?"

A. "I think..."

Judge Kaufman lent a helping hand: "She said yes."

When Kleinman asked her if she had questioned Golos about his business her reply was: "No, you don't ask questions in the Communist Party."

That was also false testimony. In her book, Bentley reveals that she knew at least as early as 1949 that Golos was a member of the GPU, the then Russian Secret Police which became the NKVD. It may have been true that Bentley never asked Golos but only because she did not need to. Certainly Bentley was totally familiar with Golos' work.[4]

When Kleinman asked Bentley if she had assumed her Party alias, Elizabeth Sherman, or whether it had been assigned to her, she was again the impatient teacher facing an oaf: "You don't get given aliases. You take your own."

Kleinman asked if she had been a communist at the time she taught school and she replied again with acerbity: "No, your dates are mixed up. I taught there from 1929 to 1932. I didn't join the Party until March of 1935."

Judge Kaufman defended that overshot with: "I don't think she is reprimanding you. I think she is replying to your questions."

Kleinman drew from Bentley that she had been employed by U. S. Service & Shipping Corp. from March 1941 to January 1947. She described that organization as having been engaged in shipping packages to the USSR, the funds for the business having been furnished by the Communist Party. USSSC was closely connected to the Intourist Agency of Moscow and its American affiliate, World Tourists. Both handled travel from the United States to the Soviet Union. Golos had been head of World Tourists in New York.

Kleinman asked Bentley about Amtorg Trading Company since Brothman had testified in 1947 that he had sought legitimate business from them. She replied that she knew very little about Amtorg. Kleinman asked her if it was not a legitimate firm doing purchasing for the USSR in the United States. Judge Kaufman himself put the question to her precisely: "Do you know whether they did their business in the open or did they do it secretly?"

Bentley did not know.

Kleinman asked her whether she did not know that Amtorg purchased large quantities of steel and agricultural equipment in the United States to be shipped to the USSR. Bentley dissembled at first and then said, "I had the idea it was a Soviet organization that carried on business for the USSR, but I was in complete darkness as to exactly what they did."

False testimony again. She had written a book about her courier escapades and had a publishing contract even before she gave this testimony. In a relevant passage in that book she wrote: "…the Amtorg Trading Corporation (was) a Russian commercial agency that handled all the Soviet business interests in the United States…."[5]

Under continued cross-examination Bentley repeated how she had met Brothman. In the spring of 1940 Golos had introduced her to Brothman as, "Helen," no last name. Brothman thought Golos' first name was "John" but it was "Jacob." Brothman paid his Communist Party dues to her infrequently and only under duress and she could not remember how much his dues were.

Brothman gave her blueprints for Golos and she surmised they were not his property but, rather, material he had stolen. And she had no idea what the blueprints were about. "Kettles," she said at one point. Sometimes she would have copies made and return the originals. She would use "obscure" shops to make the copies but did not remember the names or the locations of the shops, except the general areas of the city where they were located. She also did not recall whether the grand jury had asked her similar questions.

Bentley reiterated how and where she would meet Brothman, usually in a public restaurant where they would dine leisurely after which he would turn over his technical material to her. She described also how she instructed Brothman in Communist Party theory. He would ask questions and she would "explain things" to him.

But in March 1948, about a year and a half before this testimony, she testified before a federal grand jury that she was not an authority on the Communist Party line and that the last time she had attended a Party meeting was in 1937. The testimony ran as follows:

Q. (by Mr. Quinn of the U.S. Attorney's Office)…"So that you are not familiar with the Communist Party line from there out?"

A. (Bentley) "No, and I wasn't too familiar with it then, because I was sort of in and out of it during those two years, so that actually I think I am not a good authority on it."[6]

Her statement that she would "explain things" to Brothman was preposterous as it was irrelevant but it handily linked him to communism for the prosecution.

During the time she met with Brothman, from early 1940 to late 1941, one of her duties, Bentley repeated, was "to educate him as a communist." She did not bring him any communist literature, however, leaving it to him to get that himself.

But in her book she said that bringing literature was an important part of her meetings with the people from whom she was collecting information: "…I would give them what literature I had brought—current American Communist Party pamphlets…and the Soviet publications…"[7]

Her testimony repeatedly linking Brothman to communism should never have been allowed but Judge Kaufman did not stop it.

Defense Attorney Kleinman asked Bentley about her appearance before the House Committee on UnAmerican Activities on July 31, 1948. He wanted to know if she had mentioned to the Committee the date she first went to the FBI. She could not remember, she said. He refreshed her memory; she had testified that she went to them in the latter part of August 1945. However, she had not yet severed her connections with the Communist Party, she said. She was holding on to them to be able to provide continuing information to the FBI.

Again, a contradiction in the making. According to the FBI's own records, it was not until November 7, 1945 that Bentley began to tell them her story.[8] She did visit them the previous August, but it was in connection with her search for a missing lover, Peter Heller. (See Chapter 25.) Kleinman's next question called for a simple yes or no answer: Had Ms. Bentley told the Congressional Committee when she first approached the FBI? She dallied.

Kleinman: "Won't you please answer my question yes or no first."

She slammed back: "Mr. Kleinman, if you will put your question so that I can answer it, I would be very delighted to do that."

Kleinman then questioned her testimony about threatening Brothman. "And after he resisted this suggestion (for a replacement)…you then threatened him, didn't you?"

Her reply: "I don't know if that is the word. I told him that communists should behave. Do you call that threatening?"

Kleinman continued: "Is that all you told him, Miss Bentley, that you would be forced to the conclusion that he was not a good communist?" Bentley: "That's right; I gave him a pep talk on how communists should behave."

Brothman gave her blueprints on that occasion and Kleinman asked if he also gave her any instructions. With grand hauteur, she declared: "Mr. Brothman never gave me instructions. I gave him instructions." (Kleinman meant technical instructions, of course.)

He then queried her about testimony she had given before the House Committee on un-American Activities. She did not remember whether she told them she had stopped paying Communist Party dues in 1944, and she had no recollection of her testimony in July 1948 before the Senate Investigations Committee. As Kleinman continued to probe she snapped: "...if you testified before as many committees as I have you wouldn't remember every sentence you have said. No, I can't remember!"

Kleinman drew from her that she was a paid lecturer and a writer on the subject of communism. He then asked her how long it took to tell her story to the FBI but Judge Kaufman quickly interrupted: "Aren't we going pretty far afield? ... Now is this proper cross examination?"

Kleinman replied: "Judge, we are charged with impeding justice in 1947... This woman told the FBI everything in 1945...How then could we have impeded the investigation...?"

It was a telling point but Judge Kaufman blunted its effect. "Your clients are accused of impeding justice," he said, "in that in 1947 when they went before the grand jury they did not tell their story. That is the charge."

Kaufman was muddying the waters. I did not appear before the grand jury in 1947. I appeared in 1950 and then, after the preliminaries, I did not testify; I cited the Fifth Amendment against self-incrimination. I told no story, false or otherwise. The person who testified, along with Brothman, was Harry Gold, and Gold was not Kleinman's client.

Kleinman pressed on: "....I should be permitted to ask this witness if she told the whole story to the FBI and when she told it, so that we can determine whether or not the FBI had the story she now tells..." Kleinman sought to establish that we could not have impeded justice if the FBI had had two years to follow through on Bentley's 1945 revelations. And that could be established only if Kleinman could get an admission from Bentley that she had told the FBI her story about Brothman in 1945.

When Kleinman asked her again if she had mentioned Brothman to the FBI in 1945 she quibbled: "I can't answer your question because I don't know whether I mentioned Mr. Brothman at the beginning of my story or at the end, which was in 1946. You will have to rephrase your question."

In response to Kleinman's question Bentley admitted she had never known me.

Repeatedly, however, she could not recall what she had told the FBI or the various grand juries or the congressional committees before which she had testified. "I have told too many people too many things," she said.

Kleinman asked if she testified in July 1948 that she met some person known as Bill. Her response: "I cannot, Mr. Kleinman, tell you unless I see the testimony." Then, "I'm sorry, Mr. Kleinman, I cannot recall word for word any testimony I have given before a Committee."

Kleinman reminded her that he was asking her to recall facts, not her testimony. Again, she brushed aside his question impatiently: "I told you I cannot repeat what I said before the committee. Will you rephrase the question, Mr. Kleinman?"

Valiantly, Kleinman continued his efforts to get Bentley to admit what she told the 1947 grand jury about Abraham Brothman, but she clung successfully to that "I don't remember" mode. He turned to Judge Kaufman and asked to have the minutes of Bentley's grand jury testimony of 1947 made available to him. Or, failing that, would Kaufman, himself, he asked, read those minutes, the grounds for either request resting on the possibility that there might be revealed inconsistencies with Bentley's present testimony.

Kaufman refused and suggested that Kleinman was, in effect, asking him to act as his co-counsel. Kleinman continued to press: "...but we have the most unusual condition with this witness. She has refused to give any definite recollection of anything that she has said...And I think that it is our duty today, now, to determine whether she did tell the grand jury anything about Brothman in 1947."

His argument focused on Bentley's having said she told the FBI about Brothman in 1945 or 1946; but that she could not say whether she testified about him later, in 1947.

Judge Kaufman ruled against Kleinman and straddled the issue of the possible inconsistency of Bentley's various testimonies. But he repeatedly allowed the prosecution to use Bentley to tie Brothman to the issue of communism, although she offered no real evidence that a conspiracy existed to obstruct justice. At the same time Bentley's accusations could not possibly be refuted or challenged because she was so successfully unresponsive.

Thus ended the Bentley testimony.

It is worth noting that in 1951, some months after our conviction, a Federal Circuit Court of Appeals unanimously reversed the conviction of William W. Remington (in his first trial) citing as the second of two reasons Judge Gregory Noonan's refusal to provide the defense with the minutes of the grand jury testimony of the government's star witness, Remington's former wife.[9]

On that basis we might have been able to pursue additional legal redress before our appeals were denied, citing the Remington precedent. However, both Abe and I were locked away in prison when the Remington conviction was overturned and we did not know of it. And so, an event which might have served as a critical advantage for us slipped quietly away.

Chapter 8

Harry Gold, "I Lied Desperately"[1]

In the middle of the twentieth century the trials of so-called Soviet spies, of which mine was only one, were probably the most sensational courtroom events since the Sacco-Vanzetti case in the 1920s. Fueling them was the Smith Act, passed in 1940, which made it a crime to advocate and teach the overthrow of the government by force and violence. Coming on the heels of the Smith Act prosecutions in 1949 against the leadership of the Communist Party, the successful test, that year, of a Soviet A-bomb, and the Coplon, Hiss and Remington cases, and waiting in the wings the Rosenberg/Sobell case — these events all played on Americans' growing sense of insecurity. Unreasoning fear engendered disloyalty hearings of government workers, the prosecution of the Civil Rights Congress, the Hollywood Ten's face-off against the House UnAmerican Activities Committee in 1947, and the accusations that some of the most militant and successful union struggles were led by communists. Unions so accused were expelled from the parent body unless they purged their leadership.

On November 1, 1950, just days before our trial began, the turbulence was given a further jolt by the attempted assassination of President Harry S. Truman by two Puerto Rican nationalists, Oscar Collazo and Griselio Torresola. A guard and Torresola were killed in the resulting shootout. An ill-conceived venture but with roots in the popular aspirations for Puerto Rican independence, it tightened the unease, fanned the fear of mainland populists and radicals, and confirmed nationwide a sense of political instability. The curtain thus rose on a trial stage already littered with the shadows of events in which Abraham Brothman and I had played no role. Nevertheless, we were perceived to be part of them.

Collectively, those events revealed that a new disease had swept the country characterized by paranoid fear of a Red Menace, the rejection of commitments to social causes and world peace, and the apprehension that those who espoused them were somehow a part of that menace. A more irrational period in American history would be hard to identify.

Harry Gold took the stand at our trial as the first American atom spy arrested. As Walter and Miriam Schneir noted in *Invitation to an Inquest*, it was an important coup for Director J. Edgar Hoover and his FBI. The defeat they had endured in the Eisler and the Coplon cases had left them and their director with diminished prestige and considerable criticism. The FBI were recovering through the agency of Harry Gold.[2] His appearance at our trial followed the bombshell caused by the Bentley testimony just days earlier. The complaint the government lodged against Gold said that he had obtained national defense secrets for the Soviet Union from Klaus Fuchs and had conspired with another person for this purpose.

Fuchs, a German-born refugee physicist and a naturalized British citizen, had come to the United States in November 1943 with a team of British atomic scientists. They joined American and other international colleagues to work on the Manhattan Project in Los Alamos and New York (and at other sites) to develop the atom bomb during World War II. Fuchs served on the British team until June 1948. In February 1950, then working at the Harwell atomic energy installation in England, Fuchs confessed to having violated the British Official Secrets Act by unauthorizedly turning over information to an American contact during his stay in the United States for transmission to the Soviet Union. He did not name his American contact and gave no accurate description of him[3] but the FBI had a list of possible suspects. On that list was Harry Gold.

When the FBI agents called on Gold in May 1950, in a reprise of their interrogations three years earlier, he denied all suggestions that he was the man they were seeking. Furthermore, he said, he had never been west of the Mississippi. They had no search warrant but Gold obligingly gave them permission to search his home with the proviso that it not take place before Monday, May 22, three days hence, when his father and his brother would not be present. He put off destroying any possible incriminating evidence since he did not want his father or his brother to wonder why he was suddenly and uncharacteristically smitten with an urge to clean house. He had also forgotten how much junk he had accumulated.[4]

It is also probable that he did not regard Brothman's blueprints as incriminating, which he had hoarded in his cellar closet. This was work which the Russians had rejected and which Gold had not returned to Brothman. It had no military significance and none of it was secret or had any connection to the government, which Gold well knew. He overlooked the rest of the cosmic disorder of his life—personal material such as a letter from a former girl friend breaking off their relationship and an old memorandum to himself which described in his own code the personal traits of some of the young women he worked with. They were juvenile jottings of a grown man never meant to be seen by prying eyes. (The latter was "pure fantasy" he told the agents, and he refused to discuss them.[5])

He forgot about the out-of-date train schedules of places he had denied having traveled to, which he never got around to discard, and copies of reports in his handwriting, the originals of which he had turned over to Soviet agents, notes on questions he was to ask certain contacts, street maps of cities where he had rendezvous, plane and train ticket stubs, and other useless but incriminating items. Harry Gold's personal trademark: he never threw anything out.

Early Monday morning, immediately after his father and his brother left for work he went through those papers and destroyed a substantial part of it: but he ran out of time to complete the job before the agents arrived.[6] When they pulled a Santa Fe tour brochure from behind a piece of furniture, the effort to resist no longer seemed possible. Gold asked for a cigarette although he normally never smoked. Then he said quietly but with the effect of a megaton explosion: "I am the man who got information on atomic energy from Dr. Klaus Fuchs."[7]

Harry Gold's public debut occurred when he was ushered into the courtroom to testify against Abraham Brothman and me. He had been in custody almost six months but had not yet been sentenced. The news gatherers and the curiosity seekers were out in force, stumbling over each other and vying for a look at the man who said he had obtained national defense secrets from Klaus Fuchs and possibly others, and who had passed them on to the Soviet Union. Vivid notoriety had surrounded his arrest. Now, his first public appearance generated near-hysteria.

The courtroom was hushed as his name was called. He shuffled towards the witness stand, sluggish, defeated, monochromatic, an image of lost hope, of one cheated out of a life, but with hardly the air of a conjurer of espionage. What the spectators also saw was a diminutive man barely five and a half feet tall with an apologetic presence and a round baby face set over a plump body, with brown hair neatly combed and heavy-lidded downcast eyes. Behind those briefly raised eyes floated fear and resignation. His shoulders hunched forward and he moved slowly as though he were twice his almost forty years. His demeanor was tentative and excessively polite. "Excuse me…I don't mean to cause you any inconvenience…" He had been a serious sinner and was now, in manner, a seriously contrite one. He mounted the witness chair wearily and kept his eyes averted so that he did not have to look at us.

United States Attorney Irving H. Saypol quickly drew from Gold that he had pleaded guilty in Philadelphia on July 20, 1950 to the crime of espionage—nine days before we were indicted.

"I was instrumental in turning over information on atomic energy to the Soviet Union," he announced, speaking precisely and tonelessly.

Gold's statement was immediately prejudicial to us for now the charge against us, of conspiring to obstruct justice, was placed squarely within the context of espionage and, specifically, atomic bomb espionage.

He had not yet been sentenced, he said. That would occur on December 7, some three weeks hence.

Saypol asked: "Do you stand charged with any other crime?"

"Yes," replied Gold. "I am charged with conspiracy to commit espionage with a David Greenglass and certain other persons."

We were now swinging on the same hook as the Rosenbergs, for it was Greenglass who had led to the Rosenbergs and the public would now think that we were connected to them.

Gold told the court of his family: his father, a cabinet maker and his brother. They lived together in a modest house in Philadelphia. His mother had died in September 1947. He was not married and had never been married. He had been born in 1910 in Switzerland and was naturalized on his father's papers.

He spoke of having obtained a degree of Bachelor of Science in chemistry from Xavier University in 1940—summa cum laude. He took courses at Drexel Institute in psychology and a number of advanced courses in chemistry, distillery practice, fermentation chemistry, physiological chemistry and pharmacology, among others. His course work at Drexel had led to a diploma in chemical engineering.

Gold's significant employment history had begun in 1929 at the Pennsylvania Sugar Company in Philadelphia, and had been interrupted by educational leaves of absence and a short term layoff. When the distillery division closed in February 1946, he was laid off permanently. From May 1946 to June 1948 he worked for A. Brothman & Associates in New York City as chief chemist. From September 1948 until his arrest he worked at the Philadelphia General Hospital in their heart station carrying out research on cardiac disease.

During the short term layoff from Penn Sugar early in 1933 he had worked for the Holbrook Company in Jersey City, New Jersey, a soap manufacturer.

Prosecutor Saypol asked: "During this time was there an occasion when you began to evince an interest in communist affairs?"

Gold: "It began in this fashion." He spoke as though he were settling in for a pleasant chat. He said that the man who had obtained the Holbrook job for him, (his friend, Tom Black) had solicited him to join the Communist Party. As a result he attended three meetings of the Party in Jersey City but did not join and had never been a member.

Judge Kaufman, perhaps not sure he had heard right, interrupted: "Did I understand you to say that you have never been a member of the Communist Party?"

Leaden-voiced, Gold replied, "I have never been a member of the Communist Party."

Saypol continued: "When and under what circumstances did you enter upon espionage activities?"

(Throughout this questioning defense attorney Kleinman interposed objections because Gold's recitation had no bearing on the charge against Abraham Brothman and me and did not in any way involve us. Judge

Kaufman consistently overruled; however, he did remind the jury that we were not charged with espionage.)

Gold continued. In November 1935, as a result of a conversation with Tom Black, he began his espionage career. (This was almost six years before Brothman met him.) He came to New York to be introduced to a Paul Smith who identified himself as a representative of the Amtorg Company in New York. For about three months he fed Smith data regarding certain chemical industrial processes for transmittal to the Soviet Union. These processes were owned by subsidiaries of the Pennsylvania Sugar Company where he worked and they related principally to industrial solvents used in formulating varnishes and lacquers.

The witness divided his activities into two types. One was what he called espionage; it lasted until 1940 and it involved his stealing technical information from his company. The other he characterized as courier work, collecting information from others. He turned over that material to his "Soviet superior." The data he turned over in 1940, he said, also included "a large amount of material relating directly to military matters." He never specified what those matters were, but the reference hung over the courtroom and gave added fuel to associating us with espionage.

Saypol drew from Gold a description of the modus operandi he used to maintain contact with intermediaries and to transmit information. The arrangements were characterized by a military-like precision in meeting contacts; they allowed for no slip-ups or sloppiness and were always stealthy and clandestine. Gold would give his contact exact instructions about what information he wanted. He would extract a definite commitment from his contact as to when he could expect to receive the information. He would meet his contact on the exact date and at the exact time and place previously agreed upon to pick up the material and rush it to his Soviet superior.

(The relevant question is: with whom did Gold have such elaborate meeting arrangements? The names of contacts he gave to the FBI were Klaus Fuchs, Alfred Dean Slack, David Greenglass, and Abraham Brothman. His meetings with Fuchs were apparently arranged by others. He called on Greenglass at his home so there was no need for complicated rendezvous arrangements. He did meet Brothman sometimes on street corners, sometimes in hotel lobbies, but Brothman apparently never observed any precision about keeping appointments; he came when it was convenient for him and sometimes he did not come at all and never even let Gold know he wasn't coming. Other than Alfred Dean Slack from whom Gold was purchasing information, with whom did Gold have such complicated meeting arrangements? Or was this testimony meant by the prosecution to intensify the drama of Gold's escapades and draw us into Gold's world of secrecy, stealth and espionage – thus setting the tone for our trial?)

Gold also had meticulous arrangements for connecting with his handler:

"…we would arrange the time and place (for the next meeting). The time was to the minute…we would also arrange for a second meeting, should the first one not come off; and we would arrange for emergency meetings should any be desired." They also had fall-back system if either thought he was being followed.

The hushed courtroom listened with rapt attention as though Gold were reciting lines from the latest spy novel. The problem was that despite his meticulous arrangements he was able to implicate only three confederates in his adventures: Slack, Greenglass and Brothman. Fuchs had confessed on his own. So far as Brothman, at least, was concerned, Gold's net gain was slim pickings for such arduous, expensive and exasperating toil, for Brothman's contributions were never secret nor were they government-related. Gold's recitation had to do more with phantoms than reality, but the courtroom and the public accepted his word without question.

Judge Kaufman asked Gold: "Were these instructions…the subject of communication or discussion between you and Mr. Brothman or Miss Moskowitz?'

Gold reply was: "They were the subject of communication at a later date." Then he added, "Between Abe Brothman and myself."

Saypol showed Gold a picture of a man he identified as, "Sam," his Soviet connection from July 1940 to February 1944. Kleinman's objections were again overruled, but Kaufman appeared to throw him a sop: "…. If it is proved that it is not connected just as all the other testimony is, I would then ask you to be specific in a motion to strike and I will give proper instructions to the jury."

But of course the damage in linking us to "Sam" would have already been done and surely Kaufman understood that the jury's first impressions would linger in their deliberations.

The picture of Sam was accepted in evidence over Kleinman's objections. The questioning then turned to the crucial issue of how Gold had met Brothman.

Gold related that he came from Philadelphia to New York in September 1941 to be introduced to Brothman by Sam. The meeting never took place. Later that month another meeting was scheduled and again did not come off. Finally Sam gave him "a set of very precise and detailed instructions…" and he returned to New York on the evening of September 29, 1941. And now, in this courtroom, at this moment, Gold repudiated his grand jury testimony of 1947.

From Pennsylvania Station in Manhattan in the late evening of September 29, he traveled to an area "below 30th Street… On one of those side streets… after a wait of about 15 minutes, a car came along. This was exactly pursuant to the instructions I had been given."

Objection. Objection overruled.

"… I withdrew the card on which I had written the instructions from my wallet…"

Objection overruled again.

"… and checked the license number on the card against that of the car. They agreed. I opened the door of the car. The man inside was reassured when I gave him the rest of the recognition signal as it was written upon the card."

Once again, objection overruled.

"I said, 'I bring regards from Helen,' and then I asked him how was his wife…I introduced myself as Frank Kessler and the man said he was Abe Brothman… We drove to a Bickford's restaurant where conversation ensued according to the instructions I had been given by Sam –"

And thus, Gold's testimony corroborated Bentley's about Brothman's use of his car to connect—furtively—with her successor.

The prosecution now introduced the card containing Gold's notes as evidence. Judge Kaufman was troubled; he asked Gold questions which Saypol had not thought to explore: Did Gold remember the exact day of the week and the exact time of that meeting? Gold did not, but Kaufman urged him to look at the card…did it refresh his memory about the specific day and the time? Gold could not remember; nevertheless, Kaufman was determined:

> "Well, keep that record in your hand and tell me whether …it represents a record of the day and time when you met Brothman, and whether at the time or at or about the time you met Brothman you looked at that card or record and you knew …that the card was a correct record of the day and the time when you met Brothman."

Even as Kaufman pressed him, Gold was no help. He was not familiar enough with cars to know the type; the night was too dark for him to be able to see the color and the only thing he could "certify" was the license number since it was written on the card. His memory did not serve Kaufman's purpose which was to tailor the card's use to fit the rules of evidence; nevertheless, Kaufman admitted it. So the card which Gold had used merely like a grocery list became legal corroboration of an event which the prosecutor could not have established otherwise. Kleinman objected, uselessly.

Gold and Brothman exchanged personal information. He told Brothman he was a chemist and Brothman "was glad because he could now much more adequately begin to again funnel information through me to the Soviet Union." Gold also told Brothman he was married and had twins, a boy and a girl, which was a lie he now admitted.

Saypol probed further:

Q. "When he mentioned Helen and John (Bentley and Golos) had you ever met either of them?"

A. "I never met Helen or John."

Q. "Either up to this day?"

A. "Up to this date."

That exchange is found on page 502 of the trial minutes. Gold reiterated in four additional exchanges – on pages 628, 635, 637 and 639 – that he had never met John Golos.

But six months earlier, on May 22, 1950, Gold signed a confession for the FBI which included the following statement:

"On my return to Philadelphia (from Xavier College, Cincinnati, Ohio) I was again contacted by the people with whom I had worked before. I was called on the phone in June 1940 and I went downtown to see this man, who turned out to be Jacob Golos. He again pressed me to continue the work...and I agreed. However, it was pretty sporadic ... and, with the exception of the one contact, Abraham Brothman, nothing came of it. I was supposed to get information... from Brothman but very little came of it because he was extremely unreliable in getting material together. He gave me some data on mixing equipment which was practically all his design, and it seemed to me that practically everything he gave me... was his own invention... Brothman... wanted to know about the possibility of his doing consulting work for the Soviet Union on an open basis... (but) they discounted the idea..."[8]

Two paragraphs later Gold reiterated that he had known Golos.[9] In addition, an FBI memorandum of June 1, 1950, only two months before our indictment, says that Golos and Gold had been in contact[10] and another FBI memorandum of June 5, 1950 speaks of Gold's having given the FBI a list of his espionage superiors with a description of each and *it included Jacob Golos.*[11]

These are extraordinary statements. Despite his contradictory testimony, Gold had indeed known Golos from June 1940 until at least the end of the year and it was Golos who requested Gold to contact Brothman. Also, Gold corroborates Brothman's statement to the grand jury that he was seeking legitimate business from Amtorg, (the Soviet Purchasing Commission).

Gold does not mention here that Brothman had engaged in "industrial espionage" as he would do later. When that developed in Gold's testimony it was only after he had spent hundreds of hours (according to his own notes) with the FBI and the prosecution in preparation for his appearance at our trial.

The question now has urgency: Did Bentley and Gold conform their testimony in any respect—and did that occur with the help, suggestion or coaching from the prosecution? Could such conforming have occurred without anyone's help?

Still another contradiction must be confronted. Gold had accused Brothman of having demanded in 1947 that he cover his story to the FBI (and the grand jury). To enable him to do that, Gold said, Brothman had given him a physical description of Golos since Harry told him he had never met Golos. But Harry had hidden the truth from Brothman as well as from the government; he had indeed known Golos and did not need Brothman to make any identification or to instigate any lies in his behalf. Gold knew back in 1947 that if the government learned of his true relationship with Golos it would be trouble writ large for him—and for him alone. He made his own decision to lie.

Since Gold's testimony was crucial in convicting Abraham Brothman – and me – one cannot now avoid the conclusion that the prosecution pursued a fraudulent indictment. Not only did Irving Saypol bear the responsibility for this but also Roy Cohn, who was the witness-preparer, the prosecution staff and the FBI apparatus including Director J. Edgar Hoover. In the name of the government they had launched an illegal action against us. They knew Bentley and Gold had given meaningless, inappropriate and perjured testimony which they themselves helped develop. Judge Kaufman was a willing participant in this pursuit; without his crucial bench work the prosecution could not have succeeded.

Like the proverbial bear with a sore head, an even more disturbing question arises:

How unimpeachable were Bentley and Gold as witnesses, how unassailable was their testimony four months later when they testified for the government, with the same judge and the same prosecution staff against Julius and Ethel Rosenberg?

Gold continued his testimony. He gave Sam a detailed report of his first meeting with Brothman. Again Kleinman reminded the court that the rules of evidence should bar such testimony since it concerned events not having taken place in our presence. Kaufman overruled.

Gold said Brothman came an hour and a half late for their second meeting. Nevertheless, at that meeting Gold said he gave Brothman a verbal list of information the Russians wanted: processes to manufacture aviation gasoline, synthetic rubber, petroleum lubricants—a laundry list of non-secret commercial manufacturing procedures. He also asked him for any information he had about matters of military interest.

For their next appointment Brothman was even more inconsiderate; he came two hours late and he did not bring any information. But at the fourth meeting he was on time and gave Gold a blueprint of some chemical equipment called an esterifier. Gold explained that such equipment is used to make lacquers and varnishes. Gold dutifully turned it over to Sam but Sam rejected it because it lacked details. Instead of returning the drawing to Brothman, Gold stored it in his cellar at home. It now turned up in the prosecutor's hands and was admitted as evidence.

Again Kleinman objected. Gold's activities with Sam had not occurred in Brothman's presence and Gold was relating events which much pre-dated the events cited in the indictment.

Kaufman overruled.

Instead of telling Brothman his esterifier drawing had been rejected, Gold told him it was "excellent but not complete and it required…written or descriptive material…" Brothman promised to furnish that at a later date, but Gold did not say he ever received it.

Saypol next produced a group of nine blueprints, which he also offered as evidence. Gold said he had received these about December 1941—but could not recall what they were about. Again, he never turned any of it over to Sam because they were "fragmentary;" they did not specify the necessary processing conditions. He had stored all of this in his cellar with the other material. (But these drawings had no relevance; they did not constitute designs made for the U.S. government and there was no element of secrecy about them. They pertained to commercial, industrial work which was hardly shrouded in mystery and they were Brothman's own work. As the prosecution waved these blueprints, these drawings of technical material in front of the panel of non-technical jurors, it became clear it was merely to impress and befuddle them.)

Gold also recalled for the court that he chastised Brothman; he would have to "mend his way"; submit only completed material and keep appointments on time. Brothman did not take kindly to the criticism. He told Gold that apparently the Soviet Union's purchasing commission did not appreciate the value of previous material he had submitted to Helen and John. He had given them the complete plans for a Houdry cracking plant to manufacture high-octane gasoline, also plans for a turbine type aircraft engine and designs for a Jeep model.

(But in 1942, about the time that Gold was soliciting Brothman's work, the United States government under a Lend-Lease arrangement gave the Soviet Union information it needed on various petroleum refining methods, including the Houdry process.[12] Gold's testimony was disconnected to reality. The Russians already had the information and they got it legally from the United States government.)

Gold was to meet Brothman next on December 22, 1941 at 10 p.m. He waited at the pre-arranged site for about twenty-five minutes but Brothman never came. Gold took a cab to connect with Sam and to tell him that the meeting had not come off.

Kleinman objected: "…the details now offered serve but one purpose and that was to prejudice the defendants on matters that are not within the purview of and not germane to the indictment."

Kaufman overruled, once again rescuing Saypol from an inept examination. He instructed Saypol on the correct method of phrasing his questions: "I must ask you, Mr. Saypol…to address your questions to the witness that there has been a meeting between Sam and the defendant Brothman and either a ratification of the acts… or … something to indicate a ratification in such a way that he does not testify to what Sam said or what he said to Sam until I am convinced."

Saypol was still uncertain about Kaufman's meaning so the judge became more explicit: "He can say, 'I went to Sam. I saw him at such a time.' …And after he saw Sam, he saw Brothman. I don't want details."

Gold then described his unsuccessful effort to connect with Sam, and it was a pure cloak-and-dagger scenario. Gold was late because he had waited too long for Brothman, and therefore had just missed Sam at the appointed spot on the West Fourth Street subway platform. But he then rode to the next agreed-upon meeting site and connected with Sam there. They went to a bar and talked for about two hours. And all of this testimony conveyed the sense of conspiratorial skulking about which had nothing to do with the defendants Brothman and Moskowitz.

Sometime between Christmas 1941 and New Year Brothman told Gold he would be able to give him complete plans for a Buna-S synthetic rubber plant; it would be ready in a matter of days. Gold came to the next appointment and waited on a street corner for about an hour and a half. Brothman finally appeared but without the report; it needed another week or so, he said. Gold made a number of other appointments with Brothman, none of which he kept and to make matters even more frustrating, when Gold tried to reach him by telephone he was unsuccessful.

Throughout the early months of 1942, Gold related, he endured one exasperating letdown after another in trying to pin Brothman down for the Buna-S report. Once he rented a room at the Prince George Hotel on 29th Street east of Fifth Avenue, but Brothman never appeared.

Another time they planned to go to an upstate hotel to complete the report in a less distracting setting, but Brothman backed out at the last minute. Finally, after four months of on-again, off-again appointments Gold rented a suite at the Hotel New Yorker in Manhattan. He set a date for early April 1942 and this time Brothman came. He brought with him material he had already prepared, some reference materials and a portable typewriter. Brothman wrote additional text that night and then he and Gold annotated and assembled the report. They worked until six in the morning.

The completed Buna-S report consisted of at least two hundred typewritten pages, Gold said. Mostly it was material Brothman had prepared in advance, but it also included the pages he typed that night and "about 25 or 50 blueprints including flow sheets, the design of specialized pieces of equipment...the system for the recovery of ... butadiene and styrene. It was a complete process."

At the same time Gold hinted that except for the material Brothman had typed that night, he was not the originator of the report. He did not suggest who might have been the author other than Brothman.

Gold turned over the completed report to Sam although the residual support material from which the two men had assembled the final document remained in Gold's possession.

Saypol queried Gold about other Buna-S material he had received before this session. Gold revealed that he never turned it over to his "Soviet superior" because it was incomplete; it was "fragmentary" notes and calculations in Brothman's handwriting, and blueprints. Gold had never discarded this nor had he returned it to its original owner, Abraham Brothman. (All these years, even during his time of friendship with Brothman, he had kept it in his cellar and never let Brothman know he had it. He was now endowing it with fake relevance to compromise his former friend.)

Saypol was much interested in having Gold explain one of the blueprints which he identified as a flow sheet. Gold was marvelously well-informed and gave a classic textbook definition of what such a drawing was and what purpose it served. It was, he explained, a "diagram for a process, giving each of the steps that the material...goes through before the final product is obtained..." In the case of this particular flow sheet, he added, "this is an unusually complete flow sheet...(it) gives the temperature. It gives the capacities of the particular vessel... It describes particular pieces of equipment..."

The jury seemed rapt as he continued:

> "You see, here is your butadiene. Here is the styrene. Here is the soap solution. Here is the chain modifier. Each of those go into Treat-O-Units and they are injected into these vessels, both of which are polymerizers which are really the heart of the system. It is where the butadiene and styrene combine and form low molecular weight and high molecular weight material, which is synthetic rubber."

> "... And then the rest of the system (Gold was now referring to another drawing) ... all these over here on the right hand side is the equipment for the recovery of the unused butadiene and styrene. Butadiene is a very explosive material. You can't let it out into the air like that, and styrene vapors themselves are poisonous."

Saypol asked, "In any event, when you get all through you have synthetic rubber?"

Gold said it was called rubber latex.

He also identified the flow sheet by date: January 4, 1941. The drawing for the butadiene and styrene recovery system was dated February 8, 1942.

As he had done earlier, Saypol focused on the Hendrick nameplate on the drawings and again Gold let it be assumed that Brothman had misappropriated these drawings; they were not his to have; they belonged to Hendrick, he implied.

Saypol asked Gold:

> Q. "… do you recall whether you had any further conversation with him (Brothman) regarding the Buna-S report?"
> A. "I told Abe that a very laudatory report had been received from the Soviet Union…"
> Q. "In the interval…had you met Sam or your superior?"
> A. "I had met Sam several times."
> Q. "Was that the basis upon which you had this conversation?"

This time Kaufman sustained Kleinman's objections, but he immediately hopped in to salvage Saypol's bumbling examination:

> Kaufman: "After you met Sam, what did you tell Mr. Brothman?"
> Gold: "… I told Abe that a report giving great praise to the Buna-S work had been received."
> Kaufman: "did you tell Mr. Brothman who gave you that report?"
> Gold: "Yes, I did."
> Kaufman: "And who did you say gave it to you?"
> Gold: "I said it was my Soviet superior."
> Kaufman: "All right."

The judge had again rescued the prosecution from a validly objectionable and ineffective interrogation and helped to drive into the jurors' minds that Brothman had submitted technical material of value to the Russians, the implication being that it was secret.

Brothman told Gold at that meeting that he was working on the design of a nickel catalyst plant to make a type of catalyst which would also be useful to produce aviation type gasoline and, said Gold, to prepare various "strategic organic chemicals." He never elucidated his use of the term, "strategic organic chemicals." The use of the term 'strategic' implied that the compounds were of military value; but as it never became clear what compounds Gold was referring to, and as attorney Kleinman was unable to pin him down, the term was meaningless, although prejudicial to the defense.

Gold gave a detailed technical explanation of how a nickel catalyst was used to prepare shortening and never had these jurors had a better informed chemistry teacher. Miraculously, also, the blueprints of the nickel catalyst plant which Gold had received so long ago from Brothman now appeared in Saypol's hands to be added to the collection of government exhibits. They, too, had been rescued from Gold's cellar.

Saypol then asked Gold to identify the blueprints just produced as exhibits which were to be offered as evidence. Gold said Brothman had given them to him and he characterized this material, too, as fragmentary. Saypol again made much of the fact that the prints bore the nameplate of Brothman's then employer, Hendrick Manufacturing Co., and as he had done earlier, implied that it was not legitimate for Brothman to have had them.

The material was accepted as evidence over objections.

Saypol asked again what application the devices shown in those prints would have in industry and again Gold was informative: "First, for the preparation of shortening materials from vegetable oils; secondly, for the preparation of aviation-type gasoline; and thirdly, for the preparation of various organic chemicals by hydrogenation of other chemicals."

Gold then told about a meeting he had with Brothman when the latter gave him a report on mixing equipment. It occurred in November 1942. The report, about 300 typewritten pages, contained calculations for various types of mixers and a vast amount of theory supporting the methods of design of some of those mixers. It also contained about fifty to one hundred nomographs—charts, Gold explained, used as calculation aids. There was also printed material (bearing the name, again, of Hendrick) and related papers. Gold delivered it all to Sam.

Earlier and on cue from Saypol, Gold had said that he told Brothman that "the Soviets" wanted him either to return to his former employer, Hendrick, or to get a job with a large industrial firm such as U. S. Rubber or Goodyear, in order to obtain further information on the manufacture of synthetic rubber. Saypol had not had a chance to work this topic over before Judge Kaufman interrupted:

Q. (by Kaufman) "… when was the conversation had with Brothman at which you told him that your Soviet superior desired to have him go back to work for Hendrick or another large company…?"

A. (by Gold) "… July or so, 1942."

Q. "When you met him in November 1942, he was still engaged in his own business, was he?"

A. "That is correct."

Q. "Was there any further discussion about your previous conversation?"

A. "I received a continual barrage of orders from Sam."

Q. "Did you have any discussions with Mr. Brothman about why he would not go back to Hendrick or to some other large company?"

A. "I had a couple but I gave it up after a while."

Q. "What were Mr. Brothman's replies?"

A. "He said he thought he could function a lot better and obtain much more information for the Soviet Union by continuing at Chemurgy.

On one occasion he told me that he would try to arrange some sort of consulting arrangement with the Hendrick firm whereby he could go down there a day or so a week and thus still have access to their files."

Saypol, belatedly realizing the value of that line of questioning, now continued it:

Q. (by Saypol) "In your conversations with Brothman about going back to a large industrial concern, did you say to him at any time what the purpose was for going with a large concern?"

A. "Yes. The primary purpose that I emphasized to Abe was that the Soviet Union wanted more information on synthetic rubber and they wanted it from the horse's mouth, so to speak, from a firm or a plant which was actually in operation and producing the material."

(Gold was reporting on a conversation for which no evidence existed that it had taken place, and at a time predating the period covered by the indictment which the rules of evidence should not have allowed. This was a conversation in which no act took place and no information was passed which was germane to the indictment. But again it buttressed the prosecution's claim that stolen secrets had been involved. And Judge Kaufman revived the testimony that had earlier and justifiably dissolved into nothing when Gold first mentioned it.)

Nevertheless, for all the superhuman efforts which Harry Gold said he gave so single-mindedly in behalf of a Soviet superior to extract from Brothman the technical details for his proposed project to manufacture Buna-S, and for all the vexatious inconvenience he endured to corral Brothman for appointments to complete this project, Gold spun another contradiction with this testimony. He knew, and certainly his Soviet control must have known since this was never secret, that the Russians were already legally receiving Lend-Lease aid on the self-same Buna-S synthetic rubber project from the United States government.[12] In his pre-sentencing speech Gold's lawyer, John D. M. Hamilton, mentioned that *Gold knew the Soviet Union was receiving Lend-Lease aid on Buna-S during World War II.*[13] As with the Houdry cracking plant for high octane gasoline, it included, "...the requisite engineering drawings, operating and maintenance manuals, spare parts lists and other pertinent documents..."[14]

Although the Soviet Union was getting this valuable help from the United States its chemical industry was hardly primitive. The former chairman of the Atomic Energy Commission, Gordon Dean, said:

"....Russia needed synthetic rubber and Russia got it during that period (1921 to 1935) by means of an all-out applied research program. Independent of the rest of the world, she developed a means for producing synthetic rubber from butadiene, which is derived from alcohol."[15]

So much for stolen Buna-S secrets furnished to the Russians.

Saypol next led Gold to tell how he introduced Brothman, finally, to Sam. He told Brothman that a very important Soviet dignitary would be arriving in the United States to meet with him and talk to him about further work he might do for them. Saypol asked: "You mean work of the type that you have described here?"

Gold answered: "*Information* of the type which Abe had previously submitted." (Emphasis added.)

That meeting took place in the Lincoln Hotel in Manhattan in December 1942. Gold had engaged two rooms. He met Brothman in the lobby and together they went up to the suite. About twenty minutes later Sam arrived. Gold introduced Sam as George, "just George." This was now the making of a comic opera. Brothman knew Gold as "Frank Kessler." He was introduced to Sam who was now, "George," who did not, as Gold had announced, just arrive from the Soviet Union, but he had been in New York all the time Gold knew him. And once during the evening "George" slipped and called Gold, "Harry" instead of "Frank." All the while, Brothman was still assuming that Gold's connection to all this was through Golos and Helen. He had never known about a "Sam" and Gold had so testified.

Defense attorney Kleinman objected to Gold's entire story but Judge Kaufman disagreed: "… I say once again that they are charged with conspiring to obstruct justice in that they gave false testimony… and they (the prosecution) are attempting to show the relationship of the parties and … the falsity of the testimony and I therefore overrule…"

(The judge never identified for the jury who he meant by "they" in the first half of his statement. He might have meant the testimony that Brothman and Gold gave in 1947 (Harry Gold was listed in our indictment as a co-conspirator but not a co-defendant), or he was referring to Brothman and me. Since I was a defendant in this case and Harry was not, the jury could well have inferred that Kaufman meant me. But he was creating a damaging ambiguity here. I did not give false testimony to the grand jury; I gave no testimony at all and I was nowhere near this situation in 1942 when this meeting was said to have occurred. I had not joined the Brothman firm until October 1944, had never known Brothman before that and had not met Gold until May 1946.)

Gold continued: "George" told Brothman that the report he had submitted on Buna-S was praiseworthy and equivalent in value to two or three brigades of men. The two of them also had a long discussion about mathematics; "George" was a mathematician as was Brothman, said Gold.

Saypol interjected: "You mean one was outblowing the other, is that the idea?"

Gold said no; they were discussing a topic in mathematics in which they were both interested.

"George" again brought up the topic of Brothman's working for a large industrial firm but Brothman appeared not to be interested. Finally, the meeting broke up. "George" left and Gold said Brothman thanked him for having provided a wonderful experience.

On cue, Gold then spoke of a conversation he had with Brothman in 1942 about his Communist Party dues. "I asked Abe to pay his Communist Party dues in which he was in arrears to me, and Abe said he was short then but would try to arrange it."

(We have an incomprehensible scenario here. Gold himself was not a member of the Communist Party but he was testifying that he tried to collect dues on its behalf. On cross-examination he admitted that he never extracted dues from Brothman. But Saypol's examination never asked him specifically if Brothman had paid those dues. He simply raised the issue and then let it slide away. It was, of course, irrelevant and prejudicial.)

In February 1943 Gold hired a stenographer named Jennie who met with Gold and Brothman weekly, and the latter dictated information to her about an aerosol insecticide dispenser he had designed. Gold paid Jennie himself, $10 or $15 per session. Again there was a built-in silliness to these meetings. Jennie knew Gold as "Harry Gold" just as Sam had. Brothman still knew him as "Frank Kessler." Surprisingly, no slip-ups occurred and Gold was able to maintain the deception.

After the sessions with Jennie ended Gold spent many Sundays with Brothman helping him put together a report on the production of magnesium powder used in tracer bullets and flares. Gold explained that it involved taking an ingot of magnesium, melting it and then forcing the molten magnesium through a spray nozzle into a chamber. Pointing to a diagram, he said:

"In this chamber is the inert gas, helium. A fine mist of magnesium particles forms. These particles solidify and they fall to the bottom of the chamber and they can be taken out and packaged. The feature of this process (as) opposed to the conventional one is this: the conventional one consists in taking an ingot of magnesium and subjecting it to a series of grinding or attrition processes until very gradually the desired particle size is produced. The big difference between the two processes is that the magnesium powder is inflammable stuff and by producing it from the molten state in this helium chamber you avoided the possibilities of any fire..."

(As before, Gold was impressive about his technical grasp of still another topic in industrial chemistry. But a subplot in this series of meaningless meetings was Gold's revelations that he never turned over to Sam the material on the magnesium powder plant or Jennie's notes on the insecticide dispenser or the work on the nickel catalyst plant because, said he, the Russians already had developed these techniques themselves. Instead of returning the rejected material to Brothman, again, he stored all of it in his cellar and he never told Brothman he had it.

The only items, then, which Gold said Brothman had given the Russians were his Buna-S report and some material on chemical mixing equipment, all of which was Brothman's own work. It had nothing to do with the United States government and it was neither secret nor classified. Nevertheless, the prosecution was now offering the rejected material to support its charge that we had conspired to obstruct justice and he implied that that conspiracy had overtones of Soviet espionage.)

In an obvious effort to link Brothman to government-related work (and implicitly to secrets) Saypol brought Gold back to the aerosol insecticide dispenser and asked if Brothman's firm was under contract to the government for its production. Harry replied that the government had *purchased* the dispensers. He did not say that Brothman had a contractual obligation to the government or that it was an exclusive arrangement.

Saypol tried another route. He referred back to the magnesium powder plant and inferentially to its potential for making military material. He asked Gold to identify the notes he had made—in Brothman's presence—in July 1943. It was an exercise in pointlessness. Defense attorney Kleinman objected that these notes were being used to buff Gold's irrelevant testimony and they were immaterial. It was an inanity to discuss them; nevertheless, Kaufman again overruled Kleinman.

Gold soldiered on. He met less frequently with Brothman after 1943 and his meetings with Sam ended in February 1944. However, he performed freelance work for Brothman occasionally. He had the use of the Penn Sugar laboratory (where he continued to work) whenever Brothman needed chemical analyses or tests done in connection with his engineering tasks. Brothman also referred Gold to several business contacts for similar freelance work and their relationship was becoming one of casual friendship. In the meantime, Sam was replaced by someone named John. Gold met with John from February 1944 until December 1946, but Brothman, he said, was no longer involved. The latter by now had formed his own consulting engineering firm, A. Brothman & Associates.

In February 1946 Gold was laid off from his Penn Sugar job and he told Brothman about it. The latter was in the middle of setting up his own chemical laboratory in Queens, and offered Gold the job of chief chemist. When Gold accepted the job a few months later, in May, he revealed to Brothman that his real name was not Frank Kessler, as Brothman had known him, but Harry Gold. He had used the alias, Gold said, because he did not want his employer in Philadelphia to learn of his moonlighting.

In May 1947, on his way to the Engineering Society's library to consult the research literature, he stopped by the office to see if Brothman also wanted him to check on anything. According to Gold, when he walked into the office, even before he could say anything, Brothman seized him and said:

> "Look, Harry, the FBI was just here. They know everything. They know all about us. They know that you were a courier. It must have been that bitch Helen... They even have pictures of you and me together. You have got to tell a story to cover me up. They are coming to see you this afternoon. Did you know John?"

Harry replied he did not know John. Brothman said, "You have got to tell the same story I did to cover me up." Gold said Brothman then launched into a description of a picture the FBI agents had shown him, a picture of a man he called John Golush. Brothman said the picture was that of a man with a wizened face, a wry grin, a receding hairline and curly hair, what there was of it. He told Gold to identify that picture as John Gollush and to make up a story telling the FBI that he, Gold, met Brothman through Gollush. Gold also said that Brothman suggested he say that the two of them, Brothman and Gold, had been writing a book together, if he were questioned about their activities. "And he also told me that Miriam Moskowitz was at that very moment on her way to Gibby Needleman in the Amtorg Company." Needleman, Gold explained, was employed as an attorney for Amtorg, and he identified me, Miriam Moskowitz, as a partner and the secretary of the Brothman firm.

Continuing, Gold said Brothman told him to return to the lab because the agents would seek him out there. The latter also cautioned him to conceal from them that this conversation had taken place.

Gold returned to the lab and the FBI agents, Shannon and O'Brien, arrived later. I also appeared, said Gold and I told him privately that Brothman had driven home with a headache and that we would both contact him later that day. Then I left. Gold submitted to the questioning and identified a picture the agents showed him as John Gollush.

Now, on the witness stand, Harry Gold testified that he had told the agents a false story of how he had met Brothman. He then recited a litany of what he said were his lies in 1947: He had never been introduced to anyone called John Gollush by Carter Hoodless at a meeting of the American Chemical Society. He had never gone to a restaurant with Gollush that night. He had never been made an offer by Gollush to telephone Brothman to meet him and evaluate his blueprints. He had never telephoned Brothman and made an appointment to see him; he never met Brothman in November 1940 in a restaurant in New York City and obtained the blueprints. In fact, he had met Abe in the latter's car on the night of September 29, 1941 under covert circumstances he had just described.

He told those lies, he said, only because Brothman had demanded that he, Gold, cover him with the FBI.

Judge Kaufman interjected a series of questions:

Q. "Let me get back to something you just said, that the so-called instructions or advice from Brothman was the only reason that you had for making those statements to the FBI."

A. "That is correct."

Q. "Weren't you also trying to protect yourself...?"

A. "Your Honor, I had no choice... When I arrived in Abe's office the decision was already made for me. He told me that the FBI had pictures of Abe and me together and he told me I had to cover him up. They were coming out to see me this afternoon, and there was no choice or even time."

Q. "Don't you really have reference to the fact that the type story you were telling, in fact, *was dictated by Brothman*?" (emphasis added)

A. "That is correct."

Q. "As distinguished from the reasons so-called... I do not know whether you see my point, Mr. Saypol."

Saypol: "Well, as I see it, Brothman told him to tell a false story that he had told and directed him to conform his story with his."

Kleinman: "Your Honor, I submit it is improper for these..."

Kaufman: "Disregard that statement of Mr. Saypol's. Continue."

(But Judge Kaufman had stepped far over the line by leading the witness. We were in reality facing two prosecutors, only one of whom was the real one. The other was the presiding judge himself. In Kaufman's questioning of Gold he revealed his bias and sent the jury a message that he had already decided on our guilt even before cross examination.)

Gold continued: Brothman and I arrived at the lab later and Brothman asked him how he made out with the FBI agents. Gold said I hugged him even before he could answer and told Brothman that he, Gold, had been superbly nonchalant. Then the three of us went to a restaurant for dinner. I reported that I had been to see Needleman and that I was sure I had been followed but that I had eluded my pursuers.

Gold also claimed I told the two of them that Needleman's advice had been that Brothman and Gold should tell the FBI agents that they were busy and could not be bothered talking to them, that they had no time for such nonsense.

After dinner, continued Gold, we all returned to the lab and Gold told Brothman what he had told the agents. The latter commented that he, Gold, had made a fine choice of a story. He also asked Gold to tell him every phase of his espionage activities so that he would be prepared should he be interrogated about it later. Gold refused but he revealed his lies to him about his personal life. He did not have a wife and children; he was a bachelor and had always been one. He had lied about his brother also; his brother was not killed in the South Pacific during the war; he was alive and at home. Gold was concerned, however, about having used the alias, "Frank Kessler," not only with Abe but also with the firm's personnel. If it raised questions, however, he would say that he had feared losing his job at Penn Sugar if they discovered he was also doing work in New York City.

I was present, said Gold, during all of this conversation except when I went out for coffee later in the evening. (That was not true and that is not what Gold told the FBI originally. He told them he never discussed these matters in front of me.)[16] But with this testimony Harry established that I knew a conspiracy was afoot.

(In September 1947 Gold's mother died. Brothman and I visited the Gold family during the week of mourning. I noticed that Harry's wife and children were not there and I commented to Brothman later that I was surprised. In such times, I thought, one might expect a wife, even an estranged one, to offer help. Brothman shrugged off my comment. Neither he, nor certainly, Harry ever told me that there was no wife and no children and no one explained the presence of the young man in the house whose name was Joe but who was not Harry's brother. (I did not know his tales about being married and having children were untrue because, contrary to Gold's testimony, I was not present when he unburdened himself to Brothman, nor did Brothman share Gold's confession with me.)

Gold continued his recitative: Later, in the early hours of morning after a long evening's work at the lab the three of us drove to Pennsylvania Station to drop Gold off for his train back to Philadelphia for the weekend. It was Brothman's practice to drive Gold to the station and it was not unusual for me to ride along because I lived only a few blocks south of there. Brothman would then drop me off at my apartment. During this ride, said Gold, Brothman criticized him for having brought a man to help out in the laboratory on several occasions who might have played a part, (Brothman was guessing wildly) in Soviet espionage and might have directed the government's attention to him. Gold said I interrupted their quarrel and told them they were both acting foolishly and that this was no time to fight because a falling out was exactly what the FBI wanted.

(But this was also not true. Gold and Brothman were in the front seat murmuring; I was curled up in the back, asleep – it was almost 4 a.m.)

About six weeks later, in early July 1947, Brothman received a subpoena to appear before a grand jury. According to Gold, Brothman asked him again about his espionage activities because "he did not want to be tripped up when he went to testify before the grand jury by facts of which he had no previous knowledge."

Gold's reply was that "it would be dangerous for him to have further knowledge of my espionage activities and that he was already involved deeply enough without needing to have any further incriminatory facts on his mind." He offered no details to substantiate that Brothman was "already involved deeply enough."

Gold continued, saying that I told him that I was concerned because Brothman had said that he was considering changing the story he had originally given the FBI when he would testify before the grand jury. I said I would try to get him to stick to his original story. Some time after, all three of us went to dinner. While Brothman was away from the table for a few minutes I told Gold that Needleman, the Amtorg attorney, and I had persuaded Brothman not to change the story he had originally given the FBI.

It was this testimony which firmly tied me to the conspiracy to obstruct justice. (One need only agree in some manner or show an awareness of the existence of a conspiracy by others to become a party to it, according to my attorney.) Gold established my guilt by offering this restaurant conversation, among others. But in fact that event never took place. I never had had an occasion to talk with Needleman specifically about Brothman's testimony. I was unaware what advice Needleman had given him, and for sure I did not know what either man would testify to because they had never made me privy to their conversations. Most of all, I did not know the background of either man for I did not know them in the cited time frame and neither had ever discussed past events with me. Certainly, Harry Gold knew he had never told me anything true about himself. However, for the sake of argument, let it be supposed that I did convince Brothman to stick to his original story and not to change it. One must then assume that I knew the original story was false for the conspiracy to have been established. At no time did Harry Gold say this was so.

About ten days later Gold also received a subpoena to appear before the grand jury. The three of us were together the night before Gold was to testify. Saypol's question and Gold's reply:

Q. "Do you remember the night before you testified before the jury in 1947?"

A. "The night before I testified, Abe, Miriam and I were in the Brothman office and Miriam said that this one night she wanted to go home early so that Abe and I would have plenty of time to match our stories before grand jury the next morning."

(Gold stumbled on cross-examination. "Miriam wanted to go home early so that we could have a talk.") No matching of stories this time. But in either case, it never happened.

Gold repeated that Brothman urged him to tell the same story he had originally given the FBI, the false story regarding the time and circumstances under which the two had met. But, said he, it was at this trial, now, that he was telling the truth of how they had met.

The prosecution elicited from him that he had remained in Abe's employ until June 1948. In the interval others had entered and left, but I had been there from 1944 and had become a partner before he, Gold, had arrived. Saypol asked: "In that interval were there any occasions where you had any conversations either...regarding your continuing employment by the partnership?"

Gold's reply: "Well, from about April or so of 1947 the pay in the Brothman firm was very irregular and there were long periods during which none of the members...drew any salary... and on several occasions ... Abe told me that I had to stay with the firm regardless of the fact that there was no pay because the two of us had to be together so that we could check our stories should there be any further questioning..."

This was a preposterous lie, especially because no one anticipated that there would be any follow-up after their grand jury appearance. Indeed, there had been none for three years.

The last few questions Saypol put to Gold were short but Gold's replies were especially injurious to me:

Q. "About the time that your relationship...terminated, do you remember an incident when both Brothman and Moskowitz were absent from the business for some short interval?"

A. "Yes, Abe and Miriam late in May of 1948 went on a business trip to Switzerland together."

Q. "How long were they gone?"

A. "About a week or ten days."

Q. "Do you know whether anybody else accompanied them? Did you go with them?"

A. "No."

With this Saypol introduced the irrelevant suggestion that the relationship between Abe and me may have been other than a purely business one, but he offered no evidence of it. As for the trip, Harry had expected that Abe would invite him to accompany him to Switzerland since he was a technical person. He never forgave me when Abe invited me instead, and now on the witness stand he had his payback time; against me (for also having slighted his overtures) and against Abe towards whom he had nursed a lethal hatred these last three years.

Saypol's examination closed on this note and now it was Defense Attorney Kleinman's turn.

Under cross-examination Gold expanded on his story of his activities with the Amtorg representatives. He said they carried on a legitimate purchasing business, but they had a secondary function as well; that was to obtain information by illegal means through him as their courier. Frequently, Gold's replies to Kleinman's questions became soliloquies and rambled far into unrelated territory. Kleinman asked Judge Kaufman to instruct Gold to respond directly, but the judge encouraged Gold to continue. In one instance Gold began to give hearsay testimony which Kleinman tried to curtail. Saypol wanted to hear the answer and interrupted Kleinman's questioning. A constant wrangling hopscotched between Kleinman on the one hand and the prosecutor, usually with the judge's support, on the other; over Gold's convoluted, long-winded digressions. Kleinman usually lost.

Again, under cross examination, Gold repeated he was not a communist. He had engaged in espionage because he wanted to help the people of the Soviet Union. Also, he was obligated to Tom Black because Black had obtained a job for him during the worst months of the Depression. "We were a family with a fierce sort of pride," he proclaimed, "and we would have hated to go on relief…"

Kleinman lost a motion to strike that remark. It had nothing to do with the case and was designed only to elicit sympathy from the jury. How could anyone not feel compassion for a man and his family with such admirable principles?

"Black saved us from that," he continued. "The second reason in addition to the one of a genuine desire to help the people of the Soviet Union… was that I got Black off my back about joining the Communist Party. I didn't want to. I didn't like them."

None of this testimony should have been allowed because it had nothing to do with either Brothman or me.

Kleinman then led Gold to tell that he knew Amtorg was purchasing American industrial materials and doing legitimate business with American firms seeking to dispel the aura of furtive operations. Judge Kaufman jumped ahead of him with a point of his own, asking Gold:

Q. (by Judge Kaufman): "Wasn't there a period when Russia was an ally of Germany?"
A. "There was."
Q. When was that?"
A. "From about 1939 to 1941…"

Kleinman interjected: "Your Honor perhaps stated Russia was an ally of Germany. I didn't quite get it."

Saypol contributed: "There was some agreement, they were never allies."

Kaufman: "I will accept your statement that they had a pact."

(Judge Kaufman's insertion of irrelevant history could only have been intended to prejudice the jury against us. Americans knew that the Soviet Union had signed a non-aggression pact with Germany in August 1939. The pact did not make them allies (as some Americans viewed it) but it did buy time for the Russians to prepare for the invasion they knew Germany was secretly preparing. In fact, on June 22, 1941 Germany invaded Russia and the pact was abrogated. Kaufman's characterizing Russia as an ally of Germany was incendiary because he knew from the jury selection process that several members of the jury or their relatives had served in the armed forces during the Second World War. And of course, Kaufman's reference had no bearing on our trial.)

Gold continued. He did not see that he might be harming the United States in performing what he now referred to as "industrial espionage," that is, obtaining information from Brothman concerning engineering processes on high octane gasoline or blueprints or engineering data on processes having to do with industrial mixers or information about magnesium—and here Judge Kaufman helpfully supplied the identification—"tracer bullets."

But, said Gold, *all of that was never turn over to the Soviet Union because they already had those processes.*

Kleinman then took Gold through a list of blueprints he said Abe had given him, starting with one showing how to make lacquers and varnishes. Gold said the Russians had rejected it for lack of descriptive material. But Kleinman wanted more:

Q. "Well now, Mr. Gold, whatever is on that blueprint was nothing new, was no innovation there, is that right from known processes?"

Before our eyes Harry Gold began to mutate into a technical tenderfoot:

A. "I am no design engineer and I can't tell whether there are any features here that are unique or not."
Q. "Weren't the processes of making these lacquers and varnishes and paints well known all over the world?"
A. "You mean these solvents?"
Q. "These solvents, yes."
A. "Well, the processes for the separation of these various esters have been known for a long time, that is true, but people keep bringing in refinements whereby they get better yields and so on, which accomplishes the same thing in less time and gets less byproducts. They are small advances but they count in the long run."
Q. "And whatever possible advantages there could have been for the Soviet people was in having some perhaps newer process of making lacquers or varnishes?"
A. "It is possible, just possible, that this piece of equipment would have enabled them to conduct certain esterification operations a little more efficiently with a slightly better yield and so on."

(Gold was beginning to equivocate now because he saw where Kleinman was leading.)

Q. "All that was necessary at that time, Mr. Gold, was for anybody to go over to an engineering place like Hendrick and ask for … just what you have there on that blueprint and he could have gotten it for a fee, is that right?"

A. "That is correct, but I asked that question in November 1935 and I got an answer…(that) they could purchase processes in the United States…but…they were afraid to. They were going to purchase them anyhow, but they wanted to be sure. They wanted processes exactly as they were in operation in the United States. And they said that they had an experience (that) American firms would sell them a process, and they would take it over there and put it in operation and they would find that somewhere down the line, someone from the top man or some one down the chain of command sabotaged the thing. I was told (also) that … there were firms which refused to deal with Soviet representatives, so that the only way they had of getting the information was illegal… That was my job."

Throughout his testimony Gold repeatedly implied that even though the blueprints bore Brothman's initials they were not Brothman's work, leading to a suggestion that Brothman had misappropriated someone else's work and therefore had engaged in industrial espionage. Additionally, he would not admit that he knew that Brothman was the design engineer in charge of the Hendrick Company's operations.

Gold also dodged Kleinman's question about whether he realized he was spying for the Soviet government and insisted, rather, that he was doing his work for the people of the Soviet Union. He drew a fine distinction between industrial espionage and military espionage. What he had been guilty of was industrial espionage.

Under Kleinman's questioning Gold related that when he left Brothman's employ in June 1948 he got a job with the Philadelphia General Hospital, and was now doing biochemical work rather than industrial chemical. So, for the last two years he had been working as a lab technician in an entirely new and different field of chemistry. Nevertheless, under direct examination Gold had displayed an impressive level of technical knowledge of industrial chemistry. Yet, under cross-examination, he denied the expertise he had shown just days earlier. He was suddenly smitten with an uncharacteristic modesty.

Kleinman returned to the Buna-S topic but could not get an admission from Gold that he knew anything about the manufacture of synthetic rubber even though he had worked with Brothman to assemble a voluminous report on it in April 1942. On direct examination Gold had said the report was about 200 pages long, had many drawings and "it was a complete process." Now he was suddenly uninformed about this topic.

"That is not my field," he told Kleinman.

But in reply to Saypol's questions a few days earlier, he had gone into a lengthy explanation of one of the flow sheets Brothman had drawn for the Buna-S project. "This is an unusually complete flow sheet…here is your butadiene… here is the chain modifier…they are injected into these vessels, both of which are polymerizers which are really the heart of the system…here is the equipment for the recovery of the budadiene," Gold went on. "Butadiene is a very explosive material…and styrene vapors themselves are poisonous…"

Now, under the defense attorney's questioning, Gold persistently claimed selective ignorance.

And again, under the defense attorney's further questioning Gold claimed, "That is not my field." He added that he was a biochemist and an analytical chemist. "I deal with biological things, living processes, the human body, animal organisms."

But this was true for only the past two years. During the previous thirteen years, at least from 1935 to 1946 at Penn Sugar, and from 1946 to 1948 at Brothman's, he had functioned as an industrial chemist. His academic training had been in general organic chemistry, not biochemistry. Gold was disclaiming the authority he had displayed only days before – and the purpose soon became clear.

Kleinman tried to get from Gold an acknowledgement that Brothman had published articles in American engineering journals on the topic of Buna-S rubber manufacture and therefore the process was in no sense secret. Furthermore, because it was Abe's own work, it was not industrial espionage. Gold skirted the probing by repeating that he was not an expert in that field.

The questioning next concerned Brothman's hydrogenation process using a nickel catalyst. Kleinman:

Q. "I show you now pages 1524 to 1526 of Roger's Industrial Chemistry (marked as Government's Exhibit 16) and I ask you to look at it and to see whether it describes … a process for the production of dry reduced nickel hydrogenation catalyst such as you have discussed here…and you will agree, will you not. Mr. Gold, that what you have read… in Roger's…is but a bird's eye view of industrial chemistry and that the process described in Roger's is based on some more detailed descriptions in specialized literature of that field?"

A. "Well, I don't know anything about the specialized literature in the field of hydrogenation. I am an analytical chemist and a biochemist."

Q. "It is true, however, is it not, Mr. Gold that there is nothing secret or startlingly new in the process for dry reduced nickel catalyst as appears on Government's Exhibit 16?"

A. "I can't tell. I don't know that much about commercial hydrogenation. I was told by Abe that this was a unique process."

On direct examination only days earlier Gold had transfixed the court with his expansive knowledge of this subject. He had given a detailed technical explanation of how a nickel catalyst was used to prepare shortening in a hydrogenation process. Kleinman made to continue this questioning but Saypol interrupted: "…The testimony here is that this witness says, 'Abe gave me this; Abe told me this was novel; Abe gave me this to give to my superior.' Whether he gave it to him or not is a matter of record. Whether it compares to what is in the book or whether it is even in the telephone book is really immaterial. He is just trying to get him to qualify as an expert on subjects which the witness has stated that he does not have any expert knowledge."

Kleinman remonstrated: "I was willing to accept his (Gold's) expert knowledge when he made explanations of all these things…Our purpose is to show that there was nothing unusual about this practice of making a blueprint and giving (it) to anybody who asked for it at that time. There was nothing secret."

After more bobbing and weaving over Kleinman's questions Gold finally agreed that in general Abe's blueprints did resemble the material printed in Roger's. Then Kleinman continued:

Q. "…would it be fair to say that those blueprints contain no secret or unusually unavailable information?"

Saypol: "If he knows."

Kleinman: "Of course …Is not my statement a fair one to you, Mr. Gold? Can you answer it?"

A. "Yes, the process resembles that which is in Roger's."

Q. "There is nothing secret contained in those blueprints, is that right?"

A. "You have to start to define 'secret.'"

Q. "There is nothing unusual in those blueprints, you have just seen it in the textbook, have you not?"

A. "Yes, there is nothing unusual."

Kleinman asked Gold what the strategic materials were which he had referred to the day before on direct examination. Gold replied:

A. "Well, I don't know what you would call a strategic material."

Q. "You were the one who called it a strategic material. What did you refer to?"

A. "All – the entire organic chemical field could be classified as strategic organic material, the entire field."

Q. "You mean everything in organic chemistry may be classified as strategic?"

A. "Yes, eventually."

Q. "Everything?"

A. "Well, practically all of the industrial chemicals and hydrogenation is an industrial chemical process."

Q. "Yes, and isn't it true that hydrogenation operations are one of the most common operations in chemistry?"

A. "They are common, but that still would not make them lesser in their strategic value. In fact, the very fact that they are commonly used makes them valuable."

Q. "Tell us what you mean by a strategic value or strategic material, mention something."

A. "Strategic material?"

Q. "In connection with this hydrogenation process."

A. "Well, the production of alcohol formaldehydes, I guess could be called strategic."

Q. "You said that before."

A. "Yes, I said that before."

Q. "What else?"

A. "The hydrogenation of various unsaturated compounds."

Q. "Are you through with your answer?"

A. "I am through with my answer because I am not an expert in the field."

Q. "Could you tell us very briefly exactly what you are an expert in, Mr. Gold?"

A. "I am an analytical chemist...and a biochemist."

Q. "Can you tell us, so that we can understand it, what an analytical chemist is?"

A. "As an analytical chemist I know certain special techniques for analyzing certain material... I am a biochemist because I know the relationship of chemistry to living organisms."

Q. "You took some extra studies at Columbia after you received your degree, didn't you?"

A. "I never studied at Columbia."

(This statement did not conform to what he had told the grand jury in 1947, the minutes of which were read at the beginning of this trial. Gold said then that he had taken a course in organic chemistry at Columbia University after he obtained his degree from Xavier. It was one more of the numerous inconsistencies of his testimony.)

Kleinman returned to Gold's motivation in acting as a courier. Gold had said several times he wanted to help the Soviet people. Then Kleinman asked: "Did you intend to harm or injure the United States when you passed this information concerning strategic materials?"

Gold hedged; he did not see the pertinence of the question. As Kleinman prodded Gold, he admitted that his only motive was to help the Soviet people but he added: "I was giving the Russian people information which I thought as an ally they were entitled to; and, as a matter of fact, I considered that the atomic energy project might have been completed in less time were the collaboration of Soviet scientists included in the project."

And, he continued, he did not intend any harm to the American people.

Kleinman followed that with a question which cut to the core:

Q. "And we were not at war in 1935, either, were we?"
A. "We were not."

He admitted he had not yet been sentenced; that would take place some two weeks hence. He knew his life was at stake, Gold said; nevertheless, he did not expect any reward for testifying against Brothman and me and none was promised.

In several instances Kleinman wrung from Gold an admission that material the prosecution was using as evidence that Brothman had transmitted secrets had, in fact, been published earlier, by Brothman, and was in the public domain when Gold said he received it. For example:

Government Exhibits 14 and 15 (on the Buna-S project) contained the same calculations and process information as Defendants' Exhibits G and H. These were articles Brothman had published, the first in *Product Engineering* in 1940 and the second – a reprise of the first – in *Chemical & Metallurgical Engineering* in March 1943. Both were respected McGraw-Hill publications.

Government Exhibit 13 and part of Defendants' Exhibit H, a collection of blueprints and related text, contained the same information, Gold agreed. (This was some of the "fragmentary" material he had never turned over to his Soviet contact but had stored, instead, in his cellar.)

Government Exhibit 15, the support material for the voluminous Buna-S report with numerous blueprints which Gold said he gave the Russians, contained the same material, he agreed, as Defendants' Exhibit I. The latter was Brothman's bound copy of the original report; it also contained a published article dated December 1941 on this subject published several months *before* he gave it to Gold for transmittal to the Russians in April 1942, as Gold had testified.

Saypol was distressed throughout this testimony. Twice he objected and asked that all of Harry Gold's testimony now be stricken. Both times Kaufman overruled him but offered him comfort: "… Of course, it will be for the jury to ultimately determine how much weight they want to give to this line of testimony."

His broad hint to the jury could not have been clearer. Kaufman was permitting Gold's testimony although he, himself, thought it irrelevant.

Kleinman returned to Brothman's design of chemical mixers, the blueprints for which Saypol had presented as Government Exhibit 17. That consisted of calculations in Gold's handwriting. Gold now said the work had not been his; he had either copied it from some source or Brothman had dictated it to him. Kleinman prodded; was it not part of the original mathematics on which Defendants' Exhibit J was based?

Gold hesitated and Judge Kaufman rescued him: "You can save a lot of time by saying you are not (an) expert and you cannot therefore answer, if that is the case."

Gold finessed and declined to compare the two exhibits; the mathematics was beyond him, he said. Kleinman continued to push: was the mathematics in both papers not the same subject matter? Gold held him at bay; he was not competent to judge.

Kleinman returned to the nickel catalyst subject and asked Gold about some work he had performed on this for Brothman when he was still at Penn Sugar. Gold said it was in late 1942 or in 1943; his colleague, Morrell Dougherty, helped him. Kleinman asked:

Q. "Is Mr. Dougherty married or a single man?

A. "He is married."

Saypol: "At this time I will start imposing an objection."

Judge Kaufman: "He said he was married."

Saypol: "I am talking about the general line of questioning. I don't see its connection here."

Kaufman: "I don't either."

With that Kaufman ruled the questioning out of order.

But indeed there was a connection. Saypol had good reason to shut down any further discussion about the association between Gold and Dougherty. Judge Kaufman may not have been privy to Saypol's information but as always he was the prosecution's guardian.

Saypol's information concerned the following: In Philadelphia on the evening of November 3, 1950, five days before our trial began, Morell Dougherty, Gold's long time (and now erstwhile) friend received a telephone call from a John Terry. Mr. Terry asked Dougherty to meet with him the next day for an interview about Harry Gold on behalf of a client, the client unnamed. When Dougherty demurred Terry threatened to have him subpoenaed. Dougherty thereupon agreed to meet Terry the following day at his, Dougherty's, office.

Immediately, Dougherty called the Philadelphia office of the FBI to tell the agents of Terry's request. (He had earlier been interviewed by them about Gold.) They asked Dougherty to advise them of the results of his meeting with Terry and he agreed.

The Bureau office in Philadelphia then swung into action. They checked with the New York office and learned that Terry was a private investigator in

New York, and, they guessed, was on an assignment for William Kleinman, our attorney. They then alerted the Director in Washington, J. Edgar Hoover; they also noted that Gold had admitted that he and Dougherty had stolen alcohol over a period of years from the bonded warehouse of Penn Sugar during their employment there.[17] (The theft of alcohol is a Federal offense and a felonious crime.)

Director Hoover flashed a teletype marked "Urgent" to the staff in New York telling them of the Dougherty information and repeating that Gold and Dougherty had stolen Penn Sugar alcohol. He also told them to pass the information on to United States Attorney Saypol and his staff. Clearly, the FBI was concerned about what Terry would learn from Morrell Dougherty.

Terry was to be at Dougherty's office at 9:30 a.m. the following morning. At 10:30 a.m. Dougherty called the Philadelphia FBI and this time reported that Terry had not kept his appointment. Dougherty had telephoned the hotel where Terry was staying and learned that although he had been registered there the night before, November 3, he was no longer registered there on November 4.[18]

The FBI's flurry of alarm over Terry seemed to subside as quickly as it had come into being. Inexplicably, Terry had left town, apparently in a hurry, without interviewing Dougherty and without uncovering not only the theft of the Penn Sugar property, but other disreputable activities which Dougherty knew Gold had been involved in. The question remains unanswered: Why did Terry not fulfill the purpose of his visit? One can only guess.

In the meantime, Saypol had been forewarned, which prevented Kleinman from exploring the Dougherty connection. Judge Kaufman gave a seal of approval to thwart Kleinman, and Harry Gold's image in the eyes of the jury remained forever pure and uncompromised.

Kleinman returned to Brothman's mixing equipment designs which Gold had said he gave to Sam as part of the Buna-S report. Kleinman showed Gold a copy of that material which he called the defendant's Exhibit K and asked Gold if it was the same as what he had received. Gold thought the original was more comprehensive. The blueprints of this equipment bore the nameplate of the Hendrick Mfg. Co.

Kleinman then produced copies of two of Brothman's patents on mixers and moved to enter them as Defendants' Exhibits L and M. He asked Gold if the drawings they contained were familiar. They were not. He rephrased his question but Kaufman cut him off.

"Do you think this is proper cross-examination?" Judge Kaufman asked, "The witness says he has never seen them."

The patents on the mixers were in the public domain and therefore the mixers were not secret. All the other documents the prosecution offered were similarly not secret. Nevertheless, Saypol's direct questioning had repeatedly built an aura of secrecy around that material, suggesting that what was really involved in this case was espionage. And Brothman was caught in a labyrinth of suspicion.

Kleinman wanted to establish that the patents (granted in 1940) proved that the mixing equipment designs Gold said Brothman had given him for the Russians (in December 1941) were in the public domain and therefore not secret – and they were his own work. Saypol labeled the patents "immaterial." All the other documents the prosecution had offered were similarly not secret. Nevertheless, Saypol's direct examination had repeatedly built an aura of secrecy around that material. Because Gold, who was a critical witness against us, had earlier confessed to spying, Saypol sedulously built an aura of espionage around Brothman's activities, despite the obvious evidence that they were not.

We had now arrived at a critical point in this trial. Until now the prosecution had built its case on Brothman's having passed material to Gold which it implied was secret. Judge Kaufman began to perceive that this case could dissolve if Kleinman were permitted to use the patents as evidence. Subtly, he changed course:

Kaufman: "…whether or not (the documents) were secret is immaterial…the government offered them for the purpose of showing association between the defendants."

Kleinman protested: "That is no proof of … criminality."

Kaufman sustained Saypol's objections and the jury never got to see the patents. Kaufman's bias now was becoming ever more obvious. He seemed to lose no opportunity to disparage Kleinman's professional status before the jury as well as before the witness. One of the by-products was that Gold assumed carte blanche to go off on irrelevant answers to Kleinman's questions. He repeated that because he had his "knuckles smartly rapped" for having turned over "fragmentary" blueprints to Sam he had learned his lesson. When Abe gave him blueprints thereafter without descriptive material, he did not turn them over to Sam. Into his cellar they went.

Kleinman turned to another item for Gold's identification, a published article by Brothman on the manufacture of urea formaldehyde glue. The attorney asked Gold to identify the date of the publication and then to correlate it with when he received the blueprints of it. Saypol objected and Kaufman sustained, chastising Kleinman: "There is nothing in the record that indicates that is a publication. It is a piece of paper… Now rephrase your question."

Kleinman tried again: "I call your attention to the date on that paper, Defendants' Exhibit N for identification and ask you if the date on that corresponds to the date when you received the blueprints which you did not turn over to Sam."

Gold: "I fail to see the connection."

Kleinman: (to Judge Kaufman) "Now, your Honor, I move to strike that out. I do not want him commenting on any questions…"

Kaufman ignored Kleinman and turned to Gold: "The answer is 'No,' is it?"

Kleinman: "He did not say that."

Saypol jumped in to object. He characterized the issue as "innocuous." By now Kleinman was fed up and complained: "…throughout the entire morning Mr. Saypol has been saying that the questions are either innocuous or that they have no bearing, which are not legal objections, of course, but he has been commenting on my cross-examination all the way through and I object to it."

It was a difficult day for Kleinman. He was attempting to link Gold's testimony to non-existent secrets and Kaufman and Saypol were equally determined that the jury would not draw such inferences. In the meantime, the judge had led Gold to say "no" to Kleinman's questions even though he agreed that the dates corresponded. And again, Gold negated the value of the material because there had been no descriptive text. And what did he do with this "fragmentary" material on the urea formaldehyde project? He stored it in his cellar.

He explained, although Kleinman did not ask, how he happened to forget all about the stored material:

He worked long hours so that he could take compensatory time off whenever he needed to go on a "mission." His friend and co-worker, Morrell Dougherty, covered for him but he never told Dougherty where he was going or what he was doing. When he took off on a mission he used what he called a "one-track mind." He concentrated on the mission and forgot everything else. When he returned, "I just turned the switch and I used a one-track mind in my work."

He did not mind the long hours in the laboratory… "I am happy when I am in a laboratory." It enabled him to forget that when he ran a mission he was committing a crime – and that was the reason he was able to forget about the material he had squirreled away in his cellar. Gold also characterized the blueprints Brothman had given him as having been another firm's property which he, Brothman, had no right to have. It was larceny, he said. He denied knowing that it was a common practice in the engineering business to distribute blueprints or other information to interested prospects. He also denied knowing that such material served promotional purposes.

Kleinman drew from Gold that he had made a survey for a chemical plant in New Jersey, while he was employed by Penn Sugar, on a freelance basis. His friend, Morrell Dougherty, had helped him write the survey. Kleinman asked him if it was in the field of biochemistry and Gold replied that it was in the field of distillery practice. He skirted the answer that he did, in fact, have a good working knowledge of industrial chemistry contrary to his current denials. He then qualified the identification by calling the work, "industrial biochemistry," a neat improvisation. When Kleinman asked if it had been Abe Brothman who had recommended him for the job, Gold replied: "That's what Abe told me." (He was equivocating. Gold knew that Brothman and the man for whom he did the survey were personal friends.)

By 1945 Gold's relationship with Brothman had "deteriorated," he said. He was no longer giving orders to Brothman and was no longer his superior; they had become friends. Also, by this time his Soviet superior had said they had no further use for Brothman and that Brothman was "hot." They cautioned Gold to stay away from him. He said that Brothman's identity as a source of information had been revealed to the government. (Presumably, by Elizabeth Bentley since about this time she had defected to the FBI.) However, Gold said he had so much on his mind he just forgot about the warning. (That was hard to believe; the warning was not trivial. Gold, as he did so many times during this trial, was fabricating.)

Gold then reviewed the lies he had discussed earlier. He had assumed the name, Frank Kessler, as a cover and his cover included a wife and twin children. Kleinman asked him if it was not true that only after he became employed by Brothman in 1946 that he furnished additional details to Brothman about his home life and marriage. The judge commented: "I believe he has answered that, hasn't he? He said he did it beginning in 1941."

Kleinman: "I am asking him about the details, your Honor."

With an audible sigh, Kaufman replied: "I will let him answer it once more." (But Gold had not given those details before.)

The witness continued. He had begun his fictitious stories in 1941 and continued to embellish them even though he and Brothman had become personal friends. He had also told those stories to Brothman's staff, to me, and to people with whom the firm did business. The stories involved how he had married. His wife's name had been Sarah O'Ken. She was gawky and long-legged when he first knew her, but she became beautiful and worked as a model for Gimbel's Department Store in Philadelphia where they all lived. He met her when he was courting another young woman, a Helen Tavelman. Sarah had also been courted by an underworld, swarthy character who recruited girls for brothels. Sarah's family was disreputable; her mother was a slovenly housekeeper and her father a shiftless gambler. Because they were all so short of cash his wedding to Sarah had had to be postponed several times. Finally the neighbors contributed food to the wedding celebration and they were married. His wife gave birth to twins, a girl, Essie, and a boy, David. Essie had one blue eye and one brown eye; she had also had polio. A few years into the marriage his wife met a wealthy real estate broker, an older man, and left Gold. She took the children and the only way Gold could see them was to hide behind a tree at the playground on Saturday afternoons and watch them from a distance.

On the witness stand now Gold denied the details he had told us. He did not speak of any gambling father or the neighbors' contributions of food to the wedding; he denied the story of the brothel recruiter and he was vague about recalling other details such as watching the children at the playground. He could also not recall the many details of his fictitious family life which Kleinman now recalled for him.

Harry Gold was visibly uncomfortable as this concoction of lies unfolded but Kleinman pressed for answers. Judge Kaufman took pity; he chastised Kleinman for what he said were repetitions, cut him down and again humiliated him in front of the jury and the witness.

Kleinman bore on. Gold admitted that even though he had told Brothman his real name in 1946 he continued to embellish his other fictions. He said it was easier than to "straighten out the whole hideous mess." And he continued the embellishments, he said, even though he was no longer reporting to any Soviet superior and no longer in need of a masquerade.

Kleinman asked Gold if he had described to Brothman the first apartment he and his wife occupied after their marriage, a small, one-room apartment. Gold remembered; the description corresponded to the apartment of his friend, Morrell Dougherty. Kleinman also asked Gold about having told Brothman in 1945 that he and his wife had bought a house. Gold's reply: "That was partially false but based on truth. My mother and I had purchased a home..."

He did not recall that he had told Brothman that he had traveled a great deal for Penn Sugar in 1942 and 1943, but he might have mentioned to him that his wife resented his absences. "Actually," he said, "it was my mother."

Among Gold's other significant fictions was one about the death of his brother, an Army paratrooper, in the Pacific during World War II. However, his brother was alive and well at home. Now, on the witness stand he either did not remember having told that story or he denied having done so. He had also told us that his cousin, Joe, with the same name as his brother, had come to live with his family. Gold could not recall now that he had ever told us such a tale.

After several cues from Judge Kaufman, Gold's behavior towards our attorney was becoming insolent. When Kleinman asked him whether it was true that those stories continued until the FBI first interviewed him in May 1947, his impatient reply was, "I have stated (that) on direct examination."

Kleinman asked him about some chemical analytical work he had done for Brothman and Gold replied, "We have had this question before..."

Rudeness and insolence were hardly hallmarks of Harry Gold's behavior. He had always been known to be almost excessively polite, obsequious and ever eager to make a good impression. Now, however, he had obviously been well rehearsed by the prosecution. I guessed that because Roy Cohn had been the witness preparer of Elizabeth Bentley he had also taught Harry Gold a bag of rude tricks. But when Harry went off on one of his reminiscence jaunts, Kaufman prevented our attorney from rerouting his detour to more substantive issues.

Kleinman finally got from the witness that it was not until May 1947 after his first FBI interrogation, that he told Brothman that there was no truth to any of his fables. Also, by that time he was no longer in contact with any Soviet apparatus and his employment with Brothman was entirely a legitimate business relationship.

Gold next recounted how the dire financial circumstances of the firm prevented him and others from drawing salaries. It was a continuing state of financial emergency, he said, coupled with long work hours that made him want to leave. He did not do so, he postured, because if he had the firm would have collapsed.

Kleinman asked specifically what had stopped him from leaving. His reply: "Myself.... I have always gotten myself into my own difficulties."

He then related how he had discovered that Brothman was trying to arrange various deals for the firm's refinancing and he came to the conclusion that Brothman was about to make a deal cutting him out of a promised partnership. (He had obtained the information from the company files which were full of proposals from entrepreneurs which Brothman had rejected. Harry had jumped to wild conclusions.)

Then Gold related that when Brothman returned from Switzerland in 1948, he and two other members of the firm held "an indignation meeting" with Brothman at which Gold read him a list of charges. (I was not present and never learned about the meeting.) The charges included mismanaging a job for a Philadelphia firm as well as the unkept partnership promise. He demanded that Brothman retrench and work on a smaller scale. A major complaint also, said Gold, was that I had not treated him with sufficient dignity. He said I was unkind and that I had a violent temper.

About a week after this meeting he and one of the other participants met with Brothman to get him to sign a statement they had prepared that he, Brothman, owed them back pay. Brothman refused to sign and the meeting broke up acrimoniously.

Kleinman took Gold back to May 1947 when Brothman had told him he had just been questioned by the FBI and asked him – Gold – to make up a story about how they had met.

Kleinman asked Gold if he was alarmed when Brothman told him the FBI had appeared and if he realized that he had a great deal more at stake then did Brothman. Gold denied that he gave it any thought; he was concerned about what story he would concoct, "according to Abe's instructions." Kleinman then asked if he had not realized the enormity of what he had done.

Gold replied: "I realized that I had taken information from people who had given it to me on atomic energy and I had given it to the Soviet Union."

Kleinman countered with: "Which was, of course, far more serious than information about the hydrogenation of certain oils, is that right?"

Saypol objected, Kaufman sustained, and Gold was spared the need to agree to an obvious truth.

Kleinman asked if Brothman had told him what kind of story to make up. Gold said that Brothman, in a meeting lasting only a few minutes, told him to make up a story, any story, that would cover him. His testimony now on cross-examination matched almost word for word his direct testimony, and that in turn matched what he told the FBI on June 13, 1950: "... Brothman stated, 'The FBI were here—they know everything...they know you were a courier...look, we don't have much time...you've got to tell the same story I told about how we met...'"[19]

Again he said that Brothman had told him the agents had shown him a picture of John Gollush and when Gold told Brothman he had not known Gollush, Brothman described the man as he appeared in the agents' photograph, so that Harry could identify him: "...a man with a wizened face, a wry grin, receding hairline and curly hair, what there was of it."

And again it was word for word. (And as noted earlier, Gold's testimony was perjury; he had indeed known Gollush/Golos.) Six months earlier, on May 22, 1950, Gold signed a confession for the FBI which included the following statement:

"On my return to Philadelphia (from Xavier College Cincinnati, Ohio) I was again contacted by the people with whom I had worked before. I was called on the phone in June 1940 and I went downtown to see this man, who turned out to be Jacob Golos." (Before the trial Gold told the FBI he had met with Golos for almost half a year and gave them a description of the man. During the trial he said he had never met Golos. His admission to the FBI was made before Roy Cohn got a chance to work him over).

Kleinman asked if Brothman was a prolific writer on scientific and engineering subjects. Gold replied: "Abe told me he published many articles." He refused to corroborate that Brothman had written many technical articles; he said he did not read the publications in which they had appeared even though they were on display in the office.

During much of this testimony the Saypol/Kaufman interference was unremitting. Saypol objected; Kaufman sustained; the witness balked and Kaufman disparaged our attorney, Kleinman. Gold became belligerent. When he rambled with a sludge of unnecessary detail in reply to Kleinman's probing, Kaufman refused to support Kleinman's appeal to rein him in. Instead, Kaufman said, repeatedly "Let him answer."

The judge's bias was never more obvious than during Kleinman's closing cross-examination. It yielded a flurry of objections from Saypol which Kaufman sustained.

> Kleinman: (to Gold) "Did you intend to tell the grand jury (in May 1947) the truth if you had not been influenced, as you say, by Brothman...?"
>
> Saypol: "That is immaterial if the Court pleases."
>
> Kleinman: "I think that goes to the essence of the case."
>
> Saypol: "My objection... is that it is not what this witness intended to do. The charge is what he did as a result of Brothman's influence."
>
> Judge Kaufman: "Yes, you are right. I will sustain..."
>
> Kleinman plowed on: "What I want to find out from you, Mr. Gold, is this: was it only because Brothman spoke to you and told you what he had testified to that you lied?"
>
> Saypol: "Once again I object... I think it is immaterial. I think the proof of the charge is on the basis of the evidence and the testimony of the witness and it is for the jury to determine..."
>
> Judge Kaufman: "I will sustain it."

It is not believable that Gold would have told the truth to the grand jury in 1947. He had held off a battering from the FBI without Brothman's instructions three years later, in May 1950, but Kleinman was now barred from pursuing this. He did the next best thing; he asked Gold if he realized that had he told the grand jury the truth in 1947 he would have been vulnerable to indictment and prosecution for espionage, and his life would have been at stake.

Saypol objected; Kaufman sustained.

Kleinman continued: "In 1947... when you first spoke to the FBI agents, regardless of conversations with Mr. Brothman, did you want to tell the FBI the truth?"

Kaufman sustained Saypol's objection.

Had Gold been permitted to answer these questions he would have had to admit that in denying the truth in 1947 he was acting independently of Brothman, because he had far more to lose than did Brothman. Also, the prosecution had not shown proof of Brothman's influence and Kleinman felt that such suggestions, even if true, did not constitute a conspiracy:

> Kleinman: "When were you first aware... that Fuchs had been apprehended in England?"
>
> Gold: "In early February of 1950."

Gold testified that he learned of Fuchs' arrest and confession through the newspapers and that no Soviet superior gave him any information about it. But Gold had earlier told the FBI that he had had visits from a Soviet agent in October 1949, who told him that Fuchs was giving information, and that he, Gold, might have to flee the country. So this was then another bit of perjury Gold was committing on the stand, and he was doing it with the prosecution's implicit blessing.[20]

Gold began talking to the FBI at the end of May 1950, and he was aware that he could be implicated in the Fuchs matter. The following exchange took place:

> Kleinman: "Did you decide to tell the truth or to lie when they questioned you?"
>
> Gold: "I related that the other day…"
>
> Kleinman: "No, please answer my question."
>
> Judge Kaufman: "All right, relate it again."
>
> Gold: "I acted exactly as I decided upon. First I decided that since Fuchs had already disclosed many of the facts involving our espionage activities, that I would confess completely to my activities with Dr. Fuchs, but I would not reveal anything about any of my American contacts. In other words, I would, as they say, take the rap myself."
>
> Gold continued even though his response was not pertinent to what Kleinman had asked for: "…I realized that I could possibly fight this thing and I knew if I did that my father and brother, all of my boyhood friends, would rally around me, but I knew that once the FBI began to probe into the hideous snarl that was my life, once they pulled one thread the whole horrible skein would become untangled and inevitably… I would be exposed. So I made my choice because I didn't want these people… to be so terribly disillusioned."
>
> Kleinman: "Yes, but you did not make your choice immediately, did you?"
>
> Gold: "…I take exception…here is what happened."
>
> Kleinman: "… I move to strike…"
>
> Judge Kaufman: (To Gold) "Go ahead and answer the question."
>
> Gold: "I said, 'Yes, I am the man to whom Klaus Fuchs gave the information on atomic energy.' And I sat down… and the FBI man gave me a cigarette and I asked for one minute during which … a thousand things went through my mind… and I didn't even need that minute to come to a decision."
>
> Kleinman: "Did you at first deny that you had been west of the Mississippi?"
>
> Gold: "I had denied that the week before."
>
> Kleinman: "Beginning with the first time that the FBI spoke to you, at that time you denied any knowledge of Dr. Fuchs, is that right?"
>
> Gold: "I stated before that for a whole week I fought desperately for time."
>
> Kleinman: "You fought to save your life, didn't you?"
>
> Gold: "I fought desperately for time with my family and I fought

desperately for time to complete the work at the Heart Station.

Kleinman: "Would you lie to save your life?"

Gold: "Now? No."

Kleinman: "I did not ask you about now. Would you lie to save your life when you spoke to the FBI in May of 1950?"

Gold: "In May of 1950 I lied desperately."

Gold had admitted grudgingly that whatever blueprints or other technical material Brothman had turned over to him was not secret and much of that material had appeared in technical journals. Kleinman now called two witnesses to support that.

The first was Benjamin C. Dann, sales manager of Hendrick's New York office who had worked with Brothman. Dann corroborated that Hendrick did not deal with any classified or secret material during Brothman's tenure and that Brothman indeed had solicited and done his own sales work for processes he had designed. Dann also said that the Buna-S process was Brothman's work, as was a model of Brothman's mixing equipment which had been displayed at a trade show. Dann also said there was nothing secret about the processes depicted in the drawings which constituted the government's exhibit. These processes, he said, were based on Brothman's own ideas and that, "if he wanted a copy of the drawing he was privileged to make one."

Prosecutor Saypol pushed Dann to say that Brothman had never mentioned meeting with Golos or Bentley or Gold for the purpose of selling Hendrick's services. Kaufman asked if Brothman had told him he was prospecting for business from Amtorg. To all of these questions Dann answered no. Saypol further wanted to know if it was customary for someone like Brothman to have meetings on street corners or in doorways at night in isolated parts of the city; Dann again replied no. Saypol wrung from Dann the fact that Hendrick had indeed had promotional material available (contradicting Brothman's testimony to the grand jury), but Dann later indicated that such material was not always appropriate for the needs of a particular client. As his last question, Saypol asked the witness if paying Communist Party dues was part of his sales operation; thus he completed his intimidation of Dann.

Most of Saypol's questions were rhetorical; by means of innuendo and insinuation but without proof he had portrayed Brothman as having engaged in secret, clandestine and illegal activities in behalf of the Soviet Union.

Defense attorney Kleinman presented the court with a group of periodicals he had subpoenaed from the New York Public Library. They were professional engineering journals published by the McGraw Hill Publishing Co., specifically, nine issues of *Chemical & Metallurgical Engineering* from May 1939 through May 1945, plus an April 1940 issue of

Product Engineering. Each journal contained an article by Abraham Brothman on the very topics which Bentley and Gold had identified as having constituted secret material which they said they had received from Brothman. (Appendix B includes a list of these articles.) Gold had even characterized it as "industrial espionage" because it was material he said Brothman had no right to have; it was not his own work.

Kleinman was now building an effective rebuttal. Because Brothman had not dealt in secrets he had no motivation to engage in a conspiracy such as the government had charged. The publication of his articles proved that what he gave Bentley and Gold was hardly secret. Judge Kaufman quickly realized where Kleinman was heading and he asked: "This is in furtherance of your contention that there was nothing secret about these processes; they were published articles?"

Kleinman said yes and moved to admit the journals in evidence as defense exhibits. He made it clear that the articles dealt with each of the government's exhibits which had been massed as evidence against Brothman.

Visibly alarmed at this unexpected turn, both Saypol and his assistant, Roy Cohn, jumped up to object. Saypol refused to acknowledge that even some of the government's exhibits contained material which was the subject of Brothman's articles. He wanted the entire exchange stricken from the record and said that the rules of evidence were not being followed. Cohn complained: "Has there been any contention there were secret processes?"

In an obvious attempt to mollify both of them Judge Kaufman answered, "I am going to tell the jury....that it makes no difference whether they were secret or not. Therefore I think you ought to let them go in."

The situation was ambiguous and not resolved but Kleinman plowed on. He called Theodore Olive to the stand as a defense witness. Olive was an editor of the publications Kleinman had asked to be admitted as evidence. He testified that he had published numerous articles by Brothman on mixing equipment, Buna-S rubber, DDT and an aerosol dispenser using DDT. Olive said he had published the Buna-S report in March 1942, although Brothman had submitted it a year earlier. (Since Gold had testified that Brothman had given him the Buna-S report in April 1942, a month after it had been published, it was becoming unequivocally clear that no secrets could possibly have been involved in this matter.)

Olive also volunteered that even before the article was published Brothman had traveled to Washington to try to interest the United States government in his Buna-S work.

Kleinman moved to have the article admitted in evidence. Despite Saypol and Cohn's vigorous objections, Kaufman agreed to accept it, saying: "I will receive it but I want the jury to know now and I will further instruct them...(that) it is not material whether or not... any of the material that was given to Gold or Miss Bentley was secret... That is not the charge here."

Kleinman reminded the Court that there was no criminality involved in Brothman's having given out the Buna-S information because it was in the public domain. Kaufman snapped back: "That is not the point... (it) is that they conspired to obstruct and impede justice and all of this background was introduced for the purpose of establishing the true relationship between the parties... to show that they did actually obstruct justice..."

Clearly we did not have before us an impartial, fair judge; he was speaking as though he had already made up his mind that we were guilty and that the charges had already been proved. And again, he was careless in identifying who he meant by "they." The Buna-S event had occurred between Brothman and Gold, but surely a confused jury would have been justified in thinking the judge was referring to me, not Gold, when he said, "they."

Unexpectedly, however, he agreed to admit the publication in evidence and we were elated. It would help to counteract some of the damage the prosecution had inflicted. If those jury members could hold this evidence in their own hands, we thought, note Abraham Brothman's name listed as author of articles in respected journals about which they had been told was secret but was obviously not, they would surely have to entertain at least a flicker of a doubt about the prosecution's case.

Olive's testimony was concluded and Kleinman returned to the matter of urging the court to admit the published articles as evidence. The courtroom began to come alive as it had not been since the opening days of this trial. Cohn was agitated; he loudly protested as he paced the courtroom, waved his arms and said the government opposed admitting the articles in evidence because "there is no conceivable materiality..."

Judge Kaufman patiently rescued him:

"The conceivable materiality is that they are attempting to show it is not a secret process. If you will agree—you can solve this whole thing—the Government does not contend that these matters were of a secret nature then you will eliminate this whole issue from the case... Your contention is that he was a courier for the Soviet Government and was merely transferring industrial information to the Soviet government... Secrecy as I see it is not an issue... You are not contending there was anything secret about this."

But now a strange spirit seemed to be taking hold of Kaufman. Even as he spoke he seemed to be weighing and reconsidering and backing away from what he had just agreed to do. Petulantly, he complained that the number of publications was too numerous to handle. In a newly minted concern for Kleinman and with a new-found collegiality, he said:

"I think you have this particular point sufficiently before the jury…and you will only really be cluttering up the record by additional proof… Furthermore, the Government's contention that whether it is secret or not is not… a part of the case. (Saypol, from his amen corner, cut in: "Not of primary significance…") "And I believe you have your record amply protected and that you have what you want already in the record, and that you will merely be putting in cumulative evidence… and so it being cumulative I am going to deny it."

It was a remarkable about-face, to please the prosecution. Because it would be "cluttering up the record" Kaufman prevented the jury from seeing vital evidence in our favor. And on the spurious reasoning that the material was "cumulative" Kaufman finished off our defense.

Neither Abe Brothman nor I elected to take the stand (under the established legal tenet of the presumption of innocence), and so the testimony phase of the trial was now over.

In his summation, defense attorney Kleinman asked the question which was at the heart of this case:

"Is it reasonable to believe that the Soviet espionage system in this country sent out their courier to make contact with Brothman for the purpose of getting these rather simple and unimportant blueprints and text through all this cloak and dagger mystery… when they could have gotten them for the mere asking in libraries and textbooks?"

In all of these proceedings I had become the forgotten defendant. Bentley had admitted she had never known me. Gold's statements implicated me only by innuendo. I had had no knowledge of any supposed scheme that Gold and Brothman would fabricate a story to tell the grand jury in the summer of 1947. I also had not known what either Gold or Brothman had told the FBI on May 29, 1947, before their grand jury appearances. And the prosecution had produced no evidence that I had known whether their statements were true or false, or whether I had known they would attempt to conform their stories as Gold had said they did.

But the prosecution had a most accommodating witness in Harry Gold. His motive to cooperate with the prosecution was understandable since had had not yet been sentenced.

It was in Saypol's summation, however, that I was most harmed. He made repeated references to the fact that both Abe Brothman and I had failed to take the stand: "The truth of the testimony offered here by Miss Bentley (and) Gold is conclusively established by the failure of the defense to produce one solitary word contradicting any of the testimony."

Kaufman overruled Kleinman's objections as Saypol continued: "There has not been a word regarding what was said in conferences with a lawyer named Kiernan who was consulted at the time of their appearances before the grand jury... Not a single word has been uttered regarding that meeting on the night of September 29, 1941...Not a word has been uttered regarding that all night session at the hotel..."

Kleinman was overruled all through Saypol's performance: "Not one word was offered to show that anything Miss Bentley said was untrue... not one word Harry Gold had spoken in this courtroom has been contradicted by any evidence produced by the defense."

Kleinman asked for a declaration of a mistrial which Kaufman denied, and Saypol continued: "Now, leave Bentley and Gold. Leave them knowing that not one word has been spoken contradicting anything they have testified to. Not one word to contradict the existence of the conspiracy between Brothman, Moskowitz, and Gold... We have heard no testimony contradicting the existence of this conspiracy, negating its existence..."

Again and again, ten times, Saypol returned to the theme that the jury had not heard a refutation from us and throughout, the judge denied our attorney's protests to declare a mistrial.

Judge Kaufman then summed up in a speech that lasted well over an hour. First, he reviewed the charge and he defined the meaning of a conspiracy. He said: "It is sufficient if two or more persons, in any manner... come to a mutual understanding to accomplish a common and unlawful design. In other words, where an unlawful end is sought... and two or more persons, actuated by the common purpose of accomplishing that end, knowingly work together in any way in furtherance of the unlawful scheme, every one of said persons becomes a member of the conspiracy, although his or her part might be a subordinate one..."

At great lengths he elucidated the subtleties of the legal meaning of "conspiracy." Then, he reviewed the testimony of Elizabeth Bentley and Harry Gold, including Bentley's accusation that Abraham Brothman had been a member of the Communist Party. He put on a hypocritical display of judicial balance when he also explained that there was no claim that Brothman had engaged in espionage or that the material transmitted to Bentley and to Gold was of an illegal nature or that it was secret or that it could not have been found in textbooks and magazines publicly available.

The blueprints and technical reports were admitted, he said, to show what the prosecution alleged was the true relationship of the parties involved, that it was not a business relationship but rather that Brothman knew Bentley and Gold were couriers for Russia who wanted industrial information of any kind. Much of what he said was a review of the testimony of Bentley and Gold and a reinforcement of Saypol's accusations. In this he rendered a labored, thinly disguised repetition of the prosecution's presentation.

Kaufman also reminded the jury that the case was laid against the background of espionage and subversion which the grand jury had been investigating some three years earlier. He was careful to say that as defendants we were not required to prove innocence or to take the stand. However, he made these statements towards the end of a long speech and after Saypol's repeated assaults had had an opportunity for a lasting effect on the minds of the jury members. It was unrealistic to believe that Kaufman's cautions, coming as late as they did, could have cured Saypol's impropriety and that the jury could have overcome the prejudice Saypol had effectively planted.

We had fought this action with pitifully meager funds against the majestic might and unlimited resources of the government. Our attorneys had performed well on our behalf, but they were unable to keep at bay the legal juggernaut led by the prosecution that was given decisive assistance by an ambitious judge. We did not have the funds to hire aggressive investigators who could not be frightened off and who might have uncovered evidence which would have contradicted the testimony of Bentley and Gold. Bentley's unsavory past might have rendered her performance useless to the prosecution (and perhaps ameliorated the course of the Cold War) had we been able to uncover it. Similarly, there were inadequate funds to uncover details of Gold's lies or his thievery or his ambiguous, contradictory past. And while our attorneys gave us a full measure of their talents (and courage, for ours was not the kind of case lawyers were eager to handle in 1950) they were not prestigious, high-profile personalities who could inspire awe in a judge or a jury.

Thus, I sat in the Southern District Court of New York at Foley Square, New York City, having been charged and tried as a co-conspirator to obstruct justice. I was now awaiting the jury's verdict.

Chapter 9

The Majesty of the Law

At 8:50 p.m. on Wednesday, November 22, 1950, the jury returned a verdict. They found me guilty as charged on the one count and Brothman guilty on two counts.

Kaufman was visibly triumphant. He thanked the jury and said he thought their verdict was an intelligent and proper one. He turned to Saypol and said: "…you have my congratulations…I think the evidence was exceptionally well presented. You had your problems because… there was a most serious problem as to whether or not any indictment… could be found, and that it was due to your ingenuity in searching the statute books and finding the obstruction of justice statute, because there was a serious question about the statute of limitations having run on the matter of espionage itself…"

Even now, Kaufman's statements were incomprehensible. He was relentlessly draping us in espionage despite his earlier statements that "secrecy is not an issue," and that there had been no charge against us of espionage.

We were sentenced six days later, on November 28, 1950. Saypol spoke before sentencing. He accused Abe Brothman of having attended a communist club meeting in downtown Manhattan and he accused me of having been an active communist in 1948 and 1949. These were entirely gratuitous statements made obviously for the benefit of the media; the prosecution had never introduced this during the trial. It no longer made any difference except that it also justified his request that we be given the maximum prison sentence as punishment, as though for not only having been found guilty of conspiring to obstruct justice but also for having chosen the wrong political affiliation.

In his address to the court Mr. Kleinman said that we had instructed him not to ask for mercy in sentencing. This had been Abe Brothman's decision and I certainly concurred. Having been denied a fair trial we sought this way to show our contempt for this court and its pretensions of judicial fairness. Kleinman also said: "Since what we say here will gain some publicity, I only make this suggestion. I know that your Honor will not confuse this case with the spy investigations, the atomic bomb revelations, Gold's activities as a spy and …"

Kaufman cut him off: "it is merely a question of degree…" (Again,

Kaufman's insinuation that Brothman and I were spies.)

In his grandiloquent sentencing speech, Judge Kaufman waxed oratorical:

"The defendants in this case have not only been convicted of obstruction of justice, but what aggravated the case here is the fact that the obstruction of justice, serious by itself, was laid in the background of espionage. I said in my charge to the jury that the obstruction of justice is one of the most serious crimes on the statute books, because only by safeguarding the purity of the judicial process can it be protected... When you destroy the courts, you have made the first inroad, I believe, to the destruction of your country."

"When the verdict came in, I said it was beyond my comprehension that anyone would commit an offense of this character...and what is strange... is that the very country that these defendants sought to undermine... gave them a fair, a painstaking and impartial trial, something they could not have obtained from the country they sought to aid.

"The parents of these defendants came to America seeking a haven from oppression, so that these defendants – their children—could be brought up in a wholesome atmosphere, an atmosphere which recognized that God had created a human being, the greatest thing which God has ever done... (This judge was cruelty incarnate.)

"There are so few safe havens remaining on earth today and it seems to me that these defendants sought to undermine the staunchest supporter of freedom in the world today... I just cannot comprehend why these defendants and others seek to destroy that which protects them from tyranny..."

He intoned now magisterially:

"I have deliberated, I have spent a great deal of time giving a great deal of thought to the matter of sentence and I have come to but one conclusion and that is that I regret that the law under which these defendants are to be sentenced is so limited and so restricted that I can only pass the sentence which I am going to pass for I consider their offenses... to be of such gross magnitude. I have no sympathy or mercy for these defendants in my heart..."

Kaufman sentenced us to the maximum: Brothman, five years imprisonment and five thousand dollars' fine on Count 2 and two years and ten thousand dollars' fine on Count 1, the time to run consecutively. He sentenced me to two years on the single count and a fine of ten thousand dollars.

And so ended a theater of the absurd, an extraordinary display of an actual and real subversion of justice and it took place in an American court of law. We had been unrealistic in our hopes; it had not been remotely reasonable to expect that we would have received a fair trial in the prevailing political atmosphere, especially when dealing with ambitious political players whose first concern was not to pursue justice but to rack up a tally of convictions.

We had been charged with conspiracy to obstruct justice but the prosecution conducted this trial as though the charge was espionage – and the judge not only allowed it but he contributed to this juridical sleight of hand. The prosecution's powerful pre-trial publicity machine led by Cohn, Saypol and J. Edgar Hoover swamped the press with an incessant drumbeat that we were spies, thus effectively convicting us before we even set foot in a courtroom. That pre-trial notoriety also denied us the Presumption of Innocence which lies at the heart of the American system of justice – and in that prejudicial atmosphere it was a foregone conclusion that we would never be able to obtain an impartial jury.

Further evidence that this was not a fair trial: the prosecution knew that the one witness against me and the two against Brothman were incorrigible liars; nevertheless, it compounded that deceit by knowingly eliciting false testimony from them. The prosecution also suppressed critical evidence in our favor as did the judge – ("you will only be cluttering up the record," he said.) And we were repeatedly linked to communism when communism was not on trial. The shroud of espionage draped around us and the fawning attention the press gave the prosecution brought in a guilty verdict – and the public believed justice had been done.

This trial was a sad and expensive exercise in futility; it was a sham, a show trial. It was also a heart-breaker. It caused excruciating emotional pain for us and our families. It destroyed my father's health, it ended the army career of one of my brothers, and it made pariahs out of us and cast a permanent blight over all our lives. It was also a financial disaster; it mired us in debt—we had to borrow to pay the cost of this trial – debts that had to be paid. And it took me over twenty years just to pay off the fine. Perhaps worst all, this trial gulled the American public into accepting the increasing momentum for the Cold Warr.

When my appeal was denied (and Brothman's on the same count – although the Appeals Court overturned his conviction on the second – five-year – count) the redoubtable *New York Times* said in a headline that our guilt in the *atom spy plot* had been upheld on appeal. Other newspapers reported it similarly.

We had lost more than our freedom. We had lost a contest to preserve reason in an American court.

Abraham Brothman (L) and Miriam Moskowitz after the jury found them guilty on November 22, 1950. (*Jewish Forward*)

PART III

WOMEN IN DETENTION

Phantom Spies, Phantom Justice

Chapter 10

Jail – New York City, 1950

Built in 1927, the House of Detention for Women in New York City was an incongruously designed Art Deco building, a twelve-story medieval fortress of a jail located in the heart of Greenwich Village. The front entrance faced the eastern end of Christopher Street near the intersection of Greenwich and Sixth Avenues (known as "Avenue of the Americas"). A fenced and gated courtyard on its north side opened onto Tenth Street; here the patrol wagons and police cars entered and exited with prisoners. On the Greenwhich Street side, the cell windows faced a modern apartment building across the street and inmates could see occupants of well-appointed apartments living their comfortable lives. We watched them with great envy.

> *"Ain't no rich people in this jail. Rich people don' go to jail. While they be droppin' bombs in Korea I hope they drop a few on this place. one on Washington, DC, too; that's the Jim Crowest town I been in."*

In July 1961 New York City Corrections Commissioner Anna M. Kross tried to shame the city into tearing down the House of Detention and replacing it with a true rehabilitation center for women. Twelve years later the building was finally razed. A lovely community garden took its place—a fitting but doubtless unintended memorial to the thousands of women who had been made miserable there.

Although it was a city institution, federal inmates were detained here also, and all, city or federal, with sentences of a year or less, did their time here.

Each floor above the third was laid out around a main corridor off which were two elevators, a small desk for the guards and a day room on one side. Opposite the day room was the kitchen and mess hall. At each end of the main corridor were narrower corridors which were the cell blocks, and they were perpendicular to the main corridor– one in each corner of the floor. Off those corridors were the cells, two rows per corridor facing each other, each cell block housing about ten women. There were usually at least thirty women on the floor at a time.

Each inmate had her own cell; doubling was infrequent then. The cell was about six feet wide by nine feet on one side and twelve feet long on the other, and was narrow, dark and heavily barred. At the nine-foot length there was a wash basis in the corner. The longer length extended to a window. Below the window a metal table folded down from the wall and a backless seat faced it fixed in place. When the metal lid of the seat was raised it became a toilet. A shower curtain could be drawn to separate the toilet space from the rest of the cell giving one a small sense of privacy.

"We is having corn fritters and sausages this mornin'. Would you like a little syrup with yours? And some cream for your coffee, perhaps?"

(Bobby's cheerful roar announcing imminent breakfast call was a counter to what we knew would be served, but we loved her for her ability to make us laugh.)

The cell window was small, jalousied and heavily screened; it opened over the table in about eight slits, each about six inches wide. On a sunny day the light filtered through the screen but it made the cells look even dirtier than otherwise. A narrow cot about two feet wide folded down from the wall. Its flat spring sagged towards the center and the mattress fell into the well of the spring. One could prop up the center with newspapers but when an institution raid occurred, once or twice a month, the newspapers would be confiscated because they bred vermin.

The first message a new inmate received when she entered this world was that she would be stripped of her persona. She no longer had an identity; she was not someone's daughter or mother or wife – she was a jailbird. No one would care about her except to make sure she remained quiet and followed rules. Staff attitudes were harsh and unsympathetic.

"When you write that book you be sure and write about the food. First, the food and then how mean them officers are. Ain't for nothin' they be screws."

Visiting privileges were restricted to lawyers and family members, one visitor at a time. A lawyer could visit any time and he and his inmate client were accommodated in a small private room (which my lawyer always thought was bugged). For others, the arrangements were primitive. We were restricted to one half-hour visit on weekday mornings only, forcing many visitors to take time off from work. The women who were receiving the visits were herded into a large communal visiting room, really an oversized cage without seats but with thick walls. Each inmate stood facing a thick plate glass window with a speaker phone. The visitor would appear on the other side. Inmate and visitors talked through the speaker; they could not touch. To be heard above the din of everyone else one had to yell louder than everyone else, and in a minute one could feel the noise as well as hear it. The room was unventilated, dimly lighted and depressing. When my visitors came, particularly, my parents, I took time from my precious thirty minutes to make light-hearted conversation to offset the grimness of that visiting room.

Inmates sometimes returned from a visit more anxious and agitated than before because the news they had received was inevitably discouraging and there was no one for anyone to turn to.

"You got a boyfriend? Are you a virgin? When you get married do you think your husband will like us to visit you? Would you like me to clean your house?"

The fifth and ninth floors housed women not yet sentenced but awaiting court action. If a woman had been arrested by the city police she might have been held overnight in a station house before being brought to the jail in the morning. She would have had a difficult night and would probably not have had any food until she arrived at the jail. If she were ill or pregnant (many were) she would have had no medical attention and if she slept at all it would have been on a bench or on the floor of the holding pen with other women, some of whom might have been sick. The physical conditions were abominable and she would have arrived at the House of Detention unwashed, haggard and humiliated.

"When I git out I ain't gonna be so dumb agin and git caught with the stash on me. Hell, I can make more money in a day than them m.f. officers make a week!"

Women not sentenced usually waited many months for their cases to be heard by the courts. The probation routine was one of the causes of the delay; the probation department was understaffed and could not keep up with the caseload. The crowded court calendar exacerbated that delay. Many women were thus serving time for crimes for which they had not yet (and might not be) found guilty. They were routinely lost in the judicial system because of these delays and if they had children the problems were compounded. If there was no relative to take them the children were sent to city shelters where they received minimal care. For them it would have turned into the things childhood nightmares are made of.

"I gotta raise $25 for a $500 bail bond. I cain't git it and my case don' come up for three months so here I be. My mother cries when she comes to see me. She goes to work so she cain't take my little girls. I worry sick about them."

The eleventh floor housed the infirmary. There was no advantage to being sick enough to be sent there; medical attention was limited and no procedures were carried out on the premises. Junkies kicked their habits in "tanks" ...isolation cells on a different floor. No one could hear their screams or cries and they received no medical attention. After three or four days of continual vomiting they were brought to a detention floor, sick and weak and ravenously hungry. Some of us would feed them from our stash of commissary food if they had no funds because as hungry as they were they would be unable to eat much of the institution food.

"They be robbin' us at commissary. They charge a nickel for the paper what costs three cents outside. Frank Costello must own this here commissary."

(Costello was a criminal known as "Prime Minister" of the underworld, and a leader of the Mafia bosses. He served several prison terms before his death in 1973.)

More jailhouse food went into the garbage can at meal times than was eaten; it came to us as slop and was consigned accordingly. An exception of sorts was breakfast which consisted of recognizable dry cereal, watery milk, a slice of straw-like bread and coffee. We called it "coffee," but were never sure what it was. It was not quite coffee and not exactly tea but a combination, we suspected, of whatever was left in the urns from the day before. Since the urns were never washed the liquid we drank in desperation was always bitter and rancid. The best meal we had was on Easter Sunday, 1951, when we were treated to corned beef and cabbage. It was swimming in grease and the portions were small but it was fragrant and smelled like home.

Commissary, if one could afford it, appeared weekdays only and brought relief from the institution food. The menu was always cheese or ham sandwiches on plain white bread, sweetened coffee with evaporated milk, sometimes fruit, and always slabs of gaudily decorated, over-sweetened cake. But it was food from the outside, "free world food," we called it. The commissary cart also sold toiletries, cosmetics, candy and cigarettes and the prices were thirty to forty percent higher than on the street.

We rose at six-thirty in the morning, were called to breakfast according to our corridors at seven, and an hour later were locked in for the morning count. The night shift officer would then be replaced by the day officer who would walk up and down each corridor checking each cell. At eight we were unlocked and permitted to roam to other corridors to get cleaning supplies to clean our own cells. At nine-thirty we began primping, hoping to be called for a visit. In the meantime, the sentenced women would make their way onto the floor to clean the main corridors and the common areas. Generally there were volunteers to help among the detention women, partly to relieve their boredom and sometimes to curry favor with sentenced women. Each would affect a commissary deal for the other: the sentenced women could purchase peanut butter, crackers and cheese, which were not sold on detention floors. In exchange, the detention women paid off in more expensive cigarettes. And since sentenced women had commissary only once a week they needed a detention woman's help if they ran out of anything early. Commissary was jailhouse currency.

Short tempers abounded, petty stealing was common, and I had to be constantly alert to avoid the hostility generated by my high profile case. Boredom and monotony were our constant companions. Since detention women were not assigned work detail we would play cards or knit or gather in someone's cell and sprawl on the floor. The conversation was always the same: When would one be called to court? What were one's chances that one's lawyer would be able to make a favorable deal with the court? How much time would one get, or might one walk? All of us were obsessed with time.

Sometimes the conversation was painfully honest and insightful:

"White people don' know we is the same as they. They don' know that about the Spanish either and they don' like them no more than us. We used to it and we expec' it, but them Spanish, they be fools. They don't know what we know."

It was cold and damp in the jail no matter what the weather was outside, except in the summer when it was hot and damp. Once the tile walls and concrete floors lost their winter cold they heated up and remained so all summer. The cells sported no chairs so if one inmate visited another in her cell one of them would spread across the cot and the other would sit on the damp floor with her back against the clammy wall. One got used to sitting there despite that we had seen mice cavorting there during the night.

Punishment for rule infractions meant "deadlock." One was locked in one's cell for a day or more and lost roof, commissary and mail privileges.

No heavy-duty corporate sinners found their entry here; most of the women were held on drug or related charges: petty theft, "boosting," (shoplifting), bad checks, possession or selling (of drugs), or prostitution. Heroin (horse) was the drug of choice. Many inmates were African American, heartbreakingly young and only marginally employed. If they had jobs it was as menials for less than a living wage. Their work hours were never clearly defined, overtime pay was a rarity and no records were filed for them for unemployment insurance. Similarly, their wages were rarely credited to a Social Security account. Life was a constant struggle to buy groceries and pay the rent, and sometimes if they paid for one they could not manage the other unless they doubled up in living space. They were always in debt, always doing without and medical and dental care were never an option for them or their children. And while anger could produce a quick surge of black pride, the cry for black power was still a decade away. They had no meaningful stake in their citizenship—and drugs were easily obtainable.

"Don't call me no prostitute. I'm a sportin' gal and it ain't easy. I got to make connections just like everybody else do. And I never give nothin' for nothin' cuz that don't pay no rent."

Few inmates could afford their own attorneys, so it was up to the Legal

Aid Society to provide them. The lawyers almost never met their clients until they arrived in court. They would then urge the women to plead guilty; their expertise was concentrated on negotiating as little time for them as possible. On the basis of such limited legal representation a woman could be sentenced to a long prison term.

"My lawyer say I gotta plead guilty; that way I'll git only two years. But he a state lawyer so what do he care! Hell – ain't that somethin'!"

Some of the most compassionate and gentle women I have ever known I met at this jail. They had been stuck in unsafe domestic relationships and had injured or killed their men after years of abuse. Their acts were usually spontaneous; a handy kitchen knife, a can of lye or a hammer and a blinding despair was all it took. The courts were unsympathetic, the sentences harsh and unforgiving.

Sometimes there would be a "lineup" and then someone on the floor would have a terrible time. If a woman in jail had been involved in another crime and had not been apprehended for it at the time it occurred the police might bring the complainant to the jail to identify the guilty person. We never knew when to expect such an event. However, if the warden came through the floor picking one white women after another, or black, if the woman sought was dark-skinned, and tell her to go the day room, we knew a line-up was in progress. Of course a suspect would be among the warden's selections. We would line up in no prearranged order and out of the elevator would troop a police officer or two with the accuser. He would move slowly down the line looking at each of us carefully, and if he recognized the one he wanted he would stop in front of her and lightly tap her shoulder. She would break down and scream, knowing she was in deeper trouble now than before. I hated to participate in those lineups; there was enough misery here without them.

On alternate Saturday evenings we had movies in the chapel (on the third floor); but since the jail was usually crowded, only a few of the detention women got to go. Preference went to the sentenced women and then to those held longest in detention. I became one of the latter. The movies were always vintage Grade B. Most of the women had already seen them and they acted out the parts so vividly and noisily I had difficulty hearing the dialogue. They laughed and screamed and recited the lines or improvised obscene additions to the dialogue. After a few such sessions I stopped going.

We were able to use the day room for an hour after supper. There, we could meet up with the women from the other corridors on the floor The radio would be turned up to a deafening blast and pop music would fill the floor. TV was not yet an option.

A bright event occurred once a week when a librarian, in an act of humanitarian, free-world resuscitation, would wheel a small bookmobile onto the floor. She brought books she had carefully selected to meet the interests of the women and when she got to know an inmate she made special selections for her. I was the beneficiary of her thoughtfulness. In addition to a rich variety of books she brought me her privately purchased copy of *The Compass*, a liberal New York daily. The prison administration would not permit me to order it through Commissary; they said it was too "radical." Ever since, librarians have been my favorite people. It takes an especially civilized person to love books and want to share them.

After I was sentenced, in a rash act I signed a Waiver Not to Serve. A Waiver Not To Serve signed by an inmate granted that inmate the ability to remain in the jail instead of being shipped out to a prison, perhaps far away – but her time would now not count. (She could not be released, of course.) Abe had felt that if we could be kept in New York City until the appeals were heard we could have our attorney bring us to court for conferences and thus see each other. If we won the appeals we would have been spared the harshness of prison at some remote location. When I signed the Waiver, therefore, my time ceased to count. The appeals were not heard as quickly as we had anticipated and I rescinded the Waiver, after having squandered several precious months.

Recreation privileges consisted of an hour a day on the roof after lunch during the week and on Saturdays. It was cut to a half-hour before lunch on Sundays and holidays. The outdoor section of the roof was enclosed on the sides and the top with a thick wire mesh. Benches, heavy with soot, lined the length and sides and in good weather one could sit there or walk around the inside perimeter. The indoor section was equipped with games and a broken down piano, none of which anyone used. It also housed a ping pong table which was much in demand. I knew how to play ping pong; Abe had taught me and had frequently taken me to a ping pong parlor near Times Square in New York. When I began to accumulate longevity as the detention floor's longest held occupant, I earned the privilege of playing every day. I learned to play a good game, enough that one of the guards, an expert player, would seek me out every day to play with me. I developed a "slice" – it sent the ball spinning as it barely cleared the net and caused it to bounce unexpectedly away from the receiver rather than continue on its original path. It was a difficult maneuver to return. I also learned to hit a "touch ball," one that barely grazed the edge of the table and went flying off in an unexpected direction. This was impossible to return. Soon I was beating my opponent consistently. My sister jail mates would cheer then; it was a symbolic victory of "us" over "them."

Perhaps my most memorable jail moments were when my lawyer brought me a letter from Abe. My joy blotted out the wretchedness of my surroundings and my elation lasted for hours. I could not hold on to them, however, because they could have been found and confiscated or made their way to the FBI. My lawyer kept them for me and I reclaimed them when I was freed.

Chapter 11

Bernice

I look back on my jail experience as an egregious theft of a part of my life, yet there were moments that gave me a personal reward that never could have occurred outside.

Most of the women, particularly the young for whom jail was the rawest experience they had yet known, had no idea how the wheels of justice could grind their hopes into rubble. Rules were absolute, laws were inflexible, and these young women could not afford lawyers. Although they were street- smart enough in their escapades outside, they were bewildered when they were arrested and, frequently, had no help from family or friends. Bernice S. typified such an inmate.

In her early twenties, Bernice had recently come from the south to live with a married sister in New York. She met a young man at the hospital where both were employed. Her job was in the supply room where she had a fair degree of responsibility; she was intelligent and diligent. He was an orderly and handsome and fun to be with. She loved pretty clothes, he loved the good life, and their incomes were not adequate to cover the lifestyles they coveted. He convinced her to act as a lookout in an attempted robbery. They were caught and Bernice was brought to the House of Detention, landing in the cell opposite mine.

One could not help but notice the understated elegance of her well-tailored tweed skirt, the cashmere sweater and the paisley print silk scarf she was wearing, for they were not the typical attire of those who sojourned here. She also carried a hand-detailed leather handbag (the contents of which had been deposited in the warden's office) which matched her shoes. It was clear she had expensive tastes. In the next day or two we became friendly and she confided that her father had been a university student from Germany who had made his way to a university in North Carolina. He and her mother, an African-American, had met in the campus coffee shop where her mother worked. They fell in love, married and had two daughters. After the second, Bernice, was born, he decamped and his family never saw him again.

Bernice was numb with distress that this first and only mistake might cost her dearly and, as many I had seen before, she cried constantly.

"I wish I were dead! I shouldn't have come to New York! My sister says I've shamed them and my mother is crying her eyes out. And I'll probably lose my job and I wish I had never been born!"

She had not yet met her probation officer and from the experiences of other women I knew that her future could depend on the report the probation officer would submit to the court before sentencing. As I had done with some others in jail, I gave Bernice a pencil and some tablet paper and suggested she write a brief autobiographical statement for the probation officer. As she wrote she became purposeful and then hopeful. She described who she was, emphasized that she had a good work history and had never been in trouble before. The other inmates and I told her that the probation officer would likely be too rushed to ask her a lot of questions so this document she was writing would have to be productive.

When she finished writing, I acted as devil's advocate and grilled her as I imagined the judge might do. Did she not realize that bills run up on charge accounts would have to be paid? Didn't she realize that the young man with whom she was arrested was irresponsible? What plans did she have to pay off her bills and stay out of debt?

She wrote and rewrote her statement and we rehearsed the scenario for several days before she met with the probation officer. When she returned from that meeting she was shaken and not at all optimistic. Nevertheless, she had submitted her statement and the probation officer accepted it without comment.

Some weeks later she was called to court for sentencing. She did not return with the other women who went to court that day, so we knew she had made probation. During afternoon lockup when the guards changed shift I sat on my table looking out the cell window as I did each day at that hour. It was quiet time when the screaming and arguing and crying and cursing seemed to be turned off by an invisible hand which signaled, "Hush!" I always welcomed this time of the day.

As I stared idly at the busy street below I spotted Bernice among the passersby; she was waving up towards my window and blowing kisses. A policeman monitoring the building walked across the street to where she stood and motioned to her to move on. She continued to wave and blow kisses, then walked slowly away looking back over her shoulder until she disappeared around the corner.

I felt her triumph; I knew I would never see her again and I would miss her. But I was glad for her.

Chapter 12

Sabine

A floor officer came looking for me in my cell on a bleak, rainy day in April 1951. She said that a new inmate had arrived who could not speak English and she was crying hysterically. The office thought her language was Yiddish. Would I see if I could communicate with her? None of the other officers had been able to do so.

She led me to Sabine's cell in a different corridor from mine, opened the gate and let me enter. I sat with Sabine on her cot, held her hand and tried to make out what she was sobbing about. She was a small, undersized woman perhaps in her early thirties. In a mixture of Yiddish which I recognized, and perhaps Polish she related that she had arrived from Belgium the day before. U. S. Customs found undeclared watches she had pinned to the lining of her overcoat. They confiscated the watches and arrested her; she was now terrified and inconsolable. She had survived a concentration camp in Poland, she said, only to end up in another here in New York City. She had lost her husband and two young children in that camp. Her parents and siblings had also disappeared during the war. After the war she had been sent to a displaced persons center and there had met an older man who also had lost his family. He was leaving to join relatives in Pennsylvania and had asked her to follow him. He pointed out that she had no ties to Europe anymore and in America they could be married and start a new life together. He also suggested that she bring a supply of watches which would be useful as seed money so that they would not be totally dependant on others. Now, here in jail, she did not know how to reach him; she felt betrayed and she was once again buried in a concentration camp with no way out.

In my stumbling efforts to communicate I tried to comfort her. I was sure her friend would be notified that she was here and that she would not languish in jail for the rest of her life. I also guessed with the most optimism I could summon, that the worst she would have to endure would be a sentence of only a few months. ("Only," she gasped.) Then, I said, she could put this all behind her and get on with her new life.

It was meal time; I coaxed her into the mess hall and she managed to eat a little.

She gained a sense of hope in the ensuing days. The House of Detention, while ugly, unfit for human habitation and totally depressing, was nevertheless clearly not a concentration camp. Her friend had indeed been contacted and had come to the jail to see her with a lawyer in tow. She was called to court within a week and was sentenced to six months. With statutory time off for good behavior she would be out in four. When she was transferred to another floor in the jail to do her time she was forlorn that we would not see each other again, so I gave her my parents' address to write me there after she was released.

When I was freed a year and a half later I found her letters waiting and I was delighted and moved that she had written. However, the thought quickly sobered me that she would be applying for citizenship and her friendship with me would do her no good and probably great harm. I was a convicted felon; the charge against me had been very serious and if the Immigration and Naturalization Service learned that I was her friend she could be denied citizenship. I wrote her that it would be best that we not have further contact. I did not explain why because I was afraid it would complicate her life if she ever had to deny knowing me and I was not sure she could handle lying about our friendship in order to acquire citizenship. I let her think I had no interest in continuing a jailhouse friendship and that I was abandoning her. Immediately her letters ceased.

I have often thought with deep regret that during a time when friends were dropping away from me I had lost a friendship that might have given me comfort and enriched my life. And for many years I was troubled that I had added to the colossal pain she had already endured.

Chapter 13

Ethel Rosenberg

In the summer of 1950 Ethel and Julius Rosenberg were arrested and charged with having conspired to commit espionage in behalf of the Soviet Union. They were in their early thirties and the parents of two young sons; she was a homemaker and he was an engineer who ran his own small machine shop. Neither was able to make bail; the judge had imposed $100,000 for each, and for this family of modest means it was an impossible sum to raise. They were jailed to await their trial.

In that same summer, the government arrested Abraham Brothman and me for conspiring to obstruct justice in a case which had the same overtones of Soviet espionage. We were tried and convicted in November 1950 and remained in jail while we awaited a decision on our appeals. The witnesses against us, Elizabeth Bentley and Harry Gold, would also appear against the Rosenbergs four months later.

Ethel and I were both incarcerated in the Women's House of Detention but were kept separated, she on the ninth floor and I on the fifth, and we had never known each other before. The police van became our unplanned social outpost; we traveled together in it when we went to court, I to attend my trial and she to meet with her lawyer and with Julius to plan their court defense.

The section of the van behind the driver was paneled off and a row of benches stretched down each side. A grate cross the middle separated the men from the women, all of whom would be transported together. The men would be picked up at the Federal Detention Center on West Street. They were loaded into the front section and secured by the grate. Then the van rolled across town and picked up the women; they sat in the rear on the other side of the grate.

By the time I joined this trek to court it had become the prisoners' practice to let Julius have a seat abutting the grate on the inside; the seat on the other side of the grate was left for Ethel. Inside the van it was pitch black when the door was closed but no one cared. Except for the whispering of Julius and Ethel, conversation was desultory. This was a short trip to court and not a fun outing. Once, when a prisoner lighted a cigarette, in the flickering of the match we witnessed Ethel and Julius maneuvering to kiss through the grate. No one hooted or made coarse remarks as they would have done with anyone else. The prisoners gave these two a sense of privacy; the

Gothic dimensions of the drama engulfing them seemed to touch everyone, even the most callous.

Four months after Abe Brothman and I were sentenced, in March 1951, the Rosenbergs were tried and convicted. It was said that theirs was the most sensational court event of the decade. Just as Brothman and I were tried for *conspiracy* to obstruct justice (but not the act of obstructing justice) so the Rosenbergs were tried for *conspiracy* to commit espionage (but not the act of espionage). Prosecutors like "conspiracy" cases because the rules of evidence are not as demanding – and the evidence in both cases was certainly highly questionable. As in our trial, the Rosenbergs were prosecuted by the same prosecutors led by Saypol and Cohn, tried by the same judge, Irving Kaufman, and with the same government witnesses, Bentley and Gold. (Observers could not help but note that our trial appeared to have been a dress rehearsal for the Rosenberg trial.) Also testifying against them were Ethel's brother, David Greenglass and David's wife Ruth.

During World War II David Greenglass had been assigned to the Los Alamos laboratory (where the atom bomb came into its final stages) as an army technician; At the Rosenbergs' trial he said that, as a result of Julius' urging, he had given Harry Gold technical, secret information on the A-bomb for transmission to the Russians. Also at the trial, his wife, Ruth, who was not indicted, said that she had seen David's sister, Ethel, type the information David had sent for Julius to transmit to the Russians. (But in her grand jury testimony several months earlier she had testified that she, herself; wrote out and gave Julius those notes.)

The day the jury brought in a guilty verdict, Ethel was moved to my floor and assigned a cell at the end of the corridor nearest the guards, which permitted them to keep her within sight at all times. Presumably someone in the Department of Justice wanted to be sure Ethel Rosenberg would not do away with herself. (She commented to me later that it was ironic that they could never understand that this would be the least likely thing she could ever do.)

Her corridor was now diagonally opposite mine. I watched her settling in from behind the bars of my corridor and when the gates were opened at recreation time I walked over to say hello. She greeted me warmly and she, who faced such a monumentally more severe punishment than I did, she was concerned for me. Was I bearing up well?

She was the same with other inmates and quickly they warmed to her. She was never judgmental about whatever brought them to this hellhole; she would share anecdotes with them about her children and listen sympathetically to their sorry stories. She had a gentle presence—there was a dignity about her and as she became known to those women, their routine cursing and descriptively angry language became muted when she was near.

Many of the women were young and barely out of their teens. When melancholy seized them she became a surrogate big sister and comforted them. The outside world usually thinks of a jail population as the most outcast, most immoral and most destructive part of society; nevertheless, the women saw themselves as loyal and patriotic Americans and they separated their legal misdeeds from their love of country. One accused of treason or espionage, as Ethel was, would have been regarded with contempt and overt hostility by those women, yet they did not believe the government's accusations about her. They liked her, they accepted her, and they gave her their endorsement.

I also found her cheering to be with. At Commissary time in the middle of the afternoon we would buy a cup of coffee and sit in the mess hall dawdling over it while we talked. Our conversation was trusting, inconsequential chatter: the roots that identified us as second generation American Jews and as women, the pleasures of New York City life, our common interest in music and always, always her children. We floated free then for those few moment in a more benevolent world—until a guard would yell across to us as we finished the last of our coffee: "Hey, you two! You're not in the Waldorf, ya know! Time's up for Commissary!"

We had, tacitly, set limits on our conversation so we never discussed our legal cases; but sometimes Ethel would remark bitterly about her brother's scabby behavior towards her. She remembered David as a child, cute and cuddly and as the one who was their mother's special joy, and she much indulged him. Trying to comprehend the freakish turn of his behavior, Ethel recalled that he was always over-confident and reckless, and life had tripped him up many times. Now, she reasoned, he had walked into the FBI's arena underestimating how they could forge steel traps out of airy spiderwebs; at the same time he was sublimely, foolishly cocksure about his ability to handle himself with them. Ethel knew firsthand the awesome pressure they could exert and she visualized that when they threatened to arrest his wife and to anchor him to the death penalty he quickly collapsed and followed where they led him. She was sure that ultimately he would be unable to live with what he had done to her.

One Saturday evening the jail had scheduled the movie, *The Pearl*, adapted from Steinbeck's novel. I planned to go but Ethel refused. She had read the book and knew that the story involved the death of a child. She could not bear to relive that scene; it reminded her too much of her separation from her sons.

In our afternoon recreation hour we were allowed up on the roof and we walked around and around in the outdoor section, stretching our legs and trying to joke or otherwise pretend life was better than it was. Sometimes we would stand on the benches and crane our necks looking westward through the wire mesh and over the rooftops imagining we could see the men's prison on West Street which housed Julius.

Ethel had to summon a special inner strength when her mother came to the jail to visit her. Mrs. Greenglass would cry: "What are you doing to Davey? Tell the FBI whatever you have to, to save him! You and your husband—you're killing him and you're killing me!"

She would return from one of those visits spent and stricken, and because she was hurting and desperate for comforting, after her shower that night, as she patted perfumed talcum powder over her body, she would murmur wistfully: "Maybe Julie will come to me tonight."

She talked of her two young boys incessantly and worried about the instability of their lives now. From behind bars she was exerting heroic efforts to get their social worker to make sure they were adequately cared for and even that they continued with their music lessons. They had been lodged with her mother when she was arrested, but the social worker had removed them when she overheard the grandmother scream after some misbehavior: "You're going to die in the electric chair just like your mother and father!"

The boys were then thrown into the chaos of the New York City foster-care system and Ethel likened their suffering to hers. They would make friends with other children at the shelter but those friends would disappear when relatives or foster care people picked them up. Like her, the boys had no permanence, no continuity to their lives now. Ethel understood how emotionally devastating it was for them and she was tormented by their loneliness.

She was not surprised when Judge Kaufman imposed the death penalty. She said she knew that would happen; the guilty verdict demanded a punishment sufficiently severe to compare with what David's sentence would be. (He was sentenced after her. She had expected he would get thirty years, as did Harry Gold; instead he received fifteen.) But at least, she thought, she would continue to be lodged in the New York City jail until her appeals were heard. That would enable her to confer directly and often with the social worker about the children, and thus have a more direct hand in their care.

About a week after sentencing Ethel was called to the visiting room. As she passed me in the corridor she said, "I think Manny is here and I don't understand why. He visited me yesterday."

Manny was Emanuel Bloch, her attorney.

As Ethel entered the elevator to go down to the visiting room, an officer got off the parallel elevator coming up. Together with one of the floor guards she entered Ethel's cell, began to strip it and bundle Ethel's personal belongings. Those of us who observed this immediately understood what was about to happen and we quickly spread the word. We became agitated and noisy; alarmed, the guards locked us in our corridors but not in our cells, since this was not lock-up time and they did not want any confrontation. We crowded into the cells facing the courtyard where prison vehicles waited when they came to transport inmates, jammed ourselves against the heavily barred, screened, jalousied windows and cranked them open. A mean April wind sliced through us; we shivered in its icy blast as we waited. When Ethel emerged from the building she was surrounded by a phalanx of escorting marshals. As she entered the idling car in the courtyard we shouted to her from the different windows:

"ETHEL!"
"ETHEL!"
"ETHEL!"

There were at least a dozen women in the corridor overlooking that courtyard so she had to have heard us. Some of us wept; all of us were shaken. Ethel was being transferred to Sing Sing Prison in Ossining, New York, where she would spend the remaining twenty-six months of her abridged life in virtual isolation from the rest of the world.

The newspapers the next day showed her smiling through the window of the car as it sped away and there was some criticism in the media that Ethel seemed to be a tough bird to be able to smile at such a moment. The braying fools never understood the human spirit –but we knew better.

Ethel had heard the anguish in our voices and wanted us to buck up Ethel was smiling for us.

Chapter 14

And in the End, the Sisterhood

On June 21, 1951, some of the Smith Act defendants were jailed and two of them, Marian Bachrach and Elizabeth Gurley Flynn, were lodged on my floor at the Women's House of Detention. They were in a different corridor so I did not see them until the afternoon recreation hour. I found them sitting on the roof and I introduced myself. Marian gasped.

"You're still here!" She took my hand and greeted me warmly.

Gurley Flynn sat frozen, barely returning my greeting, and I was vaguely uncomfortable that she was signaling me that it was not a good idea for us to be seen hobnobbing together. I disregarded her signals – for me it would have been a waste of a golden moment for companionship, no matter how ephemeral.

Marian and I talked animatedly; I described the absurd customs and conventions characteristic of life in jail which she would need to be sensitive to, and I also told her I was awaiting a decision on my appeal. It was so good to talk naturally and freely with someone who shared my universe!

"We're expecting to go out on bail in the next day or so," she said. "Can we do anything for you?" She was a dear woman.

I told her I was to be transferred the next day to the Federal Reformatory for Women in West Virginia, and there was nothing now that she or anyone could do.

When we returned to the floor Marian wished me well and embraced me. Gurley Flynn barely nodded goodbye.

When I was released from prison in September 1952 I related this incident to Gloria Agrin, Manny Bloch's associate. But it was later reported that "…while women prisoners in the House of Detention purposely befriended Ethel Rosenberg, CP Leader Elizabeth Gurley Flynn studiously avoided her."

Cited as the authority on this was an interview Gloria had given on December 14, 1976.[1]

I cannot understand how my story transmogrified into such an unrecognizable caricature of the original event. Gloria, who died in 1980, would have been well aware of the chronology of events surrounding the Rosenbergs and she was never given to trivial gossip. The Rosenberg trial occurred in March 1951; they were convicted and sentenced in April 1951. Ethel was transferred to Sing Sing Prison in April shortly after sentencing.

The group of Smith Act defendants which included Flynn was not jailed until June 1951, some two months after Ethel had left and therefore Flynn could not have avoided her, "studiously," or otherwise.

In 1957 the United States Supreme Court overturned the Smith Act convictions in *Yates et al. v. United States*, 354 U.S. 298.

During the interminable and difficult eight months I spent in the Women's House of Detention I learned a lesson that would be mine for the rest of my life. Despite a world of cultural and class differences between my sister inmates and me, I now and forever belonged to them: the thieves, the petty swindlers, the pickpockets, the boosters, the junkies, the hookers, the check writers, the incredible amateurs in lawless mischief, the foolishly or temporarily strayed, the bruised, the angry, and those bred in violence who knew no other way. I was one of them. I was a member of the Sisterhood. Jail fundamentally altered the way I identified myself and the ties of shared suffering prevailed. One way or another all of us were demeaned, dehumanized and brutalized; we were all indelibly impoverished by our jail experiences.

PART IV

SERVING SERIOUS TIME

Chapter 15

Shirley

Having rescinded the Waiver Not to Serve I was transferred on June 22, 1951 to the Federal Reformatory for Women in Alderson, West Virginia to finish serving my time. I was uneasy and frightened; once again I was in threatening territory and totally alone. I searched each new face among the staff who processed my entry for some reassurance that this experience was not going to be my private hell, but no one acknowledged or seemed to care about my apprehension.

I was kept in solitary quarantine for three days and then in the general quarantine cottage for another seven, along with other new arrivals. My time was minutely organized for me. I learned how to darn socks, mend torn clothing, scrub (not mop) floors, clean the premises, make a bed with hospital corners, and pass white-glove inspection of my room. Every activity followed a rigid routine. During the solitary part of this a kite (an "illegal" note) was slipped under my door, I guessed by one of the regular inmates who delivered supplies to the cottage but with whom we in quarantine could have no contact. It was from my friend, Shirley, whom I had known back in the New York City jail before she was transferred here. I read the note twice, then tore it up and flushed it down the toilet to prevent the possibility that it would be found because that could bring Shirley a whole lot of grief.

Good old Shirley! Suddenly I felt warm and happy; I had a friend here – I was not alone.

Shirley was working at the storehouse and hoped I would be assigned there so that we could see each other. There was no chance that we might be housed in the same cottage; Shirley was an African American and living arrangements here were still segregated. By extraordinary luck I was indeed assigned to the storehouse and Shirley and I hugged and laughed and hopped around each other the first day I reported for work.

She was from Brooklyn and she was tall, well built, with proud square shoulders and a self-assured mien. She pulled her hair back off her face showing a perfectly shaped, classic head and she scorned the straightening iron as a symbol of white standards of beauty. Her easy manner was deceptive; if you read her carefully she seemed to say:

"I am me, Shirley! Take me as I am or get out of my way!"

Her quick eyes took in her surroundings in an instant, but she never let on what she saw and understood. She bore her prison time with a haughty contempt, coming close to wandering off an invisible, permissible line of behavior but she never did. When she smiled, not often, she lit up her personal space like a bonfire in the cold woods. She spoke with a down home Brooklyn twang and an inflection that was unmistakably sassy. In the brief time I had been here my ears had not yet become accustomed to the soft slur of Southern speech characteristic of most of the warders and many of the inmates. Shirley's voice, her metallic stridency, reminded me of home and was music to my ears.

She was perhaps ten years younger than I, but street smart and quick-witted. At work we maintained a steady banter in comfortable camaraderie; it helped keep us anchored in this otherwise absurd world. When we spoke seriously she revealed a contradictory sensibility: she did drugs because, why not? She got on to drugs while still in high school. Despite that, she managed to graduate with good grades—and then she hit reality.

"I will not be some white chick's cleaning lady," she said and she hammered defiantly at the wall for emphasis.

This was 1951; college was not an option and neither department stores nor offices were about to hire African American women (or men) for white collar jobs—especially not such a one who held her head high, returned your gaze without blinking and refused to use the language of servility. So, to get from fix to fix, she boosted or turned tricks and floated through a stuporous haze that ended only when she was arrested.

I said I thought she hadn't tried hard enough and she shot back with, "You mean, like you?" The sneer came from the bottom of her gut.

Wise Shirley, smart-aleck Shirley, she was far more perceptive than I. I judged the situation from my perspective as a white, middle-class woman with aspirations befitting my class, so I still believed in the world I knew. She saw it from the perspective of a young black woman with no status either as a worker or as a bourgeois and, as a racial outsider, with little maneuverability.

And oh, yes; she could be impishly mischievous. The Fourth of July was only a few days away when I had cleared quarantine. The holiday was traditionally celebrated with games and races on the lawn and there would be free cokes; truly a departure from the usual gray grind. Shirley had touted my expertise as a ping pong player while I was still in quarantine, but did not bother to tell me she had signed me up as a volunteer to play in a tournament against Axis Sally, a sister inmate. Known by her real name, Mildred Sisk, (also as Mildred Gillars), she had been an American radio actress in Germany during the Second World War and had been convicted in 1949 of broadcasting pro-Nazi messages over Radio Berlin. She was now serving a long prison sentence here. She was also reputed to have been a champion ping pong player who had honed her skills playing against American soldiers before her conviction.

I exploded at Shirley when I saw the schedule of contests while she rolled with laughter. I was hardly eager for any interaction with this inmate. I could see the tabloids back home when the news was leaked: "SOVIET SPY AND NAZI AGENT MEET IN FRIENDLY RIVALRY"

Fortunately for me, Mildred wanted no part of this either and withdrew, and of course Shirley said that was because she knew I would have beaten her.

"It would have been a match full of international significance," she sighed.

Shirley was due out two months after I was, and we exchanged addresses when I left. I would never have done that with anyone else, but I believed in Shirley and I trusted her. A week or so after I knew she was home I telephoned. She was the same wry, quirky Shirley. We agreed to meet the following Saturday at the side entrance to the New York Public Library on Forty-Second Street in Manhattan and go to lunch.

I was about fifteen minutes late—traffic had held me up—and when I arrived there was no Shirley. I sped around to the front entrance but she was not there either. I waited an hour and then telephoned. Her mother answered and said Shirley had been at the library, had waited a few minutes and then became nervous so she left. (A few minutes! She knew I was coming from out of town!)

Cool, imperturbable Shirley, nervous after waiting a few minutes? Shirley, whom nothing ever bothered, *nervous*?

Suddenly I tasted ashes. "Damn!" I choked. "Damn!"

Shirley was back on horse.

Shirley, now an ex-con, couldn't find her way. Shirley was shooting up again.

Chapter 16

Christmas with Iva

On September 29, 1949 a federal jury convicted Iva Toguri d'Aquino of a single count of treason for having broadcast Japanese propaganda to American servicemen during World War II.[1]

Born in America of Japanese immigrant parents and a graduate of the University of California, Los Angeles, Iva Toguri (later Iva d'Aquino when she married) sailed to Japan in the summer of 1941 to visit a sick relative. By the end of that year she was stranded in Japan when war broke out between that country and the United States and she could not get home.

Iva refused to renounce her U.S. citizenship so she was denied a ration card. As a result of near-starvation she ended up in a hospital suffering from pellagra, beriberi and malnutrition. When she recovered somewhat she obtained a job with the Domei News Agency, a Japanese listening post where she typed news from Europe (such as Winston Churchill's speeches.) She was also ordered to broadcast on Japan's "Zero Hour," a radio program beamed to American and Allied troops in the Pacific, the scripts for which she had to type. The scripts were created by allied POWs then being held in Japan and with whom she had contact. They consisted of light banter – disc jockey chatter – which contained satirical references or insider jokes which the Japanese would not understand but which Allied combatants would certainly recognize. After the war Iva told military investigators she had not composed those scripts, they had been written by the POWs and that she was not anti-American nor was she disloyal to her country. American soldiers in the Pacific dubbed her "Tokyo Rose" but she was one of several women who made broadcasts in English.

After the Japanese defeat in 1945 the U. S. military detained her and then released her for lack of evidence. In 1949, when the State Department said that it did not object to issuing a passport to Iva so she could return to the United States, she was rearrested (in Japan) and charged with treason. She was transported to the United States to stand trial. She defended herself as best she could but was unprepared for the waves of anti-Japanese racial prejudice which engulfed her. Her conviction was based on the testimony of two witnesses against her. (Years later those witnesses recanted.)

In September 1949 Iva d'Aquino was sentenced to ten years and a fine of $10,000 and she was hauled off to the Federal Reformatory for Women in Alderson, West Virginia to do her time. In the meantime, Iva's husband,

Felipe d'Aquino, of Japanese/Portuguese heritage, was not allowed to be with her and she could not leave. Ultimately, the marriage dissolved.

At Alderson, Iva found that prison handed her more of the ordeal she had already endured. Her sister inmates were as misinformed as the American public had been and they were equally judgmental and certain that justice had triumphed in the government's case against her.

The following year, 1950, I was convicted – wrongfully – of conspiracy to obstruct justice in a case with overtones of Soviet espionage, and I was sentenced to two years and a fine of $10,000. I, too, ended up in Alderson. Iva and I were lodged in different cottages and we had different work assignments. She was the dental assistant at the infirmary which was at one end of the campus and I worked in the storehouse at the other end so we came in contact with each other infrequently. The fleeting contacts we did have occurred when I was assigned, briefly, to work at the infirmary or on some Saturday afternoons at the Arts and Crafts workshop – and we kept those contacts impersonal but civilized. I, for one, and perhaps she, too, wanted to avoid inmate gossip about a cabal of "spies" at this institution although I never believed she was a spy any more than I was. And I, too, was enduring the harassment of sister inmates so I understood how difficult it was for her.

This petite, private young woman, who was the same age as I (thirty-four) with a gentle manner and an infrequent smile, handled the taunts and hostility with quiet forbearance. When one of the women whispered, "Jap spy" loudly enough for her to hear, as she joined them in the dayroom after supper, she never again joined them in the dayroom. When someone jostled her in the corridor out of sight of warders she pretended it was her own clumsiness that made her fall. When coffee got spilled on her in the mess hall she quietly wiped up the mess and asked permission to sit aat another table. She found solace attending Mass Sunday mornings until a peer group sat behind her and, *sotto voce* hissed "Jap spy" or "Jap whore" during the service. She stopped going to Mass.

In her free time Iva found a creative outlet in the arts and crafts shop. I put in an appearance now and then to design and etch copper coasters or simple silver bracelets – the easiest tasks I could handle because I was so clumsily endowed. But Iva truly had a depth of talent. She was good with her hands, she had an imaginative sense of color and design and she was deft with tools. In the beginning she used colorful fabric scraps to make collages and then she worked at leather carving. She made some nice handbags which she put up for sale in commissary. She was lucky and sold a few – to visitors who always checked out commissary – and the income from that gave her the funds to buy other supplies. Then her big project was a colorful 3-foot by 5-foot throw rug that she spent several months designing and looming. It transformed her room, it banished the institution drab, the clinical antisepsis, it splashed her room with gaiety and charm, and made the premises distinctly hers. It also gave her a quiet pleasure.

She found that rug cut to shreds one Saturday afternoon when she had gone up the hill to commissary.

You could not have watched her if you had been there; you would not have wanted to witness such awesome pain. She did not cry or carry on; the wound was too profound. She just seemed to shrink into herself, now ever more remote and withdrawn.

As time wore on Iva seemed to put it behind her – but she did not return to the arts and crafts shop. She also never forgot she was part of this prison landscape. In the communal bathroom in the morning she greeted her sister inmates pleasantly as they made their ablutions and hoped the day would go well for them – but she walked alone to the mess hall for meals and never paired off as most of the other women did.

Over time you knew life was moving on for her as it was for all of us; the inmate population was constantly changing as some women disappeared and new ones entered. And the new ones found her presence acceptable as some of the old ones had not, and she responded to their overtures with cautious cordiality. The healing was evident when she ambled over to the arts and crafts shop one Saturday afternoon in the fall when she was off work. She fingered the swatches of fabric and the leather scraps and played with them and folded them into funny shapes and you knew ideas were flooding through her and her life was moving back on track. As November bore on she became more engrossed – like old times. She took those scraps of colorful fabric and bits of leather and shaped them around tongue depressors. Then she fashioned them into whimsical, witty figures with flowing robes and jaunty, ridiculous hats. She added faces with adroit strokes of color and they registered merriment or goofiness or they were lugubrious expressions of what she was privately thinking She made one after another, eighteen of them, each different, brought them to her room and hid them in her dresser drawer – and no one knew they were there except the officer who ran a periodic room check. And eighteen of them matched the number of women in Iva's cottage.

As December approached Iva sketched and mailed off the annual Christmas cards to her family. She also made an extra eighteen cards, decorated each with the name of a cottage inmate, and taped each card to a figurine. And she did all this secretly and quietly and no one knew.

On Christmas Eve Iva lingered in the bathroom so that she would be the last to be locked in for the night. When her sister inmates were all abed and locked in she gathered her bundle of Christmas offerings, skipped silently through the two floors of the cottage – the officer on duty that night monitored her – and deposited a jaunty figurine with a personalized, hand-decorated card at the door of each inmate Then she whisked herself back to her room, was locked in, and perhaps she went to sleep.

The next morning, Christmas morning, she remained in her room. She couldn't bear the cries of "Merry Christmas!" floating through the building and everyone's longing, including her's, for home and dear ones – no other day on the calendar would be so freighted with such longing. She heard the bursts of surprise and laughter as the women found her gifts but she was too modest to accept their thanks so she hid in her room until breakfast call when she hastily washed and dressed. And, as always, she walked alone to the mess hall and never paired off as the other women did. Iva was ever the class act.

All this happened a long time ago but there may still be a woman somewhere of somewhat advanced age in the hills of Kentucky or on the shores of Maine – or in the pockets of despair somewhere in America – who remembers a desolate Christmas long ago and a young woman of infinite grace who turned it into a moment of joy and love when joy and love were in rather short supply.

* * * * * * * * *

A quarter-century after the events in this story occurred, President Gerald Ford granted Iva an unconditional pardon in January 1977. Her pardon was based on evidence not presented at her trial that she did not commit treason. In January 2006 the World War II Veterans Committee presented Iva with its Edward J. Herlihy Citizenship Award. She lived to be ninety years old and died in Chicago in 2006.

Chapter 17

Lady Lily and the End of the Line

S he said her name was "Liliana" but the guards called her just plain "Lily." She never said what she was picked up for and no one asked. The traditional darby here at this Federal Reformatory for Women (where I was also a guest then) was that if the FBI and not the local police picked you up you knew you were going to do time but you got better food at a federal institution and they didn't push you around so much. Or put their hands all over you, or make dirty remarks, or slip into your cell at night with a promise they'd let you go in the morning if you didn't squawk. But life was never like those local goons promised, the women said. If you were going to be picked up, it was better with the Feds.

She was a pretty woman underneath all that make-up, you could see that, but her pale, round face sometimes seemed vexed by ghostly memories. Her frequent expressions of apprehension alternated with a breezy, false confidence and it betrayed less worldliness than she seemed to want you to think she had. She kept patting her graying hair – now streaked with fading, bottled yellow – as though for reassurance – although she was as well turned out as any newly arrived prisoner could be who had just been through a humiliating arrest procedure. Her lumpy frame, all five feet of it, suggested a personal timing somewhere between mid-thirties and defiant middle-age. But it was her manner that set her up for trouble. It was "elegant" when elegance among my sister inmates got you relentless ridicule. She minced her words, she sounded at times like a transplanted, foreigner, English upper-class, perhaps, but then she would lapse into down-home regional speech so you knew she was faking. Some of the women dubbed her, "Lady Lily." And she wasn't laying out her life for anyone. Odd, I thought; what secrets was she hiding?

I had only a passing interest in what had brought her here. I guessed she might have written checks on an outdated account. The government doesn't like it when you write checks without back-up funds or when you sign someone else's name to a check that was not your own. Or maybe she crossed state lines with drugs or she swindled someone – got advance payment for expensive goods she never delivered. Or lifted someone's mail. Or perhaps she drove off in someone else's car without bothering to get the owner's permission. Or some other federal offense, probably reckless, and perhaps desperate. There were no big-time stock swindlers or Ponzi-scheme artists among us in 1951, nor did these women ever get to fracture bank laws.

Most of my sister inmates were poor and they would be poor when they were freed because that's what they had been born into. When they could get jobs they had waited on tables or worked in factories or served as maids or cleaning women. If they were white and lucky and had had some schooling they worked as cashiers or saleswomen at local shops, not always steady work. Women of color became cleaning women or tended the sick and the elderly. And when they were arrested, white, brown or black, it was usually for a crime rooted in street economics or it was drug-related – boosting, theft, turning tricks, perhaps some creative combination that looked like a way out of difficulty. It was never a big-money crime. Compounding their problems, when they finished serving time and returned to home base they would face some legal barriers and discrimination in employment and they would be barred from certain public benefits like eligibility for public housing. Even when they were able to find a job, inevitably government investigators would appear and expose them, so the job never lasted very long. Once convicted of a crime, you never finish paying your presumed debt to society.

But none of this seemed to be Lily's problem so I waited like the others, for her to reveal what had brought her to these hallowed grounds. I expected she would tell it like most of the women had done, perhaps embellishing the story and exaggerating not a little. And in her version she would have been innocent and falsely charged, and truth to tell, that was not beyond the realm of possibility. We had all had our own experiences and there were a few who had truly been sacked by the law – the arresting officer who was not above planting evidence, the paid witness who lied, the ambitious prosecutor who was never so concerned about seeking justice as he was about racking up a tally of convictions, the harassed probation officer with too heavy a caseload to have time to hear your version of what happened, the bored judge waiting for his political patron to get him a more prestigious judicial appointment with a more generous pension plan – and the hearing was routine and the conviction foretold.

Lily seemed as though by resolve not to understand that she was now doing time. Five years of it; even with good time off – was lot of time and her release date was far into the future. She just waved it away and never tried to make peace with being here. Most of us, after the gates had slammed behind us, realized that the only way to survive this misery was to buckle under, forget or at least put on hold the dreams we once had, and never complain because everyone here carried a load and no one wanted to share yours. You could make a ceremony every evening before you climbed into bed by marking off the day on a calendar, ritually counting the time left and always double-checking your arithmetic so that if you needed to think about it during the night you knew instantly how much time you still had left. "I've done five months and two days, and only fourteen more months to go." But if you had a lot of time like years, marking off the days seemed hopelessly forever, so you never even looked at a calendar.

Truth: I kept telling myself: this "home away from home" – this prison was survivable. It was not as bad as jail which was usually just a holding pen, dirty, smelly, crowded with women who were at least as forlorn as you, with no privacy, a narrow cot or bench to sleep on, terrible food and overrun with mice or rats Here, except for being separated from loved ones and friends and the comforting familiarity of home, except for the freedom to move about, to go to work each morning like everyone else, or spend an afternoon with a best friend, except for the terrible waste of time and the postponement of living, except for the intractable monotony and meaninglessness of life behind bars, except for the sense of isolation in the midst of a group of women equally wounded – many bitter and bent – except for the reminder in a thousand ways of your pariahhood, except for the heavily-gated isolation and the obsessive security, except for all that and if you kept reminding yourself it truly would end some day – you could do this time. You lived in a cottage with fifteen or twenty other women of varying personalities and ages. Many had suffered even more than you – and some had become combative and ill–tempered and were dangerous. But you had a room to yourself, small but private (prison over-crowding was not yet a problem) and if you made up your mind you could do this time without tearing yourself apart. The cottages, ten of them, were set in an oval around a grassy field and an inmate crew kept the grounds manicured. Visitors always thought the place was "picturesque." The food was a lot of pasta with beans or black-eyed peas, usually flavored with a fatty slab of bacon. Or it was something called "stew" with wilted vegetables floating in an over-seasoned sauce. (But sometimes there were biscuits – a special treat – but only one per person, alas.) The prison complex was set in a hollow at the foot of a hilly terrain far from any built-up area and it was surrounded by a tall, sturdy, barbed-wire fence. The environment guaranteed that you would be made miserable but if you made peace with the place you could survive.

When Lily first arrived a few of us, dredging up human instincts that had somehow not withered in the harsh ambience of this institution, made small, friendly overtures. She brushed us off as though we were chaff. We shrugged, now forewarned, and thereafter kept our distance. Tempers here were short, emotions raw and frequently out of control, and you learned to steer clear of complicated personalities. And Lily was complicated. She seemed to meet her problems head-on and then vanquish them with a wave of her hand.

"I'm not going to be around here long," she announced grandly. "Bugsy will get me out."

Bugsy? Bugsy Siegel? Yes, that Bugsy.

Most of us had heard of Bugsy Siegel, although he had not been headline news recently. He was the legendary gambling crook who kept the police in

Las Vegas frantic even though he regularly paid them off. Siegel was also that tricky master of the slots who so successfully engaged the whole of the U.S. Internal Revenue Service as well as the U.S. Treasury Department looking to collect back taxes on his gambling loot and the FBI, for years, had been itching to get its hands on him for running a constellation of illegal rackets.

"I'll be out of here soon," she said. "You'll see. Bugsy will get me out and then I'll laugh at all of you." Her special person, her man, Bugsy Siegel, would take care of everything. He would send her money for commissary and one day soon he'd come to get her and she would be free!

We were incredulous and she enjoyed that – she'd be out of here soon because Bugsy would arrange it. "How?" we would ask and she would smile mysteriously. "Oh, he has ways."

She never seemed to care that some of her sister inmates were making fun of her because of her Bugsy chatter and her grand manner, and she ignored the cruel comedy at her expense. I knew this was going to escalate; sooner or later someone would dump some sticky spaghetti on her. Or trip her or shove her in an isolated corridor or decorate her room with obscenities.

Rhodie, who had the room next to her, tried to tell her to tone it down – she wasn't impressing anyone but Lily was stubborn. And after a while Rhodie stopped trying. She had her own problems and they were getting at her through the letters she got from home. Her mom was sick and the social worker was concerned about placing her baby in a more stable environment. And Rhodie would have no say about where or by whom that decision would be made – or where this magical "more stable environment" would be. She fretted about it incessantly and Lily and her foolishness were just not Rhodie's concern.

But things changed.

One balmy evening in September, a few months after she had arrived, Lily decided to join some of the women to go up the hill to the institution schoolhouse for a class in office skills. A local church volunteer (who had been appropriately vetted) was teaching it and the women liked her. Lily had never before participated in anything. We watched Mrs. Smith, the officer on duty that evening, carefully check out Lily and the other women as each went through the door and we thought, "Well! That's new!" When they returned at the end of the class, they were checked back in but Lily did not come to the day room as the others did. She had gone to bed, they said. At 9:30 that evening we turned off the radio in the day room, put away our reading, folded our handwork, crossed another day off the calendar and went to bed. At ten Smith locked us in.

When Mrs. Benton, the day shift officer, unlocked us in the morning I sensed something was awry and made a beeline for the bathroom. There, the conspiratorial whispering turned into an exultant roar.

"She's gone! Lily's gone! She made bush!"

Suddenly we all had a newfound respect for this inmate – she had escaped! She did it by reviving an age-old trick – she had lumped her pillow into the shape of a human body, draped it with a nightgown, and covered it over with a blanket so that, in the dark, it looked like a sleeping form. Mrs. Smith, the night shift officer, had turned off the corridor and room lights with a master switch at 10 the previous evening and then checked each room with a flashlight before locking us in for the night. Lily's room was now dark so Smith, with the flashlight, saw what she thought was Lily, curled up, already asleep. Benton took over in the morning but when she unlocked the doors at six in the morning what she saw was no Lily.

I was mildly sorry for Smith; probably now she would be hauled up on the carpet and might even lose her job. But I was swept into the group exultation; one of us had actually broken out of this prison and was free!

We went to breakfast – the mess hall was across the field and we saw on their faces that our sister inmates from the other cottages had heard the news. They, too, were gleeful. The somber expressions belonged to the staff. We were careful not to giggle too obviously or show how much we relished Lily's knockout trick because they could vent their frustrations over this in sneaky ways and we could become targets.

We went to our assigned jobs but all day long it was hard to contain our giddiness. We whispered and laughed and said, "Good old Lily!" In the meantime the grounds were suddenly overrun with government officials – FBI, we thought, or men from the Bureau of Prisons – and as we passed them to and from work we hooted derisively. One of us had made them look helpless and foolish and there was no containing our glee.

This institution was now split, emotionally, into two opposing camps and the antagonism layered heavily over us. One side was the staff and the administration on whom this would reflect badly in concert with the whole system of American justice, and we – a phalanx never before united, traditional losers and totally without practical resources but drawing strength and unity from one inmate's idiotic trick – were the opposing side. This was new. There had always been an embittered undercurrent of hostility— inmate against inmate – usually one who imagined insults from another which sometimes morphed into retaliation with an ugly display of unreasonable belligerence and physical retribution. That had kept the discord unending among us. But in this one dazzling event it was our moment for unity and unrestrained joy – and because of its impossibility we cherished the victory which a harebrained woman had handed us. And she was now our heroine and we were captivated by the boldness of what she had done.

The next morning brought more of the same. Lily was gone; Bugsy Siegel must have indeed come to get her – how did they ever arrange this?

Mail was censored and in an era before cell phones no telephone calls were ever allowed from the office unless it was an emergency – and then, the call would be monitored. But Lily's victory was ours. And the third day was like the first two; there was balm in our souls as sweet as a baby's smile. As the frustration of the staff grew, as those long-faced investigators crawled all over the place, our delight in their humiliation became boundless.

The fourth day was our undoing.

They found Lily hiding in a small, rundown church a quarter of a mile from these grounds. When she had returned from that evening class she was at the end of the line when she got herself checked in. Then she stepped back into the dark, slipping out of the cottage before Mrs. Smith had a chance to lock the doors. Lily then headed up the hill; she crept under the barbed wire fence, suffered scratches and gashes and torn skin – and the ultimate insult – she sprained her ankle because in the dark she couldn't see the rough terrain. She hobbled in pain up to the road and as far as the church and could go no further. She found some stale food in the vestry kitchen and then waited for her ankle to heal but in the meantime the barbed wire wounds were becoming infected and she could not maneuver to wash them. There was no Bugsy Siegel.

We couldn't imagine how she ever thought she could make this work alone without outside help. She had no cash, she wore telltale institution garb and she was a stranger in the area. Our joy turned to anger – at Lily for having been caught. We fumed: "That idiot! She didn't plan it right – whatever made her think she could get away with this?" We carried on— with descriptively obscene language as could only be expressed by women locked out of the mainstream – and as though Lily had handed us each personally a searing defeat. We felt like fools and choked with fury. Lily had made bush – an almost impossible feat – was free for four days and was caught right outside the prison gate. Dumb broad! We had come to believe in her; we had desperately wanted her to make this institution – and the self-important, simpering bureaucrats, the whole benighted prison system with its entrenched office holders and political appointees and its skewed sense of justice – look like a pack of fools. We had tasted her triumph and it had become ours. How dare she renege on an implicit promise and snatch victory away from us by getting caught!

They took her to the infirmary, cleaned her up and the next day they shipped her off to St. E's, an institution for the criminally insane. We never saw her again. And of course there never was any Bugsy Siegel. We learned that he had died four years earlier – before Lily had ever sashayed into our lives.

Chapter 18

Reconnections

Some months after I arrived at the Reformatory, Rabbi Abraham Shinedling and Helen Shinedling, his wife, visited. They had driven several hours from their home in Beckley, West Virginia because they had learned there were some Jewish inmates at the institution. Those of us who were Jewish were notified that the rabbi would conduct services and meet with us on a forthcoming Wednesday afternoon. If we chose to attend we would be excused from work. I went.

Rabbi Shinedling was middle aged, a man of awesome dignity, well spoken, well informed and knowledgeable in a number of academic areas. He had been a classics major at Columbia University and still savored the literature of ancient Athens and Rome in the original Greek and Latin. He was also a formidable Judaic scholar, articulate, fiercely partisan, but never glib or pompous.

After services he met with each of us privately. When I sat with him I forgot the boundaries now enclosing me; talking with him was reminiscent of home, of what I had known with literate, informed friends—a rich intellectual exchange and an experience that shattered the confines of this prison. He voted labels, not platforms and therefore always voted the Republican Party ticket because, he said, the Democrats were the party of slavery but the Republicans were the party of Lincoln. In the south of those years, scarred by the memories of lynching black men – some accomplished legally such as the Scottsboro case, the Martinsville Seven and most recently Willie McGee, and uncounted numbers the result of extra-legal mob violence, his convictions were understandable; the south then was the Democrats' stronghold. Although I thought he was oversimplifying matters, I knew I was talking to a humanist.

He came once a month and each time after the service I would have an hour of thoughtful conversation with him. He spoke of literature, ethics, ancient and modern Jewish history and baseball—ever baseball. He exuded good fellowship and a humanity which restored my battered sense of self-worth. He was pained by my experiences although I did not complain. He endowed his concern for me with a personal respect which revived my hopes that I would be able to reenter civilian life with some degree of normalcy.

Helen Shinedling, whom I would see only briefly at the beginning of each visit, was a woman of uncommon class. I had etched some silver bracelets and copper ashtrays in an arts and crafts class which I had put up for sale through Commissary. They were suddenly being sold along with other craft items I had made at a time when no one else's work was moving. Only years later did I learn, accidentally, that she had been the purchaser.

In between his monthly visits Rabbi Shinedling would write me at least once a week. His letters were newsy and cheerful and full of his activities as though he were trying to focus my attention on things outside my prison routine. He was editing a colleague's book on an ancient Jewish civilization, he would be spending some time working on the archives at Hebrew Union College in Cincinnati; he was preparing his son for bar mitzvah; his wife was nagging him to shed a few pounds but she was such a good cook, how could he?

He never asked me for details about the cause of my incarceration, but he was patient and sympathetic when I tried to explain. I told him of my concern about my parents and the anguish I knew they were enduring because of me. Just coincidentally, he would be traveling soon, he said, to a rabbinical conference in New York City. He would plan to visit my parents in New Jersey as well. Indeed, he did so and he made them proud and happy when he arrived. He stayed several days in their home and met with leaders in the Jewish community. He was a distinguished man and an ambassador of hope, and he effectively restored the good will and the respect my parents had enjoyed in the community before my scandal had closed them off.

After my release from prison I remained in touch with them. They moved to New Mexico and I visited them there; they came east several times and I spent rewarding hours with them. Over the years we maintained a warm relationship. Knowing them and basking in their regard helped me to reconnect with my life; they were restorative antidotes to the wounds I had endured at the hands of Judge Kaufman and Irving Saypol and Roy Cohn, and J. Edgar Hoover and the whole cabal of rogues and liars who had stolen my life and profited thereby.

Chapter 19

Hope Is For Fools

Soon after I arrived at the Reformatory I applied for parole. Subsequently I was called to a meeting of the Parole Board; the members asked why I had committed the crime for which I was now serving time. I replied that I was not guilty of that crime and had so pleaded. Three months later I received the Parole Board's decision: "Parole Denied."

Abe Brothman, serving his time at the Atlanta Federal Penitentiary, also applied for parole. He submitted a written statement (with published copies of articles he had written, in support) and it rang with a more trenchant confutation than the Parole Board usually received. In a letter to a former business associate he described his statement:

"… I said that parole would enable me to alleviate the economic hardship my family was enduring and begin restitution of financial losses to others who had suffered them as a result of my arrest and conviction. It would also end an obvious miscarriage of justice. I reviewed that I had been accused of a conspiracy to obstruct justice and, implicitly, of espionage. The former, I contended, either had to be the willful, calculated design of one guilty of the latter, or it was the irrational act of one whose attachment to purpose is precarious. Or, these charges weren't true at all! I was willing to join the prosecution in dismissing the second alternative for the story of my life would hardly support such a notion. On that account I was willing to evaluate the accuracy or the falsity of the charges, not as they would be handled in a hysteria-driven court but on the basis of my public record. I have marked seventeen years of my career in the fields of engineering, physics, chemistry and mathematics by publishing up to four articles per year in the open, in recognized American journals. I have identified my philosophic record even longer by my devotion to the principle that science has nothing in common with secrets or its directly-related hangover from alchemy, black magic and wizardry. Espionage in the realm of scientific information for one with such a record and outlook could only be a game for fools whose romanticism outweighs either their stupidity or their scientific comprehension. I leave it to those captious hypocrites who have already confessed such acts to excuse them as being afflicted with schizophrenia. I am not so impaired, nor am I a romantic. I hope also that I am not a fool!"

Parole for Abraham Brothman, Prisoner 71647, was denied.

Parole Form No. 34

Department of Justice
PENAL AND CORRECTIONAL INSTITUTION
Federal Reformatory for Women
Alderson, West Virginia

NOTICE OF ACTION OF PAROLE BOARD

MIRIAM MOSKOWITZ
10069-W

SEPTEMBER 6, 1951

DENIED

On this date the above-noted action was taken by the United States Board of Parole on your application for parole. Your attention is called to the fact that any misconduct or violation of the rules of the institution may cause reconsideration of any favorable action.

Parole Officer

> Both Abraham Brothman and Miriam Moskowitz applied for parole; and both were denied in August 1951. This form, denying Moskowitz's appeal, meant she had to serve her full two year sentence. Brothman shared the same fate.

Chapter 20

Surrogate Living

My job at the storehouse demanded little of me beyond my time; it was simply a place I had to go to each morning. My duties consisted of receiving and checking in deliveries and writing them up for inventory. It took no special skills and after a few months I asked for a transfer to the hospital lab. My request was granted and I was elated because now, I thought, I could learn something new and perhaps useful.

I ran into an unexpected roadblock, however, Millie, the inmate who ran the lab and who was an experienced technician, was visibly unhappy with my presence. She had worked alone in the lab from the beginning of her assignment and because of that she enjoyed an occupational prestige few other women had in this institution. There was no full time doctor on the premises, only a nurse. I had to watch Millie closely to learn how to do a urinalysis or how to draw a blood sample from a vein for a complete blood count. Millie showed me techniques only grudgingly and never completely. I pin-pricked my fingers constantly to draw drops of blood which I could then smear onto a slide to study under the microscope and the little I did learn was primarily from that and from the few out-of-date books in the lab on elementary biochemistry and technician procedures. I quickly realized that this assignment would never prove fruitful for me. Moreover, anything less routine than what Millie and I did was done off premises because an inmate who needed complicated medical treatment was usually transferred to a full-service hospital.

My work assignment was now causing me stress and no matter how hard I tried, I could not neutralize Millie's antagonism so I asked to return to the storehouse office. My request was granted.

While I had no serious complaints about my work environment, life in the cottage was a different story. Here I was clearly not a member of any sisterhood, as I had been in the New York City jail. In this southern, rustic setting I was perceived to be an odd fish by staff and inmates alike. My prison mates came from all over the United States; this was then the only federal penal institution for women. I was the only New Yorker in my cottage, "New Yorker" being a code term for "Jew." When anyone asked me if I was from New York she was really asking me if I was Jewish.

But it was the nature of what had put me in prison that became the core of my difficulty. The notoriety of my trial had repeatedly played on the overtones of disloyalty, communism and espionage, and just the hint of someone's ideological nonconformity was enough to unravel the otherwise benign attitudes of rational people. The prison population, warders and inmates, was not different in this respect from the rest of society. On this account alone it regarded me with a well-defined hostility.

(The inmate population at the reformatory was roughly 60–40% white to black. In the New York City jail black women outnumbered white by about 75% to 25%, a rough estimate. My unscientific perception was that bank robbery, car theft, bad checks, swindling and other big money crimes evolved into federal offenses and African-American women had limited opportunities to engage in such events. When they broke the law it was usually drug-related or for lesser money offenses and that was most often handled by local systems of justice. But punishment was always severe.)

Another exacerbating factor for me was that my parents had spent a great deal of money in my defense, even if to no avail. It did not matter that the funds had been borrowed or mortgaged for; the perception was that I had sold out my country while being far more privileged than most of the other luckless women here. Many of them had been abandoned and left to founder alone when they tumbled into trouble, and for those who were mothers the system played havoc with the lives of their children. By contrast, it was unfavorable that I had a support system.

Above all else, however, I was that insufferable, quintessential outsider, a Jew.

All of this generated an undercurrent of hostility towards me and I had to learn quickly to tread carefully. In everything I said and did I maintained an unobtrusive presence. Dutifully, I followed all orders without a hint of a question or a twitch of distaste, no matter how bureaucratically nonsensical. Whatever my work assignment – kitchen cleaning crew, storehouse, hospital lab – I did my job quietly and tried to remain inconspicuous. I asked for no privileges, accepted the animosity with resignation, and minded my own business.

As the months wore on the staff's attitudes softened, probably because I generated no problems for them. But my sister inmates did not ease off. For some, prison had become the bind of escalating retaliation. There seemed to be no respite from the constant quarreling. They gossiped jealously, exaggerated the faults of others and imagined slights where none existed. Their sense of moral reality was bent; they were quick to threaten, they found ways to hurt each other and incited others against their targets. Uneasily, I soon found I had become a target for the artful harassment by a few who constituted a hermetic subculture in this wilderness.

I added layers to my already developed carapace and steered a careful course, aware that responding to provocation would only set off an avalanche of trouble for which there would be no cure. Quickly and pragmatically I learned a new set of rules: to hush my tongue and avoid conflict as much as possible. It was not easy.

So, if an inmate made a friendly overture – not often—I responded pleasantly but guardedly, but if one spat out "Jew!" or "bitch!" or "spy!" or some permutation of all three I pretended not to hear. When tablemates refused to pass bowls of food to me at meal times I pretended I wasn't hungry. And always I remained watchful when I was in my room alone. I had heard stories of how an inmate had found her room smeared with mud after she had painted it; how a hand-loomed rug another had made over many months in an Arts and Crafts class had been shredded when she was not in her room; and how photographs of still another's family had been discovered ripped and tossed into the trashcan. And there were the terrible tales of a Nisei naïf who had found solace attending Mass each Sunday but who found it the better part of devotion to cease going because a peer group would sit behind her and "sotto voce," curse her out as "Jap-spy!" as she made the responses to the liturgy.

It was a savage, bleak time and there seemed to be little humanity in this world.

In the meantime, one day flowed monotonously into another and the calendar on which I marked off the days sometimes seemed not to change. I tried to disconnect from this reality; prison was only a way station; it was not my home. I resurrected old memories instead. I would recall how my favorite uncle would tease me about my freckles as he slipped me a forbidden candy, or the bliss my father created when he presented me with the roller skates I hadn't dared to hope for, or the delicious feeling of reading in bed by flashlight under the covers long after my mother had decreed lights out – and my psyche would smile and I would be soothed. The business of doing time demanded a masquerade for daily functioning but I was always conscious of the need to keep strong and sane. I worked at it by remembering who I was and how lucky I had been.

One of the older women in my cottage, Ida, had showered me with small trinkets and gifts when I arrived – a handkerchief she had crocheted, a vest she had knitted, beads she had worn – and I was too new to prison life to comprehend the unspoken subtleties of inmate relationships. It quickly became apparent, however, that in return she expected me to become her exclusive companion, her private person in our leisure time. Many of the women had similarly paired off but I wanted none of this. I resented this institution and did not want it to redefine my persona. I returned the gifts as Ida continued to visit me. Suddenly one day, as she rose to leave, she turned to embrace me and tried to kiss me on the lips. I pushed her away and in a low voice so that it would not carry into the corridor said, "No!" She cried and I was sorry for her but adamant. She had years of time ahead without the safe haven of stowaway memories; prison had become her reality and she could no longer hold on to another perspective. When her release date would come, I guessed she would probably not be able to function outside anymore.

Inmates were permitted to send two letters a week, usually only to family members, but there were no restrictions on the number we could receive. We could write our attorneys any time and all correspondents had to be approved by the Bureau of Prisons.

We were also permitted two one-hour family visits per month, but I discouraged my father from coming. (My mother was not well enough to travel to West Virginia.) It would have been an arduous trip because there was no direct rail link between home and this remote corner of West Virginia. It would also have entailed an overnight hotel stay and cab fares back and forth, and I did not want my father to incur such expenses. In all my letters I stressed that I was comfortable and not enduring any hardship.

One of my brothers did come, however. He was in the army, on leave, and because he appeared in uniform – tall, handsome and well-turned out – the warden's office treated him like a visiting nabob. We used the special visitor's room (available to all inmates). It was furnished like a very large, well-appointed home living room. An officer monitored us unobtrusively in a far corner. With both of us talking at once the hour seemed to vanish almost as soon as it began.

Twice I was able to get permission to telephone home, collect. I made the calls from the warden's office and ~~logically~~ it seemed to me both times that someone was on the line listening in.

While a letter from home could deliver a moment of bliss, more than anything I missed Abe and I suffered a stubborn longing for him that nothing could deflect. I had so much to tell him. In this lonely wasteland my portion of misery seemed too much to bear and I needed him. Even more, I need his brave reassurance that we would yet triumph over this catastrophe.

But I envied Alva, the young woman in the room next to mine, because she had something tangible to assuage her longing. Her dearest person, Gladys, had been the previous occupant of my room. Friendships here were intense and sometimes sexual, and Alva's relationship with Gladys had become a shield against the terrible longing that could cut through the toughest emotional armor. For them it was till-death-do-us-part. When Gladys was freed, she and Alva pledged to reconnect on Alva's release date—years away. This was self-deception because each of the women had families to whom she would return; one in Texas and the other in Alabama. They would probably never see each other again. But Gladys had given Alva one of her work shirts—they had both worked on the paint crew—which Alva kept wrapped and unlaundered in her dresser drawer. In moments of great longing Alva would peel the shirt from its wrapper, clasp it to her breast and take a deep, hungry draft of the fading body scent that had been Gladys'. Then she would tenderly return the shirt to the drawer.

As I settled into a routine, with some trepidation I joined my sister inmates in the cottage living room after supper each evening. I joked with them over the latest gossip about staff doings and participated in the clumsy sociability which that generated. That summer and fall of 1951 were memorable for the baseball playoffs; it was the New York Giants against the Brooklyn Dodgers in the National League pennant race. The Dodgers had been in front by some thirteen games in mid-August and their roster included Jackie Robinson, Duke Snider and Peewee Reese. On October 3, in the most classic ball game of all time, in the ninth inning, on the last day of the season, the Giants unexpectedly took the pennant when Ralph Branca threw a fatal pitch and Bobby Thomson drove in the winning runs. The sportscaster, the pitch of his voice climbing towards hysteria, caught us on the nub of his excitement (on radio; TV here was not yet ubiquitous). As the Dodgers fell our hearts broke and we shared a sense, for the moment, of mutual loss.

When the Yankees went on to win the American League pennant the contest became a subway series. It was Joe DiMaggio in his last year, and Mickey Mantle and Yogi Berra and Phil Rizzuto against Manager Leo Durocher and Willy Mays and Sol Maglie and other noble warriors. The Yankees swamped the Series, of course.

In my other life I had been to ball games with Abe, but had never been as caught up in the imagery of baseball as I was now. It was a good feeling. It linked me to a vital part of American life that seemed to me still innocent and orderly and untainted by the fraud and deceit I had known. For the moment I was again part of the larger American community, not shut away and an outcast.

One evening after supper I joined the others in the cottage living room to listen to pop music on the radio. One of the teenage inmates pulled me out of my chair to dance with her. As the beat of the big band took hold, as we spun and swung around the room I could see that most of the women were beginning to accept me. There were fewer catcalls or curses hurled my way, fewer hissed threats or obscene notes pitched into my room. I was eating regularly now; the cottage officer had rearranged table assignments, and the jostling and the tripping I had endured out-of-sight of warders and all the other covert and threatening provocations had begun to abate. Except for a few deeply embittered young women whose lives had been mangled beyond salvage and who continued the harassment sporadically, I was becoming for most of the prison population just another of its "girls."

It was then I met up with Miss Anders. Of all the staff personnel who had processed or otherwise surveyed me after the marshals had delivered me through the gates, she was the flintiest, the most forbidding and the most threatening.

Miss Anders was the officer in charge of the music program, and that was geared to church services. On Sunday mornings it was Catholic Mass, and on Sunday afternoons, Baptist services. Since I did not participate in those events I never had any contact with her. I also never had the feeling that she cared about the personal identities of any of us. She seemed to avoid staff gossip and never much appeared to be caught up in the darby—the prison gossip—and the rumors which that usually generated. This was unusual in such a restricted environment where gossip was the most meaningful activity of the day. Anders was always prim and tight-lipped and seemingly closed off from her surroundings. When I went to see her, therefore, I knew I would find her cool, brisk, remote and perhaps brittle and indeed she was all of that.

"Do you have a violin around here?" I asked. "I used to play."

"What do you want to do with it?" she countered.

I wanted that fiddle to help me shake off my obstinate prison loneliness. I missed Abe, I missed his warmth and love, but I also wanted to be able to deal with my growing and troubling awareness that I had to rethink our relationship. The violin might also fleetingly return me to happier times and strengthen me, perhaps, to face some of the hard thinking I knew I had to do. It would even be a symbolic step of independence. In all the years I had been with Abe, I had pursued no independent activity because my interests had always been subordinate to his. Now it would be my turn.

I did not tell Miss Anders that. I indicated only that my prison time might be less wasteful if I tried to recapture old skills. She nodded thoughtfully and said she'd see.

About a month later, while I wondered irritably what was taking so long—I had heard there had once been an instrument on the premises—a violin arrived at my cottage and the officer in charge presented it to me with quiet discretion. No one was near when she called me into her office. There she made a short, self-conscious speech about how the institution was always glad to accommodate its "girls" and she turned over the instrument to me. Inside the worn, black cardboard case was a violin of nondescript origin but newly cleaned and polished and with new strings. The bow appeared to have just been rehaired. It needed rosin, and the pocket of the case yielded a fresh piece.

All I needed now was print music. Miraculously Miss Anders had seen to that, too. A stack of miscellaneous music arrived, and among the treasures were a shabby volume of Kreutzer Etudes which I had studied in my youth, some popular encore oldies of Fritz Kreisler vintage, some hymnals, and an ancient frayed copy of Anton Rubinstein's Violin-Piano Sonata, Opus 13. I had never heard the Rubinstein and when I read through it, it was like connecting with a new, exotic friend.

With permission from the duty officer, after supper that evening I went down to the basement, propped up the Kreutzer on the warren of interweaving steam and water pipes and tried to practice. The sounds I produced shocked me; they were raucous and most inelegant. I had no aural memory of a 440-vps frequency to which I could tune the A string, and my sense of harmonic proportions was now unreliable. Searching for fifths with or without an accurate A was beyond me and frustration began to take over. I sat on the steps of the basement stairway asking myself why I was embarking on this extraordinary unpleasantness. I hadn't held a violin under my chin since my days in my college orchestra; now at thirty-five my muscles were no longer able to accommodate the difficult positioning of the left elbow and my right arm could not control a steady route of the bow within the quarter-inch or so prescribed for it near the bridge. But with some fifteen months left of my sentence, yielding to discouragement so quickly meant facing a long and empty time. I reminded myself that nothing could ever again be as hopeless as the court trial I had recently endured. Even though I was a convicted felon I was no longer as despairing. Time was healing – if I had suffered I had also survived.

I began to practice. The easiest Kreutzer was a major obstacle course. I worked on it slowly phrase by phrase but the sounds I was producing made me groan with dismay.

It was no ideal environment for practicing so I sent a request to the Assistant Warden that I be permitted to go elsewhere to practice. She referred it to Miss Anders and back came a notice to my cottage officer that henceforth I was to report every evening at 7 o'clock to the school house on the hill, within the prison confines, but a walking distance of perhaps a quarter mile.

As I checked out with the duty officer the next evening I saw her pick up the telephone. She would be calling the guardhouse to report that I was legitimately walking across the field alone. Then she would call the schoolhouse where I would be clocked and checked in. The meticulous security was only a minor irritant because now, for the first time in months, I was totally private and alone without the need to be locked in my room if I wanted to be alone.

As I traipsed along the landscaped path among the faded fall flower beds and up the hill towards the

Miriam Moskowitz played the violin for church services during her incarceration at the Federal Reformatory for Women in Alderson, West Virginia. This photo was taken before her incarceration. (Miriam Moskowitz)

schoolhouse, I treasured the seven minutes or so that I would need to make that walk. The fields glimmered in the twilight and I stopped for a moment as I climbed to survey the area below. The ten dormitory cottages comprising the living area of the institution each housed, perhaps, twenty inmates more or less. These and the administration building at one end formed a quadrangle on the lower campus. Off the far end near the administration building were the garment shop, the storehouse and the laundry and further out, the cannery, the carpentry shop and the farm. They no longer seemed so grim as I trudged up and away from them. My chronic hunger to be rid of this place, my lust for freedom, was momentarily abated and the luxury of being alone, even briefly, softened my resentful awareness of the barbed wire fences off in the distance. I skipped because I was suddenly, wildly happy, then immediately slackened my pace for I wanted this walk to last as long as possible. Every muscle in my body relaxed. In the magic of the moment the moon slipped in and out of the clouds, winked, and dared me to catch it. No one was near whom I could see and I laughed giddily because now it was irrelevant if anyone was watching me from the guardhouse. I was in the open air, alone and free—for seven minutes.

Each evening I made my trek up the hill to the schoolhouse, tuned the violin to the piano in the auditorium and then chose an empty classroom at the far end of the building. There I practiced. I tried the beginning Kreutzers, then some of the pop stuff and the hymns and worked my way into the first movement of the Rubinstein. Such melodic, romantic music! I thought of Abe and felt his presence.

It was blissful, those evenings—every night except Sunday when the schoolhouse was closed. Every day at work I planned my practice sessions in my mind: which part of what etude needed most attention and what fingerings and bowings would be likely to work. I would need to attend to intonation and vibrato also, because the swooping shifts of the Rubinstein kept defeating my attempts to produce the lush, juicy sound it seemed to call for. Every day I planned and every evening I climbed eagerly up the hill to my rendezvous.

A few weeks later Miss Anders cornered me at work:

"How about playing with the choir and the organist for Sunday services next week?" She was pleasant as though she were straining to make the invitation sound casual; she even sounded friendly. "We've never had a violinist before. It would make the services especially nice."

I knew that in this isolated area many of the townspeople attended church services here at the reformatory, and a violinist accompanying the choir would be a novelty. (Church services as well as all communal activities were not segregated.)

Anders no longer seemed quite so splintery as she waited for my reply; the spun glass had vanished. One of my sister inmates had told me she had seen Anders eavesdropping at the door of my practice room, so presumably she knew what my musical deficits were. But I was grateful to her; I had lately learned from my cottage officer that she had had to take that violin to a repair shop in a distant city on her own time and probably at her own expense, to get it restored to playable condition.

Nevertheless, her request made me uneasy. If I agreed I would implicitly allow this institution to invade my privacy and become my real world, and if it did not work out I would suffer excruciating embarrassment. But as Anders spoke there was an aura of vulnerability about her and I was moved. "We need each other," I thought. Aloud, I said: "Sure. Of course."

She brightened. "I'll get you some choir robes –but you will have to wash and iron them. Okay?"

"Okay."

I went to a rehearsal the following Saturday and all went well, even though I was nervous. The next morning I arrived at the chapel early to practice some scales and warm up. Then Anders helped me dress. I put on a long black skirt, and then a black bib trimmed with white lace around the throat. Over that went a white knee-length surplice with a square neck back and front and wide sleeves. I had been wearing a blue and white enameled gold pendant on a gold chain. My mother's dearest friend, Dora Sachs, had brought it to me for good luck the morning I left for my trial, but it was my mother who had put it around my neck. The pendant was inscribed with the Ten Commandments in Hebrew. I flipped it over my bodice and wore it prominently.

Thus decked out I found the total effect stunning and strange. It was the first time I had doffed prison garb. I looked at the choir members dressed similarly and suddenly recognized not a one. They and I all radiated peace.

Such was my routine for the remainder of my prison sojourn. I worked, I knitted, I read, I formed guarded friendships, I wrote home and I played the violin. The days went by with ritualistic and monotonous sameness. Always I was suffused with loneliness. Besides the physical isolation from the surroundings and the people I wanted to be with, the interruption and postponement of living was hard to bear. But I did have that violin and because of it I had Miss Anders. Her regard for me was changing perceptibly from frozen aloofness and thinly veiled distaste to an easy friendliness.

She did something extraordinary, the first of many kindnesses, and she did it quietly as was her style. She took three of us, the young woman who played the piano (and organ), the lead soprano from the choir and me, and two afternoons a week she had us excused from our drudge jobs to come to the music room at the schoolhouse for lessons in harmony and music theory. She put us through rigorous ear training, taught us solfege, keys and chord structures and musical styles. It was a world away from prison and an intellectual exercise I found exhilarating. She also instituted a music appreciation session on Saturday afternoons when we were off work. She brought records from her personal collection and a portable record player and for an hour and a half she filled the small school auditorium with glorious sound.

In June, some three months before my release, Miss Anders put together a musical event called, "The Time of the Roses." She got hold of some surplus nylon parachutes from the Second World War which the U.S. military had declared obsolete. She prevailed upon the garment shop at the reformatory to rip them apart, dye batches of the resulting pieces of fabric into different pastel colors and make them up into pretty garden party dresses. She cobbled together a prop crew from among inmate volunteers who gathered voluminous bunches of roses from the institution grounds and positioned them effectively on the stage. Some discarded lumber from the carpentry shop had been miraculously sanded, painted and fashioned into stage backdrops. The total result transformed the schoolhouse auditorium into something charming; we could imagine it looked like an intimate lovely theater.

Each of the choir members and the pianist and I were decked out in those parachute dresses like free world players. We performed popular songs, spirituals and hymns. There were some solos, some small-group part singing and some full company singing, all with piano and violin accompaniment, and a few instrumental solos and riffs. Several of the singers had been nightclub performers and their voices endowed the event with an impressive professionalism. The audience included not only the locals and the staff and inmates but officials from the Bureau of Prisons who came from Washington to take this in.

The event cast a rosy hue on life in the institution for a brief period and one felt it like a layer of balm. We were, for the moment, a little less like outcasts and more like the women we wanted to be. There was more laughter on the grounds and less quarreling and complaining. Even the obscenities and explosive language, always a part of prison life, seemed to abate.

When my sentence was drawing to a close the Department of Justice notified me that I would have to serve an extra thirty days while it investigated my claim that I could not pay the fine of $10,000. I had been told this would happen; nevertheless, it became another in the series of blows I had been dealt and I was dispirited. I had been marking off the calendar and counting the days and I was primed to leave. I wept that night—the only time in this two-year stint that I did. But the next day I had a notice that I was being granted four meritorious days off my sentence—on recommendation from Miss Anders.

It was an unprecedented gift; meritorious days were not the same as statutory time off for good behavior; they were not automatic and were infrequently bestowed. They were particularly not awarded to political miscreants as I was perceived to be. Yet Miss Anders had maneuvered that situation around to humanize it. The four-day bounty meant more to me than the loss of the thirty days and I was overwhelmed. I thought it significant also that in my male-dominated world, the world which had so victimized me, it was a woman in this subset community of women who had reached out to soften the blows.

I was released the following month, on September 17, 1952, a luminous day with still the feel of summer. Anders came to my cottage to say goodbye as I was about to board the institution van that would take me to the train station. We shook hands and I looked long and hard at her, wondering if I would ever see her again. I wanted to fling my arms around her to keep her from slipping out of my life but I remained cool and controlled.

"Have a safe trip home," she said, "and don't come back!"

I felt awkward. "Well, I don't know. I might really learn to play that fiddle if I had another shot at it." She knew I was straining to be casual and keep my excitement under control.

I boarded the van and waved to her as we pulled away, straining to keep her in view. The van turned, went through the gate – I was on my way to freedom – and she was gone.

PART V

Life Resumes Among
The Lawful

Chapter 21

Working

I was unaccustomed to being alone, and the train was blissful for its privacy. A young man, a passenger, who had probably seen the prison guard hand me over to the conductor and who realized, perhaps, I was a released prisoner, sat down next to me and made convivial conversation. I changed my seat and he took the hint.

It was a slow train and did not reach its layover point in Washington, D.C. until the early morning hours. I remained awake throughout the night; life was so pleasant I couldn't waste any of it on sleep. I was also too excited. In Washington I had to wait for a connecting train so I bought a cup of coffee and rejoiced at the freedom I had to accomplish such a small act of independence.

The train pulled into Penn Station in New York City at mid-morning and immediately I called home. Then I got on a subway heading downtown. My destination was the office of Emanuel Bloch. I wanted to know how his charges, Ethel and Julius Rosenberg, were. I had not known Manny Bloch, but when I was brought to court during my trial he would attend each session, taking notes. He would also have Ethel and Julius brought to court to give them a chance to be with each other in the bullpen in the courthouse basement while he sat in on the court proceedings upstairs. Then he would confer with them. Always, when he saw me after each session, when I had to return to the bullpen, he would call out cheerily: "They've got nothing on you, kid!"

When I walked into his office his jaw seemed to drop and his shoulders hunched up. I reassured him quickly that I was free; I had finished my time and had just arrived from West Virginia. He breathed easily again and we talked. He told me of the status of the appeals he had filed and said that Ethel and Julius were bearing up remarkable well and continued to be hopeful. He was also solicitous about me; what was I planning to do? He volunteered:

"We'll have to get you a job. I'll talk to some people."

"No, Manny, that's not necessary!"

I thought he had enough to worry about and I did not want him to be burdened with my problems. However, for me Manny Bloch became sainted; he was the only one ever to offer help.

Before I left, I took the enameled gold pendant from my neck and gave it to him.

"Give this to Ethel for me," I said. "My mother wants her to have it."

That was stretching the truth, but my mother had indeed been concerned about Ethel. In all the visits she made to me in the New York jail she never failed to ask how Ethel was. I thought it would cheer Ethel to know that my mother, along with millions of others, was concerned about her. (After the execution the newspapers reported that Ethel left two pieces of jewelry for her sons: her wedding ring and a "religious medal.")

That done, I headed for home as though I were just another commuter. When I opened the door to our house I could hardly breathe for the rush of excitement that flooded through me. My mother had prepared one of her remarkable dinners; my father could not take his eyes off me and followed me around as I wandered from room to room. I marveled how wonderful it was to be here.

The next day I ran to see my sister; she had just given birth to a baby girl. My brothers, out-of-towners, telephoned as did other relatives. My mother spoke to the relatives in Hungarian, her native language, thinking to foil possible eavesdroppers. A sick feeling swept over me that my mother could be made to fear the FBI for nothing she had done, but merely because she was my mother.

A dear friend, Sophie, dropped by. We had been friends since high school and she remained loyal and supportive during the worst times. No one else – none of my former friends called.

In succeeding days I found a job as a public relations manager and for the moment it was a triumph I began also to thread my way through a social routine, gingerly picking up the shards of my old life and blending them discreetly with my evolving one. I could not afford my own living place, but thought that would come soon.

Abe was freed soon after I but I had difficulty reconnecting with him. He was the same Abe, unabashedly self-absorbed and irredeemably solipsistic about his own perceived place in the universe. (As he embraced me after our two-year prison separation, he said, "I had a terrible time in prison" and proceeded to give me details, but he never asked how it had been for me and I never told him!) However, I had changed. During the two years since our arrest I reviewed incessantly what had catapulted me into this cataclysmic experience. I reevaluated the past as I had never been able – or willing – to evaluate the present. And I finally saw I could never have a life unless I made drastic changes – not least because I needed, finally, to be my own person. We parted, painfully, and I had a rocky time of it when it sometimes seemed I could not endure another moment of that pain.

It took me a long time to move ahead and while I worked it out there were some who became unintended victims with me. There was that pleasant, totally guileless young man who appeared on my social horizon and seemed to complete my life again. A week before we were to wed I cancelled out. He was hurt and bewildered and I could not explain my panic. There were others towards whom I warmed initially, but for whom I could feel no juncture of either trust or desire. Inevitably, each took his leave.

Through it all, no one in my new life had known me in the old, and it needed a delicate balancing act to keep my most recent identity submerged. I was always fearful that I would be found out. Many in my old life who I thought were friends, were too uneasy to welcome my presence now. The Cold War had intensified; the increasingly strident Senator Joseph McCarthy was ransacking the nation's equilibrium as the country succumbed to political paranoia. A convicted felon, especially one so publicly condemned, was hardly a social asset. I watched my whilom friends skitter off like jittery chickens, tumbling over the refuse of their discarded morality.

In the meantime, the FBI was not done with me. In May 1953, eight months after my release from prison, they appeared at my door and asked to talk to me. In 1956, they accosted me on the street. Rather than let them into the house and alarm my parents I sat with them, both times, in their car and listened to their questions. Did I remember anything now that I cared to share with them which I had withheld before? No, there was nothing I could tell them and yes, if I thought of anything I would let them know. I was excruciatingly polite.

Less than eight months after the Rosenberg execution their attorney, Emanuel Bloch, died suddenly of a heart attack. He was 52 years old. I was among the overflow crowd who attended his funeral on February 2, 1954. The FBI, in characteristic, mindless snoopery, duly noted my signature in the condolence book.[1] (The FBI was assisted in this case by the NYPD.)

The FBI records indicate that they interviewed me a third time in October 1961.[2] That is not true and it is one of many errors about me in their files. Most egregiously, they turned a co-worker and a neighbor into informants about me,[3] thus compromising my relations with them and making my life inordinately more difficult.

I endured their questioning in the two interviews I did give because I hoped to stave off their going to my employer to expose me. They did, anyhow.

I had become the public relations manager for a kosher food firm, having sought out co-religionists to work for because I thought they might be benevolently indifferent if my past were ever exposed. That proved to be a naïve overestimate of their brotherly concern.

After my second FBI interview the board chairman to whom I reported no longer seemed to acknowledge me and no longer called me to meetings. The situation deteriorated. My secretary left and was not replaced, and no work seemed to be coming across my desk. Assignments, mail and telephone calls that I would normally have been expected to handle were going randomly to others. And when I submitted my vacation schedule my boss hemmed and hawed and murmured he was not sure my job would still be there when I returned.

I gave notice and left.

The FBI had done its work. I learned that they had visited the Personnel Office and told them I was a convicted felon and a communist.[4] Mr. Hoover and his FBI were making war against my life and it is difficult to understand the justification. I had paid my presumed debt to society. There could have been no benefit to the country for such harassment and no ensuing prestige to the FBI. The cost to the public, however, for keeping agents busy on such meaningless assignments would have been impossible to justify.

I was lucky and found a new job as a sales promotion manager with a small packaging firm. The pay was less, the firm not as large or as financially secure, but it was a job. I had been there about a year when I received a telephone call at home from a former business friend of Abe Brothman's, Bernie Pidto. Bernie and Abe had participated in a joint business venture and Abe had also borrowed money from him – although I did not know it then. Bernie would spend many hours at our office even when Abe was not present, and I often wondered how he could run his own paint business in Brooklyn and yet spend so much time at our office in Manhattan and at our lab in Queens.

The telephone call surprised me. Bernie had never been particularly attentive towards me; our conversations had been limited to perfunctory greetings. It was now more than a decade since I had last seen him. He had been present at the work site the day of our arrest. Nevertheless, he was now on the telephone. He did not make much conversation, however; he merely asked where I was working—and I told him. He commented that he knew the firm, it was small and he speculated about its future—and that was all. I puzzled over the call; he had not asked how I had been, he had given no reason for calling and he seemed to be in a hurry. He merely asked where I was working. It was one more baffling event frozen forever in my memory and I closed the chapter on it.

But coincidentally, the FBI learned of my new employment about the time of Bernie's call. As they did at my previous job, they developed an informant at my new job whom they would telephone whenever they wanted to keep tabs on me.[5] (They also harassed my mother by telephoning her, pretending to be long-lost friends trying to locate me. They frightened her and made her miserable because she always guessed their identity.)

Shortly after Bernie's call I was faced with a crisis at work. A former employee showed up at the building entrance early one morning, before I arrived, with a stack of *Spy Confidential* magazines under his arm which he distributed to my fellow workers as they arrived. The magazine was a single issue, undated, and an imitation of the then popular *Hollywood Confidential* magazine. The latter was a scandal sheet which rummaged about in the private lives of movie people. The young man was gone when I arrived but it was not until I was called to an unexpected management meeting that I realized something was wrong.

My boss, Charlie, and the company's management consultant showed me the magazine. It featured a picture of Abe and me in the police van after our conviction and the caption under it said:

"Miriam Moskowitz and Abraham Brothman behind her were part of atomic spy ring. She received 2 years in pen, $10k fine; He got 7 years, fine of $15k."

When they were done with their questions, Charlie said they would have the company's attorney check what I had told them, discuss it with the Board of Directors and then consider what action they would take. In the meantime, I could continue on the job until I heard from them.

It was a raw time for me. My father had died a month earlier and I was consumed with guilt that I had destroyed the tranquility of his final years. I also missed him terribly; he had always been my champion and now when my courage needed bolstering he was gone. While I waited for Charlie to tell me whether I would continue to have a job I considered chucking everything and fleeing, perhaps to Canada – a woman alone, without a support system, without resources and with little job prospects. I really had no way to turn. (The only possible practical solution I could think of, in my desperation, was to drive upstate to some quiet country road off Route 17, find an isolated place to park, close the car windows, remember happier times and take a nap – with the motor running.)

Subsequently I was called to a Board meeting. Charlie sat at the head of the conference table, I at the other end and the legal staff and Board members on either side. Charlie was nervous and ill at ease but as he spoke he steadied himself. He said that the Board was in agreement: if I had done anything wrong it was probably in the nature of a private indiscretion. They did not believe I had been a spy; they thought I had been swept into a political haymaker at a critical time in the country's history. I could remain on my job and in that case instructions would be disseminated discreetly throughout the office and the plant that anyone overheard gossiping about me would be fired.

A few years later when it came time for me to leave (I had been applying for a teaching position and had a job offer) Charlie gave me his blessing. He was also concerned that I would not be able to manage on a beginning teacher's salary so he arranged to have me come in for freelance assignments when I could make it.

Charlie was a compassionate person and, unlike my previous employer, a man of courage and integrity. I have never ceased honoring his memory.

DEPARTMENT OF JUSTICE

Office of United States Attorney

Southern ____ District of ____ New York

Receipt NO. U29720

(CHECKS ACCEPTED SUBJECT TO COLLECTION)

Claim Against

Miriam Moskowitz

U. S. Attorney's No.

114909

Amount Received

Seventy and 00/100 Dollars---------------$75.00--------

From

Agency & File No.

USDC, SDNY C133 - 106

PAID IN FULL

Type Claim	Amt. of Claim	DJ File No.		
FINE	$10,000.		( ) Pre-judgment	
			(X) Judgment	(X) Paid in full
			( ) Compromise	( ) Partial Pay No.

Date Payment Received

January 22, 1976

By

EdithKaltman, clerk

for UNITED STATES ATTORNEY

ORIGINAL—TO PAYER

Miriam Moskowitz's final payment in January 1976 of her $10,000 fine –
more than twenty-five years after it was imposed by Judge Kaufman in
November 1950, in addition to her two-year prison sentence.

Phantom Spies, Phantom Justice

Miriam Moskowitz,
photo in her college
yearbook, *Microcosm,*
June, 1942.
(Miriam Moskowitz)

Miriam Moskowitz
and friend, *circa*
summer 1938.
(Miriam Moskowitz)

Miriam Moskowitz on the porch of her home, about July 1946.
(Miriam Moskowitz)

Miriam Moskowitz in Puerto Rico to attend the first Casals festival in April 1957.
(Miriam Moskowitz)

Miriam Moskowitz,
about 1956, at a
food trade function
where she worked at
public relations.
(Miriam Moskowitz)

Miriam Moskowitz during an
interview by Danya Abt for
GRIT- TV that aired January
13, 2011. Ms. Moskowitz is 94
in this photo.
(GRIT-TV) (ZACH HALBERD)

Chapter 22

Broken Shadows

After I left prison in September 1952 I could hardly wait out the months until December when I planned to send Miss Anders a Christmas card. I bought an especially beautiful one and scribbled a note on the back that I was working, I had started violin lessons, and had joined a community orchestra. I thought that was rather impressive.

Back came her card; it bore her signature and nothing more. Disappointed, I realized Anders was forbidden to have any contact with former inmates except for holiday greetings and her strong sense of propriety made it unthinkable that she would violate that proscription.

For the next two years I sent Anders a Christmas card with a personal note full of chatter and each time she answered with her signature and nothing more. I let the routine fade the fourth year; it no longer seemed relevant. But the year after she sent me a card first and it had a note penned on the side and back. She signed it "Christine," and her return address was now on the west coast. Her note said she was giving piano lessons, she was also studying and she was enjoying attending museums, galleries and concerts. I knew she was not old enough to retire; she could hardly have been fifty then. I was edging up on forty.

Each year thereafter her notes were enthusiastically approving of whatever I had written the year before. Once I wrote that I was giving violin lessons to the junior members of my siblings' families and that two of them appeared destined for more serious study. She answered the following Christmas how proud she was of me.

Another time I wrote that I had changed to the viola and was now playing string quartets and other chamber music. She envied my opportunity, she replied, and continued: "I'm always so cheered to hear from you; it makes me feel I'm a part of your musical life."

The viola was larger and heavier than the violin, but I loved its deeper tone. The year I finally acquired a quality instrument I could hardly wait to tell her. It was a Contina of the modern Neapolitan school and I was rapturous in describing its mellow tone, its color and its workmanship.

"I know how thrilled you must be!" she replied. "To us who love music there is no greater joy than to own a quality instrument. I am enjoying my grand piano more and more as the months pass. For me, too, it is the realization of a lifetime of working and saving for it." Then, almost as a non-sequitur, "Have you ever tried practicing early in the morning, before breakfast? You can accomplish twice as much in half the time."

This last provoked me. I was now teaching school and had never worked so hard in my life. I exploded:

"I cannot let your remarks go until next Christmas to reply. Consider my routine, please: I'm up at six in the morning in a dark, cold house; I shiver and try to dress with lightning speed to keep from getting indoor frostbite. I put up the pot for coffee, another for cereal, maneuver the toaster into position, pour the juice and try not to spill it while shivering. I split-second dovetail all that with ablutions. At seven I drive to work to arrive before eight. There, it's a totally different world, no music but lots of stress. Leave at three, frequently later. If my mother needs attention (I bought a small cottage to be nearer to work; so my mother now lives twenty miles away) I rush to the supermarket and shop for her, deliver her groceries, spend a bit of time visiting with her listening to her fears and discontents, and I try to make palliative conversation.

Then home. Dinner, bath, collapse for an hour with a newspaper. Look at books on end table longingly; they've been waiting to be read for weeks and the library is telling me there are reserves out on them and to please return them. Open fiddle case instead and warm up with scales, finger work, etudes, literature. Two hours later lower the thermostat and creep into bed. If it is a quartet night, no practicing but bedtime is later. In between I also teach evening school two nights a week, pick up private tutoring in math and work summers on math curriculum I try to ignore that my back wants out of this routine and that I am always, always tired. Weekends I catch up with work left undone from Friday, mark papers, prepare lessons and attend to school-related paper work. A rare treat is slipping off to the theater or a concert or an excursion with a friend. Mostly my social life is on hold."

"Practice before breakfast?"

This one she, too, answered immediately: "My deepest apologies. I did not have a complete picture of your heroic efforts and your note has given me a more perceptive look into your crowded life. I do admire you. Stay warm, for heaven's sake! Love, Christine."

I hoped to bridge the formality she had imposed and to speak of more personal things: my work, my aspirations, my loneliness and disappointments and my small victories. I also wanted to know more of her but when I delicately broached questions she never locked into them.

I sent her a postcard from Cremona, where I had gone one April when I was on sabbatical. I was backpacking my way through Italy and poking about in the workshops of luthiers hoping to find an old master's instrument at a bargain price. She rejoiced that I had such an opportunity. And as always her notes were warm and endorsing and I was a focus for her concern. Once I wrote that a painful shoulder was dogging my days; her next note suggested that my diet include alfalfa sprouts—we are what we eat, she said.

So it went for some twenty years, this stillborn friendship that would never grow to term. In all this time the baneful thought occurred to me that she could be feeding my notes to the FBI, but then I rejected that possibility. It would never have been in keeping with her character. In any event, I thought wryly, Mozart and Beethoven could probably survive the scrutiny of the FBI although I was not so sure that Shostakovich or Prokofiev would. I did not share this black humor with her.

I also did not tell her that I was marching for civil rights in the great movement that was sweeping the country or that I was taking time out from music to write a newsletter as a member of a local civil rights organization. I never mentioned that I was demonstrating in front of the United Nations to ban the bomb and that I was marching for peace up Central Park or for women's rights down Fifth Avenue. And I did not think she would understand the depth of my outrage over Vietnam even though I was sure she would have been appalled had she realized what was being done there in her name. In our letters we talked only of music.

Always I wished to know more about her. Where had she grown up and studied? How had she found that zone of troubled women to work in where I met her? Why had she chosen not to marry or, as with me, had there been a failed liaison, a derailment of love because sensible judgment allowed for no risks? She was a pretty woman, spirited yet reserved, and with a subtle sense of humor. Had she found modern circuits of erotic life too treacherous to handle? And as a woman alone how had she confronted the punitive economics and the social instability of being unanchored to a man, a onesome in a twosome world?

As the years passed my need of her seemed to become more urgent. Christine Anders was the only one in my present life who had shared with me the experience of another—my prison sojourn. She had known me at a time and in a place no one else had. I had a discontinuous identity without her; I had a broken shadow. For two years, I had had no personal presence to anyone except to Christine Anders and I needed her as a witness to the continuity of my life.

One December I was harassed by a number of problems. My shoulder needed surgery, school was unusually hectic that year, my mother's health was declining precipitously, nothing was right. I overlooked sending Christine a Christmas card. It was several weeks later that I realized I had not seen her card either. The following December I sent her card early with a note telling her of my distractions and hoping all was well with her.

No card came back. I tried telephoning but found there was no listing for her now. In my restless unease I considered flying out to the west coast to find her. While I mulled that over, in January I received an epiphany, a letter from a lawyer:

"Dear Miriam," he wote, "I have your letter to our mutual friend, Christine Anders. I am sorry I must tell you that Christine passed away on January 25 last. Some years ago she had had cancer but with treatment it went into remission and remained so for a long while. However, a year and a half ago she called to tell me it was back and the doctor said she had only a few months to live. I had known Christine through our church where she was the organist. She asked me to be her executor.

She spent some time at home being quite sick, went to a hospital for three or four weeks and then to a convalescent home where she died.

She had a nice service."

Chapter 23

Abraham Brothman

In our darkest moments Abe had a recurrent dream that we would one day escape to a remote cottage, said cottage to be surrounded by a moat and accessible only by a drawbridge which would always remain in the UP position. Evil would be shut out of our lives and peace and love would enfold us forevermore. He even named the son he hoped we would have, "Sholem," Hebrew for "Peace."

In the beginning, as his personality unfolded, I chose not to see his weaknesses or his warts and I allowed him more sins than I would have accepted in anyone else. I was not alone in this. All, it seemed, who knew him generally thought that Abe Brothman's reasoning was so perceptive, his insight so special, he could never stumble; who anticipated life's pitfalls, and therefore could never be trapped by them; whose step was sure and whose decisions would always be unerringly wise. But this was also a man whose conspicuous intelligence and chronic lack of self-doubt drove him to overestimate his ability to control the forces impinging on his life, and to underestimate everyone else, and whose errors of judgment about others were so wrong they would later almost destroy him.

Brothman was barely fifteen when he entered Columbia College on a full scholarship.[*] He went on to Columbia School of Engineering and graduated as a professional engineer before his nineteenth birthday. He took a fellowship in the Department of Mathematics for six months; he had been refused one in the School of Engineering and suspected that anti-Semitism had ruled him out. This was, after all, 1932.

Despite that it was the depths of the Depression, job offers came quickly. He joined a large chemical equipment manufacturer in Pittsburgh as a chemical engineer. In a matter of months he became chief engineer; he was now barely twenty-one. His career there and subsequently with other companies was marked by strife. The issues usually involved salary disputes, but there were also his quarrels about the jesting epithets used by some of his

---

[*] I derived this official information about Abraham Brothman's education and employment from an autobiographical document he wrote for his attorney, William Messing, Esq. in the summer of 1950. A copy of that document is filed with the Moskowitz Papers at the Arthur W. Diamond Library of Columbia University Law School, Special Collections Dept.

colleagues: "Brothman, the Jewboy genius." He was scrappy about anti-Semitism and called them on it repeatedly.

He also found himself disagreeing with corporate outlook. Brothman foresaw that the future route of the American chemical engineering business would find itself at odds with the then prevailing corporate thinking. His perspective was to provide clients not merely with the equipment they needed, but also the particular chemical process if they had not already mapped it out. He urged his company to offer a packaged service; it would be a unique, advanced development in the industry. But each of the companies he had affiliated with in his career was unwilling to go this route; it was an untested idea and could be financially risky. It would require budgeting funds to set up chemical research laboratories and a staff, and would involve a complicated administrative and professional hierarchy. It was simpler and safer to follow the old path: design and sell equipment only, and let the client piecemeal his job out if he needed chemical process development.

(In 1950, while Abe Brothman sat in jail awaiting trial for having conspired to obstruct justice, and some seventeen years after he first began outlining his ideas, the bible of the chemical industry, the *Chemical Engineers Handbook*, in a new edition, credited Abraham Brothman for his pioneering work in chemical process development.)

Brothman had been bedeviled by his perceived uniqueness; he was unusually young in a position of great responsibility and, because of his youth, was cozened several times by corporate chicanery. An oral agreement he had had with a client in which he was to receive a stock participation in lieu of fees was never honored, nor was he ever paid for this work. Another client accused him of having submitted faulty designs of a plant to fill aerosol dispensers. The client reported that Freon was leaking out of the system and he refused to pay Brothman's design fees.

Abraham Brothman in August 1944 when he founded A. Brothman & Associates. (Miriam Moskowitz)

Brothman visited the plant one evening when the client was absent and discovered that although the plant operated efficiently during the day to fill the dispensers, at night a crew was employed to drain the Freon from the system and to ship it out as an air conditioning refrigerant for sale on the black market to theaters and restaurants. (These were the years of World War II and Freon was closely rationed.)

In still another instance Abe Brothman wrote a paper on a specialized field of chemical mixing. He invited two junior members of his staff to make a contribution to the paper as a means of helping them establish themselves professionally since they would be listed as co-authors. He left it to one of them to handle the mailing of the paper to the U. S. Navy in Washington, D.C., expecting that the article would generate an inquiry which could, in turn, lead to an order for equipment for the firm. It would have resulted in a handsome commission for him. Some weeks later, not having heard from the Navy, Abe inquired and learned that one of the men had removed the original face sheet containing the names of the three authors and submitted the paper as his own.

The same young man was also discovered to be acting in concert with one of Abe's clients to sell Abe's work to him in return for which the client would use his Washington influence to obtain draft-free status for the young man – this during wartime.

Perhaps the most expensive of all Brothman's business calamities was a classic swindle that he fell victim to early in his career. It involved a customer and a subcontractor. Brothman had returned to New York after five years with his first employer in Pittsburgh and had set up his own corporate entity: Republic Chemical Machinery Co. At Republic, he sought jobs to design chemical mixing equipment and to provide the equipment by subcontracting its fabrication. The sale of his services would include a royalty payment for the patents he held on the equipment design as well as a design fee.[1]

Republic obtained an exceptionally large order for equipment design and fabrication from a major manufacturer of consumer products. It duly subcontracted the fabrication to a company Abe had done business with before and to whom he was well known. When the equipment was ready to be shipped the subcontractor demanded balance payment before shipping. Abe turned to his client for the balance payment but the client refused to pay until the equipment was at its railroad siding in Chicago. No bank would lend Abe money without substantial collateral which he did not have. After several days of intense negotiations in which it became clear that the client and the subcontractor were in collusion, Abe wound up as the subcontractor's chief engineer and Republic Chemical Machinery, Inc. became the subcontractor's subsidiary. The Chicago firm paid the subcontractor directly for the equipment, Abe's patents now belonged to the subcontractor and Abe was out of business.

It would be inevitable that Abe would want to set up his own operation as a consulting engineer so that he could exercise greater control over his professional life. He was nothing if not self-confident about his ability to build such a business even without adequate capitalization. He wanted the freedom to create without the strictures of moribund corporate vision, but he had family and staff responsibilities he was not able to meet after he set up his consulting office. In 1946 Abe made me a partner in the business so that I would one day recoup financially for having foregone a regular salary when the coffers were low. He made similar commitments to others, in desperation, but he failed to tell me. Ultimately this created confusing and sometimes strained relations between the others and me because I never understood the special claims they seemed to have on him.

He sold rights to patents he owned to raise funds, but those funds did not last long. Eternally optimistic, he had no hesitancy to borrow money to keep the business afloat, not from banks but from individuals who believed in him. My father was one. Unquestionably, he meant to repay those debts but he never achieved the financial stability to do so. Yet he continued to go deeper into debt instead of setting limits on the scope of his operation or retrenching, or ending them altogether and becoming a salaried employee again.

The fallout from this, among other dire consequences, was that Brothman repeatedly and indiscriminately trusted business acquaintances who he would quickly turn into best buddies when his prior experience should have made him more cautious.

One of them became one of the FBI's "Confidential Informant of Known Reliability" (in their exquisite parlance) who furnished information about Abe from about December 1945, a few weeks after Bentley had made her revelations to the FBI. The flow of information from this source continued until about the summer of 1947. It was a

Gerhard "Gus" Wollan demonstrates one of Brothman's inventions, a pressurized canister for dispensing insecticide (referred to as a "bomb" in Gold's testimony). Wollen was a mechanical engineer and a partner in A. Brothman & Associates.
(Miriam Moskowitz)

diligently acquired hodgepodge of trifling, irrelevant detail about Abe's business dealings, his private political opinions and his social activities, all in a tedious sludge of frequently misleading information. It included his efforts to contact Amtorg (the Soviet Purchasing Commission), to interest them in his designs for vitamin plants. (He was not successful.) It also included his work in behalf of a Jewish group from Palestine (not yet the State of Israel) to design a plant to manufacture DDT.

Those reports also contained personal information about each of Brothman's partners and some of his employees.

There were other sources. One labeled, "Confidential Informant T-1," provided information about Abe's education, his professional experience and a list of technical articles he had published, information that could have come at that time only from Abe's office files. There was also information on Abe's daily activities in detail, i.e.: "Feb. 23, 1950: Abe on L. (company name); Calculations, 6 hours; evening conference with BP on Ulster Chemicals..."

T-1 gave the FBI copies of two address books; one was Abe's personal listing which he kept in his desk and the other, the business directory which I stored in my desk. Neither had any revealing information.

T-1 also furnished information about Brothman's planned business trip to Switzerland, projected for the summer of 1950. It included a copy of a letter he had written to the Passport Division of the State Department in which he offered standard verification of his need to travel.

On May 22, 1950, coincidentally the day before Harry Gold was officially arrested, the Bureau's agent, John M. Collins and his associate interviewed Brothman and he told them himself he was planning to make a business trip. On June 16, 1950 he was re-interviewed and again he told the agents he was planning to travel.

Brothman never knew that the young engineer whom he had accepted as an intern was an FBI informant. Brothman had been approached three years earlier, in 1947, by a New York engineering firm to allow the scion of one of their foreign clients to work with him to learn the process engineering business. The young man was a recent graduate mechanical engineer, heir to a large chemical conglomerate in India, and eager to serve at any task. Brothman looked on him as a younger brother and a friend. During this period Brothman wrote two technical articles which were published in an engineering journal. He shared authorship with the young man because he wanted to give the fledgling's career a boost.

Again, Abe Brothman had misplaced his trust. He also never made that last trip to Switzerland. The contract, the work on which he had spent two intensive years, was cancelled in the wake of his arrest, his ensuing notoriety and, of course, his conviction.

Neither Abe nor I had taken the stand in our defense. We knew that the prosecution would have focused on our relationship and I, particularly, would have been the object of savage interrogation. Roy Cohn himself had hoped to uncover evidence of "moral turpitude" on our part, and had inspired FBI Director J. Edgar Hoover to send the American Legal Attaché in London to search the Swiss hotel records to determine if we had "cohabited" when we were there on business in 1947. For all that expensive effort they learned nothing incriminating about us; Abe and I had registered in separate rooms.[2] Nevertheless, Saypol and Cohn would have strayed far from the legal charge against us; they would have turned the trial into a frenzied exposé of sex and scandal and would have spun the heads of the jurors and the media with prurient entertainment. *EVEN WORSE, HAD I TAKEN THE STAND ETc*

There was also the question of our old political ties. I had been a member, briefly, of the Communist Party. Brothman had been a member of the Young Communist League as a teenager in the nineteen-twenties. The trial in 1950 would have become a syllogistic phantasmagoria: (1) we were communists; (2) all communists are spies; (3) ergo, we were spies.

We also believed in the American system of justice even as it was practiced in the hysteria of 1950. To secure a conviction the prosecution had to prove guilt; the onus was not on us, the defendants, to prove innocence. This, the Presumption of Innocence, is the bedrock of American law. But we were incredibly naïve; we never realized that the temper of the times, the overwrought, hysteria-driven notoriety, and the willingness of a poorly informed public and a naïve jury to believe what the prosecution and the media told them would drown us in preconceived guilt. Worse yet, we were trapped in a deadly game in which we were merely pawns; we *had* to fall. The judge and the prosecution team in our trial would be the same who would try and prosecute Ethel and Julius Rosenberg, and Morton Sobell four months after our trial. To assure a conviction in that case, it was imperative that the prosecution establish the credibility of Elizabeth Bentley and Harry Gold since they would also testify against the Rosenbergs. With our conviction, they became unimpeachable witnesses.

Also, perhaps decisively important: in the deliberately cultivated hysteria surrounding the Brothman/Moskowitz case, with the infamous, misleading publicity the prosecution fed to an eager coterie of news gatherers, it never became understood – and no investigative journalist ever poked around to pick it up – that had I not been indicted I would have been able to testify as a defense witness for Abraham Brothman to counter Gold's fabrications. But in charging me with a felonious crime, a slick, pre-emptive action, the prosecution rendered me useless as a defense witness for Brothman. My conviction, of course, secured that situation for the prosecution.

The same sly, crafty and deceptive prosecution maneuver was true in the case involving Oscar Vago. He, too, would have been able to refute Gold, but Vago, in gross abrogation of his civil rights, was held in jail for almost two years and never brought to court for a hearing or a trial until after the Brothman/Moskowitz and the Rosenberg/Sobell trials were disposed of. The testimonies of Harry Gold and Elizabeth Bentley remained enshrined as truth and forever unchallenged while we were all convicted.

While held in the New York jail, Abe had become friendly with a father and son who were being prosecuted for tax fraud and who were incarcerated there also. The pair owned several businesses, including a factory which produced machine parts. Their business was being run by their own appointed proxy during their incarceration. The flamboyant and incendiary press releases fired out of the sanctuaries of FBI chief J. Edgar Hoover and Prosecutor Irving Saypol had endowed Abe Brothman with an aura of limitless technical expertise. It was part of their campaign to paint him as a technological benefactor of the Soviet Union; if he did not actually give that country exotic military information, Saypol implied that he *could* have.

The curiosity of the father and the son were heightened by the outlandish nonsense they read each day in the newspapers. They needed a chief engineer in their business and looked on Abe with great interest. They proposed an unusual arrangement:

While the three of them: Brothman, father and son were incarcerated, Brothman would function in his free time in prison as their chief engineer. To accomplish this they secured permission for their proxy to visit Brothman regularly in prison for conferences and instructions. They also induced Brothman to assign to them the rights to his most recent patents. In return they paid the legal fees for his appeal, and sent a weekly stipend to his family. When he was released from prison he went directly to work for them.

During our jail sojourn I received letters from him which reflected his optimism about ultimate vindication and our future. One of them opened a window into an aspect of his thinking that his persecutors would never have understood. On January 1, 1951 he wrote cheerfully about what he thought the New Year would bring, and after the personal remarks he added:

"...You will remember my recent concern with the Riccian Lemma. And you will also recall the extensions of it that I was contemplating. Well, I've made a list of the possible extensions some of which will demand the development of methods and theorems to accomplish the extensions. It adds up to a thesis with applications to cosmic and atomic space, to the motion of bodies under a variety of force-fields, constant-strength and constantly shifting strength force-fields. Perhaps, at last, the resolution of the dualism of matter—the topic with which I first plagued you! So it adds up to this: cosmic space...atomic space, the scene of the most restless shifting of behavior that man knows... and all this put together through the matchless grace and beauty of mathematics..."

Elsewhere he wrote that he was planning a book on process equipment design.

Despite all the punishment they had inflicted on him, Brothman's enemies did not have him beaten; he was still thinking and creating and looking ahead to working in ways that would leave all this present misery just a dusty footnote to our lives.

But in 1954 Abe Brothman was called before the McCarthy Committee and refused to give testimony, citing the Fifth Amendment. The event was widely televised and the government harassment continued. Accordingly he changed jobs several times after that, always restricted in the type of work he could seek out. For his own security he avoided assignments that would be tied to government projects.

In matters scientific Abe Brothman was a most rational servant. He was appalled by what he considered to be the substitution of reason by the supernatural that permeated the atmosphere of our case and, later, the Rosenberg trial. In science, he said, there can be no secrets. The atom bomb had been the historical culmination of generations of scientific inquiry and those generations were international in scope.

While the mission to build the bomb was organized under American sponsorship in the United States, the project's scientists were recruited from all over the world. Many were refugees from Nazi-controlled countries. In 1942 a special section of the Army Corps of Engineers under General Leslie R. Groves was established to assume responsibility for developing the atom bomb. The enterprise became known as the Manhattan Project or, more formally, the Manhattan Engineer District—or MED.[3]

The Manhattan Project involved the work of the world's most talented scientists and as each layer of its development took place it built on previous layers, as science always does. Abe thought that any promulgation of the idea that secrets were involved would create an artificial world of mystery around all branches of science. It would proclaim that science belonged only to an intellectual—and perhaps, a political—aristocracy. The ensuing parochialism would discourage a societal participation in rendering judgments about the use of science and the control of nature. A community underinformed about science would also be weakened in its ability to make decisions about using nature wisely. Under such conditions, Brothman thought, democracy could not thrive.

Missing from the implied debate was an understanding of why it fell to the United States to be the first to develop the atom bomb. Not only did it have the unprecedented advantage of being a refuge for an international congregation of world-class scientists, it also had not suffered hostilities on its own soil during the Second World War. American borders had not been violated by the physical havoc generated by war; its people had remained free of disease, it had financial resources no other country could match and it had unlimited access to raw materials. While it was inevitable that the United States would be the first to produce an atomic bomb it was also inevitable that the Soviet Union would not be far behind once it began to rebuild, particularly because the Russians were known to be world leaders in the field of physics.

****

As the FBI built up its file on Abraham Brothman, Hoover and his people first entertained the notion of trying to foist a charge of perjury on him. However, that would have required at least two witness and they had only one—Harry Gold.[4] They understood that I would not be a witness for them when they questioned me (before and after the trial) – and I was not cooperative. They then went to a charge of conspiracy to obstruct justice and succeeded in getting Brothman convicted on two counts. However, the five-year count was overturned on appeal because it had been brought in the wrong venue. After Brothman served his two years and was free, the FBI's legal mechanics sought to have the venue defect corrected but the statute of limitations had run.[5] As a result, Brothman served only the two years on one count, paid a fine of $10,000 and thought he was free now to rebuild his life and somehow reclaim his profession. Like an institutional Javert, Hoover and his people had other plans for him.

Even before the trial the FBI had contemplated launching a more serious charge against Abraham Brothman, that of conspiracy to commit espionage based on his having turned over a report on the manufacture of Buna-S rubber to Harry Gold. It was a report he had written about work he himself had done.[6] And as the trial revealed, it was also not a secret process. Nevertheless, to justify their crusade the FBI interviewed all the companies Brothman had worked for. Those sources each told the Bureau that Brothman had engaged "…in strictly commercial type research… and had no access to confidential, restricted, secret or other government contracts." The FBI's file concludes: "Data by Brothman not susceptible to espionage."[7]

But FBI Director Hoover was obsessed with draping a spy charge on Brothman.[8] If he had succeeded it would have lent validity and enhanced prestige to his shrill claim that the FBI was closing in on the trail of other spies after the arrest of Julius and Ethel Rosenberg. It would also have appeared to justify the public hysteria he had created that the FBI was about to capture additional members of what he called the "Rosenberg Spy Ring" which, of course, never happened. But the Bureau leader was appallingly ignorant of American technological developments. He also willfully ignored reality in his feverish chase to find non-existent atom bomb spies – or spies of any other kind. Not Buna-S, *not any other project Brothman had worked on was secret or restricted.*

In this instance, at least, more sensible thinking prevailed. On July 31, 1950 James M. McInerney, then an Assistant Attorney General, told Hoover that such a conspiracy would have to involve an illegal agreement to transmit information relating to the national defense to a foreign government in time of war with a specific intent defined by the statute. He concluded: "It does not appear... that there is evidence on this point."[9]

So that thrust died for Hoover. Nevertheless, the FBI maintained Brothman's name on their Security Index until December 1965 when the Justice Department told the Bureau to remove it.[10] Not to be thwarted, the FBI then listed Brothman on Section A of the Reserve Index "... inasmuch as he is in a position as an engineer to influence others against the national interest."[11]

They also noted:

"Subject on occasions of previous interviews by Bureau agents failed to express a willingness to discuss circumstances of his known past activities as a Soviet espionage agent and there is no information available to indicate that he has adopted a cooperative attitude towards the Bureau."[12] (What were those *"known past activities"*? They did not specify.)

In March 1973 – twenty-three years after his conviction for conspiracy to obstruct justice – the FBI reviewed its file on Abraham Brothman and concluded that although he was "...not a member or a participant in activities of revolutionary organizations, or is considered an activist in affiliated fronts, he has exhibited a revolutionary ideaology (sic) and is likely to seize upon the opportunity presented by a National Emergency to commit espionage..." (The FBI did not specify why he was *"likely ...to commit espionage."*)

They recommended that Brothman's name now be included in ADEX, Category III, instead of on the Reserve Index-A.[13] It was not until November 8, 1974 that they finally closed out the Brothman file.[14]

Abraham Brothman had first come to the FBI's attention in November 1945 when Elizabeth Bentley turned his name over to them. As a result, they instituted a mail cover,[15] tapped his telephone—illegally[16]—surveilled his comings and goings and sought informants for more information about him. What they learned was an indefensible waste of manpower and taxpayer's money; it generated only voluminous reports on Brothman's legitimate business activities which obviously no one in the FBI bothered to understand. So, for twenty-nine years the Bureau hounded and harassed Abe Brothman as (1) "likely" to commit acts of espionage because (2) of "known past activities"—never specified; and (3) because his ideology—*his thoughts*— were suspect. And this was done despite advice from a ranking Justice Department official that Brothman could not be tied to espionage.

A word about the Security Index and how it illustrates Hoover's methods. In 1939, Hoover, without any authorization, had begun compiling a list of politically suspect Americans to be rounded up during a national emergency. Termed the Custodial Detention Index, the criterion for listing was not a person's conduct; but *anticipated* conduct. Hoover's project had no congressional or executive mandate and it caused concern that it endangered constitutional liberties.[17]

When the United States entered World War II then Attorney General Francis Biddle authorized the detention of German and Italian aliens who were considered dangerous. (The detention of Japanese aliens and Japanese Americans had been accomplished earlier by executive order.) Biddle did not authorize the detention of "Communist" aliens because by then the Soviet Union was an ally in the war. He also did not consider prosecuting American citizens listed as communists in the Custodial Detention Index.[18]

In July 1943 Biddle ordered Hoover to discontinue the Custodial Detention list, among other things finding its "classification system is inherently unreliable." He also stipulated that the files (which the FBI had already developed) be stamped unreliable.[19]

In a deft sleight of hand Hoover appeared to comply with the order, dropping the original identification, "Custodial Detention List" and changing its name to "Security Index." Fearing that his duplicity would be discovered, he admonished the FBI staff that the renamed list remain strictly confidential within the Bureau.[20]

He was lucky; he acquired a soul mate. In August 1948, Biddle's successor, Attorney General Tom Clark, authorized a secret directive to maintain the Security Index program.[21] Clark had intentionally not sought legislative authorization, opting instead for a strategy of seeking *ex post facto* congressional authorization whenever (or if) that might become necessary.[22]

In September 1950 Congress passed the Internal Security Act (the McCarran Act) under which "subversive" citizens would be subject to detention. (As noted, Congress was not aware that the FBI had already set up such a list.) Because the provisions were less stringent than the standards Clark had secretly instituted two years earlier[23] then Attorney General J. M. McGrath decided that the detention lists would continue to be based on the Bureau's Security Index program which Clark had authorized in 1948.[24]

In September 1971, when Congress repealed the McCarran Act's preventive detention provision, Attorney General John Mitchell authorized Hoover to continue listing individuals for preventive detention, now changing the list's name from "Security Index" to "Administrative Index."[25]

Thus, Brothman's name was carried on the Security Index and ultimately on the Administrative Index ("Adex") for more than twenty years after his release from prison and years after his usefulness to the FBI had been exhausted. He was unremittingly subjected to and continued to endure this harassment which seriously limited his ability to earn a living while it shrank the boundaries of his professional career.

Abraham Brothman died of a stroke in December 1980 at the age of sixty-seven. His life had begun full of promise but it was brought to an unproductive, even premature end by an unstable woman and a very frightened little man. Both of them, one a vindictive liar and the other a fantasist and, in his lucid moments, a fake and a fraud, willingly let themselves be used by amoral, ambitious toads employing subterfuge and legal tricks, with the assistance of an out-of-control FBI. Their victims had no real way to defend themselves. In this most cynical of ages they turned Abraham Brothman into just another of their stepping stones.

He had sinned but his sins were personal. Nevertheless, and contrary to the maniacal accusations, Abraham Brothman was not a spy and never trafficked in espionage.

Chapter 24

Enter Venona

In July 1995 Venona burst upon the fading Cold War scene to reopen old arguments. It was the Central Intelligence Agency's release to the public of the first group of decryptions and translations of coded cable messages said to have been sent from Soviet embassies in the United States to Moscow beginning in the late-1930s. The Army's Signal Security Agency was credited with having originally picked up and decoded those messages. The work continued under the aegis of the National Security Agency and its partners in the intelligence community: the FBI, the CIA, and British Intelligence, and it was given the arbitrary code name, "VENONA."[1]

In 1996 NSA released additional translations making a total of about 2,900. Some of them appeared to be about routine embassy business. Many had critical decryption gaps, fragmented translations and admitted guesswork by the decryptors or translators in their efforts to make sense out of the material. Nonetheless, the Venona sponsors were able to identify certain Americans who, they said, had passed unauthorized information to the USSR during the nineteen-forties and it constituted a presumptive picture of successful espionage against the United States.

If one can put aside a number of questions these disclosures raise (including the possibility that the Federal Bureau of Investigation had a proprietary interest in establishing Venona's authenticity) they appear to validate information which the FBI had made public through the accusations of confessed spy-couriers Elizabeth Bentley and Harry Gold, among others.

So, while I am not mentioned in the Venona files my co-defendant, Abraham Brothman, is identified in footnotes to two of them under cover names, "Constructor" and "Expert."[2] (Venona does not indicate how the identifications were determined or when they were made, leaving unanswered the extent to which they were colored by Bentley's revelations in November 1945. This is pertinent because the first Venona message was decoded in 1946, *after* Bentley's revelations.)[3]

Harry Gold, who was not named by Bentley, is identified by the cover names, "Arno," "Gus," and "Goose."[4] Even if the two Venona files that are said to be about Brothman and Gold are correct in their identifications, they reveal no interdicted behavior by Brothman. One refers to Gold's gossip about Brothman's job problems and mentions the progress of his work on "Aerosol and DDT." The other lists a change of cover name for Gold.

Neither file indicates a direct contact between Brothman and the Soviet station. (One should keep in mind, in reading these Venona files, that before May 1946, when Brothman hired Gold, he was unaware of Gold's true identity—Brothman knew Gold as "Frank Kessler," as Gold had testified under oath.)

Nevertheless, on the basis of this material, speculations and distortions have proliferated into unsupported allegations by some writers exploiting the topic of Soviet espionage. All of it reflects a full-blown attempt to confirm the FBI's original but never substantiated accusations against Brothman. For instance in *Venona, Decoding Soviet Espionage in America*, Haynes and Klehr have this to say: "Brothman ... originally started spying for the Soviets when he worked for Republic Steel, supplying blueprints and documents on industrial processes."[5]

Brothman never worked for Republic Steel. In 1938 he set up his own corporate entity, Republic Chemical Machinery Co. and under that name he designed a chemical plant for Colgate-Palmolive Peet Co. to produce hydrogenated shortening for its consumer market. His company was absorbed by Hendrick Mfg. Co. and Brothman became its chief engineer. Their operations had nothing to do with Republic Steel.

The "blueprints and documents on industrial processes" to which the authors refer is vague and misleading. Part of Brothman's job was to serve as an adjunct to the Hendrick sales department; his income included commissions on sales.[6] Thus, he submitted proposals to a range of prospective clients, among them the Soviet Purchasing Commission (Amtorg). Those proposals included flowsheets – blueprints laying out visually the engineer's conception of the flow of materials in the ultimate design of a chemical plant. Flowsheets usually omit critical processing data, i.e., quantities and rate of feed of start-up chemicals, identification of catalysts, temperature, pressure and other processing conditions, stages and duration of processing and equipment design characteristics. Because they are in blueprint form, flowsheets are impressive and authoritative-looking to a layman but they are merely skeletal pictorials of an engineer's ideas in progress. They are not finished designs.

Brothman submitted such flowsheet blueprints in pursuit of legitimate business, in lieu of suitable printed promotional material which he did not have. None of it contained secret or classified information. The then sales manager of Hendrick testified to the truth of this in Brothman's defense.[7] And because they were not finished designs Harry Gold himself, in his testimony against Brothman, complained that Brothman gave him "fragmentary" (read "incomplete") material time and again which he, Gold, could not pass on to his Soviet handlers.[8] The authors also attribute to Harry Gold the statement that "Brothman had helped to deliver industrial processes to the USSR for producing synthetic rubber and developing industrial aerosols" (*industrial aerosols?*) – and they refer to the two Venona messages (#1390 and #1403) identifying Brothman as one of Gold's sources for espionage.

But in 1941 and again in 1943 Brothman published articles in professional engineering journals in the United States about processes he had developed to manufacture Buna-S (and also Buna-N) synthetic rubber.[9] And while he was giving this so-called secret information, the American government under a Lend-Lease arrangement was furnishing the Soviet Union all the information it needed about Buna-S[10] Furthermore, Gordon Dean, then chairman of the U.S. Atomic Energy Commission, reported that the Soviet Union had developed its own means for producing synthetic rubber some years earlier.[11]

Regarding those "industrial aerosols," (for which information the authors credit Harry Gold, but do not cite when, where, or to whom he said it) this was a hand-held aerosol insecticide device which contained DDT as the main ingredient and Freon as the propellant. It was the forerunner of modern devices now found in kitchen cabinets and on work shelves throughout the world. Brothman had designed the dispenser and the nozzle, and the machine to fill it and he had also developed a continuous process of DDT manufacture. His work was publicized in October, 1944.[12] An "industrial aerosol," whatever that is, it was not. And Gold knew that – he had seen the sample dispensers in the laboratory and in the office and had even borrowed one for use at home. Harry Gold said some silly things in his time but it is impossible to believe he would have compromised his professional reputation by morphing a squirt can into an "industrial aerosol" – and I cannot believe he committed himself to such an idiocy.

There are other errors in Haynes and Klehr's book. We were not convicted of "obstruction of justice for lying to a grand jury," but rather of a *conspiracy* to obstruct justice. There is a vast difference – the former was a misdemeanor; the latter a felony. Nor could I have lied to a grand jury in 1947 before which I never appeared. And if the authors are referring to the 1950 grand jury, I did not reply to any but the most routine questions, nor did Brothman; so we could not have perjured ourselves. At no time was Brothman (or I) accused of espionage although FBI documents, ignoring reality and turning opinion into fact, repeatedly made it appear so in its public statements and files – and always without substantiation. (But it is the rigorous benchmark of historians to acknowledge the difference between opinion and fact and to report accordingly.)

Equally indiscriminately, the authors also characterize Abraham Brothman as having been "a long time KGB asset engaged in industrial espionage."[13] As with the previous statements, no sources are cited, and it, too, is false and contradicts the record.

During the trial defense attorney William Kleinman produced a number of Brothman's published technical articles in American professional journals which he had subpoenaed from the New York Public Library. These documents proved that the information disclosed in the blueprints which Bentley and Gold had said Brothman gave them to transmit to the Soviet Union was publicly available and not secret.[14] Judge Kaufman denied the attorney's request to admit them as evidence because, he said, it was not material. "Secrecy as I see it is not an issue," he stated.[15] He reminded the prosecution that "...the Government does not contend that any of these matters...were of a secret nature..."[16] In his charge to the jury and ever on guard to protect his case against a successful appeal, Kaufman elaborated:

> *"There is no claim made in this indictment that Abraham Brothman engaged in espionage. It is not charged here that the material transmitted was of an illegal nature or that it was secret or that it could not have been found in textbooks or magazines on engineering or chemistry."[17]*

The record is clear: Brothman did not traffic in secrets nor was he charged with that. Indeed, "KGB asset" has a sinister, espionage-tainted ring. By calling Brothman a "KGB" asset, Haynes and Klahr appear to transform Brothman's legitimate attempt to market industrial processes to the U.S.S.R. into espionage. Lacking facts to substantiate any illegal or traitorous behavior by Brothman, these writers spin accusations with seeming disregard for the truth and without attribution to the source of their (mis)information.

So, eight errors about Brothman appear in this book in less than a half-page of text, and other than the meager material the authors gleaned from Venona they do not cite sources, But all the original information in the FBI files came from Elizabeth Bentley and Harry Gold,. More significantly, the voluminous FBI material I studied revealed no evidence that the Bureau ever attempted to verify or substantiate or even question the information it acquired through Bentley and Gold. They simply – and uncritically – copied everything into their files without evaluating it.

Other writers who have also written about Soviet espionage have similarly attributed acts to Brothman which he did not do. A common characteristic of most of these writings is that they are careless and imperceptive retreads of the inaccuracies in the FBI files. Repeatedly ignored is the stubborn and immutable fact that none of Brothman's work was connected with the government or the military, none of it was restricted or secret or classified information, *and all of it was Brothman's own intellectual property.* The trial record confirms that and it is a dishonest rewrite of history to claim otherwise. As Brothman himself ruefully noted to his attorneys during the trial, he could have inserted all this material into a supersize manila envelope, addressed it to "Joe Stalin, c/o the Kremlin" and dropped it off at the nearest post office box – and it would have been perfectly legal.

Leaving aside the awkward question of whether the undiscerning, unverified use of questionable material is actually scholarly historiography, or even reliable reporting, what is one to think of the validity of the FBI communications themselves – or the reliability of whoever their unnamed sources were? What is one to think of the reliability of the origins of such material? Can any of it escape the taint of being a patchwork quilt of guesswork, invention and misinformation stitched together to justify past sins of domestic political chicanery and flawed international diplomacy?

Finally, one addresses the sequence of events involving on the one hand, Harry Gold and his Soviet handlers, and, on the other, the timing of the appearance of Brothman's name in Venona.

In June 1944 the New York embassy of the USSR cabled Moscow, according to Venona, about station business involving Gold (referred to here as "Goose," his code name then). The decryption contains a gap but the end of the paragraph states, "He is wondering why the monthly payment of 100 dollars was discontinued." The reference is inferentially to "Goose."

About three months later Venona discloses again that a request was being made of "…100 dollars a month. Telegraph your decision. We shall advise in detail by post." This file was also not completely decrypted so the reference to who made the request was not spelled out. However, since the subject was "Goose," i.e., Harry Gold, it is again inferential that Gold was once more asking for money.[19]

(Later, Gold would confess to his attorney, Hamilton, after first having denied it, that he had received payment from the Soviets from his first contact with them.[20] Moscow apparently discontinued payments to him some time in 1944 as Venona reflects.)

Next, Venona says that on October 8, 1944 the Soviet embassy in New York wrote Moscow advising that Gold wanted to set up his own chemical laboratory offering as an inducement that it would be a cover for his courier activities. He proposed to work on the practical applications of the thermal diffusion of gases and thought he could market this to American firms. In December 1944 the embassy sent a follow-up cable regarding Gold's proposed venture – he was now requesting a subsidy of $2000 for the laboratory. They were wary of the project and it apparently died.[21]

Brothman's name first appears in the Venona files in October, 1944 about the same time as his insecticide device was being publicized in an American engineering journal. It also coincides with the moment when Gold reiterates a request for the reinstatement of the $100 monthly payments and when he seeks approval to set up a laboratory – with station funding.

If one accepts the Venona files for what they purport to be, it is persuasive that Gold was hawking Brothman's name to his Soviet friends to score points, first to justify the monthly payments he wanted restored and second, to win the station's financing for his laboratory. In return he was volunteering engineering inducements from Brothman, a *quid pro quo,* but about which Brothman could not have been aware since he did not know Gold's true name or identity then. Under oath, Gold had testified:

> "Brothman at that time (November 1942) knew me by two names. One, Frank Kessler, which I had told him was my true name. The other, Harry Gold, I had given him as a name of a friend of mine which he could use as a telegraph drop in case he ever had to get in touch with me."[22]

(Gold later explained the subterfuge to Brothman: he did not want his employer in Philadelphia to know he was moonlighting on a second job.)

Gold's testimony also confirms that Brothman did not learn Gold's true name and identity until several years later:

> "When I came to work for him (May 1946) and not until I came to work for him, I asked him 'What do you think my true name is?' And he said, 'Frank Kessler.' I said, 'No, it is Harry Gold.'"[23]

Defense attorney Kleinman asked Gold about the lies he had told Brothman, among them about his non-existent family and his brother who, he said, had been killed during World War II but who was actually alive. He asked if those lies among many others continued until the FBI first interrogated him in May 1947. Gold's reply: "They continued until the FBI spoke to me... in (May) 1947."

It was not until then, Gold testified, that he first told Brothman that there was no truth to his stories.[24]

With respect to Brothman, the Venona files adds nothing to the facts. They served simply as a source of baseless innuendos.

Part VI

A Confluence Of Toads

Who Benefited?

Those who rend their garments to confess grievous sins, theirs and others, real or counterfeit, and those whose careers, and perhaps their lives, depend on such confessions, develop a mutuality of interests. Elizabeth Bentley and Harry Gold were instruments employed by an ambitious judge, overzealous prosecutors and an FBI whose interests were furthered by finding Abraham Brothman and Miriam Moskowitz guilty of conspiring to obstruct justice in the context of atomic espionage – and thus involving deadly secrets.

The accusations were false and all parties knew it.

One views the accusers and their mentors and the judge who made all things possible for them, as symbiotic toads. Let us examine how they benefited.

Chapter 25

Elizabeth Bentley

"As the S.S.Vulcania sailed into New York Harbor that July day in 1934, I leaned on the deck rail and looked at the skyline wistfully. It was good to be back in my own country after a year's study in Italy, I thought, and yet what, really, was I coming back to? I had no home, no family. Nor was there much prospect of finding a teaching position. From all that I had heard abroad, the economic situation in the United States had not greatly improved. True, I still had some money left from my father's estate but that would not last too long. Somehow I must find a way to earn my living. Standing there on the deck, I felt alone and frightened."[1]

So began the saga of Elizabeth Terrill Bentley in her 1951 autobiography *Out of Bondage*. She was twenty-six years old when she returned from Italy; she was forty-three when she wrote those words.

Bentley's father, Charles Prentiss Bentley, had been a newspaper editor and department store manager.[2] Her mother, Mary Burrill,[3] had been a school teacher. Elizabeth was born in New Milford, Connecticut on January 1, 1908 and said of her childhood that it was an "overly stern, old-fashioned New England upbringing."

In 1915, and for the next eight years, the family moved several times because of the father's employment. Elizabeth graduated high school in Rochester, New York and in 1930 obtained a bachelor's degree in English from Vassar College. She taught at the Foxcroft School in Middlebury, Virginia for two years, and then went to New York in July 1934. Unable to find a teaching job she enrolled at what she said was, "Columbia University business school" to learn shorthand and typing.[4] (She testified at the Brothman/Moskowitz trial that she obtained a master's degree from Columbia University in 1935, but her dates appear to be in conflict.)

Bentleys account of her college years reveal small deceits that shade reality in her favor and foreshadow, perhaps, the more serious distortions she would ultimately live by and swear to. In 1988, Hayden Peak, then an adjunct professor at the Joint Military Intelligence College in Washington, D.C., wrote an Afterword to a reissue of *Out of Bondage*. In it he reveals that Bentley told a Subcommittee in 1948 that at Vassar she had been a member of a political association as well as the French Club and the Italian Club. However, Peake found no mention in the Vassar College yearbook of

Bentley's having been in any club or part of any extracurricular activity.[5]

As Bentley's career as a creative informant flowered, she willy-nilly cast suspicion on earlier acquaintances. In her book she mentioned her former Vassar College dramatics teacher, Helen ("Hallie") Flanagan, a much respected dramatics coach who was later involved in the commercial theater. Flanagan left Vassar to become director of the Federal Theater Project from 1935 to 1939 as part of Roosevelt's New Deal program during the Depression. (She served ultimately as dean of Smith College.) Bentley recalled Flanagan's enthusiasm for the new society emerging in Russia in the nineteen-twenties. Some thirty years later, in 1952, when FBI Agent Kennelly asked her if Hallie Flanagan had been a communist Bentley admitted she did not know but added, gratuitously, "....all her ideas pointed that way."[6]

Bentley wrote that in her loneliness she became friends with a nurse she met at Columbia and in March 1935, through her new friend, joined the Communist Party.[7] For the next three years she was also a member of and active in the American League Against War and Fascism while holding several short term jobs. She had begun her career as a teacher, then became an investigator for the New York City Emergency Home Relief Bureau for a few months After that she worked for a year as a saleslady at Macy's, did some translating work, was a children's camp counselor and worked at the magazine, Consumers Union. She described that journal as having been set up by striking "left-wing" employees of the old Consumers Research.[8]

Bentley also worked as a researcher, a secretary and a general office worker. On cross-examination at our trial she added that she had been employed briefly by the Charles William Paper Company, by an accounting firm, and by St. John's Guild among other organizations. All her jobs appeared to have been temporary.[9]

In early July of 1938 Bentley obtained a secretarial job through the Columbia placement bureau, with the Italian Information Library. When she realized it was a propaganda outlet for the Italian fascist government, she voluntarily went to the Communist Party headquarters in Manhattan to offer her services as an informant. She met with a Mr. F. Brown who encouraged her to collect whatever information she could but who did not seem to have time for her subsequently. Ultimately she was turned over to Jacob Golos and worked with him for several years thereafter. She brought him copies of correspondence, propaganda and other materials.[10]

As with her other employment, Bentley's Italian Library job was also proving temporary. "By early spring, 1939," she wrote, "my days with the Italian Library of Information were running out. The director had somehow stumbled over an anti-Fascist article that I had written for the *Columbia Spectator* back in (October) 1935. He flung it angrily on my desk and asked me what I was doing in the Library if I had such violent objections to

Fascism. So I was not surprised when I was told my services were no longer needed."[11]

Well, not quite. The October 1935 issues of the *Spectator* printed no article by Elizabeth Bentley. On October 17, 1935 it did, however, feature a story: "Columbia Student Refused Loan, Charges Discrimination by Officials at Casa Italiana." In that article Bentley charged that Casa Italiana might have been motivated to discriminate against her application for a loan because she was affiliated with the American League Against War and Fascism. The article also mentioned that Bentley said she had criticized the fascist system of education while in Italy.[12]

Bentley's inconsistencies abound. In 1951, about the time that her book was being readied for publication (in which she made much of her anti-fascist stance) she was also testifying at the William W. Remington trial. Under cross-examination, she admitted that while in Italy in 1933-34 she had belonged to a fascist student group at the University of Florence.[13] The question then arises: Did Miss Bentley lie when she said she had to leave her Italian Library job in 1939 because she had written an anti-fascist article four years earlier (for which no supporting evidence could be found) or did she lie when she testified under oath that she had joined a fascist group in Italy in 1933-34? Juxtaposed, the two statements are not reconcilable.

The undercurrent of Elizabeth Bentley's story, not only as she revealed it in her book but as disclosed during her interrogations by the FBI, by various Congressional committees and by researchers, is that of a lonely life of unremitting financial stress and emotional insecurity.[14] It is apparent that she never quite connected with the mainstream of her social group. Her New England middle class background and her first-rate education would have been expected to bring her social if not financial advantages but these apparently never materialized, despite that in the late nineteen twenties and early thirties it was uncommon for a woman to have acquired a quality education such as she had.

Bentley's situation improved markedly when she began to work for Jacob Golos in 1938.[15] Golos ran World Tourists, a travel agency promoting tourism and shipping to the Soviet Union.[16] He was, Bentley said, a high ranking member of the Communist Party of the U.S.A. and a former member of the Soviet secret police.[17]

In 1939 the Department of Justice indicted Earl Browder, then the American Communist Party leader, for passport fraud, and Jacob Golos for failure to register his firm under the Foreign Agents Registration Act. Golos pleaded guilty and received a suspended sentence.[18] Browder went to prison, but President Roosevelt freed him in 1942 "in the interest of inter-allied relations."[19]

As the business of World Tourists declined Golos, in 1941, set up a separate corporate affiliate, U. S. Service and Shipping Corp. to handle all passenger and freight traffic between the United States and the Soviet Union. John Hazard Reynolds, an independently wealthy banker and longtime friend of Golos' was named president and treasurer. Bentley was made vice-president and secretary. The new corporation, said Bentley, would be an American corporation run by Americans, not Russians.[20]

Start-up funds for the new company consisted of $20,000; $15,000 from the Communist Party through Earl Browder, and $5,000 from Reynolds himself. Between them Reynolds and Bentley held all the stock. They worked closely with Golos and World Tourists, regularly dealing with the Russian travel regulatory agency, Intourist, as well as with the State Bank in Moscow and the Russian diplomatic staffs in New York and Washington. They also had to deal with American regulatory agencies including the Department of Justice.[21]

A year or so after the new enterprise was launched, Reynolds returned to active duty as a lieutenant colonel in the United States Army. In the meantime, Golos' health was deteriorating and Bentley found she was running USSSC almost entirely alone as well as spending half her time at World Tourists.[22] At the same time, according to Bentley, she was also an espionage courier picking up secret information from her Washington contacts for transmittal to the Soviet Union.[23]

In this period she also managed to meet with Abraham Brothman to pick up "industrial information material" (never specified) which he gave her for transmittal to the Soviet Union.[24] Brothman, she said, worked for Republic Steel Co. and she met with him from early summer to the fall of 1940.[25]

Golos died in November 1943 and for a while she continued with her multiple duties. But in late 1944 the Russians decided to take over USSSC and Bentley had to resign as an officer of the company. She stayed on to help her Soviet-selected replacement, Ray Elson, while she waited for an agreement to be signed which would provide that the Russians would buy out her and Reynolds' stock and reimburse Browder for the $15,000 he had invested in behalf of the American Communist Party. She expected that the agreement would provide her with a five-figure severance settlement.

Matters did not go smoothly.[26] Bentley had moved to Connecticut without arriving at a severance settlement. She refused to return her stock, quarreled with Elson[27] and was having "considerable difficulties" with her Soviet contact, Anatoli Gromov, an official at the Washington Embassy. In late 1944 Gromov made "repeated requests" that she reach a settlement with USSSC, among other matters.[28] Meanwhile, representatives of the Communist Party's finance department were trying to get her to return the money which Browder had given for the start-up and were insinuating that Bentley had "walked off with the money."[29]

On September 15, 1945 Bentley returned to New York, rejoined the firm, helped push Elson out, and reverted to her former position as head of

USSSC.[30] But this was temporary and her situation continued to deteriorate.

When Gromov ordered her to close out her activities he indicated he had plans to pick up her contacts. Those plans, however, did not include continuing her services until a later, unspecified and indefinite time.[31] She met with Gromov in May 1945 and he subsequently offered her various gifts. In October 1945 he handed her $2,000 saying it was part of her salary.[32] At Bentley's last meeting with Gromov on November 21, 1945 she was, by prearrangement, surveilled by the FBI since she had become an FBI informant.[33] But there were several serious inconsistencies in the litany she recited to the FBI.

First, Brothman never worked for Republic Steel Co. In 1938 he had set up his own company, Republic Chemical Machinery Co., to design and market chemical equipment. Republic was absorbed by Hendrick Manufacturing Co. and Brothman became their chief engineer. Neither Hendrick nor Brothman had anything to do with Republic Steel.[34] FBI files substantiate this and it becomes convincing that when Bentley did not know facts she improvised. She also said that Brothman worked in Pittsburgh (for Republic Steel) when he worked in New York City for Republic Chemical. She also reported that he lived in Nassau County, New York when he actually lived in Sunnyside, Queens.[35]

J. Edgar Hoover himself admitted that Bentley "erred" when she referred to Republic Steel.[36]

Bentley's story of how she decided to go to the FBI is even more convoluted. As revealed in the FBI files but never mentioned in her autobiography, *Out of Bondage*, Bentley had had a romantic encounter with a Lieutenant Peter Heller in the spring of 1945. Heller had told her that he was a member of the New York National Guard.[37] After several months Heller abruptly dropped out of her life. On August 21, 1945 Bentley visited the New Haven office of the FBI to inquire about her mystery man. She visited them again for the same purpose on August 29. Both times the agents told her they did not know a Lieutenant Peter Heller and they gave her no advice.[38] Agent Roger F. Gleason reported on her visit:

> "Miss Bentley advised that she has seen Heller frequently since the original meeting and that his actions have mystified her in that he claims that he is a government investigator and at various times has described himself as a 'big shot Government spy.' He has told Miss Bentley that even though he would wish to, he cannot reveal his address even to her as his work is very dangerous…"

Bentley also said that she had told Heller she was contemplating leaving USSSC, but Heller advised that she remain with the firm so that she could obtain information for the government:

"To date he has not requested her to do anything specific... Miss Bentley related that if the man was legitimate and if she could be of any assistance to the Government she would be glad to do so, but that she was personally mystified as to how this could be accomplished."[39]

New Haven subsequently wrote the FBI's New York office about the Bentley/Heller story. According to Peake, in that letter Special Agent Jack Danahy said that Bentley had picked up Heller in the bar of the St. George Hotel[40] in New York City where she was staying. The next morning she noticed a shield in his wallet but could not tell what agency had issued it. Danahy thought that this caused her to believe she was being surveilled and she went to the New Haven FBI shortly thereafter. Danahy also said that Heller was a New York City probation officer, not a New York State National Guard officer.[41]

Apparently unsatisfied with her inability to learn more about the vanished Peter Heller and perhaps to ascertain if she was, in fact, being surveilled, Bentley wrote the New York Field Office of the FBI and then visited them on October 16, 1945. But this visit was "specifically for the purpose of furnishing information in connection with an impersonation complaint made by her concerning Lieutenant Peter Heller." She said she was also not sure whether he was a government investigator or was connected with the Communist Party or Russian espionage activity and was trying to test her loyalty towards the Party.[42]

At this meeting she gave indications that she had information about possible Russian espionage but gave no real information and did not tell the agents she expected to meet with Anatoli Gromov the very next day. She was, of course, still running USSSC and collecting a salary from them. She left her number with the FBI.[43]

Sensing that Bentley had something to tell the FBI Special Agent Buckley of the New York office made several attempts to reach her by telephone. He finally succeeded on November 6, 1945 and urged her to come in to their office. However, Bentley told him "she was upset and had a great deal on her mind" and she was undecided whether she should reveal her information. Agent Buckley explained to her that "if she had any information regarding un-American activities this Bureau should know about same and that if she allowed Agent Buckley to speak with her he could possibly offer her some assistance..."[44]

Bentley's appearance at the New York office of the FBI the next day, November 7, initiated her long career as an informant. She told the agents that she was being threatened by representatives of the Communist Party who were demanding that she return the $15,000 the Party had invested in U. S. Service and Shipping Corp. through Earl Browder. She also said she was afraid of the Soviet representatives with whom she was dealing "and whose true identities she professes not to know." She spoke of her dealings with the Russians but "the information was vague and non-specific..."[45]

Throughout November 1945 Elizabeth Bentley met with the FBI agents on fifteen separate times and on November 30 she signed a statement which reduced to writing all that she had told them.[46] They continued to question her for several months after that and it was not until January or February of 1946, she said, that she finally finished telling what she called the "whole story" – a story in which she named 150 persons she had known, or known of.

When our defense attorney cross-examined Bentley, however, she implied that her visit to the FBI in August 1945 concerned her spying confession, not the missing Heller, and as the Gromov affair was also to indicate, Bentley's believability was often questionable. In testimony before a congressional committee in the summer of 1948, Miss Bentley said that when she met with Anatoli Gromov on October 17, 1945 it was with the FBI's agreement and guidance that she had taken the $2000 from him.[47] However, FBI memoranda of July 28, 1955 reveal that the records failed to show that, as of October 16, 1945, the FBI had any knowledge of a forthcoming meeting between Bentley and Gromov.[48] FBI records do show that she told them about the Gromov meeting on November 16, a month after the fact, and on that day she turned over to them the $2000 she had received from Gromov.[49]

Reference to two other individuals against whom Ms. Bentley testified, can throw some light on her credibility. We turn to the cases of William W. Remington and William Henry Taylor.

At the end of July 1948 Bentley testified before a congressional committee about Remington. By now Bentley's role had become emblazoned on the front pages of newspapers across the country and was pivotal in a number of other cases involving government employees.

William Walter Remington was a Dartmouth College honors graduate who obtained a Master's degree in economics from Columbia University in 1940. He followed that by an auspicious career as an economist in various agencies of the New Deal government. In 1948 he joined the Department of Commerce.[50] But in 1945 and again in 1947 Elizabeth Bentley named Remington before a Federal grand jury as one of her sources for restricted government information saying she knew him to be a Communist. The grand jury returned no indictments. Thereupon she repeated the charges publicly (in July 1948) before a Senate subcommittee. Remington replied that he had indeed met Bentley and had given her unclassified information in 1942 and 1943 but claimed he had known her as a newspaperwoman doing research and treated her as he would have any other member of the press.

Bentley's charges coincided with the beginning of President Truman's

Phantom Spies, Phantom Justice

Loyalty Program and so, on September 28, 1948, the Commerce Department dismissed Remington, which dismissal he appealed. Earlier, on September 11, Bentley had repeated her charges on a radio program. Remington sued for libel and the network and the program's sponsor settled a judgment out of court. Thereupon, on February 10, 1949 the Loyalty Review Board ordered Remington reinstated.

Subsequently, during congressional hearings in April 1950, two former communists claimed that Remington had been a Communist Party member in 1937 when he was a Dartmouth undergraduate. Again, the Commerce Department dismissed him and on June 8, 1950 a federal grand jury indicted him on one count of perjury, his denial of Communist Party membership. In a trial lasting from December 26, 1950 to February 7, 1951 Remington was convicted. His conviction was based on the prior grand jury testimony of the government's witness, Remington's former wife, Ann Moos Remington, from whom he was divorced in 1949. But the grand jury hearing revealed that Ann Remington had changed her original testimony to remarks that were now crucial to conviction, after having been subjected to savage, frightening pressure in the grand jury hearing by the foreman of that jury, John Brunini. Among other things, he had threatened Mrs. Remington with a contempt citation and prison, and improperly told her she had no privilege to refuse to testify.[51]

Other peculiarities tainted this case. Bentley had been in the midst of writing her book, *Out of Bondage* purporting to be an expose of Communism and spies in America, at the same time that the Remington grand jury hearings were occurring. Remington figured prominently in her book. Clearly, the Remington indictment would be beneficial to marketing the book. Also, Brunini, the grand jury foreman, was later revealed to have been Bentley's literary assistant for the book. He had signed a contract with her publisher, Devin-Adair, and expected to share in the profits from the book sales.[52] The FBI was concerned, however, that if Brunini's role were known it would have a negative effect on the outcome of the Remington case.[53]

Nevertheless, unknown to Bentley, Remington's attorneys learned about her literary ties to Brunini. When they questioned her on the witness stand she denied such a relationship. After persistent questioning she admitted Brunini had done some editorial work but denied there had been a contract or that he had any financial interest in the book. The defense then produced two of the publisher's employees who testified that there had indeed been a Brunini contract with a promise of a share in the profits of the book sales. Bentley had perjured herself – but Judge Noonan denied the defense motion for a dismissal.[54]

In the meantime, the prosecutor warned Brunini not to accept any fees for his collaboration on the Bentley book. (He was particularly concerned that this would "jeopardize the Brothman case" as well as Remington's, if the information fell into the hands of the defense attorneys in those cases Also strange, was the role of Assistant United States Attorney, Thomas J. Donegan, one of the government prosecutors who, it turned out had also acted as Bentley's personal attorney when she sued her former employer, U. S. Service and Shipping Corp., for back pay.[55]

After Remington's conviction was overturned on appeal, the government, in a surprise and unprecedented move, convened another grand jury on October 19, 1951, some sixteen months after the first indictment. It secured a second indictment against Remington, this for perjury it alleged he had committed during his first trial. It was a novel legal maneuver and Roy Cohn was credited with it.[56] The second trial took place in January 1952 and found Remington guilty. He was sentenced to three years in prison, lost his appeal and began serving his sentence on April 15, 1953.

On November 22, 1954, a few months before his scheduled release, Remington was brutally beaten by two fellow inmates and died two days later. He was thirty-seven years old.

The Taylor case was another of Bentley's spy-naming dramas. But when she named William Henry Taylor, a former Treasury Department economist her credibility took a severe hit. [57]

In 1947 Bentley stated that Taylor had supplied her with secret government information. For the next eight years Taylor was hounded and subjected to ceaseless interrogation by congressional agencies and grand juries, all vying for the same public attention (and public funding). In 1955, when Taylor was working for the International Monetary Fund, his attorney submitted a brief that challenged Bentley's accusations. The brief, filed with the International Organization's Employees Loyalty Board on March 28, listed thirty-seven Bentley misrepresentations. Among them were the following:

1. Bentley had testified to the House UnAmerican Activities Committee that Taylor had traveled to Portugal on a government mission. Taylor had never been to Portugal.

2. Bentley had told a Senate committee in 1951 that "Bill" Taylor had given her government documents. But in a pre-trial hearing for a libel suit (July 26, 1954) Bentley under oath admitted she had never met Taylor.

3. Bentley told the Internal Security subcommittee in 1949 that the Russians were interested in RDX, an explosive. She could not explain what it was or why the Russians were interested it.[58] "...I don't know too much about it; it recently appeared in the papers," she said. The Taylor brief thought she probably lifted the story from the newspapers.[59]

4. She claimed that she and other Russian agents knew the date

of the Allied invasion well in advance. "We knew D-Day long before it happened..." she told the House Committee in 1948. The Taylor brief pointed out that D-Day was a variable date; General Eisenhower did not decide on the date until twenty-four hours before it happened. Even then, the U. S. Military to Moscow kept the Russians fully informed on the date of this invasion.[60]

5. In her book, *Out of Bondage*, she wrote that about June 6, 1944, the spy ring gave her samples of the invasion currency printed for use in liberated Germany, which she transmitted to Russia. (She had earlier set the date as 1945.) Elsewhere (at another time) she placed the time as January 1944, and in testimony before the McCarthy Committee in 1953 she said it was late 1943 or 1944. However, Treasury Department records indicate that the currency was printed by March 27, 1944 and that on April 14, Secretary of the Treasury Morgenthau informed the Russian ambassador that the plates for the currency would be made available to the Soviet Union. There would have been no need for a spy ring to turn over the currency.

The Taylor brief also mentioned Bentley's lies about the $2000 she received from Gromov, referred to above.

Taylor was never indicted on any of Bentley's accusations; but he had been subjected to cruel and merciless harassment because of her irresponsible charges. He would later present his own challenge to her.

The question arises: What motivated Elizabeth Bentley? Was it really the sudden bloom of patriotism she cited in her book? Or did she change sides at this particular moment in her life because she was fearful that she was under surveillance by the FBI and thought to fend off punitive exposure with an anticipatory confession? Her close associate, Jacob Golos (who had died two years earlier) had been indicted for failure to register as a foreign agent and Louis Budenz, a major Communist Party figure who had known her, had recently defected. Did she fear exposure by Budenz and perhaps others who were falling away? And did the Heller incident confirm her suspicions that she was being watched?

The answer may come from the FBI itself.

According to Peake, the FBI "accepted neither her moral guilt nor her Heller story as sufficient explanation for her changing sides." Bentley had told them that "she discontinued her activities in Soviet espionage because all of her contacts were taken over by the Russians and further, because of threats she had received from an officer of the U.S. Communist Party in November 1945 (who) stated if she did not return the $15,000.... that he... would 'blow her to hell.'" It was because of these reasons that she came to the FBI. But the FBI believed that she also feared exposure.[61]

There was yet even another reason, more significant in some ways than the others.

Gromov's news that he was planning to replace her, could have been a severe threat to her sense of financial stability. His plans for her to continue in some other assignment were vague.[62] He also directed her to sever her connections with U.S. Service & Shipping Corp. Thus, she faced the immediate practical problem that she would be out of a job and would have to find a new way to earn a living.

She was thirty-seven years old in 1945. Her academic credentials had been shelved for fifteen years and she was without a marketable work history. Without family or friends, a woman alone without a support network, she once again faced the prospect of being broke, unable perhaps even to pay her rent. She would have remembered the insecurity she had endured during the Depression and been paralyzed with fear.

Did it occur to her then that one way to stave off disaster was to court the FBI? And when she entered the FBI's fold, she continued working for U.S. Service and Shipping, drawing her salary as the firm's head (her sole means of support), meeting almost daily with Bureau agents as well as working with her old Soviet and Communist contacts.[63] The firm began to close down in January 1947 because of government harassment. As a final irony, she sued the firm for severance pay and a Christmas bonus. (The case, in which she was represented by attorney Thomas Donegan, was settled out of court in June 1947.)

Thereafter Bentley found work as a secretary in a succession of temporary jobs. In 1948 she began a lecture tour and on August 28, 1948, appeared on "Meet the Press," a radio program. In the meantime, in July, her story had been published in the *New York World-Telegram*. Soon thereafter she testified before a number of congressional committees.[64] In April 1951, McCall's Magazine announced the serialization of her book. Bentley was now a professional anti-communist and becoming a professional witness. In the latter part of 1948 she took instruction from Monsignor Fulton Sheen and, in November of that year, under the sponsorship of Mr. and Mrs. Louis Budenz, converted to Catholicism.[65] In December 1948, the FBI reported that the *Bridgeport Post*, some months earlier had revealed that Elizabeth Bentley had received treatment at the Institute of Human Relations at Yale University in New Haven. On inquiry, Dr. F. C. Redlich of the Department of Psychiatry was noncommittal and said all information was confidential.[66] In September 1949 Bentley obtained a job teaching political science at Mundelein College in Chicago. She left after one semester.

The personal history of Elizabeth Bentley became characterized by perpetual financial insecurity. In 1951 she received a $3000 advance against royalties for *Out of Bondage*. She spent some of it to buy a house in Connecticut but the rest was quickly dissipated. In March 1951, when she testified at the Rosenberg trial, defense attorney Emanuel Bloch asked her if she was a paid informant. She replied that she was not, but in fact, this was merely a question of timing, involving the $2000 from Gromov and given the FBI in 1945. Bentley had been asking the FBI about the money since the beginning of the Rosenberg trial in January 1951[67] and it was eventually handed over to her in March 1952, a year after the Rosenberg's were sentenced to death. The agents had forwarded Bentley's request to Director Hoover, who had to weigh the delicate question that it could "be considered as espionage money... and in that event... would have to be turned over to the Treasury Department" versus the need to keep Bentley on board. As the same agents who brought up the money's espionage taint noted, Bentley had just recently appeared as a witness in the Brothman case and was scheduled to appear as a witness in the trial of William Remington. Assistant U. S. Attorney Thomas Donegan (who, as noted, had represented Bentley in her salary suit against U. S. Service & Shipping Corp.) recommended that "this matter should remain in 'status quo' until the Remington case has finally been resolved."

In March 1952 Director Hoover approved the payment of $2000, the Remington case (and the Rosenberg case at which she had also testified) having been safely disposed of.[68] Bentley signed a combination receipt and release which said:

> "TO ALL TO WHOM THESE PRESENTS SHALL COME... I, Elizabeth Terrill Bentley...acknowledge receipt on this date of the sum of two thousand dollars... in full payment for any and all services heretofore rendered by me to the Federal Bureau of Investigation...(and) ... I hereby ... remise, release and forever discharge the United States of America, its officials... from any claim which I ever had... relating to services rendered by me to the Federal Bureau of Investigation...[69]

Thereafter, Ms Bentley's behavior became increasingly bizarre. Since she was an important continuing witness for the government in its prosecution of espionage-related trials, her actions caused considerable consternation in FBI ranks and in the office of the United States Attorney for the Southern district of New York.

In May 1952 Bentley was involved in a physical altercation with the caretaker of her Connecticut home. The melee, in which her face was badly bruised and several teeth damaged, caused Cohn and the FBI great concern. To keep the situation from becoming public, they threatened the caretaker with legal action and made him sever his relationship quietly with Bentley.[70]

On August 29, 1952 Bentley was involved in an automobile accident in Connecticut that landed her in jail because she hit another car and did not stop. Cohn somehow quashed the charges and kept the hit-and-run event out of the newspapers. The very next day she had another automobile accident and two weeks later, a third. This time she was injured and her car was wrecked.[71]

Endemically needy, she badgered the FBI for funds. They, in turn, together with prosecutor Cohn, wished to keep her in a "friendly frame of mind,"[72] for her appearances as a witness before the Subversive Activities Control Board and at the Remington trial, as well as other matters Cohn was presenting to the grand jury.[73]

Ultimately, FBI head J. Edgar Hoover agreed to pay Bentley $50 per week for nine weeks,[74] at the same time complaining that the FBI was experiencing more difficulty with Bentley since she became a paid informant *than when she was volunteering her cooperation*.[75] The FBI also paid her $500 for "past services" – noting her valuable witnessing in the Rosenberg trial – and they returned the $2000 Gromov had given her (as noted above,) and which they had intended o turn over to the Treasury Department.[76] Cohn also arranged that she be paid a more generous witness fee in the Remington trial than the Department of Justice usually paid.[77] Meanwhile, the FBI was complaining that Bentley was becoming increasingly unstable and hysterical raising concerns about her dependability.[78]

Other events threatened her peace of mind.

A lawsuit by the IRS for non-payment of taxes was staved off by Cohn who negotiated a favorable settlement for her.[79]

Influential benefactors found her teaching jobs that inevitably ended prematurely. Bentley complained of being ill; was drinking heavily and, to the FBI agents working with her, she appeared to be mentally unstable. They were also concerned that she seemed obsessed about Cohn's having promised her, as she had said repeatedly, a lump sum payment of $1000, which she desperately needed to pay some bills.[80]

Also, she needed a car to get from Connecticut to her doctor in Manhattan and thought Cohn should provide one. (In at least one instance, two FBI agents drove to Connecticut to bring her to an appointment with her doctor in Manhattan.[81]) Ultimately Cohn arranged for her to obtain a rental car for an unspecified period, at no cost to her.[82]

The most threatening event for Bentley, however, came when Harvey Matusow, a former FBI informer who had recanted, testified before the Senate Internal Security Subcommittee in February 1955 that Bentley had confessed to him in October 1952 (just when Brothman was finishing up his two-year prison stint and while the Rosenbergs, in the death house in Sing Sing Prison, were awaiting execution) that she had lied about her espionage contacts, and that she "had to do it because it was the only way she could work."[83] Cohn effectively silenced Matusow with an indictment for perjury. In a quick trial in July 1955 Matusow was convicted and sentenced to five years in prison which sentenced he served.

This did not end Bentley's problems. The Taylor matter was resurfacing and now Taylor was on the offensive. He called for a public hearing before the Senate Internal Security Subcommittee so that he could confront Bentley and have her repeat her charges against him under oath. In the nick of time, it seemed, the Loyalty Board cleared Taylor of disloyalty charges and the suit was abandoned. But Edward Fitzgerald, another of those Bentley had named as one of her espionage contacts, was now bringing suit in the U.S District Court in New York in August 1955 and his attorney planned to examine Bentley under oath. The FBI was able to have the Fitzgerald matter quashed and Bentley was also spared this ordeal.[84]

By 1956 Bentley was no longer headline news. She had shown renewed signs of stress and changed jobs twice. By October 1959 she was teaching at the Long Lane School, a penal institution for young women in Connecticut. No longer owning a house; she was living on the school grounds without even a telephone of her own and she had drifted into obscurity. She died at New Haven Hospital in 1963 after surgery for an abdominal tumor; just days shy of her fifty-sixth birthday. She had no survivors.[85]

Testifying before the Jenner Committee in November 1953, Hoover had said: "All information furnished by Miss Bentley which was susceptible to check has proven to be correct..."

But the Taylor brief proved that much of Miss Bentley's information was incorrect. How efficiently and exhaustively had the FBI checked her stories? The actions of Hoover and his staff were especially reprehensible because, as Peake noted, the FBI "got a good idea of the extent to which Bentley was willing to be flexible with the "truth."[86] They knew she was a liar.

Bentley's descriptions of a Soviet spy ring did not establish that the Soviet Union had acquired highly sensitive military and diplomatic secrets; her testimony was never corroborated and her identified sources held low-level positions in the government.[87] She never produced any document of those she said had given her information nor could she even describe the contents of those materials.[88] For all of her accusations Bentley's stories, alone, never brought about an indictment much less a conviction on the charge of espionage of any of the people she vilified or whose lives she wrecked. But she certainly threw the country into an agonized turmoil and heated up the reckless, frenetic drive to the Cold War.

Chapter 26

Harry Gold

Harry Gold never thought of himself as a spy until the government said he was. Until then he thought of himself as a self-anointed Robin Hood leveling an international political imbalance and helping what had been a valued American ally in World War II to gain information he thought it should have had through normal diplomatic or commercial channels. He knew he would be perceived as disloyal because of the postwar anti-Soviet fervor. Yet it pleased him that he might be enabling the suffering, war-torn Russian people to somehow repair their wounds and live better lives. He had, however, never been a communist and had rejected membership in the Communist Party. So he had testified.

So why did he go full throttle in his shattering confession?

Harry Gold was a simple man. The FBI threatened him with the death penalty and terrified him with the possibility of retribution towards his father and his brother. In that situation, with no one to confide in or to share his fears or to comfort him, he reasoned he would find relief from the FBI's relentless pressure by falling in line with them. A confession would lighten the load of his disabling fears and if he gave the government even more than full measure, things might somehow work out, he thought.

His abject remorse in court at the time of his indictment, and later at his sentencing were the obvious calculations of a frightened man. So, things did work out for him but not quite as he expected.

It was Harry Gold's testimony alone that sent me to prison, testimony that contradicted what he had earlier told the FBI. In June 1950 he told them he discussed nothing in front me; on the witness stand barely five months later he said I knew that he and Abraham Brothman intended to give false testimony to the grand jury in 1947. And because the Brothman/Moskowitz trial resulted in convictions, Gold (and Bentley), just four months afterwards, in March 1951, became unimpeachable witnesses against the Rosenbergs.

On the witness stand Gold testified as a modest, self-effacing sinner undergoing the agony of expiation – in self-important tones and firmly sure of the intricacies of his story. His dramaturgy was frequently in Homeric detail even when not solicited and often he rambled on to trifling events or gave personal opinions although they were irrelevant. On the stand he had finally captured an audience and he was not going to let anyone yank him off the stage before he had delivered himself of all his long pent-up ruminations.

And always, his was the ultimate humility; he had been the little man caught in a web and manipulated by evil forces against which he had been powerless to resist.

Six months earlier, on May 31, 1950, Gold had come before Federal Judge James P. McGranery in Philadelphia to request a court-appointed attorney since he could not afford one. He specified: "... I would like him (the attorney) to understand very clearly that I must continue to give information to the FBI freely, that he is to put no restrictions whatever on that regardless whether he thinks it is damaging to me or not."[1]

Gold also said that he "did not want a lawyer who would make a show; that he have no radical connections... no leftish or pinkish background whatsoever."[2] He specified additionally that the attorney would have to understand that he intended to plead guilty except for one part of the charge: he had not intended to injure or harm the United States.[3]

Judge McGranery appointed John D.M. Hamilton, a former chairman of the Republican National Committee who was also a prominent corporation lawyer. His assistant, Augustus S. Ballard, also served. (Hamilton and Ballard, both distinguished members of the Philadelphia bar, gave unstinting attention to Gold's defense. They also continued to represent and advise him in matters pertaining to his incarceration, his business affairs and personal matters for many years after he had been sentenced. They rendered Gold a service beyond what was usual or expected in court-appointed representation, probably in the finest tradition of the legal profession.)

Gold had pleaded guilty to the charge of conspiracy to commit espionage. He had not yet been sentenced when he testified against Brothman and me. Some two weeks after our conviction, Gold appeared before McGranery for sentencing. It was December 7, 1950, five days before his fortieth birthday and the ninth anniversary of Pearl Harbor. Gold's attorneys had interviewed him extensively and had obtained character statements from people who had known him. When Hamilton rose to give his pre-sentencing remarks he was well prepared. He "... took three hours and held the room spellbound," said the Philadelphia Inquirer the next day.[4]

Hamilton spoke of the poverty of Gold's parents when they emigrated to Philadelphia. Harry, a sickly child, had been sent to a camp for undernourished children in 1923 and 1924 by a local social service organization. All through his childhood Harry Gold had known poverty up close and it shaped a lasting sympathy for the underdog, Hamilton said. Because he was small Harry withdrew from social interactions and became a prodigious reader. His favorite books were the Frank Merriwell series and the stories of Ralph Henry Barbour. These were tales of athletic achievements by schoolboys and Hamilton thought that Gold had projected himself into those stories as a way of overcoming his own physical shortcomings.

When he was in high school, Gold helped fellow students with their homework, frequently doing it for them and, continued Hamilton; this desire to help others became the dominant characteristic of his later life.

In January 1929, after Gold graduated high school he was hired by the Pennsylvania Sugar Company as a janitor but with the title of Laboratory Assistant. He worked seven days a week, twelve hours a day, and sometimes overtime. Despite this, he never lost an opportunity to help some of the technicians even if it meant staying beyond his twelve-hour shift. Hamilton said his disregard for hours was characterized by some associates later at the Philadelphia General Hospital as an "obsessive compulsion."

Gold also found time to tutor some of his fellow workers who were taking courses in the area colleges. He did this gratis and at their homes because he did not want to inconvenience them by having them come to his home. He did this while he himself was taking courses at Drexel Institute and while he was working twelve-hour shifts. Years later, Hamilton said, colleagues at the Philadelphia hospital where he then worked said that Gold never measured time by hours but by the tasks to be done. The time he gave to his job not only exceeded all normal standards but went beyond what might have been expected of a conscientious research worker. Specifically, Hamilton said, if an experiment required that it be started at three o'clock in the morning, Gold was there and remained until it was completed. During a transit strike in 1949 he slept at the hospital to be available. He also usually worked on holidays and on at least one occasion returned from a two-week vacation after one week. He gave blood for tests repeatedly and to excess and he volunteered to be the subject of tests even when made with toxic substances. (The offer was refused.)

Hamilton spoke of Gold's awesome generosity, willingly lending money to fellow workers even when he did not know them. Sometimes he had to borrow the funds—at usurious rates—to be able to make those loans. One of his fellow workers characterized Harry Gold as having been "solicitous to the point of fault" because Gold said it was unimportant whether the money was ever returned to him. He never reminded anyone of what they owed him, and it was almost embarrassing to return borrowed funds because he was reluctant to accept them.

When Gold graduated from Xavier he received a sum of $145 from his Soviet agent to use for graduation fees, continued Hamilton. However, he gave those funds to other students to meet their graduation fees. He then had to write to people in Philadelphia asking for repayment of loans he had made to them years earlier and so put together enough money to meet his graduation expenses.

Hamilton observed: "Harry Gold ranks in my experience as one of the most extraordinarily selfless persons I have ever known."

The lawyer then reviewed what material Gold had turned over to the

Soviet Union. In one instance Gold's information concerned processes relating to industrial solvents used in manufacturing varnishes and lacquers. He also turned over information relating to the production of ethyl alcohol used in pharmaceuticals. This was all he produced for his Soviet agent, then Paul Smith, from November 1935 to August 1936.

His next Soviet contact was a Steve Schwartz with whom he was in contact until September 1937 and to whom Gold turned over information on the manufacture of ethyl chloride, a local anesthetic. All the information thus far, said Hamilton, was common basic information.

Schwartz also asked Gold to recruit people to provide technical information but Gold had no stomach for that. Instead, to quiet Schwartz, he gave him fictitious names and addresses of people he said he was trying to recruit.

Gold's next contact was Fred, no last name, and he appeared in the fall of 1937. Gold turned over to Fred the details of experimental processes for recovering carbon dioxide from flue gases, the recovered material being useful for the manufacture of dry ice and soda fountain refrigeration. Hamilton hinted that it was questionable whether all of this could properly be considered espionage but in any event the offerings thus far were meager.

After Fred, came Sam in September 1940, who asked Gold to contact a New York engineer by the name of Abraham Brothman. Sam also dwelt on the critical situation in Russia to impress Gold with the continuing need for his help. According to Hamilton, Gold had told Sam that as Lend Lease assistance was being given then by the United States this made further assistance from him unnecessary. Sam replied that it was slow and laborious to get supplies through regular sources, and although Russia could manufacture some of the needed supplies itself, getting trustworthy information from American industries directly through legal channels was not always possible. Some American companies intentionally supplied antiquated data or withheld basic information entirely.

Accordingly, said Hamilton, Gold contacted Brothman and met with him from October 1941 to December 1943. He was not greatly successful. Much of the data Brothman turned over to Gold was relatively unimportant, said Hamilton. Some of it concerned machinery for mixing commercial chemicals. Some had to do with a continuous process for the production of Buna-S synthetic rubber but Hamilton said that the Russians had also obtained this information through official channels. Brothman also gave Gold information about manufacturing magnesium powder and an aerosol insecticide dispenser. The last two items, said Hamilton, were of no interest to the Soviet agents: "All in all, the material obtained from the chemist (Brothman) was scarcely worth the time and effort given."

Hamilton then discussed Gold's activities with Alfred Slack, David Greenglass and Klaus Fuchs and it was only the material he received from those sources, said Hamilton, which appeared to be related to the government's charges. Gold's last meeting with Fuchs, Hamilton said, was on September 19, 1945 so his efforts to transmit secret data appeared to have predated the start of the Cold War which,, Hamilton reminded the court, began in March 1947 (with the promulgation of the Truman Doctrine.)

Hamilton also told the court that Gold had never been paid for his Soviet services. (Hamilton did not know then that this was untrue. Gold had originally told him that he had never been paid but later confessed to him that his sworn testimony before the grand jury had been "inaccurate," and that he had indeed been paid from the beginning.)[5]

Then Hamilton returned briefly to his portrayal of Harry Gold as an unusually generous man. When Gold was laid off from Penn Sugar in February 1946, "... he walked the streets looking for work... not for himself but for his friends."

The attorney reminded the court that the Soviet Union had been an admired ally during the time Gold was transmitting information to it and had also been the subject of universal sympathy and admiration. Hamilton recalled that when Germany invaded Russia (June 1941) the United States was still six months away from entering the war but it nevertheless had an interest in the allied success. On that account it had enacted the Lend-Lease Act on March 11, 1941 which provided material assistance to Russia after June. From then until December 31, 1946 when Lend-Lease ended, the United States sent a constant flow of supplies to Russia amounting to about seven billion dollars. Hamilton recalled:

> "Our sympathies and interests in Soviet Russia were cemented when we became her brothers-in-arms in December 1941. Amtorg was now supplemented by Soviet technical and military missions dealing with nearly every phase of our war efforts. Russian officers and scientists were invited and encouraged to inspect and make use of our innermost commercial and military secrets... This spirit was present in our armed forces where American youth was indoctrinated with the subject of our admiration... Organizations sprang up all over the nation bearing such names as 'Aid for Russia' and "Friends of Russia' ... Our most prominent citizens proudly permitted their names to be used as sponsors for these organizations... Praise for Russia was heard on all sides here, and as late as 1947 these Russia Aid committees were found listed in the local telephone directory. Five short years ago Russia was a respected ally."

Hamilton then asked the court to view Harry Gold's offenses "(not) in the temper of these times but as they would have been weighed had he come before Your Honor... at the times they were committed." He reiterated: "Every offense (of) the defendant occurred when Russia was in the high favor… of the American people."

He concluded by listing the punishments meted out to people charged with similar crimes in Canada and England:

Fred Rose: (1946) A Canadian member of Parliament who was charged with "delivery of information of the highest importance," to the Soviet Union. Sentence: 6 years.

Dr. Alan Nunn May (1946) A British scientist, charged in Canada in the same investigation as Fred Rose, pleaded guilty to a charge of passing atomic secrets to the Soviet Union. Sentence: 10 years.

Dr. Klaus Fuchs (1950) A British scientist, charged under the same statute as May. Sentence: 14 years.

In the May case, "Sir Harley Shawcross, the King's Prosecutor, would not ask for the maximum stating that 'the prosecution makes no suggestion that the Russians are enemies or even potential enemies,'" quoted Hamilton.

Harry Gold then addressed the court. He thanked his attorneys; he said he had received scrupulously fair treatment by the Court and also by the FBI and the authorities at the various prisons where he had been lodged. "Most certainly this could not have happened in the Soviet Union…" he observed.

He also avowed that "the most tormenting of all thoughts concerns the fact that those who meant so much to me have been the worst besmirched by my deeds. I refer here to this country, to my family and friends, to my former classmates at Xavier University and to the Jesuits there, and to the people at the Heart Station of the Philadelphia General Hospital. There is a puny inadequacy about any words telling how deep and horrible is my remorse." He had tried to make amends, he said, by disclosing "every phase of my espionage activities, by identifying all of the persons involved, and by revealing every last scrap, shred, and particle of evidence."[6]

The prosecution asked for twenty-five years imprisonment. They reasoned that if Gold were sentenced to thirty (or more) years "there is little question but that he would be bitter…Notwithstanding… it is believed that Gold could be talked into cooperating further with the FBI… because his only hope would lie (in cooperating) for a reduction of sentence."[7]

Judge McGranery sentenced Harry Gold to thirty years, the maximum possible under the law short of the death sentence. The severity of the sentence stunned his attorneys and the courtroom observers, but Gold showed no emotion.

Who was this Harry Gold and how did he rise to such baffling infamy?

Chapter 27

... And the Real Harry Gold

Harry's parents, Celia and Sam Golodnitzky, were Russian Jews who fled to Switzerland early in their marriage. Before her marriage Celia had participated in the failed Russian revolution of 1905.[1] Harry was born in Bern, Switzerland on December 12, 1910. The family emigrated to the United States when Harry was three, changed their name to Gold and, having been turned away by relatives in Arkansas from whom they had expected help, found their way to Philadelphia and settled there. In 1917 a second son, Joe, was born. Sam worked as a carpenter and cabinet maker. The children were called by their diminutive Yiddish names: "Hershele" or sometimes, "Heshie" and "Yussele" or "Yussie." It was a close, warm family relationship, mutually supportive and interdependent.

Harry an undersized child, puny, softspoken, exceedingly polite and unaggressive, was an easy target for the Irish street bullies in the neighborhood who mocked his Jewishness and routinely terrorized him[2] His home and his family were his only refuge. Both parents read the *Jewish Forward*, a social democratic Yiddish newspaper printed in New York, and they much admired Eugene V. Debs and Norman Thomas, nationally known pacifists, one, a labor leader, the other a minister, and both perennial Socialist Party candidates for public office. Harry became acutely aware of the inadequacies of an economic system that could produce the suffering his family and others endured during the Depression and although he never joined the Communist Party he held a mildly left view that a more equitable distribution of the national wealth was much to be desired.[3]

Sam found a job with the Victor Company in Camden, New Jersey, just across the Delaware River from Philadelphia. It was a good job but within five years there was an influx of immigrant workers from Italy who baited him with crude anti-Semitic remarks and targeted him with mean tricks. They stole his chisels, put glue on his tools and on his good clothes and made life miserable for him. There was no point in protesting to the foreman; Sam knew him to be anti-Semitic also.

Some six years later Sam found himself working under another foreman, an Irishman who hated Jews far more bitterly than anyone Sam had yet known. Harry recalled:

"He told my Pop, 'I am going to make you quit!' and he put him on a particularly fast production line where Pop was the only one hand-sanding cabinets. He would come home at night with his fingertips raw and with the skin partially rubbed off... Mom would bathe the fingers and put ointment on them and Pop would go back to work the next morning. But he never quit, not Pop, and he never uttered one word of complaint to us boys."[4]

Harry went to local schools and after graduating high school he landed a job with the Pennsylvania Sugar Company. His wages were an important help to his family and he dutifully turned over the major portion of it to his mother. But he also saved some of it and after two years he took a leave of absence from Penn Sugar to attend the University of Pennsylvania.[5] He had to drop out after a year-and-a-half for lack of funds so he returned to Penn Sugar.

In December 1932 when the national economy hit bottom, Harry was laid off. Desperate for a job, Harry found one with a soap manufacturer in Jersey City, New Jersey through a new friend, Tom Black.[6] During this time Black tried to recruit Harry to join the Communist Party and to satisfy his incessant demands Harry attended three meetings, but he never joined.

He worked with Black in Jersey City for about nine months. When President Roosevelt inaugurated the National Recovery Act in 1933 Harry's old firm was able to rehire him so he returned to Philadelphia. At night, from 1933 to 1936 he also attended Drexel Institute and obtained a diploma in chemical engineering. He was then transferred to the Research Department of Penn Sugar. Two years later he took another leave to attend Xavier University in Cincinnati from which he graduated with a degree in chemistry. When he returned to Penn Sugar it was now as a professional chemist. There he became friends with Morrell Dougherty, another chemist.

At Tom Black's request, Gold said, he agreed to turn over information on his work at Penn Sugar to a Russian contact from the Amtorg Purchasing Commission. Amtorg, an American firm doing business since 1924, handled the buying and selling of goods and services for the U.S.S.R. This, according to Harry, launched his secondary career furnishing secret information to the Soviet Union. Specifically, he turned over information on industrial solvents; he did this to deflect Black's nagging to join the Communist Party, primarily, although he was willing to help the Soviet Union anyhow. He was aware that the Russians were then bearing the brunt of the struggle against the growing Nazi menace and the plight of European Jews resonated with him. After 1941 he felt even more strongly about helping the Soviet Union because then it was an ally in the Second World War.

In his middle or late twenties, Gold overcame his shyness to develop a romantic interest. The young woman told the FBI that from about 1933 to 1939 she was part of a social group of young people in the neighborhood and included in this group was Harry Gold. All of them came from poor families (as did Harry) and they admired him because of his devotion to his family. Nevertheless, he remained a social outsider. She dated him several times but warned him her feelings towards him were not romantic. Gold's interpretation of the end of this relationship was that the young woman had "jilted" him.[7]

In his early thirties Harry Gold made several other attempts to connect with romance. In 1943 he dated a young assistant chemist who worked in the Penn Sugar laboratory with him. She refused to continue the relationship because Harry was Jewish and she was not.[8]

Later that year he received a poignant note from someone signed, "Marian," dated October 27, 1943 which said:

> "Dear Harry: You make it difficult for me to tell you that I cannot see you again. Please don't think that I have failed to appreciate your thoughtfulness and pleasant ways. You were always an agreeable companion, and I feel sure that there is someone very special waiting at the end of your rainbow. May happiness and success be your lot always."[9]

During their search of Gold's home in May 1950 the FBI agents found a pair of unused theater tickets for January 30, 1943 for the Forest Theater in Philadelphia. Harry explained: he had made it a practice to buy tickets in advance so that when he succeeded in getting a date, he already had the evening well-planned. When he was unsuccessful he gave the tickets away. (In this case he apparently forgot about them.)[10]

In September 1948 Gold courted a young woman with whom he worked at the Philadelphia General Hospital. This time the situation seemed more promising; the young woman went out with him for about a year. When Gold revealed he had marriage on his mind she abruptly put an end to their relationship. He continued to telephone her until about February 1950 – coincident with the news of the Fuchs arrest in England—then he gave up.[11]

At Penn Sugar he had a friend in Morrell Dougherty. Their association did not always benefit their employer. Beginning in 1937 or 1938 Gold and Dougherty stole alcohol from the still room and bonded warehouse of Penn Sugar– as much as ten gallons a week by late 1940. They would transfer it to flat one-gallon containers and carry it out in their briefcases.[12] The team sold the alcohol to employees for five or six dollars a gallon (at a time when alcohol was rationed and its distribution restricted for the national defense).

Gold and Dougherty had been working on a vitamin assay project at Penn Sugar in the early 1940s and they decided to offer that work for sale independently of their employer. Accordingly, they made arrangements with an analytical chemical laboratory, Terry and Siebert, to use their name to solicit business. They offered their services to a number of potential customers but were unsuccessful.[13] Back at Penn Sugar their efforts did not go unnoticed. Robert Tuson, Process Superintendent, recalled for the FBI that he noticed that Dougherty and Gold appeared to be withholding information regarding their work and he and other officers had the uneasy feeling that the two men were not to be trusted. Tuson also said that Dougherty had told the lab assistant not to turn in any lab analyses results without first clearing the information with Gold or himself.[14]

Gold and Dougherty were also suspected of stealing laboratory equipment. Tuson recalled for the FBI "that in approximately 1945 he received information from Richard Bowers... that numerous items of equipment were... missing ... the total items missing represented a large financial loss to the company." The FBI report continued:

"Tuson stated that, because of the actions of Dougherty and Gold, he was suspicious of them and knowing that he would tell Gold, (he) mentioned to Dougherty that ... equipment (was) missing and that he thought it would be a good idea if he checked his equipment in before leaving (for the day)... Immediately following his talk with Dougherty the missing equipment began to reappear... when it was finally checked there were no major items missing."[15]

(Tuson's accusation appears to tie in with Venona information that Gold had asked his Soviet spymaster to set him up with a laboratory of his own.[16] If Gold's proposal had become a reality some of the cost of furnishing his lab would have had to come out of his own pocket. Helping himself to Penn Sugar's equipment would have saved him the expense of purchasing it.)

Harry Gold performed many acts of kindness for his friend, Morrell Dougherty. He paid the hospital bill when Dougherty's second child was born in 1937 so that Dougherty could get his wife out of the hospital. That same year he also lent Dougherty $247, borrowed from his mother, to buy a car. Dougherty never repaid it. In 1948 Gold lent him $400 to buy another car. Of this, Dougherty repaid only half so that for this and other loans, Gold said, Dougherty owed him about $1000. The agents elicited these financial details as ammunition against any damage Dougherty could inflict if our defense attorney, Kleinman, called him to the stand. Gold thought Dougherty's debt to him might be a brake on his giving damaging information. He also guessed that Dougherty would not care to have it exposed that he stole alcohol.[17]

Another who could furnish damaging information, Gold told the agents, would be Robert Tuson, the superintendent at Penn Sugar. Tuson had told the newspaper people that Gold's work at Penn Sugar was equivalent to what could have been done by a high school student.[18] (But he may have been tearing down Gold for reasons other than truth telling.)

In February 1946 Penn Sugar closed down its distillery department and

Harry was out of a job. But there were some voiced conjectures about why he was let go. A co-worker commented:

"… it seemed odd…that Dougherty and Gold were let out of their jobs with the excuse that their positions had been terminated when there were others who might not have been as capable… who were placed in other laboratories belonging to the same company…"[19]

It does raise questions. The wartime shortage of technical personnel had hung over into the postwar period and one would have expected a chemist like Gold to be kept on and reassigned. Gold, himself, told the FBI that Penn Sugar had promised two years earlier, when the distillery would be shut down as anticipated, he and Dougherty would be returned to the research division. They were let go instead.[20]

Even more telling was the objection Prosecutor Saypol raised (which Judge Kaufman sustained) when our defense attorney began to question Gold about Dougherty. If those questions had been allowed to develop, Gold's thievery might have been exposed and the jury's image of his probity would have been more realistic.

There was also the thicket of lies Harry Gold constantly scrambled through. In order to satisfy one of his Soviet handlers' demands that he recruit others as spy couriers, Gold said he gave them two names: Joseph Schultz and Herbert Epstein. He provided backgrounds for them, physical descriptions and addresses. But the backgrounds were those he fabricated from the bits and pieces of the lives of the people he knew in his neighborhood and the addresses were those he selected randomly from a telephone directory. There had never been a Schultz or an Epstein; the information Gold provided his handlers was totally false.[21]

The agents found information in Gold's home which referred to an "Unknown American #1," an apparent spy contact who worked for the Crouse, Hinds Company in Syracuse, New York from 1941 to 1944. They went to the trouble of obtaining about 500 fingerprint cards each containing a photograph of the person employed by that company and they asked Gold to identify his "Unknown American #1" from those cards.

Gold was unable to accommodate them. He admitted that the person he had called "Unknown American #1" was a figment of his imagination.[22]

There were other figments.

Harry told Abraham Brothman that he was a member of a championship basketball team while in high school. He also said he ran on a freshman cross-country meet in Van Cortlandt Park in New York City. He claimed that he completed two and a half years at the University of Pennsylvania and did graduate work at Purdue and at St. Louis University.[23]

To de-figmentize: Harry Gold never played basketball. He did not participate in any inter-collegiate cross-country meet or in college sports or other organizations. He completed one and a half years at the University of Pennsylvania, not two and a half, and he never attended Purdue or St. Louis University.[24]

Harry Gold lived much of his life in fantasies, often clothing himself in an identity that belonged to someone else. Among his fictions were the descriptions of his fake domestic life and the tiny apartment he and his illusory wife lived in; in reality, that apartment and the domestic life resembled that of his buddy, Morrell Dougherty.[25]

On February 2, 1942 Dr. Albert B. Katz examined Gold for the Selective Service Board and recorded his blood pressure at 182/100 whereupon he rejected Gold for military service. Gold told his attorney, Hamilton, that nevertheless twice he tried to enlist.

The truth: Harry Gold had listed his mother, Celia Gold, as a dependant before the local Selective Service Board #65 on December 2, 1941. He wrote on the S.S. form: "The amount earned by my father plus that contributed by my brother is not sufficient." Three days later he followed that up with an affidavit to support his claim for occupational deferment.[26] There was no evidence that Gold ever amended his original deferment claim or that, in fact, he tried to enlist.

When Harry Gold testified before the 1947 grand jury he said his education included a course in organic chemistry which he took at Columbia University.[27] When he was arrested his claim to have studied at Columbia ` gave the FBI some consternation. They checked and then wired Director Hoover, "NO EVIDENCE OF SUBJECT'S ATTENDANCE AT COLUMBIA UNIVERSITY."[28] Under cross-examination at our trial he finally got it straight; he did not ever take a course at Columbia.[29]

Among other stories, he told the FBI that he had been drinking regularly from the time he was about seventeen or eighteen years of age. He did not drink from 1933 to 1940 while in the early phase of his Penn Sugar employment, he said, but he drank to excess during the entire period he was handled by his Soviet controls, Semenov and Yakovlev (from 1941 on). He also went on drunken sprees of two or three months' duration at regular intervals. He did not believe Semenov or Yakovlev knew of it nor did he think Brothman was aware of it. He stopped drinking in 1948.[30]

Well, now.

There was evidence that Harry Gold drank – for a very brief period. In a memo of August 15, 1950, Augustus S. Ballard, one of his attorneys, noted that he had interviewed Albert Sklar, an old friend of Gold's who told him that in their youth they would occasionally visit a tap room and he always thought Gold was a temperate fellow. However, said Sklar, Gold had been seen intoxicated once or twice within the three or four years before by a mutual friend.[31]

The dates given coincide with the end of Gold's employment at Penn

Sugar, from February to May of 1946, when he was unemployed. But Gold's story of long term drinking is difficult to believe. If Harry had been drinking when he was seventeen or eighteen it would have occurred while he was still in high school and living at home in the bosom of an intimately connected family. Drinking would never have been part of the culture of his family and he would have hardly been able to waltz that past his indomitable mother nor likely the school personnel nor classmates. Also, this was a poor family who barely made the food budget stretch from week to week on the father's meager earnings; living room furniture had been repossessed when they could no longer make the installment payments. Gold's funds for bingeing would have been non-existent.

By the time Gold came to work for Abe Brothman in May 1946 he was taking medication for hypertension – barbiturates, Abe had told me. Of all people Gold would have known not to combine alcohol with his medication. Furthermore, he could never have disguised his drinking from the lab personnel and certainly not from Brothman with whom he conferred daily, usually at the lab. Also, the three of us met for dinner almost every evening and I never saw any sign that Harry had had a pre-prandial boost nor did he order a drink at dinner, not even beer or wine. And when he stayed at my apartment in the spring of 1946 he had no liquor supplies with him and I saw no sign of any drinking.

But if the FBI and the prosecution believed Gold's story of excessive drinking they apparently did not question how reliable his perceptions could have been of my so-called efforts to exert any influence on Brothman and his grand jury testimony in 1947 or that I was aware that he, Gold, would lie in his testimony in 1947. They did not wonder how believable was even his claim to other details of his spy escapades. They appear not to have had any doubts about his truthfulness.

Perhaps the more urgent question is why Harry Gold stretched a brief reality into a long-term event when the evidence contradicts that claim. Was it his naïve effort to elicit sympathy from his tormenters, the FBI? Was it his way of hinting that the Russians drove him to drink and thus build a case for having been held helplessly in their power? Was it a reflex that Harry Gold could never tell the truth or even perceive it when a reincarnation might endow him with a more attractive persona? This was the golden age of the movies when the hero was always tall, handsome, debonair and rich, with one hand flicking a cigarette and the other clutching a cocktail in an illusory Valhalla. Such a hero was never encumbered by the mundane problems of having to earn a living and pay the rent—and he always got the girl. So Harry had his figments.

There was also the matter of how he dragged me into the alleged conspiracy.

An FBI report of July 27, 1950 says: "Gold recalls telling Brothman practically nothing in Moskowitz's presence..."

He recollected for the agents that I had gone out for coffee and while I was gone the two men compared and discussed their interviews with the FBI. Gold then confessed to Brothman that he was not married, did not have two children, his brother was not killed during the war but was alive and that he, Gold, lived with his parents and brother in Philadelphia. Brothman berated him for having told him those lies. Gold, for his part, suggested to Brothman that he not discuss those matters in front of me.[32]

And again: "Gold recalls telling Brothman practically nothing in Moskowitz's presence but later... Moskowitz had gone out for coffee... they talked of their stories to the agents."[33]

Still once more he told the agents that he never discussed his activities in front of me; he did not trust me; he said I had a violent temper and he told Abe nothing in my presence when they met after the FBI interviews.[34]

Nevertheless, from June 1950 when he first said he never talked in front of me to November 7, the day before our trial began, he altered his original remarks significantly: "Moskowitz was present at all of the above conversations in the laboratory."[35]

And again: "Gold believes that Moskowitz was present when Brothman pressed Gold about all his other activities and his personal life, for example, Gold's story about his wife and two children and his dead brother."[36]

There was also Gold's testimony that he had never met Jacob Golos when the government's own files disprove it.

According to Gold, Brothman ordered him to lie that they had met through Golos even though, Gold testified, he had never known Golos.[37] Five times on direct examination during our trial he said he had never met Jacob (or John) Golos and had not known him. But according to statements he gave the FBI before he testified he had indeed met him, talked with him and worked for him from June 1940 until the end of that year.[38] (See Chapter 8.)

So, in addition to his other lies Gold perjured himself on this issue, a perjury in which the prosecution itself was complicit.

When Gold first began meeting with Abe Brothman in 1941 he would extract a promise from Brothman to meet at a meticulously arranged place, date and time, but Brothman rarely kept his promise or would come hours late and sometimes not at all, and would not even let Gold know when he was not going to keep his appointment. Gold would wait endless late hours on lonely street corners in Manhattan in all kinds of weather for meetings with Brothman which would never materialize, inflicting acute punishment on himself. He always had to catch a train back to Philadelphia, usually in the late evening and he had to be able to function at work the next day, usually with very little sleep. He always seemed helpless to rein in Brothman while he, for his part, clearly had priorities that differed from Gold's. One must ask why Gold persisted in what any sensible person would have perceived was a hopelessly unproductive effort. Why did he endure this marathon exasperation and why did he inflict such punishment on himself, not once but over and over?

Gold had floated the story that he wanted to help the Soviet people in their mortal struggle against the Nazis and it was out of this purest of motives that he became a spy courier. So he also endured Brothman's dallying. But the real reason may have been that Gold was being paid by his Soviet control starting in 1941. (See Chapter 24 – "Enter Venona".) If the Venona information is accurate then Gold's claim to idealistic motivation is spurious. He was enduring Brothman's unreliability because he needed Brothman to justify the continuation of his monthly payments.

Gold bore much of the expense of traveling to New York to see Brothman. Sam would have reimbursed him but Gold deliberately understated his expenses to Sam, he claimed, because the Russians were not getting full value for money spent. The reason: Gold doubted that the material Brothman gave him was of much value.[40] (But later, he testified that Brothman gave him processes which he labeled, "industrial espionage," another of his self-contradictions.)

Gold maintained the tenuous relationship with Brothman for some four years. During that time Brothman did give Gold technical material. He also used Gold for freelance work, all of it non-military, not secret and not connected with the government. In addition, Brothman referred Gold to professional colleagues who gave Gold similar assignments. This was wartime; an available chemist like Gold would have been much sought after. And during all those years Brothman knew Gold as "Frank Kessler," a family man from Philadelphia. Later when he came to work for Brothman Harry gave him his true name but the rest of his chimerical identity remained in place until May 1947 when the FBI sought him out.

When I first met Harry Gold I thought he was the most woebegone person I had ever known. All of us in the Brothman firm had heard the painful details of his failed marriage. His wife, Sarah, was very beautiful. When they married they were poor but blissful. Their rented studio apartment was so tiny only one person at a time could fit in the kitchenette. Eventually, they bought a modest house and their twin children were born. Essie, the girl, had one blue eye and one brown eye; she had also recovered from polio. David was his stalwart son. The marriage turned sour because Sarah objected to Harry's frequent business absences. When the twins were four she left him to live with a much older man and took the children with her. The only way Harry could see his children was to watch them secretly from a distance in a playground on Saturday afternoons, hiding behind a tree.

It was a wrenching story, grimly told, and we ached for him.

There were other sorrows in his life. His brother, Joe, had been a paratrooper in World War II and had been shot down over New Guinea. His parents, grieving sorely, had persuaded their nephew, Harry's cousin, to live with them. His name, coincidentally, was also Joe.

When Harry arrived at the Brothman firm he stayed with me in my apartment in Manhattan. My apartment-mate had left for a long summer visit with her out-of-town parents and I was glad to offer Harry temporary hospitality, the post-war housing shortage still being a factor to contend with. He was my guest and no money was involved; my apartment mate had already paid her share in advance and I did not need Harry's funds.

I had expected that he would return to Philadelphia on weekends to see his children, and to resume whatever social life he had there but he seemed to prefer to stay in Manhattan and subtly he began to adapt his routine to mine. It gave rise to difficult social situations. If I had friends over Harry made them his friends, bustling in the kitchen with me to help serve up coffee even if I did not need help. If I planned to go out he would ask where I was heading and when I left I had the uncomfortable feeling that I should have invited him to come along, even if it was just to meet a friend and go to a movie.

I brought him with me to my parents' home early on several Friday evenings. He enjoyed the benediction of my father's Sabbath Kiddush and my mother's traditional Jewish table. He said he also liked talking with my father. I brought him with me once to a party on a Saturday night because I hated to see him so lonely. He did not stay, however; he felt awkward and left early.

On Sundays he would loll about in his pajamas all day, even though it was clear it made me uncomfortable, especially because sometimes friends would drop in. When I made breakfast for us on Sunday mornings, he liked his toast "burnt," his coffee hot and black. He would then nurse the coffee until it cooled. At lunch or dinner he never turned down a second helping of anything.

Early one workday morning he opened the door to my bedroom and entered to wake me although I had not asked him to do so and my alarm clock had not yet rung. It had been a hot, humid night; I had slept under a thin sheet and wore no nightclothes. Harry did not simply call to me from the doorway; rather, he came all the way into the room, bent over me and shook me, calling, "Get up, sleepyhead, get up!"

I awoke startled to see his face close to mine and I froze in fear, unable even to scream. Later that day, still shaken, I told Abe. Alarmed for me and sensing that he really did not know this man, he took off for the lab and told Harry that he thought my apartment was unsuitable for him—what he needed was, really, a place closer to the laboratory. Unwisely, perhaps, Abe also chastised him for having entered my room that morning. Harry broke down and cried, said Abe later, because the incident added to his misery over his wife's estrangement. Abe spent the evening with him and walked with Harry until five that morning trying to talk him out of the blues.

The incident appeared to rankle Harry for a long time, festering and forming part of his stories to the FBI four years later.[41]

Before this event destroyed our relationship, Harry had been ever eager to ingratiate himself when he stopped by the office on his way to the lab, so much so that he sometimes confounded my office routine. He would insist on trying to be helpful even if I did not need help, particularly since his lab work had a priority on his time.

"Here, let me give you a hand," he would say, picking up the mail to take it down to the box, or he would offer to proofread the technical material I had typed—well-intentioned efforts which only served to slow me down.

Once I needed to proofread and collate a long technical report I had typed and I found myself making elaborate plans to postpone doing it until I was sure Harry would be unlikely to come to the office that day. Fending off his proffered attention became a burden and I never knew how to handle him without hurting his feelings.

For his part, Abe Brothman gave Gold what seemed to be the steadiness of genuine friendship. Gold spent all his leisure time with Brothman, most of it at the laboratory. He and Abe would also go to the Julia Richmond High School on the east side in midtown Manhattan to play handball—the gymnasium and the swimming pool were open to the public on certain evenings. The two would sometimes also steal away together to see an afternoon ballgame in season. It seemed to me their bantering revealed a camaraderie of two friends neither of whom would ever do the other harm. And despite the closeness of their relationship Harry continued deceiving Brothman with his fantasies of a family life.

Brothman first learned he had been duped when the FBI agents appeared in May 1947 to question him and then Gold. It was not until then that Harry, in panic, told Abe the truth. He was not married and did not have two children. It was with his mother, not a wife, he had purchased a house, and it was his mother, not a wife who had complained about his absences. And his brother, Joe, was safe at home, not shot down over the Pacific.

In his testimony Harry said he found it easier to continue the masquerade and even to embellish it from time to time than to admit he had fabricated a domestic identity. In retrospect, however, questions push their way forward: Was it really because it was easier to continue the deception, or did he enjoy his fantasy more than the drab reality of his life? Did his stay in my apartment give him the comforting illusion of a domestic life even though it was entirely superficial? And when Brothman suggested he find another domicile, did he see me as another love object who had spurned him?

Harry's life was strange and ambiguous. He made loans he could not afford, sometimes even to strangers. He went to extraordinary lengths to do favors for people at significant cost to himself, obsequiously buying affection. He blamed himself for his mother's death because he had been away from home so much, although he was thirty-seven years old when she died. He accused a young woman who did not return his romantic interest of having "jilted" him. But in all his activities it was apparent that he was deriving significant satisfaction from them. He needed to believe he mattered because his life had been so colorless, so void and socially unrewarding. When he connected with Semenov and Fuchs he may have viewed himself as propelled into a social stratosphere, making friends in high places—and those were opportunities no one else he knew could claim. Semenov dressed and spoke and looked like an upper-class American; he was urbane, erudite, cultured; he quoted Wordsworth, had read Dickens, Browning and Robert Frost. He dazzled Harry with perceptive comments about Thomas Wolfe, Somerset Maugham, Edgar Lee Masters and Carl Sandberg. He was also a graduate of the Massachusetts Institute of Technology, an engineer and a mathematician.[42] Klaus Fuchs was, of course, one of the stars in the international scientific firmament.

Witness: On July 10, 1950, Gold signed a voluntary statement for the Philadelphia FBI office. It was an elaboration of an account of his meetings with Klaus Fuchs which he had given them the previous May 22. The last paragraph indicates how lonely he must have been and how much the Fuchs contact meant to him:

> "I would like to add that throughout our entire meetings, the relationship between Klaus Fuchs and me was that of firm friends. Further, on the occasion of the last meeting in Santa Fe, Klaus expressed the hope that sometime in the near future we might be able to meet openly as friends."[43]

When the Brothman firm ran out of funds and salaries could not be paid, Brothman tried to show good faith to Gold by adding his name to patent applications, one of which he filed for the manufacture of methyl methacrylate. This was a plastic product known commercially as "Lucite," (DuPont's trade name) or "Plexiglas," (Rohm and Hass). Brothman had broken through the existing patent structure and had developed a method of manufacture different from and cheaper than currently used methods.

Brothman also shared with Gold other patent applications for new processes to manufacture commercially useful products which he had developed as offshoots of some of this work. He had every expectation of profiting from those developments and it was for that reason he added Harry Gold's name to the patent applications.

It was an unsatisfactory financial arrangement for Gold. As we all did, Harry Gold needed the security of a regular income, not a promise of future riches. But Brothman, at his wits' end to keep the business afloat, was sublimely certain he would ultimately strike paydirt. At that time it appeared a reasonable expectation.

The patents were granted while both men were in prison but then they could no longer be commercially exploited. At least one, applied for in April 1948, was granted in January 1951 for the manufacture of acetylenic alcohol and acetylenic gamma glycols.[44] It was seized by the government to be sold and the proceeds applied to Brothman's as yet, unpaid fine.[45]

Sharing patent authorship was further evidence that Brothman did not know of the extent of Gold's secret life. And if he had not known that he would have had no motive to enlist Gold in concealing facts from the government. Brothman's personal concern that his efforts to solicit Amtorg business could be misconstrued is understandable given the hostile anti-Soviet climate then. However, it could not sensibly have generated a motive to derail the government's investigations into espionage when he, himself, had not been involved. Indeed, Gold told the FBI that, "Brothman had not the slightest idea of my work with Dr. Fuchs."[46]

But Brothman had inflicted what Gold would come to regard as the most egregious wound of all. When Brothman was interviewed by the FBI in 1947 he told them that Gold had succeeded his contact, 'Helen," (as he had known Elizabeth Bentley), in picking up his offerings for Amtorg. He also told them that Gold was then working for him in his laboratory in Queens. Until that moment Harry Gold had not existed for the FBI. As a result Gold felt, and expressed this in notes he wrote later in the fall of 1950, that Brothman had betrayed him. From 1947 on Gold's attitude towards Brothman turned into coiled resentment.[47]

I had not known how the FBI found Harry Gold until I heard his testimony at the trial – which made no sense to me then – and more specifically until I read the FBI files years later. In an FBI memorandum they recorded that Gold told them, when he and Brothman were discussing their interviews with the FBI that evening in May 1947, I went out to get coffee and while I was gone Brothman said to Gold: "You don't blame me for bringing you into this, do you, Harry?"

That memo continues: "Gold believes that Brothman waited until Moskowitz was gone to bring this up, as Brothman did not want Moskowitz to know 'that Brothman had put the finger on Gold.'" It also indicates that the two men had discussions privately, and not in front of me.[48]

Harry Gold blamed Abe Brothman for his own profound mistakes He had been warned in 1945 by his Soviet handler, John (Yakovlev) to stay away from Brothman because Brothman was "hot," presumably because of the Bentley disclosures. In his testimony, Gold said he forgot about that warning.[49] (Significantly, had Gold stayed away, Brothman would *never have learned Frank Kessler's true identity.*)

I do not believe Gold forgot Yakovlev's warning—it was not about trivia. He` simply chose to ignore it. He had been unemployed for three months after Penn Sugar let him go. Unable to find suitable employment in the Philadelphia area where he lived, he took the job with Brothman because he needed it, not because he forgot Yakovlev's warning.

Similarly, Harry Gold was angry with me. Part of that had been generated when Brothman told him to move out of my apartment. Some of his fury resulted from Brothman's having asked me to accompany him to Switzerland when Harry thought he should have been the one to go. But much of it was for another reason.

When I was interviewed by the Bureau agents in May 1950 I sensed that Harry Gold was talking to them. Trying to keep them from reaching unfavorable conclusions about Brothman and me, I warned them that not everything Gold said was true. As an instance, I told them of his imaginary wife and children and the dead brother who was very much alive. It was a classic blunder. Of course they shuttled back to Gold, told him I called him a liar and that I had further demeaned him by exposing his embarrassing lies. He would have regarded that as the ultimate tipping point even though he would have been unmasked by others to whom he had told the same mythic stories. If he were going to go down in this developing debacle he would take Brothman with him and he would take me along, too. Hence his contrived testimony that I knew that he and Brothman would concoct a false story for the 1947 grand jury and that I sought to restrain Brothman from changing his story – and by implication, keep him from telling the truth. And because Gold was so eager to cooperate with the FBI and the prosecution this testimony, like much of the rest of his information, came only after he had spent hundreds of hours with them in preparation to testify.

The pressure the FBI exerted on Harry Gold must have been the most frightening experience of his life. In a lengthy document he spoke of their initial interviews in Philadelphia before his arrest saying, "…I desperately parried each of the probing questions."[50]

But those agents would probably have begun in a disarmingly friendly manner (as they did with me) and, because he would have perceived them to be such nice, clean-cut, open-faced young men, he warmed to them. In another setting they could have been choir boys, he would have thought. In turn, they would have spoken respectfully, shown recognition for his professional status and he would have basked in their deferential treatment. His persona had taken so many cuts these last few years—his disappointing career turns and yet another failed romance just a few months earlier—he would have appreciated their esteem and would have turned away any ideas to protect his privacy.

Witness: Gold commiserated with the two agents who were interrogating him: "…(when) it seemed that Miller and Brennan began to droop with defeat I started to feel sorry for them all over—they had given it such a good try."[51]

In minutes they were all on a first-name basis; it was "Scott" and "Dick" and "Harry."[52] And then:

> "From the first I began to feel a genuine liking for Miller and Brennan; and as the weeks (of interrogation) passed this feeling increased and I discovered that there was present in me a tremendous urge directed towards earning their respect."[53]

It was at that moment that he was doomed. He was now totally alone, he had no one to share his fears with, no one to confide in and he began to view his enemies behind a cloud, transmuting them and identifying with them against himself. Harry Gold had lost his bearings.

Once he began to yield information he might have hoped they would then let him alone, relax their pressure and go away. Instead, they swarmed all over him and turned up the pressure even more. Over hundreds of hours they would have badgered him and harassed him interminably and ultimately he would have let them coax him into saying anything, true or not.[54]

In his agonizing journey to find peace, Harry Gold also obligingly identified for the FBI those co-workers who he said were communists. It included two who he regarded as close friends and with one of whom he maintained a warm relationship until only a few months before his arrest.[55] His political convictions were inconsistent. At our trial he said he thought communists were "a lot of whacked-up bohemians" and he held them in contempt.[56] But an FBI informant, T-3, reported she had seen Gold at a meeting of the Communist Party in Queens, New York, just a few months earlier, on January 30, 1950.[57] He had accompanied a friend to that meeting. One wonders if Gold's real political convictions morphed to accommodate the vagaries of who he needed for a friend at a particular moment.

Gold also named others, for instance, an obscure professor under whom he had studied briefly at the University of Pennsylvania eighteen years earlier. He told the FBI he thought the educator had been a "Soviet sympathizer."[58] He had last seen this man in 1932; what relevance his information had in 1950 was imponderable. Gold was feeding a giant maw with names but the more he fed the hungrier it became.

In January 1951 the International News Service approached Gold's attorney, John D. M. Hamilton, about having their writer, Bob Considine, interview Gold for a syndicated series of first-person articles by Gold. They would pay him $5,000. Considine thought there were also good possibilities for a book and movie rights, and those rights would belong to Gold who would also get one-half of the proceeds if any other publications picked up the series.[59]

It was a dazzling offer. Harry intended to use the initial funds to pay his attorneys and to give a large chunk of it to the American Heart Association. (His mother had died of heart disease.) Gold expected a fair income from the book and movie rights as well as the reruns of the original articles. The problem was how could Mr. Considine get to interview Gold? Hamilton suggested he go through Roy Cohn or Irving Saypol, the prosecutors, for clearance, anticipating no difficulty.[60]

The contract the INS sent Gold on February 6, 1951 specified that he be available for interviews and prepare full information on his activities which would then be submitted to the proper authorities for clearance. The contract also stipulated that if such clearance was not obtained the agreement would be nullified.

Gold began writing his document, "The Circumstances Surrounding My Work As A Soviet Agent – A Report" in anticipation of its use by INS.[61] However, the FBI thought it was extremely undesirable for the articles to appear before the Rosenberg trial, and Gold agreed to have INS delay publication.[62]

The Rosenberg trial ended with a conviction in March 1951. On April 10, 1951 INS revoked the offer because Saypol had refused to give clearance for the project.[63]

Saypol, Cohn and the Department of Justice were aware that Harry Gold had a penchant for expansive soliloquizing. It is not too much to believe that they were fearful that Gold might inadvertently reveal matters they would never want made public, for instance, his inconsistent testimonies. They would also have been wary that Gold could taint past or pending actions by disclosing the inner workings of witness preparation and other prosecution secrets.

Gold intended that the 123-page report he had written would be his autobiography, with two additional sections to come. Available files do not indicate that he ever completed that material but what he did finish is in minute detail and includes information about people he had known as a youth whom he had not seen in many years. It named old friends who in the first flush of young adulthood espoused radical political ideas and whose reputations could now be compromised for his merely having mentioned their names.[64]

He did the same in his obligingly informative conversations with the FBI when he discussed members of the Brothman staff.[65] He not only gave information about them, much of it guesswork, he even discussed friends of some of them. He discussed the young woman with whom I shared an apartment, whom he barely knew[66] and he talked about my parents. He said they were "liberals," guessed at what newspapers they read, and characterized their religious zeal.[67] He discussed my siblings, one of whom was still a teenager.[68]

But this document delivers its most revealing jolt when he says: "I must be punished, and punished well for the terribly frightening things I have done."[69]

It was part of Harry Gold's warped perspective that he could not quit groveling. The previous July he had written a 26-page letter to the judge before whom he was arraigned, in which he pleaded for understanding.[70] Now, just a few months later, he was willing to be stretched on a rack; he had turned self-flagellation into grotesque art.

In a June 14, 1951 letter he wrote from prison to his attorney, Gold discussed factual errors which had appeared in an article about him in "Look Magazine," issue of June 19, 1951. He said:

"when I went to work for Abe Brothman in May of 1946, it was solely as an employee ...our activities were completely legitimate ...the last time Brothman furnished me with data for Russia was in 1943 and this was not turned over on account of its fragmentary nature."[71]

As Attorney Hamilton noted in his pre-sentencing speech, Gold's activities (and thus Brothman's) occurred well before the Cold War and when the United States viewed the U.S.S.R. as a respected ally. But two years later Gold submitted an affidavit to the McCarthy committee in which he identified Brothman as "One of my sources of information for the Soviet espionage organization of which I was a courier."[72]

Gold's conception of his activities had steadily ballooned to justify the accusations against him and in the process he assigned a role to Abe Brothman he had not done earlier.

In 1956 Gold appeared before the Senate Internal Security Subcommittee and a few months later submitted a statement which supplemented his earlier testimony. In that statement he said of Brothman:

"... in 1943 I was experiencing difficulty in getting information from Abe Brothman. It was not that Brothman was unwilling to furnish data but that he insisted on giving what we didn't want, i.e., his own work and not supply what we wanted, that is, chemical processes in successful operation in the United States."

Here, Gold admitted that Brothman gave him his own and only his own work. But under oath six years earlier (at our trial) Gold said that Abe Brothman had committed industrial espionage because he had given him blueprints which, Gold had implied, Abe had stolen.[73]

Gold was jousting with reality. If he had unequivocally admitted that Brothman gave him his own work it could not have been industrial espionage. But when Gold damned it as such then Brothman had, therefore, stolen it. And the corollary was even worse: if Brothman had stolen the material then he must certainly have engaged in industrial espionage.

This discord had been nourished in an old competitiveness Gold had always felt towards his friend. Brothman had entered an Ivy League college on a full scholarship at age fifteen and graduated with a string of honors and awards including a Rhodes fellowship in mathematical physics.[74] Harry had not been so blessed. The university he attended was the only one which accepted him[75]; he had to pay his way and was past twenty-nine when he finally received his degree. Brothman was known and well-regarded in his profession from his early twenties. Gold had had a late start and now, forty, had yet to make his mark. Abe had published prolifically; Gold had not.

The one technical paper Gold wrote, in 1936, was on thermal diffusion and it was never published. Gold described it himself as having been written in practical layman's language and not as an academic treatise. It never captured any commercial interest. Some years later he gave Brothman a copy. He told the FBI that Brothman never paid any attention to it, "probably because it was not (his) idea."[76]

The resentment spilled over into a matter of status. Gold had come into Brothman's life, in his mind, as his superior but the dynamics of their relationship quickly changed. Instead of bending Brothman to his rules he found that Brothman was his own person and he, Gold, would have to do the bending. Status, to Harry Gold, defined his sense of self-worth but when Brothman changed the rules he cheated him out of the reassuring conviction that he was moving ahead in life. Gold's testimony reflected his bitterness:

Q. (By defense attorney Kleinman): "You had been Abe's Soviet superior in your espionage work?"

A. "For a very short while. The trouble was that from the beginning I let Abe be slovenly about keeping appointments on time. Had I been his superior, he would have shown up right on the minute when he should have."[77]

Every aspect of Gold's multiple confessions was a practical transaction he had entered into with the prosecution. He had been fearful that his father and his brother would lose the house they lived in because he, Harry, owned it – and in that case, would they be cast out to live on the street? Joe, his brother, worked for the federal shipyards in Philadelphia and might have been regarded as a security risk and fired because of Harry. Not least, he, himself, was in danger; he had not yet been sentenced and was facing a possible death penalty. To protect all of them he offered up Abe Brothman and then me, among others, to buy forgiveness. By the time the FBI and Saypol and Cohn had finished with him Gold was willing to say that he had indeed committed heinous crimes. He never acknowledged that they had manipulated him into taking on a role that was vastly exaggerated. He forgot that his acting as an errand boy between Klaus Fuchs (and to a lesser extent, David Greenglass) and the Soviet Union had been accomplished before the Cold War during a cooperative time when the United States and the Soviet Union were sharing technical information at the highest echelons and were joined in a mortal combat against a common enemy.

After Gold's 1956 appearance before the Senate Internal Security Subcommittee Benjamin Mandel, its research director, wrote Harry an inspiring letter:

"Dear Harry: It might be a good idea to place into the record a statement describing the methods by which the Communists play upon the minds of atomic scientists to bring them to do what was done to you. Such a statement could be of great use in enlightening scientists and preventing them from being misled by the recent signing of a propagandist statement by 2,000 scientists.[78]

Gold jumped with uncharacteristic speed. He sent a statement which the Subcommittee released on August 15, 1957. In it he spoke of how he came to his delayed understanding that his Soviet handlers had deceived him. He included an analysis of what he called "the Soviet techniques to influence sincere people to engage in espionage." He reviewed that he had given them information on the manufacture of various industrial chemicals used in formulating lacquers, varnishes and synthetic finishes, and then:

"I was told 'our people (the Russians) eat off rough boards. You can help them live a little better, a little more as humans should by getting up this material.' And along with that was something else: To get this data I had to steal it from my employer... So this added up to violating a trust – plus theft. (But none of that meant anything, it is all for a good end. The Pennsylvania Sugar Company is not being hurt. No one is really hurt, only good is being accomplished.)"[79]

Gold had never introduced this accusatory analysis before; it was a new theme. He forgot that he was not always concerned about stealing from his employer; he had stolen alcohol to resell at a profit and he had tried to steal laboratory equipment. These actions had not been inspired by his Soviet handlers.

Back in July 11, 1950, before he was sentenced, he gave a 57-page statement to the FBI which contained the following:

"... in December of 1943 and possibly January 1944 I was told by Sam (his Soviet handler) that there was an extremely important mission coming up for me and that before he could tell me about (it) he wanted to know would I undertake it. I unhesitatingly agreed."[80]

The mission was to become the Fuchs contact but they had not yet revealed the purpose when he accepted. In this case, again, Gold was not troubled by an aspect of violating a trust or stealing, or that in carrying out an undefined mission his principles might be compromised. He "unhesitatingly agreed."

In his July 1957 statement to the Subcommittee Gold also revealed a personal vignette:

"In February – March of 1937 a violent strike took place at the Pennsylvania Sugar Company. Some six hundred men and women stayed in the plant under ...siege for about five weeks; at least an equal number were outside. It was worth one's life to cross the picket line; food was brought in by ... motor launches... there were some thirty people working in the laboratories and though we chemists and engineers were not directly involved, it was known ... that we would be used to help operate the refinery; only one... refused to work – Harry Gold... let it not be supposed that my motives were all pure... I wouldn't remain because I had a "hot date"... ... Dr Reich... grew terribly angry... and said, 'you're through! Get out! But you'll never work as a chemist again—I'll see to that.'"[81]

(The union won the strike so Gold was rehired.)

At our trial Harry's earlier version was: "I refused to work in the plant while the men were on strike. It was against my principles."[82] In that version he had shaded the events to reflect that he had high moral values and was sympathetic to workers. The reality was that he did not support the strike; he was more interested in keeping his date than in showing solidarity with the strikers. That may be an understandable human circumstance but his testimony was false like his many other inventions.

Elsewhere in his Subcommittee statement Gold redefined his role with the Russians:

"I had made some three or four trips in one week between Philadelphia and New York (after working a full day...) and ... I was horribly tired... Abe had nothing for me. I met Semenov to report another failure and he, too, appeared weary. We spoke of the inherent troubles in attempting to get technical information and of the many disappointments; of the necessary cajoling and flattering; of the importuning and of the deceit, waiting on street corners for appointments never kept. It was deadeningly dull, dirty, sullying work Semenov said, and here we were, I a chemist and he a mathematician and a mechanical engineer, both pursuing a shabby course we only despised, both longing just to be allowed to do the work for which we were trained. A dismal job, this espionage, but a vital job, one which had to be done. Then, one glorious day Hitler would be destroyed, there would be peace-on-earth, and no such depressing endeavor would be (again) required. Neat."[83]

Mandel was surely getting his money's worth. Gold was not finished:

"About 1943-44 and 1945, Semenov and his successor, 'John' occasionally would introduce another theme (Semenov was returning to the Soviet Union.) But it was not 'Goodbye,' ... when this dreadful war is over...all nations would be friends...and people could travel freely; then I could openly go to the Soviet Union and in Moscow would renew acquaintances..."

"All I wish to point out is the idea of 'We're all going to be friends.' (So what's it matter if meanwhile I engage in a little illegal activity. Just a dab of espionage, huh?)"[84]

Gold believed those expressions of friendship when they were made and he believed them for many years. His perspective changed when he entered into a compact with the FBI and the prosecutors. Earlier, he had made no accusations of betrayal. He had even written glowingly of Semenov's concern that he, Gold, was running himself ragged trying to pin down Abe Brothman. Semenov insisted he go home and take care of himself; he was also worried that Gold seemed to have given up any idea of a personal life. He had no wife, no family, and Semenov scolded him and urged him to think of his future.[85]

His Russian handlers also went to extraordinary lengths to shield him from looming disaster. In the fall of 1949 Gold had several visits from a Soviet agent who warned him that Fuchs was giving information in England about his espionage activities. He, the agent, offered to arrange for Gold to travel to Europe where he would be safe.[86] Although Gold refused the offer, the gesture was hardly the act of callous manipulators.

Harry Gold summed up his newly hatched clairvoyance as he ended his Subcommittee statement:

"To me the true horror underneath 'buying' the Soviet way of life resides in the inevitable, inexorable demand for a payment—but the currency...is the human soul and there is the awful corollary the fact that a man becomes willing, even eager, to do any bidding, no matter how loathsome."

"I am aware that the portrait (of) the Soviets' maneuvering of my personality is delineated in harsh strokes. Looking back... it does seem as if it were another day, another age, almost another world. Yet I know what ... I did."[87]

It defies common sense and contradicts the evidence to think Gold really believed what he wrote. The remorse is synthetic, the sentiments self-pitying and written to accommodate Mandel just as several years earlier he had accommodated prosecutors Saypol and Cohn. He blamed others for leading him to do deeds he had never refused to do. Gold always had a choice to leave the apparatus but chose to remain because he wanted to help the Soviet people fight a war, he had said, against his own country's enemy. He never acknowledged that he had been paid. Now in a sudden epiphany he pleaded he had been tricked into betraying his country by his Soviet handlers. That may have been his strategy for achieving a reconsideration of his harsh sentence but it was fraudulent.

Harry Gold had let himself be used as a government witness to satisfy the calculating ambitions of unscrupulous men in their scramble for power and prestige. He had submitted to their coaching; he listened carefully to their leads; he let himself be fine-tuned into becoming their willing puppet. He was the ultimate acolyte. In a cynical wandering of conscience (and immobilized by fear), he became the means by which they were able to convict Abraham Brothman and me. Ultimately he also boosted the voltage against the Rosenbergs and jacked up the Cold War.

One of those who had worked with and prepared Gold (and Bentley) was Roy Cohn himself. In 1953, after he left Saypol to join the McCarthy Committee's legal team, Cohn had an affidavit taken from Gold in prison. Obviously Cohn knew he could count on Gold's continued cooperation and Gold did not fail him. Again he made charges of espionage against Brothman and it was a reprise of headline news from coast to coast.

At that time Brothman had just completed his two-year sentence and was a free man. But Gold was relentlessly pursuing new ways to punish him; at the same time he accommodated Cohn. It is questionable whether Gold believed what he was saying but it is not subject to doubt that he regarded Cohn as his best source of support in the parole application he would ultimately file.

Indeed, on October 1, 1954, Cohn sent a letter of support for parole to Gold's attorney. On September 20, Robert Morris of the Senate Internal Security Committee also sent a supporting letter.[88]

Twice Harry applied for parole and twice it was denied. In the end he had to come face to face with the severity of his sentence.

Thirty years!

Although he had appeared not to react when the judge announced the sentence in December 1950 he was, at the moment, I think, simply glad to have this phase of his misery over with. He knew at last that his father and his brother would be safe and that was a relief; they would not lose the house and Joe would not lose his job. But Harry had stood on high moral ground; he had readily admitted all his real and fantasized sins. He had named names; he had helped catapult the FBI and Saypol and Cohn to fame and boundless career opportunities; he was the government's most cooperative witness. And for all his willing toadying it was, nevertheless…, thirty years!

In the Lewisburg Federal Penitentiary, Gold's work assignment was in the medical laboratory, but this was not a career spiral. Life in prison for

Harry would have been severely circumscribed as it is for all prisoners; it would have been devoid of meaning and a punitive postponement of living. That is what prison is designed to be; it is not country club living. His fellow inmates would not have been those he would have chosen to become bosom buddies, and some would have been decidedly hostile and dangerous. This was, after all, the prison where William Remington would be fatally beaten in 1954.

For Harry Gold thirty years would have been ten thousand nine hundred fifty-eight repetitive daily rituals of scratching off days on a calendar. In the mathematics of prison life, thirty years would have been an infinity and even with time off for good behavior it would have been an endless succession of uncountable bits of time.

Abe Brothman did his time in the Atlanta Penitentiary, a harsh maximum security prison said to be the worst in the country. He had fought against his conviction but nevertheless was sentenced to the maximum: seven years on two counts, the counts to run consecutively. When Harry learned, as he would have, that on appeal Brothman's sentence had been cut to two years on one count, that would have made hard time harder for him. In his mind Brothman would serve only a zephyr moment compared to his thirty years.

It would not have eased his time to watch David Greenglass, his self-confessed co-conspirator, leave after serving nine years and four months of a fifteen-year sentence. Greenglass had also been housed at Lewisburg and was released on November 16, 1960. Harry would have watched him go thinking, bitterly, "Thirty years."

And it would have caused him little cheer to know that Elizabeth Bentley had come off as an honored citizen in some circles for her patriotic service, touted as such and in demand as a professional witness and a lecturer and writer on the very subject which Harry considered himself an expert. She had not only not been prosecuted; incredibly, she had been paid for her revelations!

On May 18, 1966, after several failed efforts to win parole, Harry Gold was finally freed. He had served fifteen years and five months although he had been in custody for sixteen years less four days. His conditional release (with time off for good behavior) would have occurred on February 12, 1969 so he saved two years and nine months for all of his accommodating atonement. (But of course he escaped the death penalty.) He was then fifty-five years old.

Gold obtained a job at Kennedy Memorial Hospital in Philadelphia and worked there until his death in August 1972 during a heart operation. He was sixty-one years old when he died, the same age as his mother at her death. His passing was as unmarked as his life had been before his moment of infamy. The world had taken no note of his death and learned of it only some eighteen months later. A lone survivor had been his brother.

I have often wondered if Harry Gold ever became as tormented by the false testimony he gave against me as he said he had been over his "besmirching deeds." He had no cause for the gratuitous damage he inflicted on me. He had made himself at home in my apartment; he had shared my friends and the routine of my life. Obviously he had carefully learned to ignore what his conscience might have found troubling. He had betrayed friends and dishonored friendships and he had damned me to undeserved grief. Infinitely worse, he had inflicted unbearable pain on my parents, my sister and my brothers. There were moments during his recitations when I wanted to shout across the courtroom:

"HARRY! HOW DO YOU SLEEP NIGHTS?"

I remained mute with difficulty and observed the stylized courtroom decorum while the cadence of his speech rose and fell with scripted monotony.

Nevertheless, I was sorry for Harry even as I listened to the spill of his nonsense on the witness stand. His illusions of a newfound self-respect were just that—illusions, much like the pretense of his having been duped, and his sad fantasies of make-believe achievements and an imagined but desperately desired wife and family life. He was so ill at ease he never looked in my direction nor out towards the courtroom audience where my father sat. But in those moments it seemed to me that he was never lonelier and I forgot momentarily, my own agony. As his lips moved, as he spoke those bizarre words, Harry seemed to be doggedly twisting himself in a winding sheet and there was a sadness emanating from him which once again touched me. He had sallied forth under a pretense of doing battle with evil and had become a prisoner of his own posturing, now trapped in the deadly embrace of his fellow toads. In the end the toads destroyed him, too.

I would have wished him better than he had wished me.

Chapter 28

Roy M. Cohn, Assistant Prosecutor

When Roy Cohn was about to be drafted he put in place the earliest recorded hoax of his budding adult life. It was an augury of the cunning that characterized him ever after.

Cohn registered for the draft in 1945 when he turned eighteen (as was required by law then) and was classified as 1-A, eligible for service. Thereupon, Benjamin J. Rabin, a cooperative Democratic congressman, appointed Cohn to West Point. (Rabin was known to Roy's father, Judge Albert Cohn, who had Democratic Party connections.) The appointment effected a reclassification of Cohn as 4-B which meant he was not eligible for the draft unless West Point rejected him.[1]

In fact, West Point did reject him. Nevertheless, Congressman Rabin was moved to reappoint Cohn again and yet again. Twice Cohn could not pass the required physical exam. In October 1946 the government stopped the draft whereupon Rabin withdrew the nomination thus saving Cohn the bother of submitting to a third physical. Two years later, Cohn joined the National Guard—two days before the draft was reinstated. Again Roy Cohn out-maneuvered the government and saved himself from conscription. As a member of the National Guard Cohn cut almost half of the drills. Many of his excuses were signed by his boss, Irving R. Saypol, the U.S. Attorney for the Southern District of New York.[2] It was a neat return of favor; Saypol owed his job to Cohn[3] whose father was an appellate court judge and protégé of the Bronx's Democratic Party boss Ed Flynn.

As Assistant United States Attorney, Cohn became a key aide to Saypol in successfully prosecuting several cases of national interest. These included the Brothman/Moskowitz case, the Rosenberg/Sobell case and the William W. Remington case. Then Cohn moved his arena to Washington where he became a legal assistant to Senator Joseph McCarthy and then his chief counsel, beating out Robert F. Kennedy who had expected his father's connections to get him the chief counsel's job.[4] It was 1953 and McCarthy's Senate Investigations subcommittee was conducting probes of communists serving in the government as well as in the Army. Cohn quickly became known as a brash, quick-talking lawyer who idolized McCarthy and disdained the law.

One of Cohn's first assignments was preparing an indictment of Owen Lattimore for perjury. Lattimore, a respected China expert who taught at

Johns Hopkins University, was, according to McCarthy, "the top Russian espionage agent in the United States." The indictment Cohn prepared contained seven charges of perjury, all of which were dismissed or dropped by the Department of Justice.[5] The case however, had devastating repercussions on American foreign policy. While Lattimore had not been employed by the State Department his counsel on East Asia was highly regarded. As Navasky observed, McCarthyism "... purged the State Department of the China hands whose expertise and dissenting cables might have spared us the Vietnam War..."[6]

Cohn's next campaign was ideological purification of government employees. For seventeen days, he and his friend, David Schine, who had been appointed Chief Consultant to the Committee, roamed Europe looking for misdeeds of American government employees overseas.[7] In Paris, in April 1953, they looked for inefficiency, in Bonn they sought subversives. While they were in Rome McCarthy, back in Washington, said they had been sent abroad to report on how much money had been spent in "putting across the Truman administration." This was apparently news to Cohn, who said, "Anything the chairman of our committee says goes..."[8]

Shine and Cohn, each twenty-six and McCarthy, some twenty years senior, became objects of ridicule even while they were terrorizing the United States with their wild accusations. Lillian Hellman, the author and playwright who had been summoned to appear before the House Committee on UnAmerican Activities in 1952 to testify about communists in the entertainment world, had refused to name anyone. Appalled and scornful of the antics of this Senate triumvirate, she wrote:

> "The boozy, hospital-patched face of McCarthy... Schine's little-boy college face, Cohn plump of body, pout of sensual mouth... Bonnie, Bonnie and Clyde, shooting at anything that came to hand on the King's horses that rode to battle in official bulletproof armor."[9]

Both Schine and Cohn came from comfortable middle-class backgrounds. Cohn was the only child of Dora Marcus and appellate Judge Albert Cohn.[10] Schine was the son of J. Myer Schine, a multimillionaire hotel and movie theater owner. David had been the general manager for the Schine hotels. When reporters asked him what qualified him for the post of Chief Consultant to McCarthy's committee, he referred to a six-page pamphlet he had written entitled, "Definition of Communism." He had arranged to have copies of the pamphlet left in each of his father's hotel rooms along with the Gideon Bible.[11]

When the two pilgrims arrived in Germany, Cohn asked the director of the U.S. Cultural Center in Frankfurt where he had hidden the communist authors in the library. That gentleman replied that, to the best of his knowledge, there were no communist authors in the library. Cohn then asked where the Dashiell Hammett books were and the director led him to the shelf where he found "The Maltese Falcon" and "The Thin Man." (Dashiell Hammett was a popular American writer of detective fiction in the middle of the twentieth century. In a court case in New York in June 1951 he refused to name contributors to the bail fund of the Civil Rights Congress, on whose board he sat. The Congress aided political defendants, many of whom were communists. Hammett was jailed for contempt of court. A fellow victim in this case was W. E. B. DuBois, the civil rights leader. The prosecutors were Irving H. Saypol and his aide, Roy Cohn.)

Cohn turned to the herd of reporters who had been following them and announced triumphantly that this was proof that there were indeed communists represented in the American library.[12] He denounced other overseas libraries for carrying books by authors such as Theodore Dreiser.[13] (Some of the novels of Dreiser (1871–1945) were concerned with what were considered ruthless industrialists and bankers at a time when American business was blatantly anti-labor.)

The group proceeded to the periodicals section and Cohn asked where the anti-Communist magazines were. The director pointed out those he considered anti-communist: "America," (a Jesuit periodical), "Business Week," "Time," "Newsweek," and others. Cohn asked where the "American Legion Monthly" was and when the director said they did not have that magazine Cohn proclaimed to the reporters that there were obviously no anti-communist magazines in that library. A young reporter then asked Cohn, "Sir, when are you going to burn the books here... You know, like the Nazis did in 1933?"[14]

Cohn and Schine earned themselves scorn and ridicule in the European press and the British press called them, "Scummy snoopers and distempered jackals."[15]

Back home, Cohn's single-minded devotion to Mr. Schine ignited a firestorm of troubles for them. In November 1953, when Schine was drafted into the Army Cohn energetically worked to win concessions for him such as nightly passes while he was still in basic training, and guarantees that he would be treated as an important person with no KP duty.[16] However, both Cohn and McCarthy were unable to win a commission for him.[17]

In April 1954, McCarthy accused Army Secretary Robert T. Stevens and others of trying to conceal evidence of espionage activities at Fort Monmouth, N. J. The Army, in turn, accused McCarthy and his chief counsel, Roy Cohn, of seeking by improper means to obtain special treatment for Private Schine. In his report, Stevens detailed Cohn's persistent demands, including Cohn's threats to "wreck the Army" if his requests in behalf of Schine were not honored. After thirty-six days of raucous, widely televised Senate hearings, McCarthy and his staff were cleared of the Army's charges. However, a few months later, in December 1954, the Senate cited McCarthy for contempt although by then the damage he had wrought was irreparable. The televised hearings had exposed McCarthy's often irrational behavior to a wide audience. His popularity and influence diminished.[18] Three years later McCarthy was dead.

Cohn, who had been forced to resign,[19] returned to New York and joined the law firm which became Saxe, Bacon and Bolan. Through his family's influence, as well as his own formidable connections, Cohn attracted prestigious, high-paying clients to the firm. Among them were Donald Trump and Sam Lefrak (the real estate operators), Francis Cardinal Spellman and Terence Cardinal Cooke, Carmine Galante (who had been said to be the Mafia "boss of all bosses") and Tony (Fat Tony) Salerno, also said to be a Mafia boss.[20] Cohn's influence began to spread over journalists, religious leaders, establishment lawyers, judges, government officials, politicians and socially prominent people. Unacknowledged were his friendships with known mobsters.[21] *The Wall Street Journal* noted that Cohn had acquired the reputation of being exceedingly dangerous to tangle with.[22]

Roy Cohn lived extremely well but he never married. To avoid paying taxes he drew a comparatively low salary, but received a lavish expense account. The firm paid part of the rent on his Greenwich home, provided an apartment in Manhattan, and supplied him with the use of a chauffeured limousine equipped with a telephone, a rarity at that time. Cohn conducted most of his business from that limousine. He avoided owning property as another way of getting around I.R.S. regulations. For twenty years Cohn paid no income taxes. The I.R.S. held liens against him totaling over three million dollars.[23]

Cohn's expense account provided him with a munificent standard of living. Despite that, he had a reputation for never paying his bills. He owed money to friends, restaurants, liquor stores, even the shopkeepers and vendors for ordinary household or office supplies. The judgments piled up but were rarely collectible because the I.R.S. had first call on him. Sometimes he would offer to settle with a creditor for fifty cents on the dollar.[24]

Convivial always, Cohn gave lavish parties, entertaining former mayors of New York, Democratic Party bosses, and state and federal judges. Among his friends were President Reagan, Norman Mailer, Bianca Jagger, S. I. Newhouse of the Newhouse media family, Barbara Walters, Ruppert Murdoch, William F. Buckley, Jr., William Safire, George Steinbrenner and Estee Lauder.[25] However, his well-placed and powerful friends could not stave off the legal problems beginning to barrel towards him.

In March 1964 Roy Cohn was tried for committing perjury, getting witnesses to commit perjury and for conspiring to obstruct justice. The events grew out of a five-million dollar stock fraud case of 1959 which involved the firm, United Dye & Chemical Corp. (a "bucket shop" stock operation) in which Cohn had an interest. The specific charges against him were that he had illegally prevented four United Dye principals, (two of whom were Nevada gamblers) from being indicted in 1959[26] for fraud by getting witnesses to testify falsely. One of the defendants also admitted to having paid $50,000 to Cohn which was to be split between Cohn and a government prosecutor in return for keeping the four clear of legal action.

Cohn was acquitted of all charges – although neither of the two witnesses against him was ever prosecuted for having testified falsely.[27-30]

Another of Cohn's business adventures concerned the Lionel Corp. In 1959 he took over this company, originally a toy manufacturer. Under Cohn's direction, Lionel acquired M. Steinthal Co. and an affiliate in 1961, and issued 123,000 common shares of stock then worth over three million dollars. As part of the deal, Cohn gave the Steinthals options to sell almost 45,000 shares back to him at almost $18 a share. A year later, with the stock a little more than $6 a share, Cohn refused to honor the Steinthals' options.[31] The company reported net losses of $2,500,000 in 1961 and almost $5,000,000 in 1962.[32] The Steinthals sold their stock for less than the guaranteed price, sued Cohn for the difference, and obtained a judgment. Cohn lost two appeals and ultimately had to agree to pay off the judgment.[33]

It was noted that when Roy Cohn took over Lionel he persuaded his buddies to buy its stock while he quietly depleted its assets. Cohn got richer and his friends lost money.[34]

Similarly, Cohn bought into Tower Acceptance Corp., a loan company, which he then renamed Tower Universal Corp. The revenues tripled quickly but profits were slim. A year later, after the stock had lost half its value, Cohn sold his interest and resigned his directorship.[35]

He gained control of Fifth Avenue Coach Company in New York City in 1961. At the end of 1964 Cohn was sued for having defrauded the company while he had served as its lawyer. In a ten-count indictment Cohn was charged with having committed mail and wire fraud and with having filed false reports with the Securities and Exchange Commission. The charges also included bribery and extortion. The prosecution contended that Cohn and others had conspired to bribe the city appraiser in a condemnation proceeding to obtain secret data concerning the company's assets from the city's files. The extortion charge stemmed from Cohn's attempt to force the president of Fifth Avenue Coach to relinquish control of the company (in Cohn's favor) by threatening to expose his part in the bribery.[36]

The case went to trial but Cohn did not take the stand. When the presentation of the evidence had been completed Cohn's attorney suddenly fell ill and was hospitalized. In a legal maneuver that was spectacular for its audaciousness, Cohn acted as his own attorney and gave the summation speech. He was thus able to make arguments in his own defense without ever having had to take the stand and submit to cross-examination. He was acquitted.[37]

In all his ventures Cohn left behind a trail of stunned, financially ruined ex-friends. A sub-headline in a *Wall Street Journal* article about Cohn stated, "Lionel in red; bus, Boxing Projects in Legal Snarls, Personal Fortune Mounts."[38] Despite the lawsuits, the million dollars' worth of judgments and the I.R.S. claims, Cohn remained personally untouched. Almost all his assets including his Manhattan townhouse, his limousine and his 99-foot yacht, were leased or held in separate corporations headed by his own nominees.[39]

Cohn was a clever, masterful self-promoter who manipulated the press, the politicians, and the courts.[40] He was slapped with judicial reprimands for unethical conduct and many of the civil actions brought against him were pursued by former clients. In one, a former client sued him for the return of a loan of over $100,000.[41] He was also accused of lying on his membership application to the District of Columbia bar, in which he denied that any charges or complaints had ever been made against him as a lawyer. It was these two charges that began the final unraveling of his career with two even more serious ones waiting offstage.[42]

One involved the sinking of the leased yacht, *Defiance*, in 1973. It was owned by the Pied Piper Yacht Charters Corp., a company whose borrowed funds Cohn appeared to be using as his own. The *Defiance* had been declared unseaworthy by its captain in Miami, who quit his job when ordered to sail it. It was put out to sea with a new captain, who had served time in a federal penitentiary. A mysterious fire broke out and the *Defiance* sank. The captain and two crew members survived, but another crew member lost his life. The father of the lost seaman charged that Cohn had ordered the boat destroyed to collect a large insurance policy and he held Cohn responsible for his son's death. Denying any guilt, Cohn was subjected to an S.E.C. investigation. He lied blatantly and repeatedly about the whereabouts of the insurance money which had been paid to Piper before vanishing. When ordered to produce the insurance settlement, some $219,000, or go to jail, he produced the funds.[43]

Even before the Pied Piper case was settled, Cohn had embarked on new and even more daring pillaging. In December 1975, Cohn and an associate forced their way into the Miami hospital room of Lewis S. Rosenstiel, a former client and multimillionaire head of Schenley Industries, to have him execute a codicil to his will. The comatose Rosenstiel was eight-four years old and paralyzed from a stroke. He was also suffering from Alzheimer's disease and on the hospital's critical list. Visitors other than immediate family were barred. Nevertheless, Cohn and his friend forced their way into the room and Cohn put a piece of paper in front of Rosenstiel. It was the codicil. He did not tell Rosenstiel what the real purpose of the codicil was although it is doubtful whether Rosenstiel would have understood anyhow. With Cohn's help Rosenstiel held the pen and made some marks on the paper.

The codicil would have made Cohn and others the executors and trustees of Rosenstiel's will, and would have given them a majority vote on matters relating to the administration of Rosenstiel's vast estate. It would also have given them control over the disposition of several pending claims involving over four million dollars brought by Sidney Frank, Rosenstiel's former son-in-law and two of Frank's children. Frank was the primary claimant against the Rosenstiel estate. He was also a friend of Cohn's.

Unknown to Cohn, however, Rosenstiel had placed most of the estate in a special trust for his daughter, Elizabeth, thus keeping it out of reach of Cohn and his cohorts.

A few weeks after Cohn's visit Rosenstiel died. Cohn thereupon filed the codicil with Rosenstiel's purported signature, which would surrender control of Rosenstiel's immense fortune to Cohn and his associates. This effort misfired. On June 24, 1976 the Dade County, Florida probate court ordered Cohn's codicil of the previous December to be revoked because Rosenstiel, the judge said, had been incapable of voluntarily signing it. He also accused Roy Cohn of having misrepresented the nature, content and purpose of the codicil.

Although there were other instances of Cohn's plundering it was these cases which moved the judges of the New York Appellate Division to order Roy Cohn's disbarment on June 23, 1986. They found his conduct highly unethical, incomprehensible and incredible, and his testimony misleading and untruthful. The New York State Court of Appeals on July 3, 1986, refused to consider Cohn's appeal despite his frenzied, last-ditch campaign to stave off the disaster. Character witnesses in his behalf included William F. Buckley, Jr., Barry Farber, Barbara Walters, Sidney Zion, Donald Trump, William Safire, Bishop Edward Broderick and Msgr. Eugene Clark of the New York Archdiocese under Terence Cardinal Cook, Alan Dershowitz and New York City Council President Andrew Stein. There were, in addition, the highly placed judges, David Edelstein (Chief Judge of the Southern District of New York), Roger Miner (U.S. Court of Appeals for the Second Circuit), Bernard Newman (U. S. Customs Court), Harold Stevens (former Presiding Justice of the Appellate Division of the First Department of the State of New York) and Stanley Fuld (former Chief Judge of the New York State Court of Appeals. As Bill Reuben pointedly noted in his account of this, "Judges!!"[44]

It was a stellar array of power and influence – but it did not help. Roy Cohn was no longer the armored tank who could roll over his opposition and leave it demolished in his wake. His disgrace was irrevocable and he had no further tricks. Except, perhaps, one final act.

Some five weeks after his disbarment, on August 2, 1986, Roy Marcus Cohn died. He was fifty-nine years old.[45]

Cohn had cynically participated in McCarthy's destructive campaign to rid the government of those he arbitrarily labeled communists, and "perverts," as he referred to homosexuals. He generated wild accusations and was merciless in hounding innocent victims. He lobbied against a gay rights municipal ordinance in New York and contemptuously referred to gay men as "fags," even while vociferously denying his own homosexuality. To the end, Cohn was willing to persecute others while concealing his own secret. Ever unfaithful he constantly recruited a stable of young men and traveled about with them noisily and flamboyantly to night clubs, parties, on vacations and even to political engagements. Nightly he would have one or more of them and in the morning sometimes would withhold payment or just forget to pay them.[46]

Cohn was the master dissembler; not even Dorian Gray could have matched him for cruelty, dishonesty self-indulgence and hedonism.[47] To the last he told everyone his malady was a liver ailment. In truth, he died of AIDS.[48] For fifty-nine years Roy Cohn had carried on a single-minded love affair with one person: himself. He consigned all the rest of the world to the trash heap.

Chapter 29

Irving H. Saypol, Prosecutor

In 1948 the ambitious Irving Saypol had forged his way into the culture of corruption to seek the post of United States attorney for the Southern District of New York. The appointment was a political patronage position decided on by a triumvirate consisting of Generoso Pope, Sr., Carmine De Sapio and Frank Costello.

Pope was the owner of an influential Italian-language newspaper, *Il Progresso*. He also owned Colonial Sand & Stone Co. , a construction materials supply company, and was a man to be reckoned with in the New York Democratic Party. Roy Cohn, a close friend, had had a number of business dealings with Pope and had invested money in his company. De Sapio, another friend of Roy Cohn, was head of Tammany Hall, the Democratic Party organization in New York, and a close friend of Frank Costello. Costello was a mobster.

At a critical moment in the deliberations of this trio when it seemed that the appointment might go to a political rival, Saypol called on his friend, Roy Cohn, for help. Cohn jumped quickly into the situation, and the appointment went to Saypol.[1]

After Saypol successfully prosecuted the case against Abraham Brothman and me, he prosecuted the Rosenbergs and Sobell in March 1951 and won more convictions. He also handled the prosecution of William W. Remington and a number of other high-profile cases, and then left the United States Attorney's post to accept an appointment to the New York State Supreme Court in September 1951, an appointment also reported to have been arranged by Costello.[2]

In May 1976, after twenty-five years on the bench, Saypol was indicted for bribery and perjury, both felonies. According to the indictment, Saypol and a member of the Manhattan Surrogate's Court met in the latter's office in November 1975 with the Public Administrator (also indicted) to trade favors.[3]

It was the Public Administrator's job to liquidate assets of estates and preserve their maximum value when there was no will. To prevent possible collusion between the appraiser of an estate and the auctioneer, the Public Administrator adopted a policy that forbade the appraiser of an estate from also selling the same property at auction.

State Supreme Court justices, on the other hand, have enormous power.

Among other duties, they can assign lawyers as referees in bankruptcy, or as guardians to minors. These are much sought-after assignments; they usually earn the appointees handsome fees and open doors to valuable connections.

In the case the indictment covered, the Public Administrator agreed to allow an auctioneer to handle the sale of a particular estate property that he himself had previously appraised. It would bring that person substantial commissions. The candidate for the double appointment was none other than Saypol's son Roger. The indictment charged that in return, Saypol (senior) promised to give lucrative court assignments to lawyers hand-picked by the Public Administrator.

The indictment also accused the defendants of having met to discuss the use of different names to conceal the fact that Saypol's son was both appraiser and seller of a property.

Subsequently, in January 1976, Saypol telephoned the Public Administrator to ask if he needed help for a lawyer the Administrator was interested in placing. The Administrator responded affirmatively. The indictment said that Justice Saypol gave a patronage assignment to the lawyer named by the Public Administrator.

The crimes of bribery and perjury Saypol was charged with carried a prison sentence of up to seven years. However, since the evidence against him had been based on a conversation recorded by the FBI in an illegal wiretap, the indictment was dismissed. Saypol suffered embarrassment and notoriety. He retired from the bench soon after.

Irving H. Saypol was seventy-one years old when he died of cancer a year after the indictment, on June 30, 1977.

Chapter 30

Irving R. Kaufman, the Judge

When the prosecution was preparing its case in the weeks before our trial, FBI officials noted with some pessimism that the government's suit against Brothman and me was not a strong one.[1] For our part, Abe Brothman and I were mildly optimistic because the burden of proof was on the government and the charges against us had little relationship to reality.

They, and we, reckoned without Judge Kaufman.

Although his individual actions might have been considered within the boundaries of judicial probity, the totality formed a partisan pattern and Brothman and I quickly discarded any notion that Kaufman would insure an ethical and fair dimension to this trial. He steered the jury carefully and when they brought in the verdict he was jubilant.

Kaufman delivered his sentencing speech in tones that played to the gallery. From the first he had unwittingly revealed a pattern of sadism, remanding us to jail even before jury selection. With that single act he sent a clear message that he thought we were dangerous and therefore guilty. I recalled how he had refused to provide us with Bentley's previous grand jury testimony, even though he had permitted her to be consistently unresponsive to our attorney's questions. I saw again Kaufman's tyranny in blunting our attorney's legitimate defense moves, and the constant, not entirely subtle, belittling of his efforts. On the other hand, the witnesses, Bentley and Gold, were treated with kid gloves.

Kaufman worked hand in hand with the prosecution in an incestuous relationship, frequently taking over cross-examination when the prosecutor was not nimble enough. He led Gold in formulating testimony, even putting words in his mouth when he stumbled. Kaufman's rulings on our attorney's challenges were invariably against us and were unreasonable and unfair. He had also not been burdened with the established legal tenet that a conspiracy had validity only if the truthfulness of the testifying conspirator is established beyond doubt. Harry Gold's veracity (and Bentley's) remained unproved and he would not permit us to provide evidence of their many deceptions. Sometimes he ruled first and established justifications afterwards. Kaufman fed the jury his own prejudices against us, and when it finally brought in the verdict he savored it as a personal victory.

His was an indelible image as he sat high on that bench, impervious to the requirements of humanity. He was imperial, unreachable, coldly outside the community of mere mortals, unresponsive to doubt and draped in the majesty of the robes of his office. The mahogany of his bench, burnished to a soft patina, was like an impregnable fortress. The power he wielded was palpable and my anger grew as I listened to him consign me to hell.

Four months later, Kaufman also secured a conviction in the Rosenberg/Sobell case. He had been assigned to sit on that case only after badgering Roy Cohn to use his considerable political influence to get him that assignment.[2] During that trial he conducted unlawful, "ex parte" discussions with the prosecution.[3] Had the defense attorneys been privy to this information they would have had cause to call for a mistrial and Kaufman would have been vulnerable to public and judicial censure.

The death sentence he imposed on the Rosenbergs did not sit as well with the public as he had anticipated. In 1952, he telephoned President Truman urging him to commute it to life imprisonment. Truman said that if Kaufman felt strongly enough to urge the President to take such action then he, Kaufman, should do it himself. Kaufman declined and this, it was said, undoubtedly had a negative impact on his lifelong ambition to secure an appointment to the United States Supreme Court.[4]

Kaufman had said that he reached his decision about the death sentence in a solitary struggle of conscience; seeking divine guidance by visiting his synagogue the night before he sentenced the Rosenbergs.[5] But he had told Cohn in advance of the trial, even before conviction, that he would sentence the Rosenbergs to death. And after he passed sentence he repeatedly called the FBI in an effort to expedite the executions as a means, he thought, of quieting the public clamor for mercy.

Kaufman's service was rewarded with an appointment to the United States Court of Appeals, but he was still eager to fulfill his lifelong ambition, an appointment to a seat on the U.S. Supreme Court. However, Justice Felix Frankfurter, infuriated with Kaufman's conduct of the Rosenberg trial, was determined not to let that happen. He postponed his retirement until Kaufman was too old to be considered and his candidacy was no longer an issue.[6]

The sentence of death Kaufman imposed on the Rosenbergs has haunted the national conscience ever since. In 1975, protestors forced Kaufman to cancel a speech at the Pomona College (California) graduation ceremony. He complained subsequently that the potential threat from his appearance did not arise from what he had planned to say, "but rather from a continuous pattern of harassment because of a trial I presided over more than twenty years ago..."[7]

Irving R. Kaufman died February 2, 1992 of pancreatic cancer and was buried from the Park Avenue Synagogue in New York City the following day. I went to the synagogue but did not enter, for I did not want to be mistaken for a mourner. The synagogue and the block itself were ringed with plainclothesmen and police in uniform, and police cars patrolled restlessly up and down the avenue. I assumed that their presence was because they expected disruptions.

Kaufman had enjoyed little peace over the years from the quiet but insistent drumbeat sounded by the National Committee to Reopen the Rosenberg Case. That organization had repeatedly called for reexamining the issues with a view to exonerating the Rosenbergs posthumously. It was accorded modest publicity from time to time, both in the United States and abroad. This rankled Kaufman; it was said that he complained to J. Edgar Hoover about it.[8]

I stood on the street corner in front of the synagogue and stamped my feet in the bitter cold. I waited, not sure why I had been drawn to be there, or what I was waiting for. Had I merely wanted to see his casket I could have sat inside the chapel where it was warm and comfortable but that would have imposed an obligation on me to listen to eulogies and I did not think I could handle that. (In fact, the eulogies were interrupted by a man who shouted, "He was a murderer! Kaufman was a murderer! He murdered the Rosenbergs!" The interloper was rushed out and I witnessed an exchange between the police and the man but it subsided quickly.)

I endured the numbing cold and the merciless wind and moved from one spot to another in a futile search for a cube of space where the wind would not whip so harshly. As I did so I noticed that I was being watched by several plainclothesmen. Ironically, I thought, after forty years I again merited police surveillance!

As the wind beat at me I regretted that I had never had a chance to confront Kaufman as I had so often fantasized I would someday do. (I had once been on a Rosenberg picket line in front of the Foley Square Courthouse where Kaufman had his office and where I had been tried and convicted. When the demonstration was over I made my way into the courthouse, drawn as if in a trance, and found Kaufman's office. I put my hand on the doorknob to enter, still not aware that I was doing something totally foolhardy, and tried to open the door. A guard came up to me and told me Kaufman's office was locked because he and his staff were on vacation. I thanked him, suddenly realized I needed not to do this, and left safely and very much in a hurry.)

Now at Kaufman's funeral, as I mused, there was a burst of usher activity at the side doors of the synagogue and it was apparent that the service was over. I moved down the block towards those doors and was unobserved because the police remained in front of the building. The casket rolled out and stopped in front of me; I sucked in my breath and trembled. It was a mahogany casket and Kaufman was encased in it much as I remembered he had been surrounded by the mahogany of his courtroom bench when he sentenced me to prison. The casket was laden with huge wreaths and the flowers gave off a heavy pungency.

The ushers had moved off the curb; looking for the hearse which was lumbering its way up the block, stalled in heavy cross-town traffic. While they waited they chatted among themselves. For a moment, Irving Kaufman and I were alone.

Silently I summoned the spectral Kaufman. Anyone observing me might have thought I was praying but this was no "Kaddish," no chant of an "El-ma' Aleh Rachamim."

" Kaufman," I thought, "time changes everything, so our roles are reversed. I now stand in judgment of you, the transgressor. Hear me carefully:

"I impeach you!

"I indict you!"

"I damn you for having lusted for prestige and for having fed your obscene ambitions at my expense! You corrupted justice with your relentless scramble for power and you knew what you were doing. You danced to the macabre music of cupidity; your dancing partners were tainted with the same depravity, and you gave them cynical, shameful victories.

"And Kaufman, if it was divine guidance you sought before you sentenced Ethel and Julius, did you also believe that it was divine retribution when two of your beloved sons died thereafter? It was an even exchange, Kaufman: in 1977 your Robert for Ethel, and in 1991, your Richard for Julius. Were you sick with your terrible loss? Did you cry out in excruciating pain much as two little boys did when you turned them into orphans so many years ago?

"Your name forever scalds memory, Kaufman. It is etched on the tablets of history by the acid of your inhumanity; it has become the vilest of curses, an anathema, an execration for the ages. I bear witness to that. We all die; but you, Kaufman, despised and rejected, you died a long time ago."

I stood over his coffin, still trembling, and I whispered, "You lost, Kaufman. You lost."

I had at last confronted him.

Shivering, I hurried away towards the cross-town bus that would deposit me near where I had parked my car. As I approached the bus stop, a child's friction toy rolled towards me out of control and a small boy ran to retrieve it. I stopped it with my foot to keep it from rolling further. He dove for it, then gave me a shy, sweet smile. I smiled back.

When I reached my car the wind had died down, the sun shone and the world seemed suddenly more cheerful. I slipped the key into the ignition, pulled off my heavy woolen hat, and shook my hair free. As I adjusted the rear view mirror my image stared back at me and I saw I was still smiling.

I knew then that the wounds of that terrible time had faded. My life had had its joys and modest triumphs; and I was whole and intact. I had survived the bitterness of injustice and the meanness of his court; I had survived Irving R. Kaufman.

Epilogue

I came of age in tandem with the end of the Depression and the beginning of World War II. In the ensuing years, like many Americans, I was numbed by the Cold War, and plunged into the long unease which it generated. It affected every aspect of American life and was relentless, an interminable crusade against communists and, eventually, anyone with a dissenting thought in his head. It was the longest war in American history, lasting almost fifty years and claiming millions of victims in poor countries exploited by the two adversaries. Every time it appeared that Armageddon had spent itself and things could not get worse, it did not and they did: Korea, Guatemala, Congo (Zaire), Chile, Vietnam and Indochina, Angola, Granada, Nicaragua and El Salvador and numerous other covert, destabilizing interventions and counterrevolutions all over the globe. In most instances the legacy of interference was armed anarchy and indigenous wars among regional powers, all in the name of containing communism; the legacy became an enduring blight on American national prestige.

As a dominant factor of life in the United States the Cold War also became the single most destructive influence on American hopes for the future. It almost fatally enfeebled organized labor by inciting it to expel militant affiliates as communist-dominated. Dedicated union people with a populist or leftist bent were declared *personae non grata* and hounded out of the labor movement. Organization of workers on a mass scale stopped. Collective bargaining agreements, nearly all with non-strike clauses did win higher wage settlements, but gave critical control to employers over the organization of work. Grievances were often not pursued aggressively.[1] What was left was a flabby shadow of a once winning combination of humanity and vision, now vulnerable in some instances to takeover by organized crime.

Under a counterfeit mantra of an ideological struggle, the Cold War fostered a way of life defined by violence and greed. It placed limits on the democratic process because it discouraged dissent. It stifled democratic hopes in emerging nations by purchasing the loyalty of its leaders and corrupting them while it impoverished its ordinary citizens. In its aim to destroy an economic rival, it sought to create a world in its own image in which it would remain the sole superpower. The final irony was that in pursuing the Cold War its leaders seriously compromised the country's standing among nations and weakened the institutions that had made it great.

The cost of the Cold War to Americans was a seesaw economy, growing unemployment, a widening divide between the haves and the have-nots, neglect of health care, social services, education, infrastructure and our natural heritage. It also contributed to nuclear arms proliferation which has grown to a worldwide threat, a planet of homeless children bedding down in hunger, and perhaps worst of all, impending climate change.

For the record, it must also be said that at the height of the political onslaught the left, pulverized by fear became irrelevant. Those who should have shown integrity and courage ran for cover; (except for a valiant, pitiful few) and the more frightened the left became the more intense grew the mania. A decade later African-Americans in the sixties came together in a highly disciplined struggle to demand voting rights, equal education and an end to segregation. They were followed by an explosion on college campuses of youths across the country demonstrating against a savage unconscionable war, and they were joined by Americans of conscience. Those young people had no heritage of political theory, no mantle of self-endowed political wisdom, no sense of history, no program beyond tomorrow and certainly no identification with the class struggle. They were mostly loosely organized caucuses high on their own non-negotiable furies. Nevertheless, out of their angst rose figures like Martin Luther King and Philip and Daniel Berrigan and Rabbi Abraham Jeshua Heschel, and an army of brave citizens — and the world became a more hopeful place.

The issue of anti-Semitism must also be confronted; it hovered over the Rosenberg/Sobell trial and equally over the Brothman/Moskowitz trial with an unmistakable presence. It was not for nothing that the prosecution leaders and the judge (the same in both trials) were conspicuously Jewish, as of course, were the defendants. Also, neither Abraham Brothman nor I were charged with the act of obstructing justice but rather with *conspiracy to obstruct*, thus freeing the prosecution from the otherwise restrictive demand to observe the strict rules of evidence. It became an exposure of the weakness of the prosecution's case, as well as its fury over our refusal to name others. But the Jewish establishment, perhaps fearing that an association with Jewish radicalism would revive latent anti-Semitism in the country, expediently avoided asking questions about the overzealous prosecution, never demurred about the use of tainted evidence from problem witnesses and never voiced doubts about the judge's obvious bias or the prejudicial atmosphere generated by the FBI and exploited by the media blitz. Rather, it maintained a detached and profound silence. Some leaders in the Jewish community even joined in denouncing us (and were especially vitriolic towards the Rosenbergs) as though to reinforce public perception of their own patriotism. For those of us nurtured on the ancient sanctity of Jewish brotherhood it was the ultimate coup de grace and I have never been able to forgive them.

* * * *

All documents I obtained from Freedom of Information Act requests as well as other documents related to my prosecution are filed with the Moskowitz Papers at the Arthur W. Diamond Library of Columbia University Law School, Special Collections Dept.

Afterword

M iriam Moskowitz is an innocent person who was caught up in the whirlwind of anti-communist hysteria that prevailed in this country at the time of her trial in 1950. We know that because of FBI documents she obtained through the Freedom of Information Act decades after her conviction for conspiring to obstruct justice during a grand jury investigation.

The prosecution's case depended on the trial testimony of FBI informant Harry Gold. He testified that in 1947 *she observed* a conversation during which he and her business partner, Abraham Brothman, allegedly discussed providing false testimony to a grand jury investigating possible Soviet espionage.[1] She did not testify before that grand jury.

The FBI documents Ms. Moskowitz obtained are proof that prior to her trial Mr. Gold told the FBI *she was not present* during that alleged conversation.[2] Furthermore, Mr. Gold told the FBI he didn't speak candidly in front of Ms. Moskowitz because of her possible negative reaction if he said something incriminating in her presence, and he didn't like her.[3]

Assistant U.S. Attorney Roy Cohn was one of Ms. Moskowitz' prosecutors, and an FBI document about Mr. Gold dated October 24, 1950 – two weeks before the start of her trial – is titled "Memo for Roy Cohn."[4]

Since we know Mr. Gold's testimony wasn't truthful about Ms. Moskowitz being present, it is reasonable to doubt the truthfulness of his testimony the jury relied on to also convict Mr. Brothman of conspiracy to obstruct justice. Particularly in light of Ms. Moskowitz's explanation in her book that Mr. Brothman had no reason not to be completely truthful during his grand jury testimony in 1947 because he hadn't done anything illegal in seeking business opportunities with Amtorg Trading Corporation – the Soviet Union's trade representative in the United States – when the Soviet Union was an ally of this country <u>prior</u> to the Cold War.

Yet, the U.S. Attorney's Office did not disclose the exculpatory documents – one of which is stamped SECRET – to Ms. Moskowitz' lawyers, the trial judge, the jury, or the federal appeal court judges when she sought to overturn her conviction in 1951.

Lady Justice was anything but blindfolded. Not only did the U.S. Attorney's Office vigorously push for Ms. Moskowitz's conviction while concealing evidence supporting her innocence, but it was ably assisted by Judge Irving R. Kaufman. Judge Kaufman only superficially concealed his bias favoring her conviction (and that of her co-defendant Mr. Brothman).

After her conviction Judge Kaufman sentenced Ms. Moskowitz to the maximum of two years in prison and a $10,000 fine.

Although the law has evolved somewhat in the last 60 years, one thing that hasn't changed is it was a blatant violation of Ms. Moskowitz's constitutional rights to a fair trial and due process for the government to knowingly rely on Mr. Gold's perjurious testimony to convince the jury to convict her.

The U.S. Supreme Court recognized in 1935 that due process of law is not satisfied "if a State has contrived a conviction through the pretense of a trial which in truth is but used as a means of depriving a defendant of liberty through a deliberate deception of court and jury by the presentation of testimony known to be perjured." (*Mooney v. Holohan*, 294 US 103, 112 (1935).) In a 1942 case the Supreme Court explained that a defendant's federal constitutional right to due process is violated if the State knowingly suppresses favorable evidence and knowingly relies on perjured testimony. (*Pyle v. Kansas*, 317 US 213, 216 (1942).)

Thus, even without the benefit of Supreme Court cases in the late 1950s and 1960s that are still relied on to defend a person's right not to be railroaded through the legal system by over-eager prosecutors, Ms. Moskowitz received only "the pretense of a trial" by the standards of 1950.[5] Her prosecutors – U.S. Attorney Irving Saypol and Assistant U.S. Attorney Cohn – subverted the truth and ignored the Supreme Court's admonition in another 1935 case, that as representatives of the public they had a constitutional obligation not to use "improper methods calculated to produce a wrongful conviction." (*Berger v United States*, 295 US 78 (1935).)

Consequently, if the federal appeals court had known in 1951 that the case against Ms. Moskowitz was based on Mr. Gold's false testimony, there is every expectation it would have overturned her conviction instead of affirming it. That can be stated with confidence because the appeals court ruled: "The case against the appellants was made largely by the testimony of Gold."[6] In support of that conclusion the appeals court related several instances of testimony by Mr. Gold that we now know was false. So unbeknownst to the court, their factual premise for upholding her conviction was wrong.

There is an extraordinary legal remedy known as the writ of *coram nobis* that exists for the correction of egregious legal errors after a defendant has completed his or her sentence. Ms. Moskowitz's conviction, based on false evidence knowingly presented to the jury by her prosecutors, fits squarely in the mold of the type of festering legal error the writ of *coram nobis* is intended to rectify.

However, even under the most compelling of circumstances the legal system is reluctant to correct the error of an innocent person's conviction. Whether Ms. Moskowitz's conviction is ever overturned by a federal court is in a sense a technicality that would only officially recognize what is now publicly known: She was innocent and the U.S. Attorney's Office knew that at the time it elicited Mr. Gold's false testimony which the jury relied on to convict her in 1950.

The manifest wrong of Ms. Moskowitz' conviction in spite of her factual innocence was compounded by the falsehood that continues to be repeated associating her and Mr. Brothman with the alleged atom bomb spies Julius and Ethel Rosenberg, and the fictitious "Rosenberg Spy Ring." Neither Ms. Moskowitz nor Mr. Brothman were spies, neither had known the Rosenbergs and they were not part of any so-called "spy ring." It was only after Ms. Moskowitz and Mr. Brothman were arrested and jailed that they each met the Rosenbergs. Ms. Moskowitz met Ethel at New York City's Woman's House of Detention, and Mr. Brothman met Julius at the Federal Detention Center.

Prosecutor Cohn admitted in his autobiography[7] that the U.S. government used the hurried prosecution of Ms. Moskowitz and Mr. Brothman on relatively minor charges as a trial run for the Rosenberg's trial that followed four months later. That raises the question of whether from the get-go Ms. Moskowitz and Mr. Brothman were subjected to a "sham" prosecution intended by the U.S. Attorney's Office as a real-life "mock trial" of what could be expected during the Rosenberg's trial,[8] since it was expected that it would be an international media sensation. If that is what happened – and the evidence supports that conclusion – then the U.S. government's conduct goes far beyond knowingly prosecuting innocent people. It is the grossest imaginable misuse of the criminal legal process that ought to be condemned by everyone who has even a passing interest in the concept of justice.

Apart from the sheer injustice of what was done to Ms. Moskowitz in the name of the law, was the impact on her life from the entire weight and power of the U.S. government being brought to bear against her. Thirty-four at the time of her trial, she has lived for more than 60 years with the stigma of being a convicted felon. After her release from prison she was harassed by the FBI, she suffered employment discrimination, and it took her more than a quarter-century to pay off her $10,000 fine.

We wouldn't know the truth of Ms. Moskowitz' prosecution were it not for *Phantom Spies, Phantom Justice*. Consequently, her book is much more than a personal memoir, it is a valuable well-documented first-hand account that corrects and contributes to the historical record of the McCarthy era, and in the process rehabilitates Ms. Moskowitz' reputation.

Hans Sherrer[*]
March 2012

---

[*] Editor and publisher of *Justice:Denied – the magazine for the wrongly convicted.*

Appendix A

Aside issue of Matusow's testimony about Bentley was his accusation that Roy Cohn had persuaded him to testify falsely in a case involving the trial of the thirteen Communist Party leaders in the summer of 1952. They had been indicted under the Smith Act, a peacetime sedition law passed in 1940.[1]

Under Cohn's tutelage, Matusow in this recantation, said he had accused one of the defendants, Alexander Trachtenberg, of having urged him to promote Andrei Vyshinskii's *The Law Of The Soviet State* because a passage in it contained directives for the overthrow of capitalism. Matusow told how Cohn had "prepared" him for his role on the witness stand; Cohn had said to him that the government wanted to introduce Vyshinskii's book as evidence of Trachtenberg's crime. Matusow told Cohn he had never discussed anything with Trachtenberg that would tie him to the passage. Nevertheless, during the ensuing months, Matusow said, the details of his testimony were worked out and "...in several sessions with Cohn we developed the answer which I gave in my testimony... We both knew that Trachtenberg had never made the statements I attributed to him in my testimony."[2]

Cohn vociferously denied Matusow's accusations and Matusow did not escape his wrath. He was indicted, tried and convicted of perjury on July 13, 1955 for having accused Roy Cohn of suborning his original perjurious testimony in 1951.[3] Ironically, as Kahn notes, Matusow was never punished for having earlier lied about innocent people but he was sentenced to five years for, in effect, having finally told the truth.[4]

Appendix B

Partial list of published work by (or about) Abraham Brothman.

1. "Robotization of Process Plants" by A. Brothman with R. V. Ramani, and "Designing a Robotized Plant for Resin Blue Production" by A. Brothman with R. V. Ramani, *Chemical Engineering*, November and December 1949.

2. "New Process for Acrylic Resin" (about Brothman's work in this field) by Richard W. Porter, Assistant Editor, *Chemical Engineering*, April 1947.

3. "New Analysis Provides Formula to Solve Mixing Problems" by A. Brothman, *Chemical & Metallurgical Engineering*, April 1945.

4. "Continuous Mixing and Reaction Equipment Design" by A. Brothman, *Chemical and Metallurgical Engineering*, May 1945

5. "DDT Fights Insects in War and in Peace" (about Brothman's work in this field), by John R. Callaham, Asst. Ed., *Chemical and Metallurgical Engineering*, October 1944.

6. "New Approach to Continuous Reactor Design" by A. Brothman, *Chemical and Metallurgical Engineering*, July, August and September 1943.

7. "Handbook of Plastics" by Ellis and Simonds, Section on Resin Plant Design by A. Brothman, Van Nostrand and Co. 1944.

8. "Batch-Continuous Process for Buna-N" by A. Brothman, *Chemical & Metallurgical Engineering*, May 1943.

9. "Batch-Continuous Process for Buna-S" by A. Brothman, *Chemical & Metallurgical Engineering*, March 1943.

10. "Design of a Urea Resin Plant" by A. Brothman, *Chemical & Metallurgical Engineering*, December 1941.

11. "Stuffing Box Design" by A. Brothman, *Product Engineering*, September and November, 1940.

12. "Vertical Shaft Design for Balanced Rotors, with Calculations for the High-Speed Rotor Effects" by A. Brothman, *Product Engineering*, April 1940.

13. "Resin Plant Design" by A. Brothman, *Modern Plastics*, October 1939.

14. "Introduction to Liquid Mixing" by A. Brothman, *Chemical & Metallurgical Engineering*, October 1939.

15. "Mixing Operations in the Paint and Pigment Industries" by A. Brothman, *National Paint Bulletin*, October 1939.

16. "Methods for Emulsifier Choice" by A. Brothman, *Chemical & Metallurgical Engineering*, May 1939.

17. "Statistical Approach to the Mechanics and Kinetics of Additive Polmerizations" by A. Brothman (in manuscript form as of November 1950.

18. "Criteria for Evaluation of Polycondensation Products and the Kinetics of Polycondensation Reactions" by A. Brothman (in manuscript form as of November 1950).

Appendix C

I have been targeted over the years by a few writers who wrote about espionage and who sought perhaps to spice up material that might otherwise, have fallen into a "do not disturb" bin. So it was when Sam Roberts of the *New York Times* wrote me (and my co-defendant, Abraham Brothman) into his book, *The Brother,* published in 2001. He quoted me, on the topic of David Greenglass' role in convicting Ethel and Julius Rosenberg, as having implicitly defended him: "'In his eyes he had no choice,' Moskowitz said of David. 'He had a new baby. His wife had been ill. They had him over a barrel.'" (Page 262)

The truth: Roberts telephoned me in 1999 ostensibly to ask about a research source I had looked into; he had learned I was writing a book. I gave him my opinion. Then he mentioned that he was writing a book about David Greenglass and I made a negative comment. Roberts jumped to Greenglass' defense: "No! No! You would have had to walk in his shoes to understand! In his eyes he had no choice. His wife was ill, he had a new baby. They had him over a barrel!"

Page 262 of *The Brother* puts Sam Roberts' words in my mouth but they were words I never said. And the figure of speech he ascribed to me is not typical of the way I express myself.

If this were Roberts' only misstatement I would shrug it off as I have done with other nonsense written about me. But Roberts soared far afield. I enumerate his errors here because they are so egregious. The numbers in parenthesis refer to pages of *The Brother*:

1. Roberts said I discussed Ethel Rosenberg's jail experience with him— I was a "fellow" inmate (sic), he said. I never discussed Ethel Rosenberg with Roberts. I did give interviews to John Wexley and Virginia Gardner (long ago), whose books Roberts says he consulted. (p. 314)

2. The chronology – easily verified but apparently not done – was wrong. Gold came into Brothman's life AFTER Bentley. (p. 18) Another chronology problem: Harry Gold and Abraham Brothman appeared before the Grand Jury in 1947, not 1949. This, too, was easily verifiable. (p. 166)

3. Roberts has Brothman and me convicted of perjury. On page 303 he has us sentenced for obstructing justice. Both are incorrect and, also mutually exclusive. We were convicted and sentenced for *conspiracy to obstruct justice* – vastly different. The trial minutes would have furnished accurate information. (p. 161)

4. Roberts referred to my co-defendant, Abraham Brothman as having run a spy ring. Untrue. Brothman was a chemical engineer; none of his work was connected with the military or the government; none of it was secret and all of it was his own intellectual property. Roberts could have found proof that Brothman had nothing to do with espionage if he had read the trial minutes or at least read the judge's charge to the jury at sentencing: "There is no claim made in this indictment that Abraham Brothman engaged in espionage. It is not charged here that the material transmitted was of an illegal nature or that it was secret or that it could not have been found in textbooks or magazines on engineering or chemistry." (p.168)

5. Gold did not "operate" Brothman. (p. 213) Again, the trial minutes would have provided the facts. Nor (p. 166), was Brothman one of Gold's "sources," whatever that meant. (p. 213)

6. Brothman did not serve seven years A successful appeal reduced his sentence to two years. The correct information was readily available. (p. 303)

There is also reference to Brothman's design of an aerosol insecticide "bomb" – what one today might call a squirt can. The sinister manner in which Roberts used the word "bomb" can easily be taken to mean serious war materiel, a connotation amplifying his insinuations of espionage about Brothman.

If some writers serve themselves by playing to ignorance and prejudice; they contribute little to the commonweal. How they serve the public is a question I often ponder.

Appendix D

Document 1: *FBI Report by SAC Edward Scheidt*, File No 100-96341, July 27, 1950, p. 9. ("GOLD recalls telling BROTHMAN practically nothing in MOSKOWITZ' presence but later, after all had returned to the laboratory and MOSKOWITZ had gone out for coffee or something, they talked of their stories to the agents.")

Document 2: *FBI Memo from Thomas H. Zoeller*, November 7, 1950, Subj: Abraham Brothman, Miriam Moskowitz, File No. 65-15324, p. 8. ("With regard to MIRIAM MOSKOWITZ, GOLD stated that he never discussed his espionage activity in her presence when he could avoid it, as he distrusted her because of her violent temper. ... GOLD believes that MOSKOWITZ disklikes him...")

Document 3: *Memo for Roy Cohn*, by SA Joseph C. Walsh, New York, FBI, October 24, 1950, File #65-15324-568. (As co-counsel for the government Cohn was in the loop for receiving all FBI documents related to Gold.)

Document 1

NY 100-96341

62
67D

(GIBBY NEEDLEMAN at that time was attorney for Amtorg Trading Corporation and, according to Confidential Informant ████ of known reliability, NEEDLEMAN was then in frequent contact with Communist Party members and Communist Party functionaries.

Shortly before the agents arrived at the laboratory to question GOLD, MOSKOWITZ arrived and advised GOLD that BROTHMAN had gone home with a splitting headache. The agents then arrived and GOLD believes that the interview with them was concluded about 9 P.M. Between 9 P.M. and 9:30 P.M., MOSKOWITZ, who had returned to BROTHMAN'S office, and BROTHMAN came out to the laboratory. GOLD said they may have called first to see if the agents were gone, but he is not sure about that. BROTHMAN wanted to know how GOLD carried off his conversation with the agents. Before GOLD could reply, MOSKOWITZ assured BROTHMAN that GOLD had been extremely nonchalant when the agents arrived.

The three of them then drove to "Sunny's of Chinatown" Restaurant located on Queens Boulevard, Long Island, and BROTHMAN's opening remark to GOLD in the restaurant was, "HARRY, you don't blame me for having brought your name into this do you? I thought since they (the FBI) would eventually uncover you it would be better for me to bring you in myself and in the very beginning."

GOLD recalls telling BROTHMAN practically nothing in MOSKOWITZ' presence but later, after all had returned to the laboratory and MOSKOWITZ had gone out for coffee or something, they talked of their stories to the agents.

GOLD was driven to Pennsylvania Station that night, or possibly the next night, with either MOSKOWITZ or BROTHMAN doing the driving; however, GOLD is sure that MOSKOWITZ was present. On the way to the station, GOLD and BROTHMAN became involved in such a heated argument concerning TOM BLACK (THOMAS BLACK of Philadelphia, an admitted Soviet espionage agent in the 1930's) that a fist fight almost resulted and only by the intercession of MOSKOWITZ was such a fight averted.

On the day that BROTHMAN received his subpoena to testify before the Federal Grand Jury, BROTHMAN was very angry. He said that the whole affair was ridiculous, that a great farce was being perpetrated, and that he would be no party to any such goings on. He said that instead of taking the stand and trying to lie and squirm his way out of the accusations, he would make a clean breast of the whole matter. BROTHMAN said he would tell the whole story about GOLOS, HELEN (ELIZABETH BENTLEY) and himself.

- 9 -

Document 2

New York, New York
November 7, 1950

MEMO:

Re: HARRY GOLD
ABRAHAM BROTHMAN
MIRIAM MOSKOWITZ
ESPIONAGE - R

The following information was furnished by HARRY GOLD to SAS JOHN M. COLLINS and THOMAS H. ZOELLER, while preparing a trial brief for the pending MOSKOWITZ-BROTHMAN trial. He was interviewed on November 1, 2, 3, and 4, 1950.

In connection with GOLD's friend, MORRELL DAUGHERTY, who resides in Philadelphia, GOLD was questioned as to how much information DAUGHERTY would be in a position to furnish the defense attorneys regarding GOLD.

GOLD stated that DAUGHERTY and he have been close friends for twenty-one years. He has done many acts of kindness for DAUGHERTY, for example, paying the hospital bill when DAUGHERTY's second child was born in December 1937, and DAUGHERTY could not raise enough money to get his wife out of the hospital. This amounted to about $30.

In 1947, GOLD lent him $250. to buy a car. He obtained this money from his mother, whom he told he was going to use the money to go into business with BROTHMAN. This money was never repaid by DAUGHERTY.

cc: 100-95068
100-96341

65-15324-577

F. B. I.

N. Y. C.

ROUTED TO - FILE

THZ:KDD
65-15324

MEMO
NY 65-15324

GOLD recalls that SAM's instructions were to meet him on the uptown express level. GOLD cannot recall whether this was the uptown level of the Sixth Avenue or Eighth Avenue line. However, he does recall that when he and SAM came up in the subway at 14th Street, they were not at Eighth Avenue; therefore, he must have met SAM on the Sixth Avenue level at West Fourth Street.

* * *

With regard to MIRIAM MOSKOWITZ, GOLD stated that he never discussed his espionage activity in her presence when he could avoid it, as he distrusted her because of her violent temper. He felt that someday after one of the many arguments she always was having with BROTHMAN she would, out of spite, go to the authorities and report them. Also, MOSKOWITZ made him uncomfortable and unhappy, and he stayed away from her.

GOLD stated that he came to BROTHMAN's firm in 1946 to replace GUS WOLLAN (it may be noted that GOLD never knew until the time of this interview that GUS WOLLAN's real name is GERHARD). GUS was a strong Lutheran and he disapproved of the relationship between MOSKOWITZ and BROTHMAN, and MOSKOWITZ wanted to get rid of GUS.

MOSKOWITZ at that time was also on bad terms with most of the other employees that BROTHMAN had, and GOLD's opinion is that this is due to the fact that she wanted BROTHMAN as her sole possession.

GOLD believes that MOSKOWITZ dislikes him for the following reasons:

The strong bond between BROTHMAN and GOLD due to their prior association;

BROTHMAN is an individual who likes to talk and to have people around him, and he liked to have GOLD around;

Document 3

MEMO FOR Roy Cohn

INDEX — SUMMARY RE: HARRY GOLD, was.
ESPIONAGE - R

GOLD advised that he was born December 12, 1910 in Berne, Switzerland, the son of SAM and CELIA GOLD. He said that his parents were both born in Russia, and that his father had been in Switzerland for about eight or ten years following the occupation of a cabinet maker. His parents emigrated to the United States in 1914, at which time the family name was GOLODNITSKY. GOLD explained that on arrival at Ellis Island, the family name had been spelled in several different ways, which delayed their entry into the country. To facilitate matters his father changed his name to GOLD.

The GOLD family went to Little Rock, Arkansas, where they resided with a relative for a short period of time. In the late summer of 1914 they went to Chicago, Illinois, where they stayed for approximately nine or ten months, while the father was employed in the stock yards and coal yards. On leaving Chicago SAM GOLD went to Norfolk, Virginia, to get employment in a shipyard, while CELIA and HARRY GOLD came to Philadelphia, where they were joined shortly thereafter by the father. They resided with CELIA GOLD'S brother in Philadelphia. This was in the year 1915.

Citizenship

HARRY GOLD was issued a Certificate of Derivative Citizenship under Immigration and Naturalization Service file 3-A-7159. No date was available, as the Philadelphia file had been destroyed.

SAM GOLD filed a petition for citizenship on June 6, 1921, Petition Number 48016, and was naturalized on June 6, 1922. His address at that time was 2649 South Phillip Street, Philadelphia, Pennsylvania, and his occupation was a cabinet maker. He indicated in these records that he was born January 1, 1881 in Russia and entered the United States July 13, 1914. He was married and had two children, HENRICH GOLD (HARRY GOLD), born December 12, 1910 in Switzerland, and YOSEF GOLD, born February 10, 1917 in Philadelphia. SAM GOLD'S Naturalization Certificate Number was 1591271.

65-15334-568

FBI - NEW YORK
OCT 24 1950

JCW:RK
65-15324

Acknowledgments

Several books among many which enriched my awareness of the widespread attacks on basic human rights during the McCarthy era were Robert Justin Goldstein's *Political Repression in Modern America* (Schenkman Publishing Co., Cambridge, Ma., 1978), *It Did Happen Here* by Bud Schultz and Ruth Schultz (University of California Press, 1989) and David Caute's *The Great Fear* (Simon and Schuster, New York, 1978).

Many people helped with this book. Stanley Yalkowsky turned over research material he had gathered during his writing of *The Murder of the Rosenbergs* (Crucible Press, New York, 1995) and urged me on. The late William A. Reuben, whose book, *The Atom Spy Hoax* (Action Books, New York, 1955), was the first of this genre and a groundbreaker, read an early draft and gave sensible insights and valuable advice; he also generously shared some research material he had acquired about Elizabeth Bentley. Augustus S. Ballard, Esq., one of Harry Gold's original attorneys, was most gracious in giving me access to his archives on the Gold case. The late Marshall Perlin, Esq., who worked with the Rosenbergs' attorney and later represented the Rosenbergs' sons, gave me a special understanding of some of the legal aspects of my own trial which I had never before understood. Sidney Shinedling shared reminiscences of his parents and helped prod my memory of my experiences with them. Whitney S. Bagnoll, Special Reference Librarian in charge of the Rosenberg files (known as the "Perlin Papers" at the Arthur W. Diamond Library of Columbia University Law School was tireless in serving my research requests over a period of many months as I prepared the original edition. Grateful thanks are also due the current Special Reference Librarian, Miss Sabrina Sondhi, who extended more than a full measure of help when I needed to recheck old files for this updated edition. Local public libraries were most helpful in locating arcane and lapsed material. I owe much, in this regard, to Miss Patti Boyd , a most creative reference librarian. Jeff Kisseloff encouraged me when I most needed encouragement. And Hans Sherrer of Justice Denied brought experience, patience and wisdom to the task of editing and publishing this edition of my book. To all of them I am most grateful.

About the Author

Miriam Ruth Moskowitz was born in Bayonne, New Jersey on June 10, 1916. Now 97, she lives in a suburb of New York City.

Miriam Moskowitz in November 2010 at her desk where she wrote *Phantom Spies, Phantom Justice*. (Steve Burns)

Photos and Images

"Nab Man, Woman in Spy Plot." (July 30, 1950) 8

Miriam Moskowitz and Abraham Brothman in June 1946 23

Subpoena for Ms. Moskowitz's grand jury July 17, 1950 appearance 33

USA vs. Abraham Brothman and Miriam Moskowitz, Nov. 1950 44

"2 in Spy Case Sent To Jail as Trial Begins" (November 9, 1950) 46

Mr. Brothman (L) and Ms. Moskowitz after the jury found them guilty on November 22, 1950 107

Denial of parole to Ms. Moskowitz in August 1951 144

Ms. Moskowitz playing the violin in the 1940s 151

Ms. Moskowitz's final payment of her fine on January 22, 1976 162

Ms. Moskowitz in her college yearbook, *Microcosm,* June, 1942 163

Ms. Moskowitz and friend, *circa* summer 1938 163

Ms. Moskowitz on the porch of her home, about July 1946 164

Ms. Moskowitz in Puerto Rico in April 1957 164

Ms. Moskowitz, about 1956 165

Ms. Moskowitz during a GRIT-TV interview on January 13, 2011 165

Abraham Brothman in August 1944 171

Gerhard "Gus" Wollan demonstrating an A. Brothman invention 173

Ms. Moskowitz in November 2010 264

Endnotes

Preface

1. Sidney Zion. *The Autobiography of Roy Cohn*, Lyle Stuart.Inc., Secaucus, N. J., 1988, 66.

Foreword

1. Schneir, Walter and Miriam, *Invitation to an Inquest*, Pantheon, New York 1983, p. 83.
2. Rosenberg-Sobell trial record, pp. 1191-3.
3. Cooke, Blanche Wiesen, *The Declassified Eisenhower*, Doubleday, NY 1981, pp. 345-6.

Chapter 1

1. FBI file #100-96341, Subfile #1A1-1A9, Subj. Abraham Brothman, July 29, 1950. Document signed by Frederick C. Bauckham, SA.
2. *Ibid.*
3. Bruce Shapiro, "Grand (Jury) Inquisition," *The Nation*, August 14/31 1998, 4-6. (Pertinent for is discussion of grand juries although anchored in the Clinton-Starr confrontation of 1988.) See also: Scott Turow, "A Secret Proceedings with No Secrets," *The New York Times*, August 2, 1998. Op. Ed.
4. William Bridgwater and Seymour Kurtz, Eds., *The Columbia Encyclopedia*, Third Ed., Columbia University Press, New York, 1963; 2032. Hereafter referred to as *Columbia Encyclopedia*.
5. Athan G. Theoharis, Ed., with Tony G. Poveda, Susan Rosenfeld and Richard Gid Powers, *The FBI A Comprehensive Reference Guide*. Oryx Press, 1999, Phoenix, Arizona, 85012-2297; 367 Hereafter referred to as Theoharis.
6. *The New York Times*, February 11, 1950, 1
7. H. W. Brands, *The Devil We Knew, Americans and the Cold War*, Oxford University Press, New York, 1993, 27-29. Hereafter referred to as Brands.
8. Congressional Quarterly Service, "Congress of the Nation 1945-65, A Review of Government and Politics in the Postwar Years," Washington, D.C., 1965; 1655 Hereafter referred to as Congressional Quarterly.
9. Congressional Quarterly, 1657-1658
10. Victor S. Navasky, *Naming Names*, The Viking Press, N.Y., 1980; 48-51, 409-410. Referred to hereafter as Navasky. Also: Aryeh Neier, "Taking Liberties Four Decades in the Struggle for Rights" *Public Affairs*, New York, 2003; 133-35, 137-42.
11. *Columbia Encyclopedia*, 463.
12. *Ibid.* Also *Congressional Quarterly*, 1654-1655.
13. *Congressional Quarterly*, 1657-58.
14. *Ibid.*

15. I.F.Stone, "The Hidden History of the Korean War" *Monthly Review Press*, New York and London, 1952; *Columbia Ency.*, 1148.

16. *The New York Times*, May 23, 24, 1950.

17. *The New York Times*, June 16, 17, 18, 1950; August 12, 19, 1950.

18. FBI Memorandum from A.H.Belmont to Mr. D.M.Ladd, July 29, 1950, Subj: Abraham Br Othman, Espionage.

Chapter 2

1. See: Joseph R. Starobin, *American Communism in Crisis, 1943-1957*, Harvard University Press, Cambridge, Mass. 1972; 46.

2. Howard F. Bremer, Ed., *Franklin Delano Roosevelt, 1882 – 1945*, Oceana Publications, New York, 1971.

3. James MacGregor Burns, *Roosevelt, The Lion and the Fox*, Harcourt Brace Jovanovich, Inc., New York, 1956.

4. Robert Dallek, *Franklin D. Roosevelt and American Foreign Policy, 1932-1945*, Oxford University Press, New York, 1979.

5. David M. Kennedy, *Freedom From Fear, the American People in Depression and War, 1929-1945*, Oxford University Press, N.Y, 1999.

6. Frank Kingdon, *That Man in the White House*, Arco Publishing Co., New York, 1944.

7. Arthur M. Schlesinger, Jr., *The Age of Roosevelt*, Volume I, II and III, American Heritage Library, Houghton Mifflin Co., Boston; 1957-1960.

8. University of Iowa Library, North Hall, Iowa City, Iowa, 1995; Exhibit: "Federal Support of the Arts and Public Projects in the 1930s" accompanied by a printed folder: "The Dream and the Deal." See also: Jerre Mangione, *The Dream and the Deal, The Federal Writers Project 1935-1943*, Little Brown and Company, Boston, 1972; 39-42, 53, 99, 255. Hallie Flanagan, Arena, *The History of the Federal Theatre*, Benjamin Blom, Inc., Bx. 10452, 1940 (reissued 1965).

9. Brands, 10.

10. *Ibid.*, vi, 10-11.

11. *Ibid.*, 12-16.

12. *World Almanac*, a WRC Medea Co., 2003, New York, 293

13. David M. Glantz and Jonathan House, *When Titans Clashed, How the Red Army Stopped Hitler*, University Press of Kansas, Lawrence, Kansas, 66049, 1995, 285. See also: Richard Overy, *Russia's War, Blood Upon the Snow*, V Books, (Penguin Putnam Inc.), 1997, 132-158.

14. Glantz and House, 5-6.

15. Brands, 66.

16. *Ibid.*, 55.

17. Walter Goodman, *The Committee, The Extraordinary Career of the House Committee on Un-American Activities*, Farrar, Straus and Giroux, New York (First Printing 1968); 416 and passim. See also Navasky, 21.

18. Ronald W. Clark, *Einstein, The Life and Times*, World Publishing Co., New York, 1971, 607.

19. Navasky, xxii, 12, 17.

20. Congressional Quarterly, 1420.

21. Except where otherwise noted: Robert A. Caro, *Master of the Senate*, Alfred A.

Knopf, New York, 2001; 232-303. Also: John A. Garraty, Ed., *Dictionary of American Biography*, Supplement Six, 1956-60, Charles Scribner's Sons, New York, 483-485.

22. Caro, 302-303.

23. Tom Wicker, *One of Us, Richard Nixon and the American Dream*, Random House, New York, 1991, 34-46. Also: Greg Mitchell, *Tricky Dick and the Pink Lady*, Random House, New York, 1998, 42-43.

24. Wicker, 52-70. Also: John A. Garraty and Mark C. Carnes, Eds., American National Biography, Oxford University Press, New York, 1999; 459. see also Joseph Kelner, "Kent State at 25," *The New York Times*,. Op. Ed., May 4, 1995. and Joseph Kelner and James Munves, *The Kent State Coverup*, Harper & Row, New York, 1980 – (Nixon's contempt for the students demonstrating against the Vietnam War cast its baneful shadow over the court trial that ensued as a result of the Kent State shootings). See also: Peter Davies and the Board of Church and Society of the United Methodist Church, *The Truth About Kent State*, Farrar Straus Giroux, New York, 1973, 2-9, 12.

25. Wicker, 662-663.

26. Lou Cannon, *President Reagan, The Role of a Lifetime*, Simon & Schuster, New York, 1991, 286.

27. William A. Reuben, *The Atom Spy Hoax*, Action Books, New York, N.Y., 1955, 290–291.

28. Navasky, 80-81, 338.

29. Navasky, 345-346. See also Larry Ceplair & Steven Englund, *The Inquisition in Hollywood – Politics in the Film Community 1930 – 1960*, Anchor Press/ Doubleday, New York, l980. See also *The New York Times*:

a) Patricia Bosworth, "Daughter of a Blacklist That Killed a Father," September 27, 1992.

b. Ring Lardner, Jr., Frances Chaney, Merle Debuskey, Kim Hunter and Madeline Lee Gilford, "Blacklist: Memories of a Word That Marks an Era," July 31, 1994.

c. Editorial Notebook, "Sam Wanamaker's Great Obsession," December 29, 1996.

d. "For the Blacklisted, Credit Where Credit is Due," October 1, 1997.

e. Bernard Weinrab, "The Blacklist Era Won't Fade to Black", October 5, 1997.

f. "Millard Lampell, 78, Writer and Supporter of Causes, Dies" October 11, 1997 (Obituary Page).

g. "Paul Jarrico, 82, Blacklisted Screenwriter," October 30, 1997 (Obituary Page).

h. "Winning a Battle But Losing the War Over the Blacklist," January 25, 1998.

See also: Ring Lardner, Jr., *I'd Hate Myself in the Morning, A Memoir*, Thunder Mouth's Press/Nation Books, New York 2000; 51a. Garry Wills, *Reagan's America Innocents At Home*, Doubleday & Company, Inc., New York, 1987: 249, 255, Wills cites FBI Report LA100-15732 on this.; Lou Cannon, *President Reagan, The Role of a Lifetime*, Simon & Schuster, New York, 1991; 289; and 589-738; See also: Garry Wills, "It's His Party," *The New York Times Magazine*, August 11, 1996; 32.

Chapter 3

1. *Columbia Encyclopedia*, 1336.

2. Dwight D. Eisenhower, *Crusade in Europe*, Doubleday, New York 1948; 466.

Chapter 4
1. FBI File #100-96341 -1A12, received by Special Agent J. M. Collins, 9/18/50.

Chapter 5
1. William A. Reuben, *The Atom Spy Hoax*, Action Books, N.Y., 1955: 299-326.
2. Letter from Mrs. Claire Vago, widow of Oscar J. Vago, October 15, 1996; also interview with Mrs. Vago, November 10, 1996 in New Haven, Conn.
3. *Ibid.* See also Walter and Miriam Schneir, *Invitation to an Inquest*, Doubleday, New York, 1965; 284
4. United States of America vs. Abraham Brothman and Miriam Moskowitz, November 1950, U. S. District Court, Southern District of New York, Crim. No. C133/106. Referred to hereafter as Trial Minutes. See also "Proceedings," entry dated October 1, 1950, Opinion #18935, J. Weinfeld.
5. FBI Teletype, NY SAC to Director, November 8, 1950, File #100-37069.

Chapter 7
1. Trial Minutes, testimony of Elizabeth T. Bentley, 351-400.
2. FBI Memo, New York, November 7, 1950, re: Harry Gold, Abraham Brothman, Miriam Moskowitz, Espionage; signed by Thomas H. Zoeller, SA, File #65-15324-577; 6.
3. FBI Report, New York, by SA J. R. Murphy, Jr., March 9, 1950, File #65-15136; 73-74.
4. Elizabeth Bentley, *Out of Bondage*, Devin, Adair, N,Y., 1951; 77, 78, 84, 108. Hereafter referred to as *Out of Bondage*.
5. *Ibid.*, 85
6 Minutes of the Federal Grand Jury, Southern District Court of New York, March 30, 1948; 2776-2777. This jury was impaneled June 15, 1947 and discharged December 1, 1948.
7. *Out of Bondage*, 116.
8. FBI Memorandum from ASAC William G. Simon to SAC New York, Subj. Elizabeth Terrell Bentley, July 28, 1955, File #134-182-101.
9. John A. Garraty, Editor, *Dictionary of American Biography*, Supplement Five, 1951-1955, Charles Scribner's Sons, New York, 1977; 563-565.

Chapter 8
1. Trial Minutes, 924.
2. Schneir, 71. See also Ellen Schrecker, *Many Are The Crimes: McCarthyism In America*, Little, Brown and Company, Boston, 1998, 124–128, 223.
3. Information imparted to me by Marshall Perlin, Esq., in a conversation I had with him at his office in New York City on October 1, 1998. Perlin, an attorney, interviewed Fuchs in prison in England early in 1959. The British Home Office had granted him permission for the interview through the intervention of the Honorable Sidney Silverman, Member of Parliament. Fuchs told Perlin he had NOT named Harry Gold and had NOT implicated him to the FBI. See also: letter from SAC Harry M. Kimball, FBI San Francisco to Director, 3/27/50 which includes: "...his (Fuchs') contact was totally unknown to him other than as a contact for the

transmittal of espionage information... this statement by Fuchs is consistent to what is known at their (Soviet Intelligence Services) methods of operation."

4. Harry Gold, "The Circumstances Surrounding My Work as a Soviet Agent — A Report," April 1951; 101. (In FBI File #65-57449-790.) Hereafter referred to as The Circumstances.

5. FBI Memo from SA William Hughes to SAC, FBI, Philadelphia. June 8, 1950, File #65-4307-704. See also: FBI Memo from SAC T. Scott Miller, Jr., to SAC, Philadelphia, 7/10/50 re Exhibit 65-4307-lB-13 (2) Exhibit 13.

6. The Circumstances, 101.

7. Trial Minutes, 922. See also The Circumstances, 103.

8. Harry Gold, Confession, FBI File 65-57449, Vol. 5, Serials 131-182, May 22, 1950; l, 2. Gold signed each page and his signature was witnessed by FBI Agents T. S. Miller, Jr., and Richard E. Brennan of the Philadelphia office of the FBI. The confession consisted of ten pages (but later acquired additions). Also see FBI File #65-4307, Vol. I.

9. *Ibid.*

10. FBI Memo from SAC (T. Scott Miller) Philadelphia to Director, June 1, 1950, File #65-57449-550, 6.

11. FBI Memo from Mr. Ladd to the Director, June 5, 1950, File #65-57449-309, 7.

12. Gordon Dean, *Report on the Atom*, Second Ed., Alfred A. Knopf, New York, 1953, 305. Hereafter referred to as Gordon Dean.

13. Notes for Hamilton's pre-sentencing speech are in the archives of Pepper and Hamilton, Esqs., Philadelphia, PA.

14. Joint Committee on Atomic Energy, "Soviet Atomic Espionage," Government Printing Office, Washington, D.C., April 1951, 185.

15. Gordon Dean, 299.

16. FBI Teletype dated June 13, 1950, 3–5; See also: FBI Memo, New York, November 7, 1950, from Thomas H. Zoeller, Subject: Abraham Brothman, Miriam Moskowitz, File #65-15324; 8; See also: FBI report of 2/3/54, File #100-96341, 9.

17. FBI Report made at Philadelphia, Pa., December 4, 1950 by Robert C. Jenson, title: Harry Gold, WAS, Espionage-R, File PH 65-4307; 4. Also denoted as File #65-57449, Vol. 28, Serial Nos. 722-742. Jensen's report covered interview with Harry Gold of October 2, 1950, during which Gold spoke of having stolen alcohol (with Morrell Dougherty) from Penn Sugar.

18. a) FBI Memorandum from Mr. L. L. Laughlin to Mr. A.H. Belmont, subject: Harry Gold, dated November 4, 1950, File #65-57449-718;

b) FBI teletype message to SAC New York, From "Hoover" dated November 7, 1950 marked, "URGENT" File #65-57449-717;

c) FBI Memorandum from Morris S. Harzenstein, SA to SAC, Subject: Abraham Brothman, dated 11/7/50, file #65-4307-949;

d) FBI Memorandum from SA Robert C. Jensen to SAC, Subject: Harry Gold dated 11/8/50, File #65-4307-947.

19. FBI Teletype, Philadelphia Office, to Director and SAC Bureau and New York, marked "URGENT" dated 6/13/50, no file number.

20. FBI Memorandum from Director to Assistant Attorney General J. McInerney, dated 8/10/50, File #65-57449-634; 3. See also: FBI Memorandum from Jos. C. Walsh, SAC, New York, 9/23/50, File #65-15324 RM Title: Harry Gold, WAS (also

using number #65-57449, Vol. 29, serials #743-770).

Chapter 14
1. Ronald Radosh and Joyce Milton, *The Rosenberg File: a search for the truth*, Holt Rinehart and Winston, New York, 1983; 535-36.

Chapter 16
1. *Tokyo Rose Orphan of the Pacific*, by Masayo Duus, translated from the Japanese by Peter Duus, Kodansha International Ltd., Tokyo and USA Ltd (New York City 10022) 1979; (55, 60–80, passim). Iva Toguri d'Aquino was sentenced to 10 years in prison and a $10,000 fine.

Chapter 21
1. FBI Memorandum to SAC, N.Y., (sender's name blacked out). SUBJECT Miriam Moskowitz, #100-96341-232, NY File #100-99876–220 file date 5/12/54.
2. FBI Report of October 24, 1961 re: Interview of October 13, 1961, Subject: Miriam Moskowitz, Newark File #100-33937, 3.
3. Letter to Director from SAC, Newark, dated June 26, 1964, Subject: Miriam Moscowitz (sic) File #100-370679-60. Also: Report by Newark Office FBI dated 7/28/64 re Miriam Moskowitz file #100-370679-63. Also: Memo to Director from SAC, Newark, 9/30/64 re Miriam Moskowitz, File #100-370679-66. Also Memo to Director from SAC, Newark, dated 11/13/64 re: Miriam Moskowitz, File #100-370679-67 and Report from Newark office, FBI dated Dec. 31, 1964, File #100-370679-68.
4. FBI Report dated July 12, 1956 covering period from April 27 to July 13, 1956, Newark File #100-370679, 1-2.
5. FBI Memo from SAC Newark to Director, 6/26/64, File #100-370679.

Chapter 23
1. This included U. S. Patent #2,212,260 covering two types of chemical mixers: an injection mixer and a superturbine mixer.
2. Teletype from FBI New York Office to Director, Washington, Oct. 12, 1950, File #100-365040-263. Also: telegram to Legal Attaché, London from Hoover, October 17, 1950, File #100-365040-263. Also, copy of cable to SAC New York from Hoover, October 26, 1950, File #100-365040.
3. Except where otherwise credited: I am indebted to Kenneth M. Deitch for his lucid description of the Manhattan Project which I used in this passage. See: Kenneth M. Deitch, *Introduction, The Manhattan Project: A Secret Wartime Mission*, Edited by Kenneth M. Deitch, Discovery Enterprises, Ltd., Carlisle, Mass., 1995; 5-14. I also found useful: Peter Bacon Hales, *Atomic Spaces: Living on the Manhattan Project*, University of Illinois Press, Urbana and Chicago, 1997; 134-135; Richard Rhodes, Introduction, *Picturing The Bomb: Photographs from the Secret World of the Manhattan Project*, by Rachel Fermi and Esther Samra, Harry N. Abrams, Inc., N.Y. 1995, 18; I also found useful: Richard Rhodes, *The Making of the Atomic Bomb*, Simon and Schuster, N.Y.; 1986, 654-655.
4. FBI Memoranda: A. H. Belmont to Mr. Ladd, July 18, 1950 and July 28, 1950

Subject: Abraham Brothman (no file number).

5. FBI Memorandum to Director from SAC, New York, January 31, 1955, Subject Abraham Brothman, Espionage, Obstruction of Justice, Internal Security Act of 1950 (no file number).

6. See Appendix B.

7. FBI Memorandum to Director from SAC, New York, June 30, 1950 (No filenumber.); also: Memorandum to Attorney General from Director, July 20, 1950, Subject: Thomas L. Black, Abraham Brothman, Harry Gold, et.al., Espionage.

8. FBI Report by SA Lloyd S. Goodrow, File #65-1393, Nov. 2, 1950.

9. Hoover's memorandum to the Attorney General of July 20, 1950.

10. Memorandum to J. Edgar Hoover, director, FBI from James M. McInerny, Assistant Attorney General, Subject: Thomas L. Black, Abraham Brothman, Harry Gold, et.al., Espionage, File #146-41-15-131, -132, July 31, 1950.

11. Memorandum to SAC, Newark, From Director, FBI, January 5, 1966; Subject: Abraham Brothman, Espionage – R.

12. FBI Memorandum 2, date not discernable, probably 1971.

13. Ibid.

14. FBI Memorandum, hand dated March 5, 1973; 2.

15. FBI Memorandum to SAC from SA (name of agent blacked out) Subject Abraham Brothman, November 8, 1974, File #100-33638-190.

16. FBI report made by H. C. Clinch, New York, March 6, 1947, File #65-14603, 4.

17. FBI Memo to D. M. Ladd from A. H. Belmont, Subject: Abraham Brothman, Miriam Moskowitz, dated November 8, 1950, File #100-370679, 1-3.

18. Theoharis, 20, Col. 2.

19. Ibid., 20, 21.

20. Ibid., 21, Col. 1.

21. Ibid.

22. Ibid., 158, col. 1.

23. Ibid., 368, col. 1.

24. Ibid., 158, col. 1.

25. Ibid., 369, col. 1.

Chapter 24

1. Robert Louis Benson and Michael Warner, Editors, *Venona – Soviet Espionage and the American response 1939-1957*, National Security Agency – Central Intelligence Agency, Washington, D.C. 1996; v, vii.

2. Venona Files #1390, New York to Moscow, 1 October 1944 and #1403, New York to Moscow, 5 October 1944.

3. John Earl Haynes and Harvey Klehr, *Venona, Decoding Soviet espionage in America*, Yale University Press, New Haven, 1999; p. 9.

4. Venona identifies Gold in several files; one is #1797, New York to Moscow, 20 December 1944.

5. Haynes and Klehr, pp. 289-290.

6. Trial Minutes, testimony of Benjamin C. Dann, Sales Manager, Hendrick Manufacturing Co., 948-951.

7. Ibid., 949, 952, 954.

8. Trial Minutes, Testimony of Harry Gold. 541-542, 547, 568-569, 703, 800-802.

9. Abraham Brothman, *Batch-Continuous Process for Buna-S, Chemical and Metallurgical Engineering*, McGraw-Hill Publishing Co., New York, March 1943; also: Abraham Brothman, *Batch-Continuous Process for Buna-N, Chemical and Metallurgical Engineering*, McGraw Hill Publishing Co., New York, May 1943.

10. Joint Committee on Atomic Energy, "Soviet Atomic Espionage," April 1951, Government Printing Office, Washington, D.C., 1951; 185.

11. Gordon Dean, *Report on the Atom*, Alfred A. Knopf, N.Y., Second Ed., 1959; 299 (See also, p. 89 herein.).

12. John R. Callaham, Assistant Editor, "DDT Fights Insects in War and in Peace," *Chemical and Metallurgical Engineering*, October 1944.

13. Haynes and Klehr, 344.

14. Trial Minutes, 1000-1003.

15. *Ibid.,* 1024.

16. *Ibid.*

17. *Ibid.*, 1129-1130.

18. Haynes and Klehr, 9.

19. Venona, KGB File #912, New York to Moscow 27 June 1944.

20. Gold to Hamilton.

21. The letter is referred to in Venona/KGB File #1797, New York to Moscow, 20 December 1944.

22. Trial Minutes, 610.

23. *Ibid.*, 831.

24. *Ibid.*, 848.

Chapter 25

1. *Out of Bondage*, 1.

2. John A. Garraty, Ed. *Dictionary of American Biography*, Supplement Seven, 1961-1965, Charles Scribner's Sons, N.Y., 1981; 51-53.

3. This may be a misprint in the *Dictionary of American Biography*. Elizabeth's mother's maiden name was probably "Turrilll," not Burrill." An address the FBI had for Elizabeth Bentley was "c/o Marian Turrill, 82 McDougal Street, New York, N.Y." Bentley said Marion was a relative of her mother's. (FBI Inventory of Documents, 11/7/75-263, Vol. 3, Serial #122.) Several FBI documents also refer to her as "Elizabeth Turrill Bentley" as well as "Elizabeth Terrill Bentley."

4. *Out of Bondage*, 1.

5. Hayden B. Peake, "Afterword" to *Out of Bondage*, 223, 279 (see notes 32, 33); hereafter referred to as Peake.

6. Peake, 224 and note 38, 280.

7. *Out of Bondage*, 17-18.

8. *Ibid.*, 54.

9. Trial Minutes, 376.

10. *Ibid.*, 377-379, Also, Peake, 231.

11. *Out of Bondage*, 70.

12. Peake, 231-232.

13. William A. Reuben, *The Atom Spy Hoax*, Action Books, N.Y., 1955; 489.

14. Peake, 223. Bentley's assumption that the FBI was surveilling her runs throughout her book and she is quoted on this in many of the FBI memos cited.

15. *Out of Bondage*, 66-67 (Throughout her book Bentley also speaks of her responsibilities to train cadres and exert leadership, implicitly not a job entrusted to ordinary members.).

16. *Ibid.*, 77.

17. *Ibid.*, 89, 93.

18. *Ibid.*, 79-81.

19. Robert Louis Benson (and) Michael Warner, eds., *VENONA, Soviet Espionage and the American response 1939-1957*, National Security Agency (and) Central Intelligence Agency, Washington, D.C., 1996; xii.

20. *Out of Bondage*, 85.

21. FBI report by SAC Thomas C Spencer, 12/5/45, subj.: N. Gregory Silvermaster, was, *et al.*, File #65-56402 -220; 2, 8, 14. This report contains the full text of Elizabeth Bentley's signed statement of November 30, 1945. Hereafter referred to as Bentley Statement.

22. *Out of Bondage*, 112-113. Also Bentley Statement 14, 16, 100.

23. *Out of Bondage*, 108-127, 156, 164.

24. *Ibid.*, 90.

25. Bentley Statement also bearing File Number 65-14603, November 30, 1945. See also FBI File #65-564002-2.

26. *Ibid.*, 58, 62, 80, 86, 100.

27. *Ibid.*, 60-61.

28. *Ibid.*, 61- 86-87.

29. *Ibid.*, 64. Also: *Out of Bondage*, 205.

30. Bentley Statement, 60-61 and *Out of Bondage*, 200-202.

31. *Out of Bondage*, 184-185.

32. *Ibid.*, 201. See also FBI Memo from SAC, New York to Director, Jan. 4, 1951, re: Payment to Elizabeth Bentley of $2000 by Anatoli Gromov.

33. Bentley Statement. See also: Peake, 290, note 139.

34. From a detailed account of Brothman's employment history dated June 23, 1950 which he prepared for his attorneys. Also see Trial Minutes, testimony of Benjamin C. Dann, 962.

35. FBI Memorandum, file #65-15530, dated 6/20/50; 16.

36. Memorandum from the Director, FBI to the Attorney General, July 5. 1950 + Subject: Abraham Brothman, Espionage.

37. Peake, pp. 219-220.

38. *Ibid.*

39. Agent Gleason's report of August 23, 1945 is given in a letter to D. M. Ladd from H. B. Fletcher, Gregory file #65-56402-3398 of August 9, 1948.

40. Probably the Prince George Hotel on East 28 Street, New York City. In *Out of Bondage* (p. 204), Bentley said she sometimes stayed at the Prince George because it was around the corner from her office which was on 25th Street and Fifth Avenue. The St. George Hotel was a Brooklyn landmark.

41. Peake, p. 276, note 11 (based on Danahy interview).

42. FBI Memorandum from The Director to the Attorney General, August 20, 1948, Gregory File #65-56402-3399. See also FBI Archives, Elizabeth Bentley Files, #65-56402, letter of August 29, 1945, titled, "Lt. Peter Heller, Impersonation, Espionage-R from New Haven FBI to New York FBI. Also see FBI memorandum prepared by

SA Frank C. Aldrich captioned: LT.PETER HELLER, IMPERSONATION, ESPIONAGE-R, NY File #47-5081, memo typed 11/5/45.

43. FBI Memo from SAC, New York, File 134-182-102 to Director, Attn. Inspector Carl Hennrich, re: Elizabeth Terrell Bentley dated 7/28/55, p. 1.

44. *Ibid.*, p. 2.

45. Gregory file, Memo for Files by A. J. Tuohy, New York Office, FBI File #65-14603-3984 concerning discussion with Asst. Director D. M. Ladd, dated August 18,1948. See also memo from D. M. Ladd to the Director, 11/9/45, File #65-56402-8 re: Elizabeth Terrill Bentley/Internal Security-R.

46. Bentley Statement; report made by Thomas C. Spencer dated 12/5/45, captioned "N. Gregory Silvermaster" was, *et al.*, FBI file #65-56402-220. This document contains a list of the dates of Bentley's interviews with agents Kelly and Spencer.

47. House Committee on Un-American Activities, 80th Congress, Hearings on Communist Espionage, pp. 555-556.

48. FBI memoranda (three) 1) from ASAC William G. Simon to SAC New York dated 7/28/55, File 134-182-101; 2) from SAC, New York to Director, FBI attn: Inspector Carl Hennrich, 7/28/55, file #134-182-102; 3) from ASAC William G. Simon to SAC, New York, dated 7/28/55, File 134-182-103.

49. FBI Memorandum from SAC, New York to Director, FBI dated January 4, 1951, File 134-435 (also recorded as #65-14603).

50. Except where otherwise cited all biographical material on Remington has been excerpted from John A. Garraty, Editor, *Dictionary of American Biography*, Supplement Five, 1951-55, Charles Scribner's Sons, New York, pp. 563-564.

51. Peake, p. 296, note 212. See also: Schneir. 314.

52. *Ibid.* (Peake, and Schneir)

53. FBI memorandum from D. M. Ladd to Mr. Belmont, October 16, 1950, File #134-435; and FBI Memo from Mr. A. H. Belmont to Mr. D.M. Ladd, subject Harry Gold (and) William Walter Remington, Perjury, October 23, 1950.

54. Peake, p. 252.

55. FBI Memo from D. M. Ladd to Mr. Belmont, October 16, 1950, File #134-435.

56. Nicholas von Hoffman, *Citizen Cohn*, Doubleday, NY, 1988, p. 91.

57. For information on the Taylor brief I used the news reports of William V Shannon, correspondent for *The New York Post* published in *The Post* on April 19 and 20, 1955, particularly the latter date. That appeared on p. 4, col. 1 and p. 45, cols. 1-5, headlined, "Elizabeth Bentley Silent as Ex U.S. Aide Hits Back." See also Schneir, p. 318-321.

58. RDX was indeed an explosive and had been in the news since 1950 and later in connection with the prosecution of Alfred Dean Slack. Bentley would have been well aware of that event.

59. Bentley's statements remarkably recalled the evasive generalities which characterized her testimony against Abraham Brothman. She said he gave her "blueprints" but never specified what they were and she disclaimed any knowledge that could have explained their content. She also could not "remember" many details of other critical events. (See, Trial Minutes, pp. 407-409, 412, 416-417, 435-36, 478-82, 491.)

60. Dwight D. Eisenhower, *Crusade in Europe*, Doubleday, N.Y., 1949; 250.

61. See note 48.

62. *Ibid.*

63. Peake, 236; and see FBI files referred to in note 48.

64. Peake, 221. FBI Memo from L.B. Nichols to Mr. Tolson, Jan. 24, 1951, File #134-435-35. Also McCall's Washington Bureau announcement of a Washington press conference for Miss Bentley on April 19, 1951 issued by Christina Sadler; also McCall's press release of that date in FBI file # 65-56402.

65. *Out of Bondage*, 184-185.

66. FBI Memorandum from SAC William C. Simon to SAC, New York, Subject Elizabeth Terrell Bentley, July 28, 1955, File #134-182-101.

67. *Out of Bondage*, 204-211; also Peake 267-268.

68. Peake, 268.

69. The elipses denote legal language only and do not alter the sense of the document. Document attached to Memorandum from director, FBI (65-56402) to SAC, New York (65-14603) March 12, 1952 which ordered SAC, N.Y. to pay Bentley the $2000 and have her sign the receipt. File #134-182-13.

70. FBI Memorandum from Mr. W.V. Cleveland to Mr. A.H. Belmont, May 8, 1952; subject William Walter Remington; also FBI Memorandum from SAC, N.Y., 65-14603, to Director, Attention A.H. Belmont, Subject Gregory, Espionage-R, My 13, 1952.

71. Peake, 268.

72. Memorandum from SAC NY (65-14603) to Director FBI, July 10, 1952; subj. Gregory Espionage-R; 1; similar memo dated 9/26/52, p.5.

73. FBI Memorandum from Mr. W.V. Cleveland to Mr. A.H. Belmont, May 8, 1952, Subject: William Walter Remington. Memorandum from SAC, New York, 65-14603, to Director, FBI, 5/13/52, Subj: Gregory Espionage-R; 93. Memorandum from SAC, New York (65-14603) to Director, FBI, July 10, 1952 Subj: Gregory Espionage-R; 1. Memorandum from SAC, New York (65-14603) to Director, FBI, 9/26/52 Subject: Gregory Espionage-R, File #134-435-66, p. 6. FBI Memo from Mr. W. A. Branigan to Mr. A. H. Belmont, Subject Elizabeth Terrill Bentley Confidential Source, October 15, 1952, p. 2.

74. Memorandum from Director, FBI (#65-56402) to SAC, NY (#65-14603) Subject: Elizabeth Terrill Bentley, Confidential Source, July 10, 1952, File #134-435-59. FBI Memorandum from SAC, N.Y., (65-14603) to Director, Subject Gregory Espionage-R, 10/3/52. FBI Memo from Director, to SAC, N.Y. Subject: Elizabeth T. Bentley Espionage-R, Feb. 3, 1953. FBI Memorandum from Director to SAC, NY, File #124-435-69, 10/22/52. FBI Memo from Director to SAC,NY; subj. Elizabeth T. Bentley Espionage R. Feb 3, 1953.

75. FBI Memo from Director to SAC,NY, File# 124=435-69; 10/22/52.

76. Teletype from FBI NY to Bureau signed 'Boardman,' 2/15/53.

77. Memorandum from SAC, NY (65-14603) to Director, FBI, 9/26/52; subj. Gregory Espionage R-1; file #134-435-66; p. 6.

78. *Ibid.*, p 6-7; Memo to J. McAndrews, SA, NY (for files) Sept. 22, 1952; file # 65-14603-4441.

79. *New York Herald-Tribune*, June 10, 1955, late city edition, p. 13; Peake, 271.

80. FBI Memo to Director from SAC, NY, 9/26/51; file # 134-435-66; p 2.

81. Memo from SAC, NY (65-14603) to Director, FBI, 9/26/52, Subject. Gregory Epionage R, Sept. 26, 1952, p 5.

82. See note 80; p 2.

83. FBI Memo from Director to SAC, NY; subj Elizabeth T. Bentley, Espionage-R; Feb 3, 1953.

84. Teletype from FBI New Haven to Director FBI and SAC New York 8/11/55 signed Casper, File #134-181-110.

85. *The New York Times*, December 4, 1963, Obit. page, col. 1,2.

86. Peake, 236.

87. Theoharis, 26.

88. Robert Louis Benson and Michael Warner, Editors, *VENONA, Soviet Espionage and the American Response 1939-1957*, National Security Agency, Central Intelligence Agency, Wash., D.C. 1996, p. xxxiii. More information on Ms. Bentley can be found in following FBI correspondence: memorandum from Mr. C. A. Hennrich to Mr. A. H. Belmont, Sept. 22, 1952 which contains the statement: "Special Assistant to the Attorney General Roy Cohn has in the past been assigned to handle Bentley in her appearances before the courts in New York..." File 13-435-65; 91. Memorandum from SAC, New York, 65-14603 to Director, FBI, May 16, 1952, Attn: Assistant Director A.H. Belmont; 3-9; Memorandum from Inspector C. E. Hennrich to Mr. A. H. Belmont, Sept. 22, 1952; File #134-435-65; memo from SA Gallaher, Sept. 23, 1952 recipient not indicated; FBI Memorandum from Thomas J. McAndrews, SA, New York Re: Elizabeth Bentley, Sept. 29, 1952, File #134-182-6 (addressee not indicated); FBI Memorandum from Mr. A. H. Belmont to Mr. D. M. Ladd re Elizabeth Terrell Bentley, September 26, 1952 (134-435067), p. 2; FBI Memo from Lester O. Gallaher, SA re Elizabeth T. Bentley, 10/29/52 (Office Files); FBI Memo from SAC, New York (65-14603) to Director Subject: Elizabeth T. Bentley, 1/16/53, File #134-435-72; FBI Memorandum from SAC, N.Y, to Director, Subject Elizabeth Terrill Bentley Confidential Source Re Maurice Hyman Halperin Espionage-R, 2/5/53; FBI memo to SAC, New York from R. A. Collins, Subject: Elizabeth Bentley, Feb. 3, 1955, NY File #100-98062;. FBI Memo from SAC, N.Y. to Director, 3/24/55; FBI teletype from New York office, to Bureau (Headquarters) marked "Urgent" signed by Kelley, 2/15/55, File #134-181-72; FBI Memo from SA Lester O. Gallaher to SAC, NY., Subject Elizabeth T. Bentley Confidential Source, 2/25/55 File #134-181-59, two pages; FBI Memo from A. H. Belmont to L. V. Boardman, Subject Elizabeth Bentley 6 June 1955; FBI Staff Conference Notes, 2/14/57, NY File #134-182-144; FBI Memo from SAC New York (100-138981) to Director (100-426205)9/21/59; 2; FBI Memo from SAC, New Haven (100-17332) to Director (100-426205) Subj. Stephen Francis Vause Security Matter-C, 10/22/59;; Teletype from SAC New Haven to Director, FBI and SAC, NY 12/3/63; 62, 117; also in Peake, 270, 305.

Chapter 26

1. Trial Minutes, p. 752. Also: Proceedings of May 31, 1950, p. 3, U.S. Federal District Court, Philadelphia, Pa.

2. Statement to the press by U. S. District Court Judge James P. McGranery, June 1, 1950 (See Files: "Harry Gold, trial of..." Archives of Pepper & Hamilton, Esqs., Philadelphia, Pa.

3. Trial Minutes, p. 752.

4. Hamilton's remarks are taken from his typewritten notes lodged in the Archives of

Pepper & Hamilton, Esqs., Philadelphia, Pa. I am given to understand that he read those notes as typed.

5. *Invitation to an Inquest*, 420.

6. FBI Files, Subject Harry Gold, File #65-57449 Vol. 29, Serials 743-770.

7. FBI Memo from Mr. Ladd to The Director, October 24, 1950 re: Sentencing Of Harry Gold; File #65-57449-706.

Chapter 27

1. FBI Memo from SA T. Scott Miller to SAC, Philadelphia, File #65-4307-185(56), July 7, 1950.

2. "The Circumstances," pp. 2-3; also see FBI Files #65-557449-790.

3. The information about Gold's early life is recalled from the reminiscences he shared with the author when he worked at the Brothman firm from 1946 to 1948.

4. "The Circumstances," pp. 5-7.

5. FBI Memo from SA Joseph E. Spivey to SAC Philadelphia, May 25, 1950, File #65-4307-78, pp. 1-4.

6. On Black's advice Gold denied he was Jewish on his job application since the firm did not hire Jews. See "The Circumstances," p. 15.

7. FBI Memo from SA T. Scott Miller, Jr., to SAC Philadelphia, June 23, 1950, Subject Harry Gold, File #65-4307-614.

8. FBI Memo from SA William H. Naylor to SAC, May 26, 1950, re: Harry Gold, File #65-4307.

9. FBI Memo from SA William H. Naylor to SAC, June 7, 1950, subject Harry Gold File #65-4307-694.

10. FBI Memo from T. Scott Miller, SA to SAC, Philadelphia, subject Harry Gold, June 7, 1950, File #65-4307-735.

11. FBI Memo from SA James F. Helmer to SAC, June 6, 1950, Subject Harry Gold, File #65-4307-258.

12. FBI Memo from SA Joseph J. Walsh to Roy Cohn, October 4, 1950, p. 7, File #65- 15324-568. Also see: FBI Report made at Philadelphia, Pa., December 4, 1950 by Robert G. Jenson, Title: Harry Gold, WAS, Espionage-R, File PH 65-4307, p. 4. (Also marked File #65-57449, Vol. 28, Serials 722-742.)

13. FBI Memo from SA T.Scott Miller, Jr. to SAC, Philadelphia, July 10, 1950. Subject Harry Gold, WAS, Espionage-R Exhibit 65-4307-1B-5 (19-9).

14. FBI Memo from SA William H. Naylor to SAC dated May 26, 1950 Subject: Harry Gold, p.1, File 65-4307-82.

15. *Ibid.*

16. Material from Venona files says that on October 24, 1944 the Soviet station in New York wrote to Moscow that Gold wanted to set up his own laboratory. At first he thought their financial help would not be needed. On December 20, 1944 the station sent cable #1797 telling Moscow that Gold was asking for $2000 to help defray costs. They indicated misgivings about the proposed venture and apparently it did not go forward. See chapter entitled "Enter Venona."

17. FBI Memo by Thomas H. Zoeller, SA, New York, November 7, 1950, p. 2, file #65-15324-577.

18. *Ibid.*

19A FBI Memo to SAC from SA Joseph E. Spivey, May 31, 1950, Philadelphia,

Subject: Harry Gold, file #65-5407-148.

20. FBI report made at New York, multiple dates from October through December, 1950, title: Abraham Brothman, was, p. 21, file #100-95068.

21. Report by SAC Albert L. Pierce of the Philadelphia FBI office July 19, 1950 regarding a statement Gold made when interrogated on June 5, 1950 by Agents Miller and Brennan.
Also: FBI Memo from Albert L. Pierce to SAC, (Philadelphia) June 8, 1950, file #65-4307-1B5 (29-18).
Also: Memo from William H. Naylor, Philadelphia FBI dated August 3, 1950.
Also: Report from Philadelphia to New York FBI dated 7/7/50 by Robert G. Jensen which mentions a third fictitious person, Malcolm Schwartz (p. 13) besides Schultz and Epstein; file #65-57449-542.

22. FBI Memo from SAC Philadelphia to SAC, Albany, June 15, 1950, (initials on memo: RGJ) File #65-4307-420. (P. 31 of No

23. FBI Memo for Roy Cohn signed by Joseph C. Walsh, SA, October 24, 1950, Subj.: Harry Gold, WAS. File #65-156324-568, p.6.

24. *Ibid.* Also see FBI File 65-4307, Dec. 4 1950, p. 2 Also: FBI teletype from Philadelphia to Director and SAC, NY, October 16, 1950.

25. Trial Minutes, p. 835.

26. Files, "Harry Gold, Trial Of," archives of Pepper and Hamilton, Esqs., Philadelphia, Pa.

27. Trial Minutes, p. 319.

28. FBI Teletype to The Director and SACS NY and Philadelphia from M. Ostholthoff, May 26, 1950.

29. Trial Minutes, p. 732.

30. FBI Memo, New York Office for Roy Cohn, October 24, 1950, File #65-15324-568, p.6.

31. Files, "Harry Gold, Trial Of," Archives of Pepper and Hamilton, Esqs., Philadelphia, Pa.

32. Teletype from Philadelphia office of FBI to Director and SACS, New York, June 13, 1950, pp. 3-5 (no file number).

33. FBI Report made by SAC Edward Scheidt, Re: Miriam Moskowitz dated July 27, 1950, File #100-96341, p. 5.

34 FBI Memo, New York, from SA Thomas H. Zoeller, November 7, 1950, November 7, 19950, Subj.: Abraham Brothman, Miriam Moskowitz, File #65-15324-577, p. 8.

35. *Ibid*, p. 12.

36. *Ibid.*

37. Harry Gold, Confession, FBI File 65-57449, Vol. 5, Serials 131-182, May 22, 1950, p. 2. Also see FBI File #65-4307, Vol. l.

38. *Ibid.*

39. Venona File #912, New York to Moscow, 27 June 1944 and File #1390, New York to Moscow, l, October 1944 National Security Administration, Washington, D.C.

40. FBI Memo from Thomas H. Zoeller, SA, ll/7/50, File #65-15324-577, p. 3. Also see FBI Report made at Philadelphia by Robert G. Jensen, SA, May 31, 1950, File #65-4307 (also listed as File #65-57449, Vol. 7, Serials 185-185x.) The latter refers

to Gold's statement that he never took money from his Soviet friends although they offered it.

41. FBI memo from SAC Philadelphia to Director, BU File 100-9634v also listed as File #100-37069-21, October 25, 1950, p. 2.

42. FBI report made in New York by SA James E. Freaney who quotes Harry Gold, November 21, 1951, p. 2, File #100-47083-188. Also see NY File 100-54127, p. 2.

43. Memorandum, SAC Philadelphia FBI to Director, subject: Harry Gold, July 12, 1950.

44. Teletype to the Director and SACS from SA Cornelius, Philadelphia FBI, Jan. 4, 1951; File #65-57449-757.

45. Memorandum from Augustus S. Ballard, Esq. to John D. M. Hamilton, Esq. (Gold's attorneys) November 24, 1954; Archives of Pepper and Hamilton, Esqs., Philadelphia, Pa.

46. From Harry Gold's Confession, FBI File #65-57449, Vol. 5, May 22, 1950, p. 9.

47. Harry Gold, personal papers, Temple University Library, Special Collections, Philadelphia, Pa. (Unclassified as of March 1998).

48. FBI memo #65-15324, dated November 7, 1950, p. 12.

49. Trial Minutes, p. 280.

50. "The Circumstances," p. 100.

51. *Ibid.*

52. *Ibid.*, p. 102.

53. *Ibid.*, p. 119.

54. In a letter to the Parole Board, Sept. 30, 1960, Gold's attorney, Hamilton, said Gold clocked 350 hours of interviews with the FBI and other government interrogators in 1950 alone. He also recorded 100 hours in 1951, 75 hours in 1952, 50 hours in 1953, and 25 hours in 1954. (Files marked, "Harry Gold, Trial of..." Archives of Pepper and Hamilton, Esqs., Philadelphia, Pa.).

55. Report of Interview by SA Robert G. Jensen, Philadelphia, FBI, August 24, 1950, File #65-4307-l-b-15 (25).

56. Trial Minutes, p. 700.

57. FBI Report by SA John R. Murphy, New York FBI, June 8, 1950, (no file number), pp. 1, 14, 15.

58. FBI Teletype from Philadelphia to Director and SACs, August 15, 1950, File #65-57449-635, p. 4.

59. Information in letter from Harry Gold to his father and brother; in files of Temple University Library, Special collections; unclassified as of March 1998, letter dated January 1951.

60. Letter from Hamilton to Gold dated January 31, 1951, copy at Temple University Library, Special Collections, unclassified as of October 1998

61. FBI memo to SAC, New York from Director, FBI dated July 5, 1951, File #655-57449-790.

62. Letter from Hamilton to Gold, February 15, 1951, in Temple University Library, Special Collections Dept., unclassified as of March 1998.

63. Letter from International News Service to Harry Gold, April 10, 1951; also letter from John d. M. Hamilton, Esq. to Harry Gold dated April 11, 1951 in which he says: "...it is seemingly impossible to obtain clearance from the proper authorities." both letters in Special Collections, Temple University Library, Philadelphia, Pa. Also

see FBI Memo from A.H. Belmont to D.M, Ladd, Feb. 8, 1951, File #65-57449-769.

64. "The Circumstances;" 8, 11.

65. FBI report, New York, by Joseph C. Walsh, SA, File #65-15324. March 3, 1951; 6.

66. FBI report, New York, file #15324, March 5, 1961; 7.

67. *Ibid.*, 7-8.

68. *Ibid.*, 6.

69. "The Circumstances;" 121.

70. Archives of Pepper, Hamilton, Esqs., Philadelphia, Pa., files marked, "Harry Gold, Trial of..."

71. Correspondence between Hamilton and Gold, Archives, file #558, Correspondence 1951-1955, Box 1, ID 31012.

72. Senate Internal Security Subcommittee, Hearings, "Scope of Soviet Activity in the United States," March 29, April 2, 3, and August 15, 1957, United States Senate, Eighty-fifth Congress; 3815. Hereafter referred to as Senate Subcommittee Report.

73. Trial Minutes; 710; 814.

74. FBI Report made at New York June 30, 1950 by John R. Murphy, Jr., SA covering Personal History of Abraham Brothman.

75. Report made at Philadelphia by Robert G. Jensen, SA, Sept. 5, 1950, File #65-4337; 3-4.

76. FBI Memo from D.M. Ladd to Director, May 18, 1950, File #65-57449-42; 5

77. Trial Minutes; 903.

78. Letter from Benjamin Mandel, Senate internal Security Subcommittee to Harry Gold at the Federal Penitentiary, Lewisburg, Pa., dated July 8, 1957, lodged with Gold's Personal Papers at Temple University Library, Special Collections, Philadelphia, Pa. (Unclassified as of March 1998).

79. Senate Subcommittee Report; 3814.

80. FBI Memorandum made at Philadelphia, Pa., File #200-95068-1B11; 37, 56.

81. Senate Subcommittee Report; 3815.

82. Trial Minutes; 692.

83. Senate Subcommittee Report; 3815-3816.

84. *Ibid.*, 3816.

85. "The Circumstances;" 69-72.

86. FBI Memo from Joseph C. Walsh, SA, New York, 7/23/50, File #65-15324 RM (also using number #65-57449 Vol. 29, Serials 743-770), re Harry Gold, WAS. Also: Memo from Director to Assistant Attorney General J. M. McInerney, 8/10/50; 3; File #65-57449-634.

87. Senate Subcommittee report; 3818.

88. Those letters are in the Temple University Library, Special Collections Dept., Files marked "Harry Gold"; Copies of correspondence between Hamilton and the Parole Board on file at Temple University Library, Special Collections, files marked; "Harry Gold," not otherwise identified.

Chapter 28

1. Nicholas von Hoffman, *Citizen Cohn*, Doubleday, N.Y., 1988; 73-74; (hereafter referred to as von Hoffman).

2. von Hoffman, 74.

3. Sidney Zion, *The Autobiography of Roy Cohn*, Lyle Stuart Inc., Secaucus, N.J.

1988; 62-65 (hereafter referred to as Zion).

4. von Hoffman; 141.

5. *The New York Times*, August 3, 1986; page 33, col. 3.

6. Victor Navasky, "Dialectical McCarthyism," *The Nation*, July 20, 1988; 31.

7. *The New York Times*, August 3, 1986; 33.

8. National Jewish Ledger, Washington, D.C., "Mr. Cohn and Mr. Shine: The Saga of Two Inquisitors," August 14, 1953; (Referred to hereafter as National Jewish Ledger).

9. Lillian Hellman, *Scoundrel Time*, Little, Brown, Boston, 1976; 150.

10. See note 5.

11. *Ibid.* Also see: National Jewish Ledger.

12. Hans N. Tuch, letter to the Editor, *The New York Times*, August 27, 1986, Editorial/Letters page. Tuch was a retired career minister in the U. S. Foreign Service. See also *National Jewish Ledger*.

13. *National Jewish Ledger*.

14. Tuch.

15. *National Jewish Ledger*.

16. *The New York Times*, Sept. 5, 1963, col. 2; and August 3, 1986; 33.

17. von Hoffman, 183-184.

18. See note 5.

19. Zion; 151-152.

20. *The New York Times*, August 3, 1986; 33, col. 1.

21. William Lambert, "The Hotshot One-Man Roy Cohn Lobby," *LIFE Magazine*, Sept. 4, 1969; 26-30. Hereafter referred to as Lambert.; Also see von Hoffman, p. 414, "A one-man network of contacts that have reached into City Hall, the mob, the press, the Archdiocese, the disco-jet set, the courts and the backrooms of the Bronx and Brooklyn where judges are made..." von Hoffman quotes the *New York Daily News* on this passage.

22. *The Wall Street Journal*, February 28, 1963; 1, col. 1.

23, von Hoffman, 409-414; also see *The New York Times*, August 3, 1986; 33; and, von Hoffman, 252, 318, 320-21, 411-413, 426.

24. von Hoffman, 409-414.

25. *The New York Times*, August 3, 1986; 33.

26. *The New York Times*, Sept. 5, 1963; 1, 25; *The Wall Street Journal*, Sept. 5, 1963; 2 and *The Wall Street Journal*, March 24, 1964.

27. *The Wall Street Journal*, Sept. 5, 1963; 2, col. 2; *The New York Times*, Sept. 5, 1963; page 25, col. 1; *The Wall Street Journal*, April 4, 1964; 4, cols. 3. 4.

28. *The Wall Street Journal*, March 24, 1964.

29. *The Wall Street Journal*, April 3, 1964.

30. *The Wall Street Journal*, April 6, 1964; 5, col. 1, 2.

31. *Dow Jones Report*, April 24, 1963; also, *The New York Times*, Sept. 5, 1963 and August 3, 1986. *The Wall Street Journal*, November 5, 1963 and March 23, 1964 under byline of Ed Cony.

32. *The Wall Street Journal*, October 17, 1963; 26.

33. *The Wall Street Journal*, May 31, 1966; 4, col. 2.

34. von Hoffman; 273.

35. *The Wall Street Journal*, Feb. 28, 1963, page 15, column 1.

36. *The New York Times*, Dec. 14, 1969; von Hoffman, 349-352.
37. *The New York Times*, Dec. 14, 1969; von Hoffman, 348; Zion, 187-189.
38. *Ibid.*
39. Lambert, 27.
40. Lambert, 26-30.
41. von Hoffman, 455-456.
42. William A. Reuben with Alexander Cockburn, "No Sense of Decency, Why Cohn Was Disbarred," *The Nation*, July 19/26, 1986; 48-51. This essay discusses the Pied Piper case, the Rosenstiel event and Cohn's disbarment.
43. *Ibid.*
44. *Ibid.*, 48.
45. See note 5.
46. von Hoffman, 363-369.
47. Oscar Wilde, "The Picture of Dorian Gray," *Lippincott's Monthly Magazine*, 20 June 1890 (republished by Penguin Classic, among others.).
48. See note 5.

Chapter 29
1. von Hoffman, 82; Zion, 60-65.
2. Zion, 65.
3. *The New York Times*, May 14, 1976, 1/B-4, December 21, 1976, page 1; July 2, 1977, page 1.

Chapter 30
1. FBI Memo (Washington) from Mr. Belmont to Mr. Ladd, Sept. 5, 1950, File #65-57449-667, 3.
2. Zion, 65-67.
3. Zion, 68. Also: *The New York Times*, Feb. 3, 1992, D-10; also von Hoffman, 99-101.
4. *The New York Times*, Feb. 28, 1992, Letter to the Editor by Harvey M. Spear, former special assistant to the Attorney General in 1952.
5. *The New York Times*, Feb. 3, 1992; D10.
6. *Ibid.*
7. *Ibid.*
8. *Ibid.*

Epilogue
1. Michael D. Yates, "Braverman and the Class Struggle," *Monthly Review*, January 1999; 5.

Appendix A
1. Alfred E. Kahn, *The Matusow Affair, Memoir of A National Scandal*, Moyer Bell Ltd., Mt. Kisco, N.Y.; 1987, 155.
2. Harvey Matusow, *False Witness*, Cameron & Kahn, N.Y., 1955; 132, 134.
3. Kahn, 240-245.
4. *Ibid.*

Afterword

1. The indictment identified Mr. Gold as a conspirator, but he wasn't named as a defendant. (*United States v. Brothman, et al*, 191 F.2d 70 (2nd Cir. 1951).

2. There are three relevant documents. "GOLD recalls telling BROTHMAN practically nothing in MOSKOWITZ' presence but later, after all had returned to the laboratory and MOSKOWITZ had gone out for coffee or something, they talked of their stories to the agents." *FBI Report by SAC Edward Scheidt*, File No 100-96341, July 27, 1950, p. 9. (Note: See Document 1 in Appendix D.); Gold suggested to Brothman that he not discuss their espionage activities in front of Moskowitz. *Teletype from the Philadelphia office of the FBI to Director and SACS*, New York, June 13, 1950, pp. 3-5.); and, on November 7, 1950, the day before Moskowitz' trial began, an FBI memo stated: "With regard to MIRIAM MOSKOWITZ, GOLD stated that he never discussed his espionage activity in her presence when he could avoid it, as he distrusted her because of her violent temper." *FBI Memo from Thomas H. Zoeller*, November 7, 1950, Subj: Abraham Brothman, Miriam Moskowitz, File No. 65-15324, p. 8. (Note: See Document 2 in Appendix D.)

3. *FBI Memo from Thomas H. Zoeller, November 7, 1950., Id.*

4. Memo for Roy Cohn, by SA Joseph C. Walsh, New York, FBI, October 24, 1950, File #65-15324-568. (Note: See Document 3 in Appendix D.)

5. In 1945 the Supreme Court clearly stated: "And we have often pointed out that a conviction, secured by the use of perjured testimony known to be such by the prosecuting attorney, is a denial of due process." *White v. Ragen*, 324 US 760, 764 (1945).

6. *United States v. Brothman, et al*, 191 F.2d 70 (2nd Cir. 1951). Mr. Brothman and Ms. Moskowitz were sentenced on November 28, 1950 to two years in prison and a $10,000 fine for their respective conspiracy convictions. Mr. Brothman was also given a consecutive five-year sentence and a $5,000 fine for his conviction of endeavored to persuade a witness (Gold) to give false testimony before a federal grand jury. That conviction was vacated on appeal, but the appeals court affirmed the conspiracy convictions of Ms. Moskowitz and Mr. Brothman.

7. Zion, 66. ("... The Brothman-Moscowitz (sic) case was a dry run of the upcoming Rosenberg trial. We were able to see how Gold and Bentley fared on the stand, and we were able to see how we fared, Saypol and I.")

8. Mr. Gold and Elizabeth Bentley (who only testified against Mr. Brothman), subsequently testified during the Rosenburg's trial, and Cohn and Saypol where the prosecutors and Judge Kaufman presided.

Index

60 Minutes (television program)..........4
aerosol insecticide dispenser ...74, 75, 99,
171, 184, 207, 257
Agrin, Gloria.....................................125
Alman, David.......................................5
Golos, John (Jacob) ...14, 15, 47, 48, 50-
4, 64-6, 73, 95, 98, 191-3, 199, 217
American Chemical Society 48, 76
American Civil Liberties Union.........18
American Federation of Labor..........25
American League Against War and
Fascism................................191, 192
Americans for Democratic Action.....18
Amtorg Trading Corporation 14, 15,
51, 54, 62, 65, 76, 79-81, 98, 174, 183,
208, 211, 222, 250
Anders, Christine 149-155, 166, 168,
169
Atlanta Federal Penitentiary 143
atom bomb 4, 17, 31, 33, 42, 59, 121,
177, 178, 252
Bachrach, Marian..............................125
Bagnold, Whitney S..........................263
Ballard, Augustus S. 205, 215, 263
Bentley, Charles Prentiss 190
Bentley, Elizabeth (also known as
Helen)...15-17, 29, 44, 49, 50-57, 59,
64-66, 92, 93, 98-103, 120, 121, 125,
173, 175, 176, 179, 182, 185, 189-204,
222, 231, 232, 240, 244, 253, 256, 263
trial testimony 49-57
personal history 103, 191, 203
Bernice S. (jailmate of M. Moskowitz)
....116, 117
Biddle, Attorney General Francis 180
Bill of Rights (U.S. Constitution) ..5, 18
Black, Tom 61, 62, 81, 211
Bloch, Emanuel ...123, 125, 157, 159,
200
Bowers, Richard 213
Bridgeport Post...............................200
Bridges, Harry 24, 36
British Intelligence...........................182
British Official Secrets Act...............59

Brothman, Abraham ...3, 4, 6, 9-11, 14-
16, 20, 22, 24, 32, 33, 42, 47, 48, 50-
52, 54-84, 87-96, 98-102, 104-106,
120, 121, 143, 144, 158, 160, 161,
170-187, 189, 190, 193, 194, 197, 201,
202, 204, 205, 207, 214-223, 225-227,
230-232, 234, 242, 244, 249, 250, 252,
254-258
arrest & background. 9-24
FBI interest. 32-33
trial opening & Bentley testimony. 47-
57
Gold's testimony. 58-102
verdict. 104-106
parole application.......................143
background. 171-184
vis-à-vis Venona. 182-187
working with Gold. 216-226
Afterword.................................252
Browder, Earl.............49, 192, 193, 195
Brown, F. 50, 191
Brunini, John 197
Buckley, Special Agent...................195
Budenz, Louis 29, 199, 200
Buna-N (synthetic rubber) 184, 255
Buna-S (synthetic rubber) 68-70, 72,
73, 75, 83, 84, 87, 89, 98-100, 178,
184, 207, 254
Burrill (Bentley), Mary 190
Cacchione, Pete..............................24
Cambodia..30
Central Intelligence Agency (CIA)..182
Chambers, Whittaker 29, 30
Chemical & Metallurgical Engineering
....254
China.............................17, 19, 234
Churchill, Winston....................33, 131
City College of New York...........22, 35
Civil Rights Congress 58, 236
Clark, Attorney General Tom 180
Cohn, Judge Albert 234, 235
Cohn, Roy Marcus ...4, 44, 66, 93, 95,
99, 100, 106, 121, 142, 175, 198, 201,

202, 225, 227, 231, 234-242, 245, 250-253, 258

Cold War ...29, 31, 36, 37, 103, 106, 159, 182, 203, 208, 226, 227, 231, 248, 250

Collazo, Oscar 58

Colonial Sand & Stone Co. 242

Columbia College 170

Columbia Spectator 191

Columbia University 49, 86, 141, 170, 190, 196, 215, 249, 263

Committee on Immigration and Naturalization 52

communism 2, 24, 28, 29, 47, 49, 53, 55-57, 106, 146, 248

Communist Control Act 18

Communist Party of the USA (CPUSA)... 15, 18, 24, 29, 32, 36, 37, 47-50, 53-56, 58, 61, 74, 81, 98, 102, 175, 191-193, 195, 197, 199, 204, 210-211, 224, 253

Confidential Informant T-1 174

Congress of Industrial Organizations 25

Considine, Bob 224, 225

Consumers Union 191

Coplon case 58

Costello, Frank 112, 242

Coughlin, Father Charles 24

Custodial Detention Index/List 180

Daily Worker 37

Danahy, Jack 195

Dann, Benjamin C. 98

Dartmouth College 196, 197

Davis, Jr., Benjamin 24

DDT 99, 174, 182, 184, 254

De Sapio, Carmine 242

Dean, Gordon 72, 184

Debs, Eugene V. 210

Defendant's Exhibits H-N 89

Defiance (yacht) 239

Depression (Great) 24-26, 34, 36, 81, 170, 191, 200, 210, 248

disbarred 4, 240, 241

Donegan, Thomas J... 44, 198, 200, 201

Dougherty, Morrell...88, 89, 91, 93, 211-215

Douglas, Helen Gahagan 30

Dreiser, Theodore 236

Drexel Institute 48, 61, 206, 211

DuPont 221

Einstein, Albert 29

Eisenhower, General Dwight 4, 36, 199

Eisler case 58

Elson, Ray 193, 194

Epstein, Herbert 214

Ernst, Morris L. 18

Federal Arts Project 26

Federal Bureau of Investigation (FBI) ... 3, 6, 9, 11-15, 17-21, 29, 31-33, 37, 40, 43, 44, 47, 49, 52, 53, 55-59, 62, 65, 66, 76-79, 88, 89, 92-98, 101, 115, 122, 123, 135, 138, 139, 158-160, 168, 173-176, 178-187, 189, 191, 192, 194-197, 199-205, 209, 211-218, 220-225, 227, 228, 230, 231, 243-245, 249, 250, 252, 258

Federal Circuit Court of Appeals 57

Federal Employees Loyalty Program...17

Federal Power Commission 29

Federal Reformatory for Women .. 125, 128, 131

Federal Theater Project 191

Fifth Amendment 16, 56, 177

Fifth Avenue Coach Company 238

Fitzgerald, Edward 203

Flanagan, Helen 191

Flynn, Ed 234

Flynn, Elizabeth Gurley 125, 126

Foley Square Courthouse....11, 39, 103, 246

Foley, John M. 44

Foreign Agents Registration Act 192

Foxcroft School 190

Frank, Sidney 240

Frankfurter, Justice Felix 245

Freedom of Information Act...4, 6, 250, 251

Fuchs, Klaus...17, 19, 42, 43, 59, 60, 62, 63, 96, 97, 208, 209, 212, 221, 222, 227, 228, 230

Gleason, Roger F. 194

Gold, Harry (aka Frank Kessler)...3, 4, 15, 16, 17, 19, 20, 32, 33, 42, 44, 47, 48, 51-53, 56, 58-104, 120, 121, 123, 173-175, 178, 182-187, 189, 204-218, 220-233, 244, 250-252, 256, 257, 263

trial testimony 59-102

re Verona 182-187

early years to sentencing. 204-209

later life................................ 210-233
Golodnitzky, Celia....................210, 215
Golodnitzky, Sam 210
Goodyear Tire & Rubber Co..............71
Government's Exhibits 13-17............87
Government's Exhibits 14-17......84, 88
GPU (see also, NKVD).....................53
grand jury...3, 15-17, 20, 32, 42, 47, 48,
    52, 54, 56-57, 63, 65-66, 73, 78-80, 86,
    96, 98, 101, 102, 121, 184, 196-198,
    202, 204, 208, 215, 216, 223, 244, 249
Greenglass, David....4, 19, 61, 62, 121,
    208, 227, 232, 256
Greenglass, Ruth.............................4, 19
Gromov, Anatoli......... ..193-196, 199-202
Groves, General Leslie R.................177
Haganah (Jewish defense force in
    Palestine) 17
Hamilton, John D. M. .. 3, 72, 186, 205-
    209, 215, 224-226
Hammett, Dashiell 236
Hebrew Union College 142
Heller, Peter 55, 194-196, 199
Hellman, Lillian 235
Hendrick Manufacturing Company...70-
    72, 83, 89, 98, 183, 194
Hiroshima 17, 33
Hiss, Alger 30, 49
Holbrook Company 61
Hollywood Ten 31, 58
Hoodless, Carter 48, 76
Hoover, J. Edgar...17, 18, 20, 21, 29, 40,
    44, 58, 66, 89, 106, 142, 160, 175, 176,
    178-180, 194, 201-203, 215, 246
House Committee on UnAmerican
    Activities (HUAC)...29-31, 51, 55, 56,
    58, 198, 199, 235
House Investigative Committee.........26
House of Detention for Women (NYC)
    ....12, 109, 111, 116, 118, 120, 125,
    126, 253
Humphrey, Senator Hubert H. 18
Il Progresso 242
Immigration and Naturalization Service
    ....22, 35, 119
Institute of Human Relations 200
International Monetary Fund 198
International News Service..............224
International Organization's Employees
    Loyalty Board 198

Intourist Agency (see also, World
    Tourists)................................53, 193
Israel 16, 174
Italian Library of Information....49, 51,
    53, 191, 192
Japan...28, 131
Jenner Committee 203
Jewish Agency for Palestine 16, 17
Jewish Forward 210
Johns Hopkins University................235
Johnson, President Lyndon 27, 29
Joint Military Intelligence College ..190
Katz, Dr. Albert B............................215
Kaufman, Judge Irving R. ...43, 45, 49,
    53-57, 61-64, 66-68, 70-73, 75, 77, 81,
    82, 87-102, 104, 105, 121, 123, 142,
    185, 214, 244-247, 250
Kennedy, President John F. 30
Kennedy, Robert F...........................234
Kennelly, FBI Agent.......................191
Kent State University........................30
Kessler, Frank (aka Harry Gold)...15, 64,
    73-75, 78, 92, 183, 187, 218, 222
KGB..184
King, Reverend Dr. Martin Luther.....29
Kleinman, William W. ...44, 49, 51-57,
    61, 63, 64, 66, 67, 70, 73, 75, 77, 80-
    102, 104, 184, 187, 213, 227
Korean War...................................17, 19
Kross, Anna M.................................109
Lane, Myles K. 44
Lattimore, Owen 234
Lawson, John Howard 31
Lend-Lease 67, 72, 184, 208
Lewis, Sinclair 35
Lewisburg Federal Penitentiary 232
Liliana (prison friend of M. Moskowitz)
    135-140
Lionel Corp..............................238, 239
Long Lane School............................203
loyalty oath 2, 18
Loyalty Program 17, 197
Loyalty Review Board....................197
M. Steinthal Co................................238
magnesium powder..............74, 75, 207
Mandel, Benjamin...........228, 230, 231
Manhattan Project.....................59, 177
Mann, Thomas 29
Marcus, Dora 235
Marshall Plan....................................27

Martinsville Seven............................ 141
Massachusetts Institute of Technology
.... .221
Matusow, Harvey 29, 202, 253
May, Dr. Alan Nunn........................ 209
McCarran Internal Security Act 18
McCarthy, Senator Joseph...17, 18, 30,
    47, 159, 177, 199, 226, 231, 234-236,
    240, 252, 263, 264
McGee, Willie 141
McGranery, Judge James P. 205, 209
Medicare... 27
Messing, William L. 44, 170
Mitchell, Attorney General John 180
Morris, Robert................................. 231
Mundelein College 200
Nagasaki 17, 33
National Housing Act........................ 25
National Recovery Act 211
National Security Agency 182
National Youth Administration 26
Navasky,Victor............................... 235
Needleman, Gibby................. 76, 77, 79
New Deal ...25-27, 29, 31, 37, 191, 196
New Haven Hospital 203
New York City Emergency Home Relief
    Bureau 191
New York World-Telegram 200
Nixon, Richard 30, 31
NKVD (see also, GPU) 53
Noonan, Judge Gregory............. 57, 197
Ohio National Guard 30
Olive, Theodore................................ 99
Out of Bondage (1951)...190, 194, 197,
    199, 200
Parole Board................................... 143
Peak, Hayden.................................. 190
Pennsylvania Sugar Company.... .61, 62,
    206, 211, 228, 229
Perlo, Victor 49
Philadelphia General Hospital.. ..61, 83,
    206, 209, 212
Pidto, Bernie................................... 160
Pied Piper Yacht Charters Corp. 239
Pope, Generoso 242
Product Engineering............ 87, 99, 255
Progressive Party............................. 37
Purdue University.................... 214, 215
Quinn, Thomas Vincent 54
Rabin, Congressman Benjamin J..... 234

RDX (explosive also known as cyclonite)
.... 19, 198
Reagan, Ronald 31, 237
Red Menace.............................. 29, 58
Redlich, Dr. F. C. 200
Remington, Ann Moos 197
Remington, William 49, 52, 57, 58,
    192, 196-198, 201, 202, 232, 234, 242
Republic Chemical Machinery Co. ...172,
    183, 194
Republic Steel Co............. 183, 193, 194
Republican National Committee 205
Reuben, William A............ 31, 240, 263
Reynolds, John Hazard.................... 193
Roberts, Sam 256
Robeson, Paul............................. 24, 36
Roosevelt, Eleanor 29
Roosevelt, President Franklin Delano25
Rose, Fred 209
Rosenberg, Ethel...4, 19, 44, 66, 120-125,
    157, 158, 175, 178, 247, 252, 256
Rosenberg, Julius...4, 19, 44, 66, 120-
    122, 157, 175, 178, 247, 252, 256
Rosenstiel, Elizabeth 240
Rosenstiel, Lewis S. 239, 240
Ryan, Judge Sylvester J..................... 42
S.S. Vulcania................................... 190
Sabine (jailmate of M. Moskowitz). 118
Sacco-Vanzetti case........................... 58
Sachs, Dora 153
Sattler, Mortimer 44
Saxe, Bacon and Bolan.................... 237
Saypol, Irving H. ...4, 43, 44, 47, 49, 50,
    53, 60-64, 66-75, 77, 79-81, 84, 85,
    87-91, 95, 96, 98-104, 106, 121, 142,
    175, 176, 214, 225, 227, 231, 234, 236,
    242, 243, 251
Schenley Industries 239
Schine, David 235
Schine, J. Myer................................ 235
Schultz, Joseph.............................. 214
Schwartz, Steve 207
Scottsboro Boys 24, 141
Screen Actors Guild 31
Securities and Exchange Commission
.... .238
Security Index 179, 180
Semenov, Sam 215, 221, 229, 230
Senate Internal Security Subcommittee
.... 202, 203, 226, 228, 231

Senate Investigations Committee.....52, 56, 234

Shawcross, Sir Harley.......................209

Sheen, Monsignor Fulton.................200

Sherman, Elizabeth...........................53

Sherrer, Hans 253, 263

Shinedling, Rabbi Abraham and Helen 141, 142, 263

Shirley (prison friend of M. Moskowitz) 128, 129, 130

Siege of Leningrad............................36

Siegel, Bugsy 137-139, 140

Signal Security Agency 182

Silvermaster, Nathan G.....................49

Sing Sing Prison 124, 125, 202

Sisk, Mildred (aka Axis Sally).........129

Sklar, Albert....................................215

Slack, Alfred Dean... 19, 42, 62, 63, 207

Smith Act............. 18, 58, 125, 126, 253

Smith, Gerald L. K............................24

Smith, Paul...............................62, 207

Sobell, Morton.....3, 4, 19, 42, 58, 175, 176, 234, 242, 245, 249

Social Security...............22, 25, 27, 113

Social Security Board 22

South Korea...................................19, 28

Spanish Civil War.........................24, 36

St. John's Guild 191

St. Joseph's School 48

St. Louis University 214, 215

Stalin, Joseph.............................37, 185

Stevens, Robert T.............................236

Stevenson, Adlai................................29

subpoena 78, 79, 88, 98, 185

Tavelman, Helen................................92

Taylor, William Henry.... 196, 198, 199, 202, 203

Terry, John..88

The New York Times 4, 20, 106, 256

Thomas, J. Parnell.............................29

Tokyo Rose....................................131

Toguri, Iva 131

Torresola, Griselio 58

Tower Acceptance Corp. 238

Trachtenberg, Alexander. 253

treason....................2, 19, 122, 131, 134

Truman Doctrine.......................33, 208

Truman, President Harry...2, 16, 17, 19, 31, 33, 37, 58, 196, 208, 235, 245

Trumbo, Dalton.................................31

Tuson, Robert 213

U. S. Atomic Energy Commission....72, 184

U. S. Attorney's Office......20, 54, 242, 250, 252

U. S. Customs 118, 240

U. S. Military Academy at West Point.. 234

U. S. Rubber 71

U. S. Service & Shipping Company (USSSC).......53, 192-195, 198, 201

U. S. Supreme Court........126, 245, 251

U.S.S.R. (Union of Soviet Socialist Republics)....2-4, 14, 15, 17, 19, 20, 24, 25, 27, 28, 29, 31, 36, 43, 47, 49, 52-55, 58-60, 62-65, 67, 69-73, 75, 78, 81-83, 86, 87, 92-94, 96, 98, 100, 101, 120, 174, 176, 178-180, 182-187, 192, 193, 196, 199, 200, 203, 204, 206-209, 211, 213-215, 218, 222, 224-228, 230, 231, 250, 253

United Dye & Chemical Corp..........237

United Federal Workers of America..22

United Nations...........................28, 168

University of Florence 49, 192

University of Pennsylvania......48, 211, 214, 215, 224

Unknown American #1 214

Vago, Oscar J....................................42

Vassar College.................49, 190, 191

Venona Project........ 182-187, 213, 218

Vietnam War..............30, 168, 235, 248

Voorhees, Jerry 30

Vyshinskii, Andrei...........................253

Wagner Labor Relations Act 25

Waiver Not to Serve 115, 128

War Manpower Commission 22

Watergate break-in............................31

Weinfeld, Judge Edward....................43

White, Harry Dexter 49

Works Project Administration (WPA) 25

World Tourists..................53, 192, 193

Young Communist League..16, 47, 175

Made in the USA
Charleston, SC
12 May 2014